The Leveling Wind

George F. Will

The Leveling Wind

Politics, the Culture and Other News, 1990–1994

VIKING

VIKING
Published by the Penguin Group
Penguin Books USA Inc., 375 Hudson Street,
New York, New York 10014, U.S.A.
Penguin Books Ltd, 27 Wrights Lane,
London W8 5TZ, England
Penguin Books Australia Ltd, Ringwood,
Victoria, Australia
Penguin Books Canada Ltd, 10 Alcorn Avenue,
Toronto, Ontario, Canada M4V 3B2
Penguin Books (N.Z.) Ltd, 182–190 Wairau Road,
Auckland 10, New Zealand

Penguin Books Ltd, Registered Offices:
Harmondsworth, Middlesex, England

First trade edition
Published in 1994 by Viking Penguin,
a division of Penguin Books USA Inc.

10   9   8   7   6   5   4   3   2   1

*A leatherbound signed first edition of this book
has been published by The Easton Press.*

LIBRARY OF CONGRESS CATALOGING IN PUBLICATION DATA
Will, George F.
The leveling wind: politics, the culture, and other news,
1990–1994 / George F. Will.
p.   cm.
ISBN 0-670-86021-2
1. United States—Politics and government—1989–1993.
2. United States—Politics and government—1993–
3. United States—Social conditions—1980–   4. Political
culture—United States.   I. Title.
E881.W55   1994
973.929—dc20   94-27749

This book is printed on acid-free paper.
♾

Printed in the United States of America
Set in Caledonia

To Erwin Glikes

1937–1994

Friend, Publisher

Come let us mock at the great
That had such burdens on the mind
And toiled so hard and late
To leave some monument behind,
Nor thought of the leveling wind. . . .

—William Butler Yeats
"Nineteen Hundred and Nineteen"

Contents

Introduction

In the 1990s Americans have been thinking incessantly about the leveling winds of cultural forces. They have been worrying about the power of those winds swiftly to level the works of governments, such as laws and schools, and of centuries, such as families and standards of taste and traditions of civility. Those winds are chilly just now, like the winds that pour off Lake Michigan and through Cabrini-Green, a housing project that is paradigmatic of much that has gone wrong in urban America.

With the concision for which he was famous, Mayor Fiorello La Guardia explained what used to be the melancholy lot of the urban politician. You can't, he said, get people excited about sewers. Perhaps not, but sewers are not the cities' principal problems nowadays. Would that sewers were. No one in the 1990s thinks a mayor's job is boring, or that the issues with which mayors struggle—crime, illegitimacy, addiction, dependency—are banal. It is not too much to say that in the years covered by the essays collected in this volume Americans have come to an unsettling conclusion. It is that their nation is in danger of evolving into a kind of civilization heretofore unknown in the modern world, one in which cities are important not as centers of commercial and cultural vitality, but rather as burdens.

There has been no single catalyst of this conclusion. Rather, it is the result of a relentless bombardment of unsettling sights and sounds, from rap music and the gang culture to the reinforcing pathologies of too many children with too few fathers attending them. What has the political system—particularly at the highest and most attention-getting levels, in the federal government—got to say about all this? Much, and not much.

Americans are arguing about an agenda of problems remarkably different from the agenda that preoccupied them just ten years ago. The epidemic of illegitimate births, the desensitizing effects of violence and other coarseness in entertainment, the politicization of higher education that is turning intellectual life into a power struggle, the Balkanization of America by "identity politics" that produces a truculent jockeying among groups seeking preferment in a racial, sexual and ethnic spoils system— these and related developments are now at the center of our national conversation. Indeed, one of the heartening developments of this decade is an abrupt expansion of the range of the discussable.

Of course not everything is discussable everywhere. On many campuses, where inquiry should be most wide-ranging and controversy should be least inhibited, the attempt to define "sensitive behavior" broadly, and to make it obligatory, has had a chilling effect. But America's political discourse is more open than it was, say, three decades ago when Daniel Patrick Moynihan brought down upon himself an acid rain of obloquy, by merely noting the early signs of the crisis of the black family.

On the other hand, there is frank bewilderment about what is to be done. That is not necessarily bad. In politics, bewilderment is preferable to misguided certitude. Still, it is striking that the range of discussable subjects has expanded as the range of things we can take for granted has contracted. Fathers attentive to the children they conceive, streets free from stray bullets, popular entertainment that does not make one wince, or worse—these are among the things no longer taken for granted. One consequence of this "reduction of the assumable" is a shrinkage of the status of politicians, and even of the political.

Suetonius, with a journalist's eye for the telling detail, wrote that Julius Caesar, although stabbed 23 times, nevertheless arranged his toga as he fell. Politicians do have a nice sense of decorum, even in defeat, do they not? In the period covered by this volume, the electorate, for the second time in a generation, cashiered a president after a single term. A Republican this time, a Democrat last time—the electorate is in a no-nonsense, take-no-prisoners mood. It is saying to politicians what Coach Bear Bryant of Alabama used to say to his football players on the first day of practice: "Be good or be gone."

In explaining the misadventure that was the Bush presidency, a poem by Kingsley Amis is apposite:

That horse whose rider fears to jump will fall,
Riflemen miss if orders sound unsure;
They only are secure who seem secure;
Who lose their voice, lose all.

The Bush administration, recollected in tranquility, and with difficulty, was a sort of marvel—the sort of marvel a man would be who could walk across a snow-covered meadow and leave no footprints. President Bush almost always—always when not organizing Desert Storm—seemed flummoxed. It was fascinating to watch him make a sow's ear from the silk purse of the strong political legacy bequeathed by his predecessor. Oh, well. Perhaps Bush's syntactical fender-benders were a blessing. As Arthur Balfour once said, Herbert Asquith's clarity was a liability because he had nothing to say.

The decline and fall of a particular politician is less interesting than the decline of the entire political process as a focus of national expectations. This is not to say that governance does not matter, or that politics has been drained of its cathartic and entertainment values. The new crowd in Washington is nothing if not entertaining and is certainly not reconciled to a modest role for politics in the nation's life.

Bush, who talked with difficulty, was defeated by a man who talks incessantly. Teachers have been called people who never say anything once, and Bill Clinton wants to be America's teacher. Whether the nation is in a mood to be instructed from political offices, time will tell. Meanwhile, let us note how beside-the-point much of national politics seems to much of the nation.

"Boredom," says a character in Saul Bellow's novel *The Adventures of Augie March*, "is the shriek of unused capacities." It does Americans credit that they are bored to tears by the stylized dance of partisan politics that seems terribly stale—Democrats saying Republicans are marble-hearted, Republicans saying Democrats are fiscal dipsomaniacs. In the 1992 election the nation watched the dance and then gave a continental shrug: Well, we might as well try someone else. But Washington's narcissism, or perhaps it is provincialism—its reluctance to be interested in, and its inability to understand, anything but itself—has become pronounced precisely at a moment when things other than the traditional spoils of distributive politics—public works, entitlements—are worrying Americans.

Much that makes news nowadays mocks the stirring words of the third stanza of "America the Beautiful":

> Thine alabaster cities gleam,
> Undimmed by human tears!

More and more Americans understand that the nation's most intractable problems derive from disregard of the wisdom expressed by other words from that stanza:

> Confirm thy soul in self-control.

Our problems are not confined to inner cities, or even to cities. Rather, they are facets of the enveloping social atmosphere. And to a significant extent they are prompted and communicated from the top down. By "the top" I mean the tone-setting intelligentsia, in academia and in the information and entertainment media, that decisively influences the messages the culture transmits. If I seem to be suggesting something like a "unified field theory" of our disorder, so be it. Society is not an assemblage of cells hermetically sealed from one another.

One of the benefits a writer gets from putting together a collection such as this is a shock of recognition. Suddenly the writer sees some hitherto unnoticed patterns and tendencies of his writings. I am struck by how much I am now writing about books. That is as it should be in an era when the condition of the culture, and the culture's consequences, are national preoccupations. Many books should be treated, journalistically, as news events. History is the history of ideas, and the more journalism I do, print and broadcast, the more convinced I become that books are still the primary carriers of ideas.

The subtitle of this volume—"Politics, the Culture and Other News, 1990–1994"—stresses something that events insistently demonstrate: The culture is news. These have been years in which education, entertainment, social theories formulated by the professoriate and other aspects of the culture have become bigger news than most of the activities of the people we commonly, but less and less accurately, call "newsmakers."

In this decade, the last decade of what need not be the last "American Century," Americans are wondering: What kind of people were we not so long ago? What kind are we now, and what kind are we becoming? The controversies arising from these questions concern many practical policy choices, from school curricula to immigration, and the controversies are as old as the nation. Ever since the opinionated Puritans waded ashore for their errand in the New England wilderness, such questions have been tangled up in American politics. For example, in 1908 the Democratic presidential candidate, William Jennings Bryan, said his Republican opponent, William Howard Taft, was unfit for the White House because, being a Unitarian, Taft did not believe in the virgin birth of Jesus Christ. The Republic survived Unitarianism in high office. Whether the Republic can long thrive while such institutions as families fray and schools decay is, to say no more, an intriguing question. Most Americans now living will live to see it answered, one way or another.

Impermanence is one of life's few constants. We have the Gershwins' word for it that the Rockies may tumble and Gibraltar may crumble. And scientists tell us that the continents themselves are wandering around. Of course, social winds that level things are not necessarily misfortunes. It is good that the Thousand Year Reich fell 988 years short and the Berlin Wall is a zillion souvenirs. Furthermore, impermanence is, in a sense, a permanent aspiration of this nation that was—and still is—largely made up of people in flight from nations resistant to change. However, when family structure begins to crumble, when parents feel themselves parenting against the powerful pull of debasing popular entertainment, when "diversity" and "multiculturalism" become aspects of an aggressive agenda for organizing Americans into grievance groups asserting group rights, and when violence seems so pervasive and random that normal urban wariness is insufficient prudence, then the sense of impermanence becomes oppressive and frightening.

In the pages that follow there are many expressions of anxiety and dismay about such things. However, cheerfulness keeps breaking out in America, and the following thought keeps popping up:

Sonny Liston was a heavyweight boxing champion who had trouble staying out of trouble, and jail. What a fight manager once said of Liston can be said of any nation: "Sonny had his good points. The trouble is his bad points." But America, unlike Sonny, has a lot more good points than bad ones. That fact can be lost sight of by those of us who, by vocation or as readers, become too immersed in journalism. Journalism, as the saying goes, does not report the planes that land safely. However, most planes do.

Be that as it may, being a professional participant in our nonstop national churning is not only a privilege, it is more fun than anything I can think of, other than making the acquaintance of David Will, as you, valued reader, are about to do.

PART 1

The Climate

Buckled by Love to David Will

Earthquakes may strike, the stock market may crash and locusts may devour the crops, but 1992 will be remembered as a banner year for the Republic because of the birth of David Maseng Will. He is doing well at life. The kid's a natural.

Of course, being a baby is like playing the bagpipes. That instrument sounds much the same when played by a master or a novice, and babies get the hang of babyness straightaway. Still, David, just completing the second week of the 3,640 weeks that the Bible says is man's allotted span, already is showing signs of prodigious promise.

Well, all right, to be precise, he surely would be showing such signs in the intervals between eating and sleeping, if there were intervals. There are not, which means he is in the pre-prodigy stage that babies pass through, a stage properly described as winsome barbarism. It is cute, but it is barbarism nonetheless.

A barbarian has been defined as someone who regards his passions as their own excuse for existing. David does. His as-yet narrow repertoire of passions, voiced with Wagnerian crescendos, are for nourishment and dry diapers. In considering his desires self-justifying, David is suited to this city that is planted thick with insistent interest groups. But he is just a baby. What is their excuse?

He cries frequently and has a strong sense of entitlements, so he may be a liberal. However, he has the breezy indifference to other people's interests and convenience that we associate with conservatives. It is unclear whether a political predisposition lurks in David's DNA.

What is, and is not, in our genetic material is a modern puzzle. It gives rise to the nature-versus-nurture controversy about what shapes individual development. All babies, be they Oliver Cromwell or Mark Twain, arrive looking pretty much alike and created equal in the sense that they are, in the language of the Book of Common Prayer, "unspotted from the world." But that does not mean babies are blank slates on which ambitious parents can inscribe a destiny of their choosing. Every parent holding a newborn feels the certainty that a sturdy, unique personhood, unlike any other, is present.

The modern parent is offered a torrent of advice and many devices for nurturing the perfect child. The wonder is that young parents, especially, do not crumble beneath the weight of the responsibility. Many do dissolve in guilt about the probability that they are neglecting some nuance that would give their child momentum toward success in the meritocracy. "As the twig is bent," and all that.

Now the good news: Children are not twigs. They will ricochet around the world as they choose, and their choosing can be influenced only up to a point.

Nature and society combine to cause most children to be born to parents who are not yet 30, parents still physically strong and emotionally resilient. However, just as schools require us to read great literature before we have lived enough to fathom why it is great, so, too, we have babies too soon. At least there is much to be said for having a baby when you more fully understand what they are getting into: life.

This is not because older parents can offer plentiful advice. By the time a parent has seen sound advice bounce off the hard shells of several previous children, that parent is apt to offer hopes rather than advice. My hopes for David include this: That he have the foundation of happiness—a great passion for some excellence. Such a passion erases the distinction between work and play, turning toil into recreation—literally, re-creation.

In one of his Palliser novels, Anthony Trollope says it is important for a young person entering life to decide whether he or she shall make hats or shoes, but that is not half as important as the decision whether to make good or bad hats or shoes. Cézanne, after putting a subject through 115 sittings for a single portrait, said, "I am not entirely displeased with the shirt front." That is how to paint, and live.

Such are the night thoughts of a father who knows that disturbed nights are to be anticipated with certainty and borne philosophically in homes where infants take up residence. But when night with slow retreating steps departs, and David sinks into the almost invertebrate slumber that adults can only envy, a father feels not fatigue but exhilaration.

It is the thrill of being again buckled by love to all the coming astonishments—the first firefly, first ice cream, first dog, first friend, first baseball game—that keep adults connected, through wide-eyed children, to the world's eternal freshness.

July 26, 1992

Karen McCune's Resilience

CHICAGO—The day Dantrell Davis died, Karen McCune wrote: "I thouht my life will better than what it turned to be." That summing-up of a life was made recently by a nine-year-old.

Today Karen is a 47-pound miracle of resilience. She is more than a match—so far—for the pounding that cities give childhood in this era of urban regression.

The shooting of Dantrell might have elicited a "so what?" shrug of this city's broad shoulders. After all, Chicago averages a shooting every 34 minutes and a murder every eight hours, and the more than 13,000 shootings so far this year have killed 17 children under 14. Dantrell was the third pupil at Jenner Elementary School shot dead this year. One of Dantrell's schoolmates said: "I hope that next time it won't be somebody that I know." He assumes there will be a next time, a fourth time.

Dantrell was killed by a sniper firing from a nearby high-rise as Dantrell and his mother began the 40-yard walk to Jenner from their high-rise, through the killing zone of the Cabrini-Green housing project. Today, beneath the lead-gray sky of a Chicago November, the hard wind off the lake is gusting razorlike rain horizontally and Karen is chatting in a classroom overlooking a growing puddle on the spot where Dantrell fell.

Cabrini-Green is 70 acres of appalling public policy less than a mile from Michigan Avenue's "Magnificent Mile." About 7,000 people live in the 31 high-rises and 60 other buildings in this public housing project. More than half the residents are under age 20. Nine percent of the residents have paying jobs.

Karen, her hair neatly braided, her white blouse and blue jumper (the voluntary school uniform that most pupils wear) immaculate, her eyes bright and her smile dazzling, patiently tells a columnist that life's not so bad if you stay indoors. "My mommy won't allow me to go outside. I stay up in the house and read books."

She usually stays away from windows. "I be scared because my bed is by the window." But the apartment where she and some siblings live with her mother is on the seventh floor, safe from most gunfire. However, "When the Bulls won [the NBA championship] a car ran into the store [across the street from her apartment] and they were shooting up and my mommy had to duck down."

Jenner School shows its 90 years but is a wonderfully clean haven for children from a neighborhood run by armed children. For now there is a truce between the gangs, a result of a heavy police presence since Dantrell's death. The truce is a respite from the recurring need to move children into inner hallways on whichever side of the school shooting has erupted.

Karen, who even in repose has the happy can't-stop-wiggling-my-shiny-black-leather-shoes fidgets of the normal nine-year-old, nevertheless practices the prudence of the street-wise urban child: "I don't wear any Starter [a brand name] jackets because they're bad for us." Six days after Dantrell was killed, a 15-year-old from another school was killed evidently because he was slow to give robbers his Miami Hurricanes jacket.

Twenty years ago Jenner had 2,500 students. Today it has 630. Some of them have symptoms—short attention spans, difficulty sustaining relationships, a tendency to think only in stark opposites—often associated with survivors of a battle area. Small wonder. Shortly after Dantrell's death, Karen shared with a local newspaper reporter the sort of memory that marks childhood in this other America:

"They couldn't find my friend's mother. They looked and looked but they couldn't find her. Finally one day they found her body stuck in the sewer. It was all mushy and it stinked real bad. I'm glad Danny wasn't like that."

Her prescription for neighborhood improvement is commonsense and contrary to public policy: "Take the gangbangers (gang members) out and take away all the guns." With an imperious sweep of a spindly arm in the direction of the high-rises, she decrees: "Mow down those buildings. Don't need to be high-rise. Five floors enough."

Social scientists debate the concept of a "culture of poverty," the intergenerational transmission of passivity and fatalism. There is such a culture but it has not claimed Karen. Her small face wreathed in a huge smile of serene certainty, she announces that she's going to college: "I'm not going to have no boyfriend or no husband or child when I'm fifteen or fourteen or thirteen. I'm going to wait until I get real, real big, until I'm"—she plucks a number from her imagination—"twenty-seven."

One of her best friends is a boy who wants to be a lawyer: "He uses big words, like 'interject.'" Karen says she is going to be a teacher. She already is.

November 19, 1992

"If I grow up . . .": Life in Cabrini-Green

CHICAGO—Paul O'Connor, a white middle-class businessman who coaches baseball and basketball teams for young black men from the Cabrini-Green public housing project, recalls telephoning one of his players. Because O'Connor was having trouble hearing the player over the roar of what sounded like a war movie, he asked him to turn down the television. The player said the television wasn't on, that what O'Connor was hearing was a firefight—perhaps two gangs settling a business dispute from the drug trade—outside the player's apartment.

The U.S. Constitution's preamble begins, "We, the people of the United States, in order to form a more perfect Union, establish justice, insure domestic tranquility . . ." "We the people of the state of Illinois," begins another constitution, have ordained and established government in order to provide for the "safety" of the people and to "insure domestic tranquility." Hold it right there.

The federal government, in its eerie self-absorption, declares "war" on this and that—drugs, poverty, crime, whatever. But in America's cities, where the irrelevance of government, often including state and city governments, is increasingly assumed, the word "war" is less a silly metaphor than a reasonable denotation.

"This," says O'Connor, driving through an intersection, "is the DMZ." Crossing this street means moving from one gang's turf to another's, no minor matter. O'Connor's baseball team plays on a field inferior to another field a few blocks away, but to get to the better field his players from "the whites" (white high-rises in Cabrini-Green, controlled by one gang) would have to walk by "the reds," which are controlled by another gang. There is too little domestic tranquility—too many snipers—for that.

O'Connor, who commutes to his suburban office, and his wife, Holly, who works downtown, live a few blocks from the lake in a tidy, placid neighborhood near Cabrini-Green, which is another world. You know, muses Paul, how country kids can imitate the sounds of various birds? One of Paul's players can replicate the sounds of different guns—.357 magnums, semiautomatic weapons—including the different sounds of gunshots echoing off bricks and concrete and cinder blocks.

Paul and Holly frequently have some of the players overnight at their home. Last night's guests were Tim and Abdul, who at age 15 have almost made it out of childhood. That is no mean achievement in a neighborhood where some mothers hard-pressed to put food in front of their children nevertheless pay monthly premiums for their children's burial insurance.

Tim is an alert, slight sparrow of a boy who is determined to be a college athlete. Where? "UNLV [University of Nevada, Las Vegas]," he answers, seeming amazed that such an obvious answer needs to be given. Many young men in Michael Jordan's city cling to the hope that sports will be their way of getting out of the city.

Abdul, a lanky amateur rap singer and clothes designer, seems more focused on life's foreground. Understandably. He lives in the high-rise where Dantrell Davis, aged seven, lived and recently died, shot by a sniper. Abdul knows the 33-year-old man charged with the shooting. The man umpired some of Abdul's baseball games.

Both boys heading off for a day in ninth grade have made it past one of the milestones of uncertain life in the inner city. It is a melancholy fact, O'Connor says, that many Cabrini-Green parents—mostly single women, of course—make a great ceremony of eighth-grade graduation, renting the graduates tuxedos for a big bash. Given the high school dropout rate of more than 50 percent, and given the gunfire, pride in the eighth-grade achievement is mingled with the bleak realization that there may never be an occasion for another graduation celebration.

In 1991 Alex Kotlowitz of *The Wall Street Journal* published a remarkable book about two boys growing up in the "jects" (the Chicago public housing projects). The title of the book was the mother's response to his proposal to write about her children: *There Are No Children Here.* When Kotlowitz asked a 10-year-old what he wanted to be when he grew up, the boy said, "If I grow up, I'd like to be a bus driver." If, not when.

When (not if, not if Paul and Holly have anything to say about it) Tim and Abdul grow up, they will have achieved adulthood with precious little help from governments, far or near. Representatives of the city government recently toured Cabrini-Green, picking a spot for a small park perhaps to be dedicated to one, or all three, of the pupils at the neighborhood elementary school who have been murdered in the last eight months. A park is better than nothing—people in Cabrini-Green lack parks and every other necessity and amenity—but, really, what a spectacle. This is government's competence: providing memorials to young victims of its dereliction of its elemental duty to insure domestic tranquility.

November 22, 1992

Soon after this column was written, Tim's mother moved first to Florida, then to Milwaukee. There Tim found friends, and enemies, in the streets. One day he exchanged angry words—not for the first time—with another young man. Tim crossed the street to a group of friends, borrowed a gun from one of them, recrossed the street and killed the person who had "dis'd" him. Tried as an adult at age 16, Tim was convicted of first-degree murder and sentenced to life imprisonment. He will be eligible for parole in 25 years, when he is 41.

The Boats at the Bottom

Before the City of New Orleans and other passenger trains got the disappearing railroad blues, the Illinois Central was, for hundreds of thousands of rural blacks, a steel highway to the promised land. They left from small depots in the Deep South and arrived at Chicago's cavernous 12th Street Station. There they turned a few miles south toward what became the largest concentration of black Americans.

Now comes *The Promised Land*, Nicholas Lemann's riveting report on the Mississippi-to-Chicago component of the northward migration of 6.5 million blacks, one of the world's largest and swiftest migrations.

Lemann's book resembles Jacob Riis's *How the Other Half Lives*, written in 1890 about immigrants from Europe. Riis wrongly said they "carry their slums with them wherever they go." Sharecroppers carried the culture of poverty to cities, but not forever.

Whereas the 19th-century immigrants' experience convinced Americans that slum life was a temporary fate for one generation, today the intergenerational transmission of poverty in ghettos suggests that the principal cause of continuing poverty is the enveloping set of urban poverty conditions. To say poverty is self-perpetuating is not to blame the victims by saying that it is produced by irremediable flaws that are finally the fault of the poor. But it is to define the challenge, which is to acculturate the underclass to the disciplines and rigors of urban working life.

The underclass, writes Lemann, "lacks a human face—its most publicized members are criminals, and otherwise it is a mass of frightening statistics." He has found faces to illustrate our history, faces like that of Ruby Lee Haynes.

She was born in Mississippi in 1916 to an unwed 15-year-old. Lemann tells her story from Mississippi to Chicago and back to Mississippi where, when Lemann takes leave of her, she is living next door to an unwed 15-year-old mother of two.

Most American blacks are middle-class, broadly, but reasonably, defined. However, a disproportionate share of the 20 percent of American children who live in poverty are black. Many are in female-headed households in urban settings where ways of life transplanted from the vanished world of sharecropping have been intensified by urban density and hazards.

Mechanical cotton pickers destroyed the sharecropper system that had replaced slavery and had itself been virtual slavery buttressed by real terror. It was peonage: In 1965, Martin Luther King met Alabama sharecroppers who, having been paid all their lives in plantation scrip, had never seen U.S. currency. In the sharecropper society of enveloping despair, there often was no money for weddings, and no formal divorces because there were no possessions to divide. All the weaknesses of the urban underclass were present—illegitimate childbearing, female-headed households, violent crime, substance abuse (mostly home-brew whiskey, but drugs, too).

The arrival in America's cities of millions of internal immigrants, a sizable minority of whom were singularly unprepared to prosper there, reached a crescendo just as the political will and economic means to cope with the challenge collapsed, and many of the jobs that had drawn them north dried up. In the 1960s, Watts and Vietnam shattered the liberal consensus. Bewilderment replaced confidence among policymakers because of a startling "disaggregation": Welfare cases rose as unemployment fell.

Since the oil shocks of the 1970s and the deficits of the 1980s and now the 1990s, the nation has felt unable to undertake new social programs. Furthermore, Americans do not see the urban underclass as composed of people like Rosa Parks of Montgomery or the children of Birmingham or the marchers of Selma—decent people handicapped by clear obstacles that will yield to crisp government actions.

Lemann, having immersed himself in the chaos of real lives, has the authority to say that we now know what will not work in the way of ameliorative policies, and that we have not adequately tried what might work. The cure for poverty is neither income redistribution nor the acquisition by the poor of political power. There is no longer a link between political empowerment and individual economic advancement.

In ghettos, "self-help" means moving out, away from high crime and bad schools. So for those left behind, a "services strategy" rather than an "income strategy" may be best after all. For a fraction of the cost of the savings-and-loan bailout, or a small fraction of the annual debt service component of the federal budget, more police could be put on foot on the meanest streets, schools where the tax base is worst could be improved, Head Start and other forms of early intervention in the most vulnerable lives could be expanded.

The richness of Lemann's reporting, which rises to the level of literature, demolishes both fashionable despair about government policies and the facile optimism that economic growth will cure the ghettos. A rising tide does not raise all boats. Lemann's unforgettable book—this reader has never learned so much about contemporary America from a single book—demonstrates that those stuck in the mud have unique problems and a uniquely powerful claim on our help.

March 24, 1991

The Surgeon General's Lament

"Society," says the Surgeon General, "wants to keep all sexuality in the closet." Which makes one wonder: What society is Dr. Joycelyn Elders living in? Surely hers is an interesting sensibility if she lives in today's America and frets that there is insufficient thinking and talking about things sexual.

This is a society in which parents can hardly watch television with their children without wincing, in which a walk past a magazine rack is a walk on the wild side, in which before or after the steamy soap operas have got the afternoon television audience panting, on come Geraldo, and Montel and Sally—"Next, bisexual grocers and the lingerie they love!" Someone should send the Surgeon General some tapes of the "shock jocks" now flourishing on radio—Howard Stern and the rest. That would assuage her anxiety that sexuality is being repressed by Victorian morality in an America that needs "to be more open about sex."

The Surgeon General should be gratified by the out-of-the-closet television commercial for little Hyundai automobiles. In it, two women speculate that men who buy big cars are compensating for their small penises. Observing the driver of a large car, one woman says, "He must be compensating for a . . . shortcoming?" Of the man who drives up in a Hyundai, the other woman says, "I wonder what he's got under the hood." A columnist for *Ad Age* notes that, in the argot of advertising, this is an ad campaign based on "penis-length positioning."

Imitation really is the sincerest form of television: Last Monday two consecutive CBS comedies, *Murphy Brown* and *Hearts Afire,* featured penis jokes. Given that such is now the stuff of mass entertainment and advertising, it is a mystery what the Surgeon General thinks is left back there in the recesses of the nation's sexuality closet, and why she wants it—whatever it is—out.

You may well think the river of national life is silting up rather rapidly with sexuality in all its permutations—gays in the military, gays in the

Saint Patrick's Day parades, Bob Packwood, Michael Jackson, Madonna, MTV, "date rape" seminars for freshmen, and so on, and on. But the Surgeon General, in an interview with *The Advocate,* a magazine for homosexuals, indicates that she thinks the nation is suffering from sexual reticence.

In the process of endorsing adoption of children by homosexuals, and embracing the fiction that 10 percent of young people are homosexuals, she says, "Sex is good, sex is wonderful." Verily it can be, but Elders's effusions are not exactly all that the nation just now needs to hear from its principal public health official.

Is it good and wonderful sex that is making so many 14-year-old mothers? From boom boxes carried by young males down city streets comes 2 Live Crew's song "Me So Horny," and lyrics about how fun it is to "bust the walls" of vaginas. Not good. Not wonderful.

The New York Times reports a resurgence of what it delicately describes as "commercial establishments where people meet for sex." It means places like the Adonis theater, a cinema on Eighth Avenue between 43rd and 44th streets in Manhattan. The city is estimated to have about 50 similar establishments where people go for sex, often for anonymous sex with multiple partners. The city government knows that it will have to care for many of the more than 80,000 "AIDS orphans"—children whose mothers died of AIDS—that the nation will have by the end of this decade. The city closed the Adonis in January because not all sex is good and wonderful.

When used by advanced thinkers like Elders, the phrase "in the closet" means "unliberated." But would-be liberators like Elders have a problem, there being little remaining in the way of laws or mores from which anyone can be liberated. Sure, in some cities children who are not yet in the sixth grade are denied information about anal intercourse, but such minor imperfections in American liberty make for an uninspiring agenda for sexual liberators.

It really is no longer daring to say, as Elders did to *The Advocate,* "I feel that God meant sex for more than procreation," and of course Elders has a right to construe God's will as she pleases. But can someone explain why a government official, and particularly this one, is favoring us with such thoughts? Where in the job description of the Surgeon General does it deal with the duty to issue public lamentations about America's sexual repression? Repression is what she implies by her remarkable judgment that American society—has she seen Calvin Klein underwear ads?—"wants to keep all sexuality in the closet."

March 31, 1994

America's Slide into the Sewer

I regret the offensiveness of what follows. However, it is high time adult readers sample the words that millions of young Americans are hearing.

Which words are lyrics, which are testimony?

In a Manhattan courtroom testimony continues in the trial of young men accused of gang rape and other sadistic violence against the Central Park jogger in last April's "wilding" episode. "We charged her and we got her on the ground. Everybody started hitting her and stuff, and she's on the ground and everybody's stomping and everything. . . . I grabbed one arm, and this other kid grabbed one arm and we grabbed her legs and stuff. And then we took turns getting on her." They did it for fun, for entertainment.

"After she was hit on the head with the pipe, did someone take her clothes off?"

"Yeah."

"Okay, who took her clothes off?"

"All of us."

"Did somebody have sex with her?"

"Yeah."

"Did a lot of people have sex with her?"

"Yeah."

When arrested a defendant said, "It was something to do. It was fun." Where can you get the idea that sexual violence against women is fun? From a music store, through Walkman earphones, from boom boxes blaring forth the rap lyrics of 2 Live Crew:

To have her walkin' funny we try to abuse it
A big stinking p——y can't do it all
So we try real hard just to bust the walls

That is, bust the walls of women's vaginas. 2 Live Crew's lyrics exult in busting women—almost always called bitches—in various ways, forcing anal sex, forcing women to lick feces. "He'll tear the p——y open 'cause it's satisfaction." "Suck my d——k, bitch, it makes you puke." That's entertainment.

This is medicine. The jogger lost most of her blood, her temperature plunged to 85. Doctors struggling to keep her alive had to tie down her arms and legs because, even hours after the attack, while in a coma that would last weeks, she was flailing and kicking as if "in a fighting stance." Her face was so disfigured a friend took 15 minutes to identify her. "I recognized her ring."

Do you recognize the relevance of 2 Live Crew?

I'll break ya down and d——k ya long
Bust your p——y then break your backbone

The furor (if anything so evanescent can be called that) about 2 Live Crew has subsided, for two reasons. Saturation journalism, print and broadcast, around the clock, quickly wrings the novelty out of subjects, leaving them dry husks. Then, if someone raises the subject again, the answer is a journalistic shrug: "Not again. We've already done that." But for 2 Live Crew the tour rolls on and the money rolls in.

Anyway, the "fury" over the lyrics was feigned. It had to be because everyone dependent on journalism did not learn what the offending words were. Media coverage was characterized by coy abstractness, an obscuring mist of mincing, supercilious descriptions of the lyrics as "explicit" or "outrageous" or "challenging" or "controversial" or "provocative." Well, now. Provoking what, precisely?

From the jogger trial: "Steve was holding her with his leg and someone was ripping off her clothes and pulling her down. She screamed and Steve held her while Kevin pulled down his pants and had sex with her. Steve hit her with a brick twice."

Fact: Some members of a particular age and social cohort—the one making 2 Live Crew rich—stomped and raped the jogger to the razor edge of death, for the fun of it. Certainty: The coarsening of a community, the desensitizing of a society, will have behavioral consequences.

Juan Williams of *The Washington Post* is black and disgusted. The issue, he writes, is the abuse of women, especially black women, and the corruption of young blacks' sensibilities, twisting their conceptions "of good sex, good relationships and good times." Half of all black children live in single-parent households headed by women. The black family is falling apart, teen pregnancy regularly ruins lives, the rate of poverty is steadily rising and 2 Live Crew "is selling corruption—self-hate—to vulnerable young minds in a weak black America."

In such selling, liberals are tools of entertainment corporations. The liberals and the corporations have the morals of the marketplace. Corporations sell civil pollution for profit; liberals rationalize it as virtuous tolerance in "the marketplace of ideas." Not to worry, yawn *The New York Times* editorialists, "The history of music is the story of innovative, even outrageous styles that interacted, adapted and became mainstream." Oh, I see: First Stravinsky's *Rite of Spring*, now 2 Live Crew's "Me So Horny." ("I won't tell your momma if you don't tell your dad/I know he'll be disgusted when he sees your p——y busted." Innovative. When that is "mainstream," this will be an interesting country.)

2 Live Crew, who are black, resemble the cretinous Andrew Dice Clay, the white "comedian." There is nothing new about selling the talentless to the tasteless. What is new is the combination of extreme infantilism and menace in the profit-driven degeneration of popular entertainment. This slide into the sewer is greased by praise. Yes, praise. When journalism refuses to present the raw reality, and instead says only that 2 Live Crew's lyrics are "explicit" and "controversial" and "provocative," there is an undertone of approval. Antonyms of those adjectives are "vague" and "bland" and "unchallenging." Somehow we never reach the subject of busting vaginal walls.

America today is capable of terrific intolerance about smoking, or toxic waste that threatens trout. But only a deeply confused society is more concerned about protecting lungs than minds, trout than black women. We legislate against smoking in restaurants; singing "Me So Horny" is a constitutional right. Secondary smoke is carcinogenic; celebration of torn vaginas is "mere words."

Words, said Aristotle, are what set human beings, the language-using animals, above lower animals. Not necessarily.

July 30, 1990

Hear America Singing: Saturday's Songs

SEATTLE—Seasonal sounds—brittle leaves crackling underfoot, migrating birds calling overhead—will soon surround us. None is more stirring than the strange music that issues from American campuses as football crowds serenade themselves with songs expressing eternal devotion to alma mater and a desire to eviscerate this Saturday's opponent.

However, here at the University of Washington the music of autumnal mayhem is notably peculiar in one particular. The song in question should be sung at the other edge of the continent, as the anthem of the federal bureaucracy. Titled "Bow Down to Washington," it sternly says:

Heaven help the foes of Washington:
They're trembling at the feet of mighty Washington.
The boys are there with bells,
Their fighting blood excels,

> It's harder to push them over the line
> Than pass the Dardanelles.

Many fight songs are spiced with odd ejaculations like "Oskee-wow-wow" (Illinois) and "Ski-U-ma" (Minnesota) and "Chig-ga-roo-gar-em!" (Texas A&M). Such songs are for football fans and so are supposed to encourage dementia. But what must today's undergraduates—or their parents, for that matter—make of Washington's reference to the Dardanelles?

Anachronisms, of language and sentiment, are part of the charm of such songs. Where but in pep songs do you still find fine old words like "pluck" (Bates), "grit" (Alabama), "vim" (Kansas) and even "sand":

> We'll back you to stand
> 'Gainst the best in the land,
> For we know you have sand,
> Illinois Rah! Rah!

The forces of political correctness probably have long since banished much retrograde language. ("Purdue has men who dare and do, and comely coeds too." To call a young woman a coed is sexism; to call her comely is "lookism.") In these days of exquisitely honed sensitivities it is safer to stick to stuff like:

> On the breast of Old South Mountain,
> Reared against the sky,
> Stands our noble Alma Mater,
> Stands our dear Lehigh.

When a song begins "Where the . . . ," stand back. A cataract of adjectives is coming.

> Where the peaceful calm Chenango
> Starts its journey thro' the vale,
> There the gleaming light of Colgate
> Flamed forth to never fail.

Songs about alma mater are supposed to be syrupy. The second campus genre, the fight song, should be bloodthirsty. As in an ancient Arizona rouser: "Smear 'em! Spear 'em! U. of A., you never fear 'em!" Rummaging around in the Library of Congress's music collection, one learns that long ago Kansas combined fierceness with flair:

> Looning down the valley,
> The lord of all he views,
> The Jay-hawk sees some tombstones in the vale.

Beneath which, presumably, Sooners and Cornhuskers are buried.

Some old songs show, alas, that the lyricist neglected to give his craft the old college try:

So give a Cheer for the Orange and Blue,
Waving forever!—forever!
Pride of old Florida, May she droop never!

"Droop"? Well, could have been worse. Could have been Davidson's "You've got the stuff, men, and that's enough then." Or Arkansas's "Here are the Razorbacks . . . never in duty lax." Oregon's song sounds defeatist: "Rally, fellows, stand behind them, they are doing all they can." A Carnegie Institute song shows only a cold-eyed homage to the tycoon who buttered the Institute's bread: "Andy was the grand old man we loved so well, Carnegie . . ."

But only the stony-hearted can resist such scrumptious goo as:

Where the western lights' long shadows
Over boundless prairies fling
And the mountain winds are vocal
With thy dear name, Wyoming.

Corny? You bet, and that's not all that's splendid about such anthems. They are pleasant whiffs of local patriotisms, unrefined sentiments of our regions, robust hymns of preference for particular parts of the national mosaic. We are all members of the great American regiment, but we also are members of little platoons—states, communities, colleges, even, each with its own marching cadences, such as South Dakota's alma mater:

Oh, the pine-crested peaks of the storied Black Hills,
The Missouri that ribbons thy plains;
Where the slant summer sunshine so lavishly spills
Over prairie and pasture and grain.

It is now possible to drive from sea to shining sea on clean, safe, convenient, antiseptic—even the billboards have been banned—highways. "Limited access" highways, they are called. They limit the traveler's access to America. Along we roll, our cars "conditioning" the air, our car windows sealing us off from the scent of northern fir and southern pine, stopping only for fuel at a franchised service station, eating at franchised restaurants, sleeping at franchised motels, listening all the way to network news blurbs and Top 40 music and arriving at the coast unmarked by any encounter with America's sweet particularities— with anything not relentlessly contemporary and remorselessly homogenized.

How nice, then, to know that almost any turn off the turnpike will take us to some place where, if we open a window and cock an ear, we may hear something quaint and quirky and wonderful like:

> Oh, let us sing of Idaho
> The Queen of all the West . . .

Yes, let's.

October 24, 1991

The Fecundity of the Fifties

Narcissism being natural, we who are in our fifties and were formed by the Fifties naturally consider that decade fascinating and resent the clichés of contempt with which it is routinely denigrated. It was, we are told, mere chrome and conformity, featuring a "silent generation" for which Ike was "the bland leading the bland." Such inanities often issue from people who, being products or admirers of the Sixties, can't think clearly about anything.

It is high time to honor the astonishing fecundity of the Fifties, and to acknowledge the decade's signal flaw, the fact that it was pregnant with the Sixties. Now from David Halberstam comes *The Fifties*, a 1958 Buick Roadmaster of a book, large (733 pages) and comfortable for a long trip. It is chock-full of fodder for Fifties chauvinists. And it should be required reading in myopic Washington, which believes that politicians make the world hum.

Halberstam gives politicians their due, and more, but the book gets into high gear with his deft sketches of captains of commerce such as Harley Earl, Detroit's "Cellini of Chrome," who loved jets and sharks and gave cars tailfins just as Ike was giving the Interstate Highway System to Americans who suddenly were never far from Ray Kroc's multiplications of the McDonald brothers' San Bernardino hamburger stand. When Americans drove away from the homes they bought for $7,990 from William Levitt—he was finishing 36 a day on Long Island—they could stay at the Holiday Inns that Kemmons Wilson was building, a new room every 15 minutes. A "quiet" decade? More like a roaring one.

The decade's most important sound emanated from Memphis, where on July 5, 1954—49 days after the Supreme Court's school desegregation ruling—a Tupelo, Mississippi, truck driver partial to black slacks and pink shirts recorded "That's All Right." The night a local disc jockey played the Mississippian's record, the station's switchboard lit up. (Disc jockeys were cultural arbiters for young people who were defining their generation with music heard on cheap transistor radios that circumvented parental control.)

Eager to interview the singer, the disc jockey sent the singer's parents in search of him. Found at the movies, he asked, "Mama, what's happening?" "Plenty, son, but it's all good," said Gladys Presley.

The most important question the disc jockey asked him was what high school he had attended. The answer told listeners what his music didn't: Elvis was white. The crossover of whites and blacks in pop music—Bill Haley, Fats Domino, Little Richard, Chuck Berry—made the radio dial America's most integrated institution.

Shrewd Jackie Gleason understood something else about Elvis of the curled lip and sullen look: "He's a guitar-playing Marlon Brando." Elvis worshiped James Dean, who worshiped Brando. When Elvis met the director of Dean's movie *Rebel Without a Cause*, he fell to his knees and recited Dean's lines. He knew them all.

When in 1951 Brando was cast in the movie of Tennessee Williams's *Streetcar Named Desire*, the decade was ready for Hugh Hefner's magazine making sex an entertainment choice. When in the movie *The Wild One* Brando, leader of a motorcycle pack, was asked by a small-town girl, "What are you rebelling against?" he replied, "Waddya got?" The silliness of the Sixties was foreshadowed.

Dean's *Rebel Without a Cause* was made because "juvenile delinquency"—how quaint the phrase seems in today's era of crack-dealing, Uzi-toting youth gangs—was romanticized and sentimentalized as "protest." It was protest not against material privation or tyranny but against the supposed "sterility" of American society.

In *Rebel*, Dean played himself—a mumbling, arrested-development adolescent—to perfection. Feeling mightily sorry for himself as a victim (of insensitive parents), the character he played prefigured the "alienated," oh-how-vulnerable-I-am, nobody-understands-me pouting that the self-absorbed youth of the Sixties considered a political stance.

Halberstam's history, although capacious, has a large lacuna. In 1950 the decade's emblematic liberal, Lionel Trilling, wrote that it was a "plain fact" that there were no conservative ideas in intellectual circles. Reading Halberstam, you might think that was still true at the end of a decade during which (Halberstam does not note) three future Nobel laureates—Milton Friedman, George Stigler and Friedrich von Hayek—were at the University of Chicago honing ideas that would help lift the century out of its statist rut.

Halberstam bestows the adjective "historic" on Allen Ginsberg's October 13, 1955, reading at Gallery Six, a converted auto repair shop in San Francisco, of his poem "Howl." ("I saw the best minds of my gen-

eration destroyed by madness, starving hysterical naked" and so on.)
But Halberstam nowhere notes the really historic harbinger of cultural
change that began one month later when Bill Buckley published the
first issue of *National Review*. That event is just one more reason for
saying that from the Fifties came most of the best of the rest of the
century.

June 20, 1993

The Death of the Sixties

Jim Morrison is dead, dead as a doornail. He has been since 1971,
when he expired, bloated and burnt out, in a bathtub in Paris at 27, not
a moment too soon. His life was a bad influence. His death was a cautionary reminder of the costs of the Sixties stupidity that went by the
puffed-up title of "counterculture." Morrison himself is not particularly
interesting, except that he is an obsession to the sort of people who root
around reverently in the shards of the Sixties. Now Morrison is back.
He is the black hole at the cold heart of the movie *The Doors*, which
tells the short, sick story of that rock group and Morrison's role as
singer.

Oliver Stone, a Sixties-aholic, is the director of the movie, which is
fresh evidence that necrophilia—Yo! Elvis!—is a growth industry.
Stone, a confused man, says, "There is a major time warp going on
here. . . . We all feel the Sixties are coming back." No, the Sixties are
now just nostalgia, kitsch junk among the clutter in the nation's mental
attic. That good news suggests that America has matured, even become
middle-aged. Not a moment too soon.

Age 27 was something of a ceiling for drugged rockers. Jimi Hendrix
and Janis Joplin died at 27. But for many pop culture figures, an early
death was a good career move. James Dean, a three-movie cult figure,
died in his Porsche at age 24. Keats, Shelley and Byron, dead at 25, 29
and 36 respectively, left serious legacies. Morrison left some embarrassing poetry and a few mediocre rock albums. He resembled Byron only
in being "mad, bad and dangerous to know." He was infantile, unsanitary (how odd that he died in a bathtub), dissolute, sadistic (he sometimes was sexually aroused only by inflicting mental cruelty and
physical brutality), occasionally homicidal (as when he locked his
girlfriend in a closet and set it afire) and eventually semi-suicidal.

Universities, self-contained communities congenial to the questioning of all authority, were natural incubators of Sixties radicalism and

today are its last redoubt. Morrison had a smattering of university experience, enough to acquire a patter of ersatz profundity from French poets. The Doors took their name from William Blake's yearning for more immediate, more intense, more real understanding, or at least sensations: "If the doors of perception were cleansed everything would appear to man as it is, infinite." In the Sixties, many people intoxicated by such talk thought the cleansing needed chemical assistance. Morrison, an icon of the drug culture, ingested his share of drugs but was basically a drunk.

Morrison's short, shabby life, and its peculiar echo today, express a longing that waxes and wanes like a low-grade infection but never quite disappears from temperate, rational bourgeois societies. It reflects a vague—very vague—desire to (in the words of The Doors' anthem) "break on through to the other side." Through what? To what? Don't ask. The Doors didn't. People who talk like The Doors are not, as such people say, "into" details.

Their point, if a notion so gauzy can be said to have anything as sharp as a point, is that the existential hero is in permanent revolt against society's repressiveness. By being in touch with nature and his vital urges he breaks on through the walls of the mundane world to "authenticity." Evanescent figures like Morrison, manufactured by the music industry, were given inflated importance by the romantic idea that artists are heroes and rockers are artists. How democratic: Anyone can qualify. (In the movie, a friend encourages Morrison: "You gotta be able to sing better than Dylan." How true.)

The juvenocracy of rock sniffed the air and decided that the times they were achanging. Elders were saying so. In 1960, Walter Lippmann said, "We're at the end of something that is petering out and aging and about finished." In 1962 Arthur Schlesinger, Jr., announced "a new epoch" of "vitality" and "new values . . . straining for expression and release." Break on through to the other side.

Morrison was not Schlesinger set to music, but both were symptoms of a Sixties disorder. Schlesinger's words "expression and release" were part of the mantra of the decade that made Morrison a shooting star, and soon a cinder. The cult of self-validating expression contributed to the debasement of education, which came to be considered a process of letting something out of students rather than of putting something into them. The craving for "release," from reason and other intolerable restraints, led to the confusion of narcissism with freedom.

Warming up for the Sixties, Norman Mailer wrote "The White Negro," praising "the primitive" in the urban jungle, the "nihilism" that wants "every social restraint" removed. That was in 1957, the year of *West Side Story*, a sentimentalizing of juvenile delinquents as Romeos and Juliets. In 1960, Mailer decided "there is a subterranean river of untapped, ferocious, lonely and romantic desires, that concentration of ecstasy and violence which is the dream life of the nation." Seeing John Kennedy, Mailer swooned: "The hipster as presidential candidate . . . a cool grace which seemed indifferent to applause . . . the poise of a fine boxer . . . a good lithe wit . . . a keen sense of proportion . . . an elusive detachment . . . manners which were excellent, even artful . . . a subtle, not quite describable intensity, a suggestion of dry pent heat . . . the eyes of a mountaineer . . . like Brando . . . Mickey Mantle-cum-Lindbergh . . ."

Teenagers say such stuff when they have a crush on somebody. Clearly some people were turning to politics for almost erotic excitement. Mailer's other heartthrob was the man Kennedy tried to kill, Castro. Mailer loved Castro for "giving us psychic ammunition" for the "desperate silent struggle we have been fighting with sick dead hearts against the cold insidious cancer of the power that governs us." Whew. Castro sure lit Mailer's fire.

The passage of time has broken the big progressive hearts of the people who looked to politics and rock music for salvation and truth, and who regarded tyrants and rock stars as existential heroes. Those dabblings with serious subjects now seem inexpressibly childish. Has there ever been such politically barren radicalism as that of the Sixties? Morrison said he liked anything having to do with "revolt." So what did this little Lenin do to overthrow "the system"? He unzipped his trousers on stage.

Devotees of the Sixties sensibility have broken on through to the other side, all right. Here they stand, blinking in the light, wondering why Americans, including young Americans, are more excited by Norman Schwarzkopf than Jim Morrison. This complicates the task of arguing that "there is a major time warp going on here."

And yet there are faint echoes of those dead days. Now, as then, any moneymaking and publicity-generating bit of popular culture, however trivial or tawdry, can, like The Doors, be tarted up to look like a highly moral exercise of "concern" and social criticism. And there are always members of the chattering classes eager to join in the puffery. Consider the case of Bret Easton Ellis.

He is a three-book writer. Formerly a prodigy-by-publicity, he now is a pornographer. He is 27. His first novel, *Less Than Zero*, was short (208 pages) but too long. It was a mildly interesting sketch of self-absorbed rich and drugged youths in southern California. His second novel really was less than zero. His third novel proves that he was at most a one-book semiwonder. Simon & Schuster gave him a big advance for *American Psycho*, then, to its credit, flinched from publishing it. This refusal generated a gusher of publicity for it. Vintage Books, dressing up its greed as anti-greed, rushed to publish *American Psycho*, which supposedly is a terribly serious "indictment" of the—you guessed it—Reagan Years of Greed.

Although Ellis is conventionally dressed and barbered, he is a Morrison for the Nineties. He is, at most, a mildly talented young man. But he is marketed by older people. Some are cynical, others are just incorrigible. (Stormin' Norman Mailer is back.) Presto! Ellis, a triumph of packaging, is a serious critic of America generally but especially of the last decade. *American Psycho* is short on plot and shorter still on characterization. It is long on sexual atrocities interlarded with minute descriptions of designer clothes and pretentious menus and other objects of status-conferring consumption. It is about a Wall Street Yuppie, a serial killer who especially enjoys torturing women, as when he inserts a starving rat into a victim's vagina.

It is (so we are invited to believe) a "satiric" look at callow youth rendered degenerate by the Greed Decade, depraved by effortless wealth and pursuing instant gratification of ever more extreme fantasies. Needless to say, the torturer himself is, well, sort of a victim. Of what? Consumption-crazed American society. You say Ellis's prose is pedestrian? Ah, the banality is a device for brilliantly conveying the barrenness of contemporary America. The book is absurdly padded with brand names? But of course: such a clever way to lampoon America as all surface.

Actually, Ellis is the 2 Live Crew of the literary set, making money from today's depraved appetite for imaginary violence against women. The desensitizing of Americans is a tragedy for an increasingly violent nation but a market opportunity for the likes of Ellis. It may seem paradoxical to call his pornography boring, but it is. Making sadism boring may seem to be a literary achievement of sorts, but pornography always is boring, for the same reason Morrison's frenetic attempts to be "outrageous" were boring. Adult infantilism is not interesting, other than clinically.

However, Norman Mailer offers an equivocal defense of Ellis served up (in *Vanity Fair*) with wheezy bromides ("Without serious art the universe is doomed") and the faintest possible praise: The novel "is not written so badly that one can reject it with clear conscience." Mailer says it is a "serious" book, a "black comedy." Useful, too. "Art serves us best precisely at that point where it can shift our sense of what is possible." Ah. Perhaps that is the purpose of the rat in the vagina. Mailer's idea seems to be that the book is provoked by, and needed by, our rotten society. Ours is "a world which, by spiritual measure, if we could measure it, might be worse than any of the worlds preceding it."

Mailer limps to a lame, utilitarian conclusion: Perhaps *American Psycho* will prevent sadistic crimes. (Harmless catharsis for potential homicidal maniacs?) Ellis's shockingness may be, Mailer thinks, good for us all, blasting society out of its death-of-the-spirit that has been caused by greed, Reagan, etc. "Ellis," says Mailer, "wants to break through steel walls." Go for it, Bret: Break on through to the other side.

Ellis is, as Morrison was, his own fault. If society has made some small contribution to such shambles, it is this. Ellis in his way, and Morrison in his, illustrate a particular fate for certain youths. In Randall Jarrell's novel *Pictures from an Institution* a foreign visitor says, "You Americans do not rear children, you *incite* them; you give them food and shelter and applause." The problem is juvenophilia. It is the foolishness of listening for wisdom from the mouths of babes and hoping that youthful vigor (the favorite word along the New Frontier when the Sixties were aborning) will liberate by smashing suffocating old structures. Remember the Founding Father, Chuck Berry: "Hail, hail, rock and roll, deliver me from the days of old."

"This planet is screaming for change, Morrison," says one of The Doors in Stone's movie. "We have to make the myths." The central myth of the Sixties was that the wretched excess was really a serious quest for new values. And there always will be a few who seek salvation from cathartic rock music, orgasmic politics and pornography masquerading as social profundity. Today there are many people who are willing to plunk down good money to see Morrison brought back to life, and death, for two hours. But for today's audiences, Stone's loving re-creation of San Francisco's Haight-Ashbury district is just a low-rent Williamsburg, an interesting artifact but no place for a pilgrimage. As the years pass, more and more Americans will say, "The Sixties? I never was there—but I saw the movie." The Sixties are dead. Not a moment too soon.

March 25, 1991

Italian-Americans Achieve the American Dream: Victim Status

Five hundred and one years ago an Italian started American history, which, sensitive people say, has been a blood-soaked tale of unrelieved exploitation, racism, sexism, genocide, violation of the rights of old growth forests, and victimization all around. But today the sensitive City University of New York awards Italian-Americans a coveted place on its affirmative action list of official victims deserving therapeutic preferences.

Strange, New York State has an Italian-American governor who is from New York City. And that city has an Italian-American mayor-elect. Yet the city university believes that Italian-Americans are oppressed. Professor Lawrence Castiglione, a founder of the Italian-American Legal Defense Fund, explains: "The general image is that we are affiliated with organized crime and thuggery. People think Italian-Americans are anti-intellectual."

Perhaps there ought to be a law against such images and thinking. The *Chronicle of Higher Education* reports:

> Italian-Americans admit they have never been burdened by racist laws and policies that have prevented other groups from advancing, but they say they too carry particular burdens. Stereotypes persist of Italian-Americans as dumb guys named Guido with links to the Mafia, they say. . . . Italian-American professors tell of colleagues asking them who their Godfather is and whether they brought their brass knuckles to class.

Perhaps there ought to be a law against dumb jokes about dumb guys named Guido. Perhaps there is such a law. Today Italian-Americans' litigation about various grievances at CUNY is as tangled as (is this an insensitive simile?) linguine.

Turbulence occasioned by tender sensibilities is busting out all over. Consider the following survey of current skirmishing on the sensitivity front, and of new developments in the victimization industry. The survey is offered in the spirit of the holiday season, a time when we count our blessings, which may include not being a victim, or being one.

Last year Cincinnati's city council passed a human rights ordinance forbidding discrimination on the basis of all the usual things—race, sex, sexual preference, marital status, color, religion, national origin and disability status. But it added a new wrinkle. It forbade discrimination based on "Appalachian regional origin."

That means "birth or ancestral origin from that area of the eastern United States consisting of the counties listed in an Appalachian Regional Origin Document" kept on file by the council. If California had been as sensitive in the 1930s as everyone is today, it would have forbade discrimination based on "Oklahoma origin." Okieism was then rampant.

The University of California, Riverside, recently suspended a fraternity for the offense of distributing, in conjunction with a "south of the border" party, T-shirts depicting, among other things, a man in a serape and sombrero, sitting on a beach with a bottle of tequila. This was judged an insensitive stereotype.

The fraternity challenged the suspension, citing the First Amendment and a new California statute protecting free speech on campuses. The university surrendered, and under the terms of the settlement, the administrators who suspended the fraternity were sentenced to undergo five hours of sensitivity training about the First Amendment, at the hands of constitutional law professors. People who applaud this mandatory consciousness-raising need their sensitivity to totalitarianism raised.

In Marietta, Georgia, the informal nickname of the Kennesaw State College "Fighting Owls" had been "the Hooters." The basketball team played in "the Hooterdome" and the baseball team at "Hooter Field." The college has dropped the nickname now that it reminds sensitive people of a chain of restaurants where the waitresses' attire (T-shirts, orange shorts) is not calculated to cause patrons to think of women as Supreme Court justices.

The University of Illinois homecoming committee, practicing the central skill of college governance—preemptive capitulation—this year banned depictions of the university's venerable Indian symbol, "Chief Illiniwek," from homecoming floats, lest offense be given. When the University of Alabama at Birmingham decided it needed a mascot, it came up with "Blaze," a Nordic warrior looking mighty aggressive. An Aryan overdosed on testosterone? He's gone.

Until 1972 they were the University of Massachusetts at Amherst Redmen. Deemed insensitive, the school's mascot was changed to the Minuteman. Now advanced thinkers say: Are you kidding? A gun-toting white male militarist? Protests have been led by a black student who says the Minuteman "is culturally biased and promotes racism."

This student went on a four-day hunger strike that ended, according to the *Chronicle of Higher Education,* when he and his mother and the school's chancellor "went out for Italian food." It was, perhaps, a gastronomic gesture of solidarity with another victim group.

November 28, 1993

Giving Some Feminists the Vapors

"My grandmother lived in a world of manicures, hair salons, and no place to go in the morning." That felicitous first sentence is the fuse that lights Katie Roiphe's bombshell of a book in which she argues that a perversion of feminism is reviving stereotypes that constricted her grandmother's world.

In today's victimization sweepstakes, many prizes, including media attention and therapeutic preferences from government, go to those who succeed at being seen as vulnerable and suffering. So hell hath no fury like that directed against someone like Roiphe, who casts a cool eye on the claims and logic of some women who consider their victimhood compounded by any calm analysis of their claims. This Roiphe provides in *The Morning After: Sex, Fear and Feminism on Campus.* It is giving some feminists the vapors.

Roiphe, 25, a Ph.D. candidate in English at Princeton, dissects the contemporary feminist obsession with sexual harassment and rape, both broadly—very broadly—defined. Behind this obsession Roiphe detects the old image of woman as exquisitely delicate, "with her pure intentions and her wide eyes," constantly on the verge of victimization.

Into what Roiphe calls "the normal libidinous jostle of coeducation" has come a gothic feminism. It portrays men as predators and women as prey—women who by nature are innocent, passive, manipulable and almost asexual and whose fragile composure crumbles when they encounter male sexuality.

This feminism explains a feature of contemporary campus life, the "Take Back the Night" marches. At these rituals, "survivors" of sexual "violence," very broadly defined, "speak out" about their "voicelessness." They describe being "silenced" by a shadowy force with several names— "men" or, for the intellectually upscale, "patriarchic hegemony" and "phallocentrism."

As Roiphe dryly notes, being "silenced" is an experience of the articulate, whose tone is often self-congratulatory: I have survived victimization, so I am very brave. Participants in these marches-as-therapy, says Roiphe, are "more oversaturated with self-esteem than with cholesterol."

Today, when certified victim groups surely aggregate to at least 200 percent of the nation's population, one often-repeated statistic of suffering is that one in four college women is a victim of rape or attempted rape. One study that popularized that factoid has interesting flaws. Seventy-three percent of the women categorized as rape victims did not themselves define their experiences as rape. Some feminists say that just proves how much those women need their consciousnesses "raised."

But at Berkeley, with 14,000 female students, only two rapes were reported to the police in 1990. And Roiphe considers it remarkable that she supposedly lives amidst an epidemic, with 25 percent of her peers encountering rapists, yet she never noticed it. "Somebody," she says, "is 'finding' this rape crisis, and finding it for a reason."

They find it by postulating that women are trapped in a "rape culture" where they are powerless and hence true sexual consent is problematic, perhaps impossible. The chorus about the ubiquity of "date rape" or "acquaintance rape" generates a climate of constant fear that Roiphe says sequesters feminism "in the teary province of trauma and crisis." In the process, the brutal crime of rape is trivialized.

Pamphlets titled "Is Dating Dangerous?" and "Friends Raping Friends" warn freshmen women to "be on your guard with every man." Such literature expresses what Roiphe calls "the old sugar-and-spice approach to female character." It infantilizes women, portraying them as helpless before the onslaught of insatiable male desire.

"We've come a long way," writes Roiphe, "and now it seems we are going back." In its portrayal of female competence, character and free will, "rape crisis feminism" echoes an 1848 book warning young women about verbally adroit men who will "dazzle and bewilder her mind" using "a subtlety almost beyond the power of her detection."

The preoccupation of rape crisis feminists with explicit, verbal, step-by-step consent to everything sexual—anything less supposedly is rape—rests, Roiphe says, on antique assumptions about the way men and women experience sex. Men are supposedly lascivious; women are innocents who, like children, have trouble ascertaining or communicating their desires.

One pamphlet defines rape to include "a woman's consenting to unwanted sexual activity because of a man's verbal arguments not including verbal threats of force." By means of "verbal coercion," cunning rakes (the language of Victorian melodramas seems natural here) turn the pretty little heads of weak-willed women. No wonder feminists who think like this are so smitten with that quintessential contemporary victim, the woman whose story was so uncannily—or perhaps cannily—congruent with this latest fashion in feminism, the woman who herself said she passively followed her supposed sexual harasser from one job to another: Anita Hill.

October 24, 1993

Catharine MacKinnon's Angry Serenity

Catharine MacKinnon, author of *Only Words* and campaigner in the culture wars on campuses, is more than just another full-time victim, ubiquitous and loud in proclaiming that she has been silenced. This professor at the University of Michigan law school also is a leader of the most radical assault on free speech in American history.

McCarthyism, the "red scare" after the First World War and the Alien and Sedition Acts were the products of political factions with familiar kinds of interests and passions. But today's assault on free speech is launched by intellectuals citing the core values of contemporary liberalism—compassion, fairness and equality.

Like all monomaniacs, MacKinnon believes in One Huge Fact. Hers is: We live "in a world made by pornography." She makes two arguments for aggressive censorship of pornography and—although she does not acknowledge it—for censorship of much more as well.

One argument is that pornography is not "only words" (or only pictures), it is a form of assault, causing violence against women and reducing them to mere commodities. So government should treat pornography as action to be regulated, not expression protected by the First Amendment.

Her second argument is that free speech is, for most people, a chimera in sexist, racist America, where most people are members of "subordinate groups." Pornography, a tool of male domination, must be censored to promote the constitutional value of equality.

Her argument sweeps far beyond pornography. Government has not only a right but a constitutional duty to suppress all expression that exacerbates any "historically oppressed" group's subordinate status. MacKinnon says that pornography and all other expression that imposes ("constructs" is the preferred jargon) subordination really silences groups, so such expression is itself really a form of censorship, and censorship of it is really an expansion of freedom.

According to the theory behind the proliferation of campus speech codes, there is this new entitlement: the right of certain groups not to have their sensibilities hurt. So censorship is progressive when it suppresses expression that offends subordinate groups. Such groups include almost everyone except white heterosexual males, Jews (interesting, that) and perhaps Asian-Americans.

Free speech must wait until all groups achieve equal status. When MacKinnon says, "Society is made of words, whose meanings the powerful control, or try to," she rationalizes something familiar: despotism— government control of words—made virtuous by the goal of equality.

Although she bases her case for despotism on an empirical claim (about pornography's power to impel behavior), she shows scant interest in evidence. However, Judge Richard Posner, reviewing *Only Words* in *The New Republic*, notes some evidence. Denmark, where pornography is completely unregulated, and Japan, where pornography featuring rape and bondage is especially popular, have rates of rape far lower than here; the rate of rape has been declining as pornography has proliferated; women's status tends to be lower where, as in Islamic nations, pornography is suppressed.

The point is not that pornography is harmless. It contributes to the coarsening of American life and so conduces to social crudeness, perhaps even violence. But the First Amendment is a nullity if it protects only expression that is without consequences, or that has consequences universally considered benign.

And even if pornography were proven inconsequential regarding violent behavior, MacKinnon and like-minded feminists would still want it censored as part of a government program to impose on society a progressive "consciousness." Furthermore, the logic of her position leads to censorship of all depictions, in popular culture or advertising, of women in "subordinate" roles.

For someone who so strenuously loathes American society, which she says is defined by pornography, MacKinnon is remarkably eager to vest in this society's representative government vast powers to regulate expression. She simply ignores the familiar contradiction in radical programs for therapeutic government: If society is so sick that it needs radical therapy, what reason is there to trust the government produced by that society to be therapeutic?

MacKinnon reasons serenely, as fanatics do, within a closed circle of logic: If you do not see our wicked society as she does, that just proves how wickedly society has "constructed" your false consciousness. Thus all critics are dismissable.

This professor, made rich and famous by a tenured position at a prestigious public university, proclaims her voicelessness in a volume published by the Harvard University Press. Here is the final sign of fanaticism—no sense of the ridiculous.

October 28, 1993

Sex Amidst Semicolons

The social air is heavily scented with sex. It saturates commerce and amusement—advertising, entertainment, recreation. Eros is rampant everywhere. Make that almost everywhere. In Yellow Springs, Ohio, home of Antioch College, the god of love has a migraine, the result of reading that institution's rules regulating "interactions" of a sexual sort.

Declaring the frequency of "sexual violence" on campuses "alarming," Antioch displays nice evenhandedness regarding eligibility for the coveted status of victim. Antioch notes that most victims are female but "there are also female perpetrators and male victims." Furthermore, "there are also many students who have already experienced sexual violence before arriving at Antioch; healing from that experience may be an integral part of their personal, social and academic lives while they are here." Having postulated a vast supply of unhealed victims and probable new ones, Antioch lays down the law:

> *All sexual contact and conduct* between any two people *must be consensual;* consent must be obtained *verbally* before there is any sexual contact or conduct; if the level of sexual intimacy increases during an interaction (i.e., if two people move from kissing while fully clothed—which is one level—to undressing for direct physical contact—which is another level), the people involved need to express their clear verbal consent before moving to that new level; if one person wants to *initiate* moving to a higher level of sexual intimacy in an interaction, *that person is responsible for getting the verbal consent of the other person(s) involved before moving to that level;* if you have had a particular level of sexual intimacy before with someone, you must still ask each and every time. . . . Asking "Do you want to have sex with me?" is not enough. The request for consent must be specific to each act.

Antioch meticulously defines terms ("'Sexual contact' includes the touching of thighs, genitals, buttocks, the pubic region, or the breast/chest area"), although some terms seem somewhat spacious. For example, "insistent and/or persistent sexual harassment" includes, "but is not limited to, unwelcome and irrelevant comments, references, gestures or other forms of personal attention which are inappropriate and which may be perceived as persistent sexual overtones or denigration." Imagine being charged with making a "gesture" that was "irrelevant" or "perceived" as denigrating.

Campuses, being concentrations of young people, are awash with hormones, which are powerful. However, hormonal heat may be chilled by Antioch's grim seasoning of sex with semicolons. This is what happens when sexual emancipation comes to a litigious society. Antioch's many dense pages setting forth procedures for prosecuting and reforming offenders will keep batteries of lawyers busy debating whether a particular request for consent was sufficiently specific. ("May I touch that?" "Is a caress more than a touch?" "May I unbutton that?" "Have you consented regarding all the buttons?") Imagine the litigation that can arise from questions about what constitutes movement from one "level" to another. (Is the movement of a hand from this body part to that one necessarily a movement to a new level? If only John Marshall were alive to help us cope.) And what is the significance of the "(s)" attached to the word "person" in the quotation above? Sexual freedom sure seems to require an elaborate regulatory apparatus.

Our nation opted for the moral deregulation of sex a decade before deregulating airlines. About 20 years ago colleges, like a lot of parents, stopped acting *in loco parentis* regarding sexual matters. Official indifference about what students do with their bodies includes all organs except the lungs: about smoking, colleges are as stern as they once were about copulating. (Health care may be paid for partly with a "sin tax" on cigarettes. A million abortions a year is a mere matter of "choice"—an achievement of the "pro-choice" movement—but choosing to smoke is a sin. Interesting.) Today students can do anything their physiognomies will permit regarding sex, but they must observe due process.

Rules like Antioch's are both causes and effects of an odd "crisis" on campuses. Such rules are written in response to supposed "sexual violence" that supposedly is so frequent that "many students" arriving at Antioch already are victims in need of "healing." By punctiliously codifying due process regarding "levels" of consensual "interactions" with "other person(s)," the rules multiply the opportunities for, and increase the probability of, sexual offenses. All this serves the interests of two classes that have much in common.

The rules, and the assumption of "crisis" that they reflect, give the "caring professions," as they like to be called, lots of victims to care for. These professionals include counselors, "gender equity" bureaucrats, sensitivity "facilitators" who conduct "safe sex workshops," and others. And the rules, by postulating a culture of female victimization and by creating many permutations of sexual offenses, delight those feminists who consider America a predatory "rape culture." The title of Antioch's Sexual Offense Prevention and Survivors' Advocacy Program encourages a sense of intense peril, of life lived precariously in a sexual jungle. People who experience, say, "irrelevant comments" are *survivors.*

One function of the "caring professions" is to heighten the sensitivity of persons who might not "perceive" sexual harassment where they should. Professionals can help young people be as offended and frightened as they should be in phallocentric America. A really caring professional can get a young woman to see that if she has no memory of being a victim of sexual violence, that may prove either how awful the memory is that she has "repressed," or how inadequate her definition of "sexual violence" is.

At Antioch, as young people go from level to level in their interactions, they are taught that there is one cardinal value: consent. The rules say, "Do not take silence as consent; it isn't. Consent must be clear and verbal (i.e., saying: yes, I want you to kiss me now)."

Actually, not now, dear. I have a headache.

October 4, 1993

The University of Chicago: Fun in a Cold Climate

When word reached the University of Chicago that a magazine published by Harvard students had ranked 300 universities in terms of the fun to be found there and had ranked Chicago 300th, a Chicago undergraduate, probably bundled up against the razorlike wind off the lake, jauntily said: "Fun isn't linear." His riposte had the wittiness, and the obliqueness, you expect from the school that expresses its intellectual brio in a song: "Anything you can do I can do meta."

Today this column rises in disinterested defense of fun as the University of Chicago understands it. I have no connection with the place, other than friendships, and I do not begrudge the top ranking for fun given to Florida State, which I assume is a university worthy of its football team.

However, if Chicago had not gone, almost ostentatiously, from being a football power—long ago, under coach Amos Alonzo Stagg—to seeming to fancy itself too damned serious for such stuff, perhaps it would not have had to suffer so many suggestions that only the slightly weird would choose to enroll there. "The largest collection of neurotic youths since the Children's Crusades," and so on.

The university was founded by a no-nonsense Baptist who did well in the oil business, John D. Rockefeller. His wizened visage—he, not the sainted Calvin Coolidge, looked as though he had been weaned on a pickle—suggested a soul lacking a spacious conception of fun. Nowadays freshmen assemble in September for their first lecture, on the aims of education, in the chapel named for him.

For many years the chapel was open 24 hours a day, a policy changed by President Robert Maynard Hutchins because, he said, "Unfortunately, more souls have been conceived at Rockefeller Chapel than have been saved there." See? The libido is frisky at Chicago as well as at Florida State.

In the most recent such address to the freshmen, Professor Richard Shweder, an anthropologist in the Department of Psychology, offered his listeners some commandments conducive to fun.

First, "Don't stand up when your professor enters the room."

Not that there is any danger of an American undergraduate doing that, but in some cultures students do. It is wrong to do it, Shweder told the freshmen, because we should detach our evaluation of ideas from the social identity of the person voicing them.

It has taken humanity eons to rise—that portion that has risen— above the fallacy that all knowledge is parochial and is the property of particular groups. Today we must be vigilant against people who would retribalize knowledge. They say there must be a black theory of this and a woman's "perspective" on that, and so on. Shweder says, "The authority of a voice has a lot to do with what is said and very little to do with who says it."

Another commandment is: "Never take a Puritan to the Monty Python show."

A Puritan, says Shweder, exaggerates a virtue until it becomes a vice, and there are as many kinds of Puritans as there are virtues, because any virtue can be overdrawn. A world that looks increasingly like *Monty Python's Flying Circus* offends Puritans, who want "a world governed by some perfectly enforced virtue." Imagine the nightmare of such perfect enforcement.

Perfect justice would require a world of watchful accountants and severe prosecutors—accountants of moral infractions, noting every error, indiscretion or dark desire, and prosecutors enforcing appropriate punishments. Protecting people from harm also is a virtue, and yet, says Shweder, if carried too far, the idea that you should protect everyone from everything they might consider harmful is a recipe for "a society of thin-skinned complainers." It would be a society with a constant acid rain of complaints about "abuse" or "harassment" or—is this beginning to sound familiar?—"victimization."

Shweder's commandment for preserving equilibrium is: "There are only two things you need to know to do dermatology."

They are: "If it is dry, make it wet. If it is wet, make it dry." The analogue for Chicago freshmen is: "If someone asserts it, deny it. If someone denies it, assert it." But, says Shweder, bear in mind that "the world is incomplete if seen from any one point of view and incoherent if seen from all points of view at once."

Such is fun in a cold climate, at the University of Chicago, where, as Shweder told the freshmen, "the brain is an erogenous zone and provocation is a virtue."

November 14, 1993

Professor Shweder later reported that in the spring after the publication of this column applications for admission to the University of Chicago jumped 24 percent. The power of the press? Sure. "When," wrote Stephen Leacock, "I state that my lectures were followed almost immediately by the union of South Africa, the banana riots in Trinidad and the Turco-Italian war, I think readers can form some opinion of their importance."

A Lunch with a Wicked Man

NEWPORT BEACH, CALIFORNIA—Amidst the genteel tinkle of restaurant lunch sounds, Mark Weber is having difficulty doing justice to his salmon, such is his passion for justice, as he pretends to understand it. He is trying to persuade me that the Holocaust never happened. It is not going well.

I am a hard sell, having visited death camps (Auschwitz-Birkenau, Majdanek, Treblinka) with survivors. But the fact that some Jews survived is part of the Holocaust deniers' "proof" that the Nazis never intended extermination.

Weber edits *The Journal of Historical Review*, a recent issue of which advertises a book "that dares to ask: Who benefited from the 'Crystal Night,' " the November 9, 1938, anti-Jewish rioting. If you guessed that the Jews benefited, you have got the drift of Holocaust "revisionism."

"Revisionism" is a term of scholarship hijacked by pseudoscholarship in the service of anti-Semitism. Holocaust deniers present any conflict among, or amendment of, survivors' testimonies, or any historical refinement of previous understandings, as "proof" that the Holocaust is a myth. Weber allows as how maybe a million Jews were victims—of the rigors of confinement, and of excessive Nazi security concerns. But Holocaust deniers say victims exaggerate, and after the war Nazis made false confessions to appease their captors, who were serving the mythmakers—Jews fabricating martyrdom for political and financial gains.

The deniers' "arguments" always return to what Weber, like the Nazis, calls "the Jewish question" (*Judenfrage*). The gas chambers were really showers. Zyklon-B gas was too weak to kill. Or too powerful to use for mass murder—it would have killed those who emptied the "alleged" gas chambers. When Hitler promised "the annihilation of the Jewish race in Europe" (January 30, 1939) he was, says one denier, merely using heroic hyperbole—"the kind of defiance that was hurled by the ancient heroes." And so on.

For some people, historical partisanship, such as defending Richard III against the charge that he ordered the murder of the princes in the Tower, is a hobby. But what kind of person makes a career of denying the reality of an almost contemporary event that was recorded graphically, documented bureaucratically and described in detail by victims, bystanders and perpetrators? Such a person tortures the past in the hope of making the future safe for torturers.

In her new book *Denying the Holocaust: The Growing Assault on Truth and Memory*, Deborah Lipstadt of Emory University argues that the deniers' work "is intimately connected to a neofascist political agenda." She says the deniers' aim is to rehabilitate Nazism and reevaluate its victims, thereby delegitimizing Israel and vilifying Jews.

Hitler, says Weber at lunch, was "the most philosophical" figure of the 20th century, and "his understanding of this century was more on the mark than that of any of his contemporaries." And "Hitler has the 'rep' he has because he opposed the whole development of the 20th century." Anti-Semitic and antidemocratic, Hitler understood the necessity for severely hierarchical and racially homogeneous nations.

Applying these ideas, Weber says that America "has two ways to go." It can become a "Third World" chaos of tribes, or can be sundered into racially pure entities.

The Webers of the world are few and their "arguments" are farragoes of dizzying non sequiturs and mock-scientific analyses of a sort concocted only by lunatics or sinister cynics. But the deniers' increasing echoes, and their ability to insert themselves into the conversation of society, are cultural symptoms.

Holocaust deniers play upon contemporary society's tendency toward historical amnesia, and its gassy notion of "tolerance" that cannot distinguish between an open mind and an empty mind. Thus a young reporter for a respected magazine interviewing Lipstadt (without reading her book) asked this question: "What proof do you include in your book that the Holocaust happened?" That reporter passed through college unmarked by information about even the largest events of the century, but acquired the conventional skepticism of the emptyheaded: When in doubt, doubt.

People as ignorant as that reporter know nothing, so they doubt everything except how sophisticated they are when they assume that nothing is certain. This assumption is irrigated in the badly educated by fashionable academic theories of epistemological indeterminacy. The vocabulary and mentality of literary "deconstruction" seeps everywhere, relativizing everything, teaching that history, like all of life, is a mere "narrative," a "text" with no meaning beyond what any individual reads into it. No event, no book, nothing has a fixed content; the individual's "perception" or "reaction" to it is everything.

That is the bad news. The good news is that this year 2 million people will pass through Washington's new Holocaust Memorial Museum, which will survive the survivors and be their testimony.

August 29, 1993

Darkness on the Mall

Strange thoughts beat upon the brain. Such as: Who held the camera so steadily, and why?

In the black-and-white photograph, a naked girl, perhaps six years old, dangles, gripped by the neck in the coarse hands of a strong woman (we see nothing of the woman above her biceps). The child, eyes closed, looks uncomfortable but resigned to, and used to, rough handling. Her face is being wrenched around to face the camera. The description of the photograph in the display in the new Holocaust Memorial Museum reads: "A mentally disabled girl photographed shortly before her murder."

We know the minds of the articulate haters whose ideologies fuel mass murder. But who can fathom the mind of the unknown photographer?

The murder of the mentally handicapped was rehearsal for the Holocaust, the story of which is told with cold, controlled fury in the museum's artifacts and images. Visitors to the museum will see film (on screens behind walls too high for children to see over) of mob animalism and other cruelties so savage that they seem to suck the oxygen from the room. But the museum also tells horrifying truths with blander images.

Near the photograph of the dangling girl is a photograph of a big building, taken from across the tops of a town's leafy trees. It is summer yet dark smoke pours from the building's chimney. The building is a euthanasia center with a crematorium. The residents of the town had to know.

The Holocaust Museum inflicts a kind of excruciating knowing. Architecture is high art when the way it frames space compels a frame of mind. The Holocaust Museum—the building and the experiences it synchronizes—is a masterpiece in response to an obscenity.

The hard, assaultive building is made of brick framed by bolted steel—the Nazi solution to the problem of the intense heat of hard-used crematoria. The building suggests a closed world without softness, other than that of flesh. The building seems contorted by anxiety: Angles are odd, implying fissures in the foundation of things. Visitors have a sense of being loomed over by structures evoking guard towers. A rising stairway intimates a railroad, and leads to an arch that insinuates into the mind's eye the gate over the tracks at the Auschwitz-Birkenau concentration camp.

Visitors begin their journey into darkness in elevators, rising to the fourth floor while hearing the voice of an American soldier in Germany 48 Aprils ago. The soldier is saying that his unit has stumbled on a horror down the road. The elevators' dark steel doors part and visitors face a wall-sized picture of charred bodies stacked like cordwood. Thus begins an immersion in evil, and an encounter with heroism in the face of it.

A square three-story tower within the museum is lined with photographs from a Lithuanian community where a 900-year tradition of Jewish life was machine-gunned to death in two days. The soaring tower of strong images of Jewish vitality suggests how much the number 6 million understates the loss. Think of all the generations that will not happen.

Some people will wonder: Why situate this museum, this experience of darkness, amidst the Mall's glistening monuments to the success of our society? One answer is: Because one message of the museum is that there is no permanent safety in social arrangements. The Mall's welcoming openness and reasonable geometry make it an analogue of our national experience, which is the best of the West. However, the Holocaust Museum, by holding up for scrutiny a radical evil that erupted in the middle of the West in the middle of the 20th century, reminds us that the most that can ever be said with certainty, anywhere, is: So far, so good.

But it almost diminishes the museum's dignity to cite its usefulness. A sufficient reason for it is to keep faith with those who suffered, by telling their truth. This the museum does, with the power of literature.

In 1989, I visited death camps in Poland as part of a delegation accepting some of the artifacts now displayed in the museum. That trip, although harrowing, did not prepare me for the power of this museum, which left me literally short of breath, suffocated by a sadness related to something Primo Levi wrote.

Levi was an Auschwitz survivor. (Perhaps, in a sense, not. In 1987, still a prisoner of his memory and haunted by the thought that the world's memory of the Holocaust was fading, he killed himself.) Levi wrote about the "interminable death" that a survivor of torture suffers. He quoted a Belgian Jew who survived Auschwitz: "Anyone who has suffered torture never again will be able to be at ease in the world." That man killed himself in 1978.

The Holocaust Museum, experienced deeply, will annihilate the possibility of feeling quite at ease. Be warned, but do not be deterred.

April 22, 1993

The Anti-Slavery Society: Still with Work to Do

LONDON—South of the river, in a slightly seedy section of the city, in a down-at-the-heels building that has seen better days but not better uses, the Anti-Slavery Society is still in business, because slavery is, too. Founded in 1839, it is the world's oldest human rights organization.

As it raises its small voice amid the incessant clamor for public attention, it faces the problem of stark incredulity concerning its threshold assertion: Slavery exists.

Today there may be as many, perhaps many more, people in conditions properly denoted as slavery as there were when the Society was founded. So says the Society's director, Lesley Roberts.

She is not one of those flurried people one so often sees in the world of altruism, the kind who perpetually look as though they had risen late and dressed in haste. She has the brisk manner of one who has worked in banks, which she has done, and she has the restlessness to have been bored by that, which she was. In an office lit only, and dimly, by watery sunlight that struggles through unwashed windows, she enumerates the Society's concerns, beginning with chattel slavery—the total ownership of one person by another. It was officially outlawed in the Arabian peninsula less than 20 years ago, and may even be expanding in parts of northern Africa, particularly Sudan.

Far more prevalent, and properly called slavery, is debt bondage, especially of children. Such laborers are bound for payment of debts and are entirely subservient to a power from which there is no appeal.

There are workers in servitude in both hemispheres. Roberts says that many Haitians living illegally in the Dominican Republic have been, in effect, sold to state-owned sugar plantations. But the biggest problems are in Asia, where slavery often is a particularly odious, because routinized, form of child abuse.

Children are, in a sense, "natural" slaves—a renewable source of slaves—because they are born into total dependence on adults. Children are sometimes sold outright, with common prices ranging from $20 in the Sudan to $200 in Bangkok.

Social traditions no longer sanctioned by laws—traditions of caste and class—can still be as strong as iron fetters. There is the tradition of giving a child for, say, a year in payment of debt—sometimes a debt incurred by parents who borrow from loan sharks, using children as collateral. At the end of the year, the person holding the child in bondage may say the child has eaten so much that the bondage must be extended.

No one knows even within several scores of millions how many children are enslaved in domestic service, in sweatshops or in Asia's huge sex trade. When computing the probable numbers, says Roberts, "it is not hard to get up to 200 million."

In India, for example, the government says there are fewer than 200,000 bonded laborers. The Society's sources say 5 million. Look down, dear reader, you may be walking on them.

Demand for Indian carpets soared when the price of Iranian carpets rose after the shah outlawed child labor in the early 1970s. Today in India's main carpet-weaving region (small hands, such as those of seven-year-olds, tie especially tight knots), there are 100,000 malnourished children employed. Some 15 percent of them, according to the Society, were sold into bondage in spite of the fact that India outlawed debt bondage 14 years ago.

They often work 12-hour days (poorly fed; subjected to corporal punishment; often sleeping at their looms six, sometimes seven, days a week, for a weekly wage sometimes as low as $1). Today, as two centuries ago, slavery pays. The labor costs of a carpet that may sell in London for $6,000 can be as little as $20.

While sifting abundant evidence of such slavery (and worse—millions of children, male and female, are devoured by Asia's prostitution industry), the Society maintains a remarkable emotional equipoise, advocating piecemeal remedies for absolute evils. For example, it does not favor banning imports of carpets made with coerced labor. It knows that destroying the carpet industry would destroy many lives. An existing industry can be improved.

Publicity, embarrassment, persuasion, organized labor—these are among the remedies required. But the first requirement is the patience of politics, which acquires special dignity in the face of such shattering facts.

Roberts and the Society (180 Brixton Road, SW9 6AT) are echoes of the distinctive moral earnestness that redeemed the 19th century and leaven this one. "I get bored easily," she says. "This is not boring."

June 21, 1990

1990: "That Last Guy Hit Me Hard"

In 1990 Americans refought their Civil War, on television, and Daisy Cave of Sumter, South Carolina, collected her 57th annual pension. But in October, the last living widow of a Confederate Army veteran died. She was between 97 and 105. But the Union, now 214, made it through another year.

The cover of *Newsweek* dated January 1, 1990, pictured two U.S. soldiers in full combat gear, rifles at the ready. The cover headline asked, BUSH'S INVASION: HOW HIGH A PRICE? HOW LONG A STAY? The subject was Panama, and the questions were still unanswered in December, but by then other questions were on American minds, such as: What is a Kuwait? But few war scenarios envision as many Americans dying in the desert in 1991 as were killed—about 16,000—in America in 1990 by homicides with guns.

Most of the people who suffered under communism in 1988, the year before the Cold War ended, suffered worse under it in 1990. They are Chinese. According to China's government there are 1,113,682,501 of them now—minus those whose political heterodoxy got them executed. China enlisted in the crusade to punish Iraq for doing to Kuwait what China has done to Tibet. Syria, another partner in building President Bush's New World Order, pocketed a billion-dollar gift (bribe?) from Saudi Arabia (crusades can be profitable) and went on a weapons-buying binge, perhaps for its next aggression against what's left of Lebanon.

The international left lost its last pinup when Nicaraguans, who know the guy, were given a chance to vote against Daniel Ortega. Albanians began rattling their chains. Looks like North Korea and Cuba are the only candidates for the role of Museum of Communism. Western nations sent aid to the stricken Soviet Union, which continued sending billions of dollars' worth of annual subsidies to Cuba. Gorbachev, the toast of every town not in the Soviet Union, and of none in it, won a Nobel Prize (not for economics). Like Kerensky in 1917, Gorbachev gathered unto himself *de jure* power as *de facto* power flowed elsewhere in his disintegrating nation, where various republics were appointing foreign ministers.

In the Balkans, the region which long ago became a verb ("to Balkanize"), Yugoslavia, too, began what looks like terminal crumbling. Unless a stupendous life is lived by some baby born in 1990, only one date from this year, October 3, will stand out in history. That was the day Germany unified. (Joke of the year: Germany's eastern and western parts have agreed on the city that should be Germany's new capital—Paris.)

What is being called the heroic age of conservatism came to a close with the departure of Margaret Thatcher. In a budget deal that settled everything for five years, or until spring, whichever comes first, President Bush drove a hard bargain: He sacrificed his dearest principle, no new taxes, but in return got rising spending and a rising deficit.

Nelson Mandela got free and made a beeline for America. Virginia inaugurated the nation's first elected black governor, whose presidential aspirations resulted in a button: "Wilder, not Gentler." November's elections virtually guaranteed that the year 2002 will be the 48th consecutive year of Democratic control of the House of Representatives. About 97 percent of all incumbents running were returned. Incumbents were shocked—shocked!—when voters began enacting term limits. David Duke, the well-barbered ex-Nazi, prepared for a gubernatorial campaign by rolling up 44 percent of Louisiana's vote for senator. Marion Barry, master of the contemporary confessional style, admitted that his cocaine problem came about because he cared too deeply, for too long, about too many other people's needs. Jesse Jackson ran headlong away from real power, deciding not to become Washington's mayor. Instead, His Shadowship became a chat show host (and Shadow Senator). In the Senate the Keating Three said we didn't do it and we did it because everyone does it. In 1991 the Senate will learn what it wrought when it confirmed David Souter.

Bonfire of the inanities: Donald Trump kept the country posted on his glandular life. Said he of Marla Maples: "Better than a 10." Said she of The Donald: "Best sex I've ever had." But he could not pay his debts. Michael Milken was sentenced to jail for acts that undermined the trust in capital, and the senior shysters at Drexel Burnham Lambert lavished on themselves $195 million in bonuses, then declared bankruptcy.

Drinkers of designer water were driven to drink stuff from the tap—tacky-city!—because of gunk in Perrier. Don't have a cow, Dude, but the nation, another year older and deeper in debt, turned to watching a TV cartoon about a 10-year-old underachiever. The nation in which automobiles' rearview mirrors bear the warning "Objects in mirror are closer than they appear" launched the Hubble telescope with a flawed mirror.

Americans, whose politicians employ speechwriters as ventriloquists, were shocked to learn of Milli Vanilli's lip-syncing. 2 Live Crew showed that misogyny can make millionaires. Madonna did something shocking: She caused MTV to reveal that it has standards. People were shocked when Roseanne Barr, a professional vulgarian, behaved in character when singing the national anthem.

Disgusted by labor troubles pitting millionaires against multimillionaires, baseball fans vowed to stay away from the ballparks in droves. Attendance declined 6/10ths of 1 percent. Nolan Ryan—the Smithsonian has dibs on his arm, when he is done with it—won his 300th game. In southern Illinois Pete Rose watched on television as the Reds won the World Series. George Steinbrenner was damned, so the Yankees may not forever be.

Hall of Famer Joe Sewell, who died at 91, used only one bat in his 14-year major-league career and struck out only 114 times in 7,132 at bats. Aaron Copland, Leonard Bernstein, Mary Martin and Sammy Davis, Jr., also were American artists, as was, in his robust way, Bronko Nagurski, tackled by death at 81. This Minnesotan, on a touchdown run for the Chicago Bears in the 1930s, trampled four successive would-be tacklers, bounced off the goal posts, smashed into a brick wall and, returning to the huddle, said, "That last guy hit me awfully hard." Navigating 1990 was a bit like that.

December 31, 1990

1991: Fate Wields a Blackjack

By a circuitous route but with wonderful precision, 1991 taught an old truth: Life is indeed a series of dark corners around which Fate lurks, wielding a blackjack. This odd year ends with Saddam Hussein as secure in his job as George Bush is in his. The year began with a bang—lots of bangs—in Baghdad. It ends with the last whimper from what was the Soviet Union. There hunger, disease, crime, collapsing transportation and pandemic incivility show that living under peacetime socialism is like losing a very violent war.

The arms control fetish reached its final absurdity when an American zealot said we should help hold the Soviet Union together because it is the entity that signed the arms control agreements. The British Communist Party changed its name but not before getting caught committing capitalism, earning $270,000 speculating in stocks and real estate. Gus Hall, 80, head of the U.S. Communist Party (we have one, Russia doesn't), still believes: "If you want a nice vacation, take it in North Korea."

It is progress that the butchery in the Balkans is not igniting the continent, as it did 77 years ago. Bush ("The mission of our troops is wholly defensive. . . . They will not initiate hostilities") was lionized as a war leader. He rented a coalition (by forgiving Egypt's debts, China's repression, Syria's terrorism, etc.). Then the coalition, especially the Saudis, rented the U.S. military and Kuwaiti feudalism was restored.

On the home front, Treasury Secretary Brady showed why he and Bush are soulmates. Brady, the administration's Churchill, sent the English language into battle to shore up consumer confidence, saying, "The rush to judgment that this recession is the end of the Western world as we know it is entirely premature" and, "It always looks dark at the bottom of a recovery." For some reason, consumer confidence did not perk up. Bush took time out from fixing the Middle East and testily denied he was neglecting domestic policy. He said he would try to fix Cyprus.

The right passion for the wrong reason: Americans, having watched Congress misgovern, finally became enraged—about members bouncing personal checks. The year of living dangerously: Bush ventured to live without the chief of staff who commandeered airplanes so he could constantly be in "secure voice contact" with the White House. No team had ever gone from last place one year to the World Series the next. This year two teams did. Democrats took heart.

Two hundred years ago the center of America's population was calculated to be at Chestertown, Maryland. In 1991 it was at Steelville, Missouri, heading southwest. The interesting white population of Louisiana gave a majority of their votes to a 41-year-old gubernatorial candidate who said his Nazi and KKK activities were youthful indiscretions. A Los Angeles citizen with a video camera caught a gang of criminals in brutal action, and in LAPD uniforms. On the cutting edge of concerned parenting, a Texas mother was sentenced to 15 years in prison for trying to arrange the killing of the mother of her daughter's principal rival for a spot on the high school cheerleading squad.

Sex of various sorts made much news. In Palm Beach, a 78-year-old prospective juror said of the defendant's uncle, "Somebody was running around without his pants. I think it was Kennedy, the fat"—pause—"the senator. He's idealistic, but maybe a little horny." That senator and his Judiciary Committee colleagues discussed the Constitution and pubic hair. Senator Robb said he just got a massage. In basketball's centennial year, perhaps the sport's greatest player ever was proclaimed a hero for endorsing "safe sex" rather than the kind he practiced while "I did my best to accommodate as many women as I could." A college-bound New York City student said he was glad the schools were distributing free condoms because "I don't want to get no disease." Schools give children condoms before, or instead of, grammar. First things first.

San Francisco's government declared the city a haven for war resisters and conscientious objectors to Desert Storm. It denied a request that it erect signs along freeways to declare the city a "sanctuary for sexual minorities." In the 1990–91 academic year the nondiscrimination policy of the University of Massachusetts at Amherst forbade "discrimination on the basis of race, color, religion, creed, sex, age, marital status, national origin, disability or handicap, veteran status, or sexual orientation, which shall not include persons whose sexual orientation includes minor children as the sex object." In the 1991–92 statement the last 15 words were deleted. Is pedophilia becoming a civil right? A feminist marketed an alternative to the Barbie doll, one with a thicker waist, shorter legs, larger hips. The feminist called it "responsibly proportioned."

On the 500th anniversary of the birth of Henry VIII—not a feminist—a London headline announced that he had been REALLY A FLOP IN BED. Seems that after his third marriage he was virtually impotent. He may have died of scurvy, brought on by vitamin C deficiency.

Citrus fruit was scarce even for royalty in 16th-century England. Our middle class is feeling sorry for itself, but it is still living a lot better than a king lived in the good old days.

Good news came from France, where folks eat 30 percent more fat than Americans, smoke more, exercise less and yet have fewer heart attacks. "Wine, particularly French red wine, has a flushing effect on the heart's artery walls." So says an ad for French wines, citing a French institute of health. And pâté de foie gras may also be good for the heart, according to a scientist (French, of course).

Death tackled pro football's first superstar, Red Grange, the Galloping Ghost. James (Cool Papa) Bell, dead at 87, retired the year before Jackie Robinson broke in with Brooklyn, so major league fans never got to see for themselves if Bell, a centerfielder in the Negro leagues, really was so fast he could snap off the light and jump into bed before the room got dark. We know he once overthrew third base, raced in to catch the carom of his throw off the dugout roof, and tagged the runner at third. The scoring on that putout was 8–8. You can look it up.

December 30, 1991

1992: Came the Revolution

Like Lenin and Trotsky returning from Swiss and Siberian exiles, the American left, at long last a winner of a presidential election, has, as it were, surged forth from the Finland station and stormed the Winter Palace, so now America's propertied classes are at the mercy of . . . Lloyd Bentsen. Only in America.

The presidential sock-buying spree at J.C. Penney in February did not reverse the Republic's slide into the Slough of Despond. Two Arizona Republicans who finished in a dead heat in their primary settled matters with a hand of five-card stud. "I want to sit in Grandpa's place," said the former actress, a stunning blonde, after winning a seat in Italy's Parliament. Alessandra Mussolini is 29.

Unsurprising headline of the year: MANY L.A. RIOT SUSPECTS FOUND TO HAVE CRIMINAL BACKGROUNDS. Media coverage stressed the rioters' "rage," but pictures showed many of them merrily conducting a shopping spree and ethnic cleansing at the expense of Korean merchants. A U.N. arms embargo was maintained, evenhandedly, on both the well-armed Serbs and their virtually unarmed victims. From the Halls of Montezuma to the shores of *Nightline*, Marines fought their way ashore in Somalia through television cameras. "Who Will Disarm the Thugs?"

asked a *New York Times* editorial about Somalia, not Brooklyn. The liberal mayor of liberal Boulder, Colorado, is sad because her city has too few poor people.

Carcinogen alert: Chemicals occurring naturally in many foods can cause cancer in animals. Ban food! Now that you have given up butter, scientists say margarine may be harmful. Even worse, some diets and drugs that lower cholesterol may produce personality changes that raise the risk of violent death. Order french fries! Rhetoric at the Rio ecofest worsened global warming. Florida, a geological afterthought, rose from the sea later than the rest of America, but too soon: Hurricane Andrew smacked it. There is a 2,400-page North American "free trade" agreement. Amazingly, there is free trade between North and South Dakota without so much gobbledygook.

Bob Packwood voted against the confirmations of Robert Bork and Clarence Thomas primarily because he is so very sensitive about women's rights. Murphy Brown and Woody Allen illustrated variations on "family values," and two members of Britain's seedy royalty agreed to continue their parasitic lives in separate palaces. Grand Duke Vladimir, direct descendant of the Romanov tsars, died at a Miami press conference.

To foster AIDS awareness, Connecticut printed 600,000 cocktail napkins with a picture of a condom and the message PLEASE LET THIS COME BETWEEN US. The Condom Hut is Rhode Island's first drive-through condom shop. Marvel Comics' gay hero Northstar came out of the closet. Superman, born in 1938, died. Not a Nineties guy. "Very phallic," said a culture maven.

And what did you learn at school today? A science historian reported that ever since the "Teddy Bear Patriarchy" of Teddy Roosevelt's day, the public representation of primates has reflected America's racism and sexism. A labor-education specialist reported that "waitressing reveals the deeply gendered expectations surrounding the world of work. . . . The food service encounter is structured by a gendered and class-bound culture." A feminist professor says she teaches "ovulars," not seminars. And for some reason, for the first time in American history state support for higher education declined for a second consecutive year.

Berkeley commemorated the 500th anniversary by renaming Columbus Day "Indigenous People's Day." A machete-wielding 20-year-old woman killed by Berkeley police left a note: "We are willing to die for this land." She had been angry about construction of volleyball courts in People's Park. A conundrum: What are liberals to do about spray-painted graffiti on the granite disc commemorating Berkeley's Free Speech Movement?

The Dream Team waxed the world in basketball, and Mike Tyson was KO'd by 12 Hoosier jurors. Prior to playing the Texas Longhorns, Mississippi State football coach Jackie Sherrill inspired his student athletes by having a bull castrated at practice. Mississippi State 28, Texas 10. During the five days the baseball owners met to fret about the game's supposedly parlous financial condition, those owners signed 34 players to contracts guaranteeing $257,925,000. Next year Barry Bonds will make more than $45,000 a game.

It's a toddling town: Anthony J. (Big Tuna) Accardo, who died peacefully at 86, was also called Joe Batters because he used baseball bats to enforce the whims of Al Capone, of whose servants Big Tuna was the last survivor. An inventor, the last surviving child of an inventor, died. Theodore Edison was 94. Sam Walton, whose Wal-Mart empire eclipsed Sears as the nation's largest retailer, was one of the world's richest men, and the richest who drove a battered pickup, when he died at 74. Eric Sevareid, North Dakota's gift to journalism, was 79. At 84 Walter Lanier (Red) Barber ascended to the catbird seat in the sky.

Workers widening a Jerusalem road unearthed a tomb that may contain the bones of the high priest who tried Jesus and turned him over to the Romans for crucifixion. Look what he started. Palm prints in New Mexico clay reveal that humans were living here 28,000 and perhaps 38,000 years ago rather than, as hitherto thought, 11,500 years ago. So why do we call this the New World? Because a skull found in Kenya has pushed back the antiquity of *Homo sapiens* half a million years to 2.4 million years.

Census data reveal that America's most typical town is Tulsa, and that by 2050 barely half the nation's population will be non-Hispanic whites. But scientists say that on August 14, 2126, a huge comet named Swift-Tuttle may smack the Earth without first filing an environmental impact statement or even getting Al Gore's permission. If it hits a spotted owl habitat there will be litigation.

And speaking of earthshaking developments: Leavened by lots of fire-breathing freshmen hot for "change," House Democrats caucused in December and . . . reelected the old batch of leaders and all but one committee chairman. Mississippi's ailing Jamie Whitten, 82, was replaced by Kentucky's William Natcher, 83. Only in America.

December 28, 1992

1993: Nature's Hysterics, and More

Peering, with trepidation, toward 1994, with fascism rising in Russia and a father-son pair of North Korean paranoiacs acquiring nuclear weapons, we can cherish the memory of 1993. In America, the year's most impressive event resulted not from man's hysterics but from nature's—rain that caused the Father of Waters to flow unvexed across farmland. The Midwest squared its broad shoulders and gave the nation a lesson in fortitude. On the banks of another river, the Kwai, in Thailand, two survivors, one British and one Japanese, both former soldiers, both 75, shook hands where a bridge had been built, long ago.

Broadcasting from the White House lawn the day the Israeli-PLO accord was signed, Connie Chung sighed, "A hundred years of hostility, of hatred, evaporating miraculously." Oh? As the Holocaust Museum opened in Washington, a poll showed that one third of Americans think it "possible" that the Holocaust never happened. Jan Gies died in Amsterdam 49 years after he smuggled food to the young girl and her family in hiding: the Franks. The GATT free(er) trade agreement was signed but Europe's governments, unhappy about the entertainment preferences of Europe's peoples, limited imports of American films and TV programming in order to protect "European culture." In 1993 that culture consisted primarily of sclerotic welfare statism, soaring unemployment and ethnic cleansing. Japan's rising sun suddenly seemed like a bubble.

On January 20, with Chelsea Clinton safely enrolled in a private school, the party primarily responsible for the condition of contemporary government took control of the executive branch. Democrats declared that their previous handiwork needs "reinventing." Said the director of the Office of Management and Budget: "We have 22 pages of regulations just telling someone who wants to make brownie cookies how many raisins and nuts they're supposed to put in the damn things. What we don't define is how many nuts it takes to explain how many nuts you need to put into a brownie cookie." The 40,000 pieces of mail "misplaced" en route to Arkansas and Tennessee before Christmas 1992 (including Inaugural invitations) were being delivered in December 1993. The Clintons proposed turning health care over to this government. The fourth branch of government, Rush Limbaugh, was not amused.

The party of taxes and compassion had servant problems: Some people were disqualified for high office because they had not properly paid taxes for their domestics. The party of diversity produced a Cabinet that the president said "looks like America." Twelve lawyers. "Lawyers," said one of them, Attorney General Reno, "are what make people free." (The Founders had a different idea: ". . . are endowed by their Creator with certain unalienable rights . . .") Reno had jurisdiction over a bloody debacle in Waco and promptly became Washington's pinup.

The nation's 19th most populous city, Washington, D.C., which thinks it should be a state, had a crime wave even in its police department. The applicants recently accepted to its police academy included a man who listed his address as 2700 Martin Luther King Jr. Avenue, S.E. (Saint Elizabeths psychiatric hospital, where he was an outpatient) and another man whose prior arrest for drug distribution was not known until, at police headquarters, he bumped into the officer who had arrested him.

Immigration became a boiling issue, particularly in California, where a Dodger game was broadcast in English, Spanish, Mandarin Chinese and Korean. Somalia, Haiti and Florida remained unpacified by American power. East Palo Alto, California, with a high homicide rate, considered providing students with life insurance, including burial benefits. During the 10 days of fires, 60 people died in Los Angeles County—of gunshot wounds. In Los Angeles, defense attorneys for the men who smashed Reginald Denny's skull with a brick successfully argued that what used to be considered especially culpable behavior—becoming intoxicated by mob violence—now excuses criminal behavior.

In premodern, superstitious ages, people who behaved badly said, "The Devil made me do it." In this age of reason, a fired Northwestern professor says his disability made him do it: For six years after his mother died he deposited almost $40,000 of her Social Security checks. He blamed "extreme procrastination behavior" caused by depression. A Penn State student complained to police about a breach of contract: A student she had hired to take an exam for her flunked it. Sensitivity was busting out all over: An AP headline said WASHINGTON GOVERNOR DROPS "CHIEF OF STAFF" TITLE AFTER INDIAN COMPLAINT.

In Dallas a 44-year-old woman filed an age discrimination suit against a bar that wouldn't hire her as a topless dancer. The male Berkeley student who attended classes stark naked was suspended for—you guessed it—sexual harassment. Gender bending among the dolls: Ken, Barbie's boyfriend, got streaked hair and an earring. A Nineties gift of caring is a $395 sterling silver condom case. An eight-year-old boy who found condoms in his parents' bedroom exclaimed to his mother, "Wow! I didn't even know you guys were gay!"

Death came to two particularly elegant people—Arthur Ashe and Holly Golightly (as Audrey Hepburn shall be remembered). Anyone wanting to understand middle-class America in the postwar period can start with the novels of Peter De Vries, dead at 83. Matthew Ridgway, like the Korean War in which he rallied U.S. forces, was more heroic than most Americans understand.

Charlie Gehringer never said much. His manager said, "Charlie says 'hello' on opening day, 'goodbye' on closing day, and in between bats .350." He died this year, as did two great catchers, Roy Campanella and the man who was the answer to a trivia question: Who was the sixth hitter, who singled, after Carl Hubbell struck out five other future Hall of Famers in a row in the 1934 All-Star Game? Bill Dickey. During the 1929 Rose Bowl California's Roy Riegels scooped up a Georgia Tech fumble on Tech's 20-yard line and ran toward the end zone. Wrong end zone. For the rest of his 83 years he was known as Wrong-Way Riegels.

December 27, 1993

PART 2

Cities

I Hear American Bullets Singing

A nine-year-old girl was shot in the head early yesterday in Brooklyn when a bullet the police said was fired by a man shooting wildly at an old enemy crashed into the car where she lay asleep, waiting to be carried up to bed after a day at an amusement park.   —*The New York Times*, July 23.

A one-year-old girl was critically wounded yesterday after her father was shot dead by a mystery gunman, sending the family auto careening wildly for two blocks in Brooklyn.   —New York *Daily News*, July 25.

A teenager who had danced on Broadway was killed in the Bronx early Tuesday morning when a sniper with a machine gun fired on his car and riddled it with bullets. The shots came from an apartment-building roof where young drug-gang members regularly shoot their weapons for thrills, the police said yesterday.   —*The New York Times*, July 26.

A three-year-old Brooklyn boy was killed yesterday when gunmen fired more than 18 rounds from semiautomatic pistols through a steel-covered door as he slept in his family's apartment.   —*The New York Times*, July 27.

A 10-month-old boy standing in his walker was shot to death yesterday by a gunman who fired repeatedly through the door of the boy's grandmother's apartment on the Grand Concourse in the Bronx, the police said.   —*The New York Times*, July 31.

Don't worry, be happy.   —Bush campaign song and theme.

Pardon me, Mr. President, but many Americans are having a hard time getting with the program. Five children became random victims in one city in nine days. That's a record that would shock Ulster, maybe even Beirut. Two years ago this month, accepting your nomination in New Orleans, you mentioned a thousand points of light. Muzzle flashes?

The day the one-year-old was shot, the President was in Manhattan in the Waldorf Astoria, in the presence of a thousand or so points of light (contributors), throwing down the gauntlet to the forces of darkness (Democrats): "Republicans want to allow the women of this state to be able to defend themselves with Mace, and liberal Democrats don't."

New York's Assembly, controlled by Democrats, killed a bill that would have legalized Mace devices. It is utopian to think that women, or men, could be safe venturing forth, from behind their triple-deadbolt locked doors, without a chemical-warfare capability.

Of course infants are not safe behind steel-covered doors, so powerful is the ordnance that perforated the apartment door behind which the three-year-old died while curled up asleep on a sofa bed with his 15-year-old sister. The apartment is in the Walt Whitman Houses.

I hear American bullets singing.

The one-year-old, shot when her father was, died the next day in the hospital where, at about the same moment, the body of the nine-year-old was being prepared for the morgue. The one-year-old's father had been driving to court for sentencing. On a firearms charge.

The *Times* says the death of the dancer, 18, "came as no surprise" to residents of the building from which the fusillade came. "They nightly hear the jackhammer rattle of automatic gunfire from their roof." He was driving a car bought with money he earned dancing in *The Tap Dance Kid.*

His father had planned to move the family to North Carolina this week to escape the urban mayhem that in recent months has claimed a five-year-old hit in the head while sleeping by a stray bullet fired by his mother's former boyfriend, and a 10-year-old killed by stray bullets in a store when an argument between a customer and the owner erupted in gunfire.

But there is good news from New York. A two-year-old sitting on a window ledge survived a wound from a stray bullet fired in a fight in the building's courtyard. A 13-year-old survived the five wounds he received in the chest and abdomen when, walking to a store, he was caught in a shootout.

Last week, America's patience snapped. With a single voice the nation thundered, "Intolerable!" We are a people slow to anger but fierce when galvanized, as by Pearl Harbor or, as last week, by Roseanne Barr's rendition of "The Star-Spangled Banner." The President weighed in, wasn't pleased.

Ms. Barr is a star and a slob. She is a star because the country has a robust appetite for slob television, the theme of which is: Crude is cute. Up to a point. There are limits.

Of course the national anthem is hard to sing, even when you are trying, as Barr was not, to do it right. That is why some people want to replace it with "America the Beautiful." Trouble is, one verse of it says about America the Beautiful:

Thine alabaster cities gleam,
Undimmed by human tears!

Not now they don't, and they aren't.

August 2, 1990

The Meaning of a Metropolitan Majority

Unheard amidst the roar of war was a small report from the Census Bureau. It resonates with the largest themes of American history: By 1990 half of all Americans lived in metropolitan areas—39 of them—with populations of one million or more. We have passed a milestone on a journey from what we once were proud of being to what we never wanted to be.

One hundred years ago the superintendent of the 1890 Census reported, "The unsettled areas have been so broken by isolated bodies of settlement that there can hardly be said to be a frontier line." Three years after this report of the closing of the frontier a 31-year-old historian, Frederick Jackson Turner, wrote what still ranks as the most influential essay in American historiography, "The Significance of the Frontier in American History."

His thesis, simultaneously inspiriting and unsettling, was that for America, geography had been destiny. The abundance of western lands explained, he said, the nation's development, moral as well as material. It shaped our democratic values of egalitarianism, individualism, pleasure in physical mobility, confidence in social mobility and faith in the possibility of rebirth through a fresh start out yonder, over the next mountain. In short, optimism.

But it was a peculiar optimism. It made the idea of progress problematic: If the "unspoiled"—by population—frontier was so fine, what was progress to be?

Turner's thesis was that the pedigree of our values, character and institutions ran not east across the Atlantic but west across the Alleghenies and the wide Missouri. His thesis implied American exceptionalism, a uniqueness and exemption from the rest of the world's woes and vices. It also implied that Americanism was unexportable. However, in the 1890s American energy leaped outward in "the splendid little war" with Spain that presaged America's entry into world history.

Turner's theory called into question the Jeffersonian tradition. Jefferson is considered the quintessential American optimist. But he was sanguine about democracy only for societies unlike what we have become. He said, "cultivators of the earth are the most valuable citizens" and government could be virtuous only "as long as there shall be vacant lands." Urban workers, merchants, financiers ("speculators"), all are sources of corruption when "piled up upon one another" in cities, all of which he considered "sores" on the body politic.

When the first census was taken in 1790, 90 percent of Americans lived within 100 miles of the Atlantic. But westward was the course of empire for Americans fleeing European, and then East Coast, congestion.

In fact and fiction, Americans came to define freedom as a function of physical space and particularly the West's vastness. Daniel Boone fled west from the sound of axes, Natty Bumppo escaped into the wilderness from "the temptations of civilized life," and Huck Finn lit out for the territories.

The problem was—is—this. The frontier may be fine for the flowering of "natural virtue." But if freedom depends on living beyond the sight of smoke rising from a neighbor's chimney, then the idea of freedom has no connection with the idea of, or need for, civic virtue.

When freedom is defined in terms of space, what becomes of the idea that man is a political animal, fulfilled in civic life? An idea of freedom, and hence of government, formed by the idea of the frontier did not prepare Americans for today's America.

As recently as 1930 only 13 million Americans lived west of the 100th meridian which skirts Dodge City, Kansas. Today, even the West is feeling congested.

In 1893, the year of Turner's essay, a friend who had been a student at Johns Hopkins when Turner studied there—Woodrow Wilson—wrote: "Slowly we shall grow old, compact our people, study the delicate adjustments of an intricate society. . . ."

Rapidly we grow dismayed by the intricacies of our society and the fact that civility is a casualty in America's cities. This could be because we have an attenuated idea of civic responsibilities, an idea unsuited to a compact people.

The latest war has loosed an extraordinarily intense collective feeling from Americans. Clearly this nation, though steeped in the severe individualism of the frontier notion of freedom, has a yearning for the community feeling that comes from collective undertakings. As America passes the milestone that marks the advent of a metropolitan majority, the question is whether any enterprise other than war can tap that yearning.

March 3, 1991

Straight Line to Calamity

The Senator glanced at the numbers and saw in his mind's eye something frightening: a straight line, ascending. Pat Moynihan had in hand the 1991 natal statistics which, together with those from 1970–1990, produce a graph line pointing straight to calamity.

Fifty years ago 5 percent of American births were to unmarried women. That began to change in the 1960s. By 1970 it was 10 percent. Since then the increasing rate has produced a virtually straight line—almost one percentage point a year for 21 years.

We bandy the word "crisis" so casually it is drained of power. However, America's real crisis can be presented numerically in the percentages of births to unmarried women:

	All Races	Whites	Blacks
1970	10.7	5.6	37.5
1975	14.3	7.3	46.8
1980	17.8	10.2	55.5
1985	22.0	14.5	60.1
1990	28.0	20.1	65.2
1991	29.5	21.8	67.9

What makes the natal statistics alarming is the ascending straight line for the whole society. What makes the statistics terrifying is that the graph line of births to unmarried black women remains straight. That is, the rate of increase is not slowing even at extraordinarily high levels.

Minority births are primarily responsible for the fact that the percentage of births to unmarried women is over 70 percent in Detroit, over 60 percent in Atlanta, Baltimore, Cleveland, Newark, St. Louis and Washington, D.C., over 50 percent in Chicago, Miami, Philadelphia and Pittsburgh. But Moynihan surmises that San Francisco's lower ratio—31.5—is the result of a minority: Asian-Americans.

Lee Rainwater, a Harvard sociologist emeritus, testifying to the Finance Committee that Moynihan chairs, foresees 40 percent of all American births, and 80 percent of minority births, occurring out of wedlock by the turn of the century. In 1976 there was an ominous portent during the Bicentennial: The percentage of black births to unmarried women passed 50 percent. Forty years after that, in 2016, if the ascending line on the graph stays straight, 50 percent of births to all races will be out of wedlock.

Now, trends are not inevitabilities. However, rising illegitimacy is a self-reinforcing trend because of the many mechanisms of the intergenerational transmission of poverty. The principal one is: People tend to parent as they were parented.

What has all this to do with the subject of the hearings—"Social Behavior and Health Care Costs"—at which Moynihan examined the natal statistics? Lots.

America is undergoing a demographic transformation the cost of which will be crushing. Why? Because poverty is, strictly speaking, sickening. The children of unmarried women are particularly apt to be poor. And poverty, with its attendant evils—ignorance, dropping out of school, domestic and other violence, drug abuse, joblessness—is unhealthy.

In the inaugural issue of *MediaCritic,* a new quarterly devoted to analysis of contemporary journalism, Fred Barnes, a senior editor of *The New Republic,* examines various myths purveyed by some journalism concerning the "health care crisis," including the myth that there is such a crisis. Two supposed signs of the "crisis" are America's high rate of infant mortality and low rate of immunization of preschool children.

Barnes notes that America's high rate of teenage pregnancy means a large number of low-birth-weight babies and a high mortality rate. "Doctors," says Barnes, "make heroic efforts to save these babies, many of whom would be declared 'born dead' in other countries and thus not counted toward the infant mortality rate."

Regarding immunization rates, Barnes reports that about 98 percent of children are fully vaccinated by the time they are of school age because vaccination is required for admission to school. Says Barnes, "Faced with a mandate, parents comply." Negligent or otherwise incompetent parents behave responsibly only when required. Such parents are particularly apt to be young and unmarried.

High infant mortality rates and low immunization rates are less health care problems—less problems of the distribution of medicine—than problems of social behavior, although the political class, other than Moynihan, is reluctant to say so. Moynihan quotes Dr. Reynolds Farley of the University of Michigan: "Shifts in attitudes imply that our norms may no longer abjure childbearing by unmarried women." What can be done?

One clue may be in William Buckley's words that Moynihan cites: "It is increasingly recognized that the most readily identifiable tragedy in modern life is the illegitimate child."

To many people today there is something anachronistic about the word "illegitimate." They find it jarring because it is "judgmental." But reviving the value judgments behind that locution may be the only way to bend down the line on Moynihan's graph.

October 31, 1993

A Sterner Kind of Caring

Enough of kinder and gentler. The nation is casting a cold eye on traditional notions of government "compassion" for poor people. As a result, Democrats' presidential hopes may depend on their ability to promise more sternness toward some of the poor. And many Republicans, despite their antistatist stance, seem more ready than most Democrats to base antipoverty policy on strong government.

There is an emerging consensus that government has an interest in, and a right to attempt, behavior modification among those who are sunk in dependency on public assistance. So there is a need to know more about what government can legitimately do to nurture in citizens the character traits requisite for personal independence. There is a less sentimental and less politically timid assessment of what constitutes "caring." Americans are recurring to the Victorian distinction between the "deserving" and "undeserving" poor. The deserving work and are decent parents, having only children they can and will care for.

Many states are implementing or contemplating laws to make some entitlements contingent on comportment. On the principle that entitlements from the community entail obligations to the community, welfare benefits may be linked to work requirements. Unwed teenage mothers receiving benefits may be required to live with parents and stay in school. Some stipends are not increased for additional children born to mothers already on welfare, or may be cut if a recipient misses parent-teacher meetings. A frequently truant teenager can cause a family's payment to be cut. Arkansas Governor Bill Clinton's "personal responsibility agenda" includes a law revoking drivers' licenses of students who do not maintain C averages.

Such laws are difficult to administer and easy for unsympathetic bureaucracies to sabotage. They also raise thorny questions, such as: Is it sensible to assume that parents can control teenagers? Does one risk increasing child abuse and other domestic violence by providing financial incentives for teenage parents to marry? Does this "new paternalism" or "moralistic, strong government conservatism" rest on a fallacy to which some conservatives are particularly prone? The fallacy is the idea that people are primarily moved by economic calculations and hence can be controlled by altering financial incentives. Economic incentives are more effective when they mesh with social norms. On the other hand, causing people to stay in school or go to work can give them healthy habits and disciplines.

Professor Lawrence Mead of New York University writes about "The Democrats' Dilemma" in *Commentary*. He says Democrats want political debate to turn on economic inequality, but most voters are more distressed about government's failure to fulfill its elementary functions, such as educating children, maintaining roads and fighting crime. People are outraged about paying for a portion of the population that is perpetually dependent on welfare because they cannot or will not behave responsibly.

Democrats, says Mead, "do not approve of the disorders of the ghetto, but they find it impossible clearly to *dis*approve of them." The lethargy of the dependent is a result of the ghetto's ethos of resignation and must be countered by policies that promote responsibility. Minimal standards of behavior must be insisted upon regardless of racial or other excuses that teach the poor that they cannot be expected to cope or conform.

Most welfare recipients are white. Most blacks are middle-class. But as Mead says, many ghetto blacks have responded to their dilemma in effect "by seceding from mainstream institutions—breaking the law, dropping out of school, not learning English, declining to work." Mead may be wrong in saying that this "internal secession" is as threatening to the nation as the South's secession in 1861, but like the South's secession, today's threatens the Democratic Party. "Most liberals," says Mead, "believe that less can or should be expected in the way of work and other civilities from the poor than most voters want."

Republicans, who are generally hostile to expansions of government's scope, are more disposed than Democrats to use political authority for behavior modification and character formation. But conservatives want to use government to decrease dependence on government; they favor prophylactic statism to increase self-reliance.

Mead's question is: Can Americans, and especially Democrats, overcome the legal and political obstructions to enforcing work and other civilities? James Q. Wilson's answer is: It's worth a wary try. In his new book, *On Character*, Professor Wilson of UCLA says character and the social settings that influence it are not beyond the influence of public policy in a free society. Wilson's definition of good character includes two qualities—empathy, meaning regard for the needs, rights, and feelings of others, and self-control, meaning the ability to act with reference to the more distant consequences of current behavior. Character is shaped by public forces—by general opinion, neighborhood expectations, artistic conventions, elite understandings, "in short, by the ethos of the times." Public policy primarily reflects that ethos, but can shape it a bit.

Some people will say that it is too costly, in money or freedom, for statecraft to attempt soulcraft. However, the alternative to attempting it may be an indiscriminate backlash against welfare for the deserving as well as the undeserving. Government, says Governor Clinton, is a limited gadget, but its capacities expand when its programs can presuppose "a receptive culture where everybody is willing to assume some responsibility for the future."

Clinton has read Peter Brown's new book, *Minority Party: Why Democrats Face Defeat in 1992 and Beyond*, so Clinton knows what he is up against. Brown reports that three years ago a task force of Democratic congressmen was debating a new social agenda and many members wanted it to declare that the work ethic is the core value of society. Representative Augustus Hawkins, then the senior black member of Congress, strenuously objected, saying the declaration would be seen by welfare recipients as a slap in the face. The statement was dropped. Behavior modification and character formation are needed near the top as well as the bottom of society.

January 13, 1992

The Poverty of Inner Resources

Passion is a prerequisite for driving the discussion of some subjects past boundaries set by political prudence. President Clinton's passionate philippic in a black church in Memphis last Saturday demonstrated that, regarding inner-city violence, the range of the discussable is expanding, but we still are a far cry from candor.

Clinton, a government man, instinctively believes that the underclass, which he says might better be called the outer class, principally lacks what governments can provide—services, work. His instinct is reinforced by reading sociologist William Julius Wilson's analysis of how, in Clinton's words, the inner cities "have crumbled as work has disappeared."

That "as" is an artful equivocation. To a significant extent, work, and willing workers, were driven from the inner city by multiplying pathologies not caused by scarcity of work. And millions of Asian and other immigrants have recently traveled not just beyond neighborhoods but across oceans in search of work and found it in American cities. Clearly there is a poverty of inner resources on the part of many persons whose desperate conditions derive from various kinds of destructive behavior.

Clinton knows this. He told the Memphis congregation that there are changes that government can make "from the outside in"—more police, job training and so on—but "there's some changes we're going to have to make from the inside out, or the others won't matter." So he sidled up to the edge of the issue.

Martin Luther King, he says, did not fight for "the freedom of children to have children and the fathers of the children walk away from them." He recurred to "the breakdown of the family," the need for "coherent families," the fact that there is chaos "where there are no families."

Yes, but Pat Moynihan moved the discussion further 28 years ago when he wrote: "From the wild Irish slums of the 19th century Eastern seaboard, to the riot-torn suburbs of Los Angeles, there is one unmistakable lesson in American history: A community that allows a large number of young men to grow up in broken families, dominated by women, never acquiring any stable relationship to male authority, never acquiring any set of rational expectations about the future—that community asks for and gets chaos."

That community gets what we have got, what the social scientist Charles Murray calls an inner-city culture of "*Lord of the Flies* writ large, the values of unsocialized male adolescents made norms—physical violence, immediate gratification and predatory sex."

Thirteen days before Clinton spoke, Murray spoke via *The Wall Street Journal*'s editorial page. His thesis is as clear as his prescription is stern. Bringing a child into the world when one is neither emotionally nor financially prepared for parenthood is a grievous wrong. When it occurs, "the child deserves society's support. The parent does not."

Throughout history a single woman with a small child has not been a viable economic entity. To prevent this, societies have channeled elemental forces of sexuality between embankments of rewards and penalties to buttress marriage. But in just 30 years the embankments have crumbled. In 1991 there were 1.2 million illegitimate births, an illegitimacy rate of 22 percent for whites, 68 percent for blacks, 30 percent for the nation, over 80 percent in some inner cities.

Government now subsidizes such behavior. It should, Murray says, end all economic support for single mothers. Marriage should be the sole legal institution through which parental rights and responsibilities are defined and exercised.

This, he thinks, would force young women who should not be mothers to seek the support of more mature adults, and would help to regenerate the deterring stigma of illegitimacy. Furthermore, it would lead many young women to place their babies for adoption.

Lift all restrictions on interracial adoptions, Murray urges, and restore the traditional legal principle that placing a child for adoption means irrevocably relinquishing all legal rights to the child. For children not adopted the government should spend lavishly on orphanages. "I am not," Murray says, "recommending Dickensian barracks. In 1993, we know a lot about how to provide a warm, nurturing environment for children, and getting rid of the welfare system frees up lots of money to do it."

Democracy, he says, depends on virtues which depend on socialization of children in the matrix of care and resources fostered by marriage. This is no longer a "black issue." The title of Murray's *Journal* essay was "The Coming White Underclass." The clock is ticking. The rising illegitimacy rate—the white rate is now just four points behind what the black rate was in 1965 when Moynihan sounded the alarm about the crisis of the black family—may make America unrecognizable before political institutions recognize the necessity of measures as bold—as boldly traditional—as Murray recommends.

November 18, 1993

Shayna Bryant Fell Through the Cracks

NEW YORK—Shayna Bryant's four siblings say that when her parents wanted to punish her they gave her a choice of a beating or going without food for two days. After she was found dead on her fourth birthday on a Formica table in her family's Bronx apartment, an autopsy revealed that she had died of blunt impact wounds to her head and torso, which also showed signs of healed wounds. Her face and hands were scarred by cigarette burns. The four surviving children say the father often used his fists, the mother a shoe. The children say Shayna received the fatal beating because she sipped water from the toilet. The police, called by the father, who claimed Shayna had an asthma attack, say there was no food in the apartment. The children say the parents would sit them in small chairs in the darkened hallway, sometimes overnight, their arms tied with cloth. Two of Shayna's siblings say the mother poured scalding water over her. Her sister Joy, five, has just been released from the hospital where she was treated for a severely burned hand and beating injuries.

The parents have been indicted for murder.

Shayna died more than a month ago. Recently some Legal Aid Society lawyers gathered in their office opposite city hall to explain why the city knew so little about the children's passage of pain, until it was too late.

Because three of the children, including Shayna, tested positive for cocaine at birth, they were put in foster care for a while, a fact unknown to some of the city child abuse and neglect specialists who have had intermittent contact with the family since 1988. When in 1991 the father of all five—at that time he had never lived with the mother—won custody of the children, neither the judge nor anyone else involved in that decision knew he had served a prison term for drug and assault convictions. The abuse and neglect personnel who last had contact with the family, in December, did not even know how many children there were.

Part of the problem is a confidentiality system that compartmentalizes information and inhibits oversight, even by the city council. Part of the problem is normal bureaucratic creakiness. But most of the problem is the mismatch between the mounting social disintegration and the social services personnel struggling to stem the tide.

There is mandated reporting by doctors and teachers concerning suspected child abuse and neglect, but nonmandated reporting, as by neighbors, is vital. Unfortunately, shouting parents and crying children often attract no attention because they are part of the standard soundtrack of life in many poor neighborhoods.

Abuse and neglect investigators, among whose ranks there is an understandably high turnover, are required to have only a college degree, in any subject, and a few weeks of training. Then they are sent out into often dangerous situations to make life-and-death decisions. They walk up to apartment doors where they are apt to encounter adults weaving about or otherwise manifesting drug use. To those adults, and to children, the investigators are supposed to ask pointed questions.

In 1984 the Legal Aid Society, a nonprofit organization, handled 3,310 abuse and neglect cases in the city. By 1989 it was handling more than 24,000. What happened? Crack did, beginning in 1985. Sixty percent of abuse and neglect cases involve drug allegations.

The society's lawyers are almost nostalgic for the era when heroin was the drug of choice. Heroin, they say, does not always annihilate the feelings essential to mothering. Crack produces volatility, or stupor, that causes loss of emotional contact with children.

Babies testing positive for cocaine often are immediately put in foster care until the mothers undergo treatment. That can take 12 to 18 months, by which time the babies often have bonded with the foster mothers. Furthermore, children exposed to cocaine in the womb have behavior problems—often they are volatile, even unable to make eye contact. They lack the attributes that cause parents to fall in love with children. So a fragile mother reacquires custody of a difficult child who is further disoriented by broken bonds.

This is a setting for child abuse. It also is a reason for parenting programs, where mothers learn what many mothers, especially very young ones, do not know, such as that when a child cries, the correct response is not anger acted out.

Small things, such as children, can fall through even small cracks, and the cracks in the abuse and neglect prevention system are not small. Caulking them requires resources of money and hope that are scarce and rapidly becoming scarcer relative to the growing need for them.

May 1, 1994

Lucky Linda, Age Fifteen

The judge, told why Linda Marrero's parents chained her to the radiator in their Bronx apartment, reduced the charge. Besides, Linda, 15, says her parents were acting in her best interests. She is what is called an "at risk" child. And how.

The New York Times details the long trek through the social services labyrinth that convinced Linda's parents that her problems "were not going to be solved through government." In the two years since she dropped out of sixth grade she has taken to disappearing into the New York nights where gunfire resonates. She was gone days, then weeks, doing drugs, returning battered. In July, when drug dealers returned her at gunpoint, demanding money, her parents chained her.

The most important point about Linda is how lucky she is. She has a father at home, and a mother who said to him, "Go buy me a chain and two locks." Imagine how it is for single mothers when the siren of the street calls, particularly to male children.

In 1960, 5 percent of American births were illegitimate. In 1988, 26 percent were, including 63 percent of black babies. This behavioral change is the main reason almost one-third of all children are paupers at some point before they are 18.

It was in the mid-1960s that some dry data began signaling a dangerous disjunction. The welfare of children was no longer varying directly with the labor market. Before then, when unemployment declined, so did new welfare cases. But suddenly dependency was an independent variable, increasing irrespective of the economy's performance. As Lawrence Mead of New York University says: "The inequalities that stem from the workplace are now trivial in comparison to those stemming from family structure. What matters for success is not whether your father was rich or poor but whether you had a father at all."

Last February, Senator Moynihan wrote a passage for a Democratic report about children being the largest portion of America's poor and so many of them being paupers at some point. He wrote: "All this is new. This circumstance did not exist during the era of the New Deal, a half century ago. It did not exist during the era of the Great Society, a quarter century ago."

Some Democratic staffers "corrected" what they assumed was an error, so Moynihan's passage read: "This circumstance was not as recognized during the era of the New Deal, a half century ago, nor during the era of the Great Society, a quarter century ago."

Such flinching from the fact that the problem is radically new is, Moynihan says, "becoming the liberal orthodoxy." Flinching is a way of clinging to this comforting assumption: Macroeconomic conditions, which government can influence, can be relied on to improve the conditions of poor people. That is decreasingly true for the millions whose life chances are spoiled by family structure.

This crisis has come upon us at a time when, and partly because, children are a direct concern to only a minority of adults. This, too, is new.

A century ago only 20 percent of American households were without children under 18. Today 65 percent are. So only a minority of adults, and a minority of adult incomes, are involved on behalf of children. Government policy reflects the fact that children now are a minority interest.

We know precious little about how government policy can get a purchase on the problem of "behavioral poverty"—poverty rooted in habits and character traits. The challenge, to which government is now at most marginally relevant, is to stimulate what has been called (by Professor Chester Finn of Vanderbilt) "social capital accumulation."

By social capital Finn means the morals, mores, habits and norms that are the lessons learned from billions of human experiences over thousands of years. Many of the lessons pertain to families and parenting.

As Finn says, we need to teach and preach and be as censorious about these things as we are about smoking, cholesterol, recycling aluminum cans, experimenting on animals and saying rude things on campuses. For starters, people must come to believe that if they are going to have children, they have an obligation to care about them as fiercely as Linda Marrero's parents care about her.

September 26, 1991

Rebecca, Age Thirteen

BALTIMORE—Begin here: In 1990 nearly 10 percent of Baltimore girls aged 15 to 17, almost all unmarried, gave birth. That is why in 1993 the city is embarking on a program to make Norplant, a long-term (five-year) contraceptive implant, available to teenage girls at school clinics and elsewhere.

The case against the program can be put concisely: By substituting chemical protection for moral restraint, it sends a message of resignation regarding behavior once considered deviant and reprehensible but now redefined, in the name of "realism," as normal.

The case *for* the program can be put even more concisely: Rebecca (not her real name).

She is wearing sneakers, clean jeans and a lavender sweatshirt. She sniffles constantly, the consequence of a cold, or perhaps of the substance abuse (sniffing paint thinner, as well as using PCP and alcohol) that got her sent to a residential treatment center. There she heard about Norplant from a public health official. Now at a hospital clinic she is listening impassively as a nurse gives her all the information necessary for informed consent for the insertion in her upper arm, by a 10-minute procedure, of six matchstick-size capsules.

Rebecca, who has been sexually active for two years, is told that the implant will not protect her until after her next period, which is two weeks away, and she is asked if she needs a supply of condoms for the interval. Oh, yes, she says emphatically.

She is 13.

Now, consider some numbers provided by Douglas Besharov and Karen Gardiner in *The American Enterprise* journal. This year 10 million teenagers will engage in 126 million acts of sexual intercourse resulting in more than one million pregnancies, 406,000 abortions, 134,000 miscarriages and 490,000 births, about 64 percent (313,000) of them illegitimate. In 1988, 11,000 American babies were born to females under 15. In 1990, 32 percent of ninth-grade females (ages 14 and 15) had sexual intercourse. Seventeen percent of 12th-grade girls have had four or more partners.

Such numbers suggest that any message communicated by a Norplant program will not have a measurable effect on the mores of an age in which more teenagers are having sex more often and at an earlier age, and much of the increase has been among middle-class teenagers, most of them white. Rebecca, by the way, is white.

The question is how to limit the social costs of all this, given the fact that (in Besharov and Gardiner's words) "adolescents who cannot remember to hang up their bath towels may be just as unlikely to remember to use contraceptives." Norplant is "teenager proof" because it requires neither a daily action (as with the pill) nor foresight (as with a diaphragm) nor a partner's cooperation (as with condoms).

Times have changed? Yes, but let's be clear about how. Forty years ago teenage pregnancy rates were higher than today. However, most pregnancies occurred in, or were promptly followed by, marriage.

Today few teenagers who become pregnant wanted to. (A study suggests that the "wantedness" rate is higher for whites than for blacks.) But for those who do become pregnant, incentives and social reinforcements are apt to be markedly different for whites and blacks.

A white suburban teenager who becomes pregnant is apt to get an abortion and go on to college. A black inner-city teenager's pregnancy is not apt to disrupt similar expectations. Many inner-city female teenagers have not seen a man in the role of economic and emotional provider for a family. And given the savage harvest of homicide, drugs and jail, the cohort of marriageable inner-city males is small. Furthermore, the pregnant teenager is apt to have a supportive matriarchy to rely on if she decides to have the baby resulting from the unwanted pregnancy.

But the prospects for such babies are at best problematic. Better the unwanted pregnancy had not occurred. And Norplant may be the most feasible preventative.

Norplant has been embroiled elsewhere in controversial welfare and criminal justice policies raising questions of morally or legally dubious coercion. There have been proposals for monetary incentives or sanctions for unmarried welfare mothers to agree to implants. Judges have proposed implants in lieu of prison for women convicted of drug or child abuse. But leaving aside the question of when it might be acceptable for society to encourage Norplant use, Baltimore's evolving program seems careful, consensual and needed. And those black activists who profess to see Norplant as a "genocidal" attack on black fertility should answer this:

What is more dangerous to the flourishing of black America, Norplant for teenagers or a growing number of black adolescents headed for a life of poverty because they were born into poverty to a single mother whose life chances were blighted by a pregnancy at age 15?

March 18, 1993

The Sixties, a Second Time Around

The "urban crisis" is, by now, a hardy perennial. In 1968 *Glamour* magazine carried an editorial titled "The Urban Crisis: What Can One Girl Do?" By then the federal government was on the job, doing things.

The bill creating the Department of Housing and Urban Development was signed into law by President Johnson on September 9, 1965, 30 days after the beginning of, and partly in response to, the rioting in the Watts section of Los Angeles. Twenty-eight years and hundreds of billions of dollars later, welfare dependency, homelessness, substance abuse, family disintegration, the intergenerational transmission of poverty, teenage pregnancy, illegitimacy, sexually transmitted diseases, public schools, violence and other crimes are all worse.

Recently Henry Cisneros, the new secretary of HUD, was asked why it is reasonable to expect Washington to do any good. He said, among much else, this:

> I think one of the things America has to address very, very squarely is whether or not we can live with continued vast spatial separations between the poorest of our populations, concentrated in public housing in central cities, and the vast differences that exist across our urban geography to the suburbs, which are essentially white. What we've got to do is break up the concentrations by making it possible for people to live in newly designed, thoughtfully scaled public housing, negotiated with outlying communities, because many of the problems . . . are a symptom of large concentrations of poor people with few role models and no lift.

One's heart sinks. The Sixties were bad enough the first time around.

The government, having exacerbated problems by concentrating the poor in public housing, is going to redouble its efforts with more, better public housing, thereby conquering the spatial separations of the social classes. This is a 1960s impulse.

In the 1960s there began the explosive growth in the number of subjects considered political and suited to government attention. Perhaps this had something to do with Lyndon Johnson being the first president to have spent virtually his entire adult life in Washington.

By the end of the 1960s Pat Moynihan was worrying about the increasing introduction into politics and government of ideas originating in the social sciences, ideas which promised to bring about social change through manipulation of society's most basic processes. This was, he said, part of a transformation of politics:

> Not long ago it could be agreed that politics was the business of who gets what, when, where, how. It is now more than that. It has become a process that also deliberately seeks to effect such outcomes as who *thinks* what, who *acts* when, who *lives* where, who *feels* how.

But even then there was a growing sense of governmental overload. "How one wishes," wrote Nathan Glazer, in the mid-1960s, "for the open field of the New Deal, which was not littered with the carcasses of half successful and hardly successful programs, each in the hands of a hardening bureaucracy." Nearly 30 years on, how one wishes government would at least learn the lesson formulated by Glazer's academic collaborator, Professor Moynihan: "The role of social science lies not in the formulation of social policy, but in the measurement of its results."

The aroma of fresh-baked, or perhaps half-baked, social science hovers over Cisneros's idea of combating spatial separations by means of "newly designed, thoughtfully scaled" public housing projects. Cisneros knows the requisite 1990s rhetoric—"I know we can't go back to the big bureaucracy answers of the 1960s"—but when explaining what should be done, he stresses better uses of Washington bureaucracies: "We think in terms of how we bring together a Department of Education on schools, and a Department of Health and Human Services on child care and welfare. We change the rules . . ."

Better rules from Washington. Back in the 1960s Moynihan, too, thought government should pull up its socks, square its shoulders and do better:

> Government has got into the business of promising more than it knows how to deliver; as there is little likelihood of cutting back on the promises, the success of the society turns on its ability to improve its performance. It is probably not a good thing to have got into this situation, but the social dynamics of an industrial society everywhere seem to lead in this direction, and to do so with special vehemence in the United States.

But is improved government performance really more likely than more judicious promising? Performance and promising are linked. Injudicious promises like Cisneros's drive government into disappointing performances.

As this is written the nation is celebrating the 250th anniversary of the birth of Thomas Jefferson, and lamenting the condition of its cities. For perspective, remember that Jefferson considered cities "pestilential" at a time when America's largest city, Philadelphia, had approximately 55,000 residents, which would not even fill Veterans Stadium for a Phillies game today.

April 15, 1993

Mr. Jefferson Comes to Town

Remarks delivered April 13, 1993, on the Lawn at the University of Virginia on the occasion of the commemoration of the 250th anniversary of the birth of Thomas Jefferson.

On March 4, 1809, in the United States Capitol, in the newly completed hall of the House of Representatives, Thomas Jefferson attended the Inauguration as president of his friend and fellow Virginian, James Madison. Observers noted—they could hardly fail to, such were Jefferson's high spirits—that he was elated to be leaving public office. One week later, on March 11, Jefferson, his packing done, left Washington. He would never return. Indeed, he would never, in the remaining 17 busy years of his life, leave Virginia, or even venture far from Monticello.

We are met today in an elegant setting that, in its elegance, expresses the spirit as well as the craftsmanship of the philosopher-statesman-architect who planned it. This space is the heart of the place—this university—where, we may safely say, Jefferson's heart came to rest late in a long life of strenuous usefulness.

I am honored and stirred to have been asked to participate in this splendid celebration. But I have come here today to pose a question which may, at first blush, seem, in its bluntness, an impertinence. The question is: Is Jefferson still instructive to us? Or has he become a glittering anachronism, with little to say that is pertinent to our nation's current discontents?

These discontents are, essentially, of two kinds, and they are, I suggest, related. One is physical, the other is cultural and moral. But, then, it was an aspect of Jefferson's genius that he knew that the elemental physical facts of social life have cultural, and hence moral, consequences. Our physical discontent is that we feel crowded together. Our cultural discontent is that this crowding gives rise to an uncomfortable sense of dependency.

Put plainly, we have become a nation of cities, and we are uneasy about this. We are uneasy not just because our cities are so dismaying in so many ways. We also are uneasy because there echo in our national memory Jefferson's forebodings about urbanization.

Jefferson inveighed against cities at a time when the largest city in the nation, Philadelphia, had a population about the size of Rapid City, South Dakota, today. Jefferson's dislike of urban life was not merely an esthetic recoil, although it certainly was that, too. His dislike flowed from his political philosophy, and reflected the radicalism of American political thought—the sharpness of our break from ancient patterns of political philosophizing. Let me elaborate.

Jefferson is sometimes caricatured as a person who was optimistic to the point of simplemindedness. He did, indeed, have the innate confidence of a natural aristocrat, and the expansive intellectual expectation of progress that characterized the 18th-century Enlightenment of which he was a conspicuous exemplar. But look at what he actually said about the problems of governance, and about the many lurking threats to the goodness of America.

Democracy, he said, depends on the nurturing of certain virtues in its citizens. But those virtues, and the strength of character that we recognize as true independence in individuals, depend, Jefferson warned, on a certain kind of social order. Those virtues depend, he said, on a rural society. Hence he warned against "piling up" people in cities. Cities are, he said (forgetting, for a moment, how much fun he had living in Paris), inherently and everywhere dreadful. He exhorted Americans to let Europe have the cities—and the workshops as well.

Jefferson was hardly unacquainted with metropolitan living. He lived with his customary flair and zest in the Paris of the 1780s—Paris fermenting with cultural and political upheaval. And having seen urban crowds abroad and at home, he still said, "I am not among those who fear the people."

But let us not flinch from this fact. Cut the people off from connection with the land, from a life of rural husbandry, and Jefferson's trust became as attenuated as he said the people's virtue must then become.

Jefferson believed that human nature presented political problems. But he believed that those problems could be ameliorated by nature itself—by the education in hardihood, independence and various other virtues that comes from a life engaged in labor on the land.

The contrast between Jefferson's political philosophy and the philosophies of the ancients is stark. The words "civic," "citizen" and "city" have a common root, and classical political philosophy taught that man could only become "civilized"—literally made suitable for life in the city, and for "citizenship"—by the close proximity to and involvement with other people that is required by the life of a polity compact enough to be walked across in a day. Compactness was a necessary condition for the flourishing of a political community—or so said most political philosophers prior to America's Founders.

Jefferson's, and America's, break with that classical tradition was complete. He wanted space not only between the citizen and the government, but also between citizens. Hence the alacrity with which he leapt at the opportunity to make the Louisiana Purchase for our suddenly very "extensive Republic." So from the beginning, American virtue was linked with space, meaning room enough for Americans to develop the virtues that undergird personal independence.

Classical political philosophy taught that the fulfillment of human life depended on active engagement in the civil, the political life of the country. Jefferson lived such a life. But he did not live it contentedly, or even happily, and he did not recommend it. To him, political engagement was a duty to be done, but not a career to be sought, still less a pleasure to be relished.

Again, remember the undisguised pleasure Jefferson took from shaking the dust of Washington from his shoes. Government, he knew, should not be at the center of American life, or at the center of the life of any American who could honorably avoid it. Serving in government can be a duty; but distrust anyone who does it for pleasure. In 1813, speaking after what he called "an intimacy of forty years with the public councils and characters," he said: "An honest man can feel no pleasure in the exercise of power over his fellow citizens."

A distinguished historian, John P. Diggins, author of *The Lost Soul of American Politics: Virtue, Self-Interest, and the Foundations of Liberalism*, rightly says that American political thought, both liberal and conservative, has emphasized *Homo faber*—man as a creature fulfilled in, and improved by, work. American political thought has not emphasized *Homo politicus*—man as the classical philosophers understood him, as a creature fulfilled and improved through participation in politics. In American political thought, and especially in Jefferson's thought, it is work, which takes place in the private sphere of life, not politics in the public sphere, that is the primary source of American dignity.

In this regard, Lincoln was squarely in the Jeffersonian tradition. Lincoln came (in the words of his campaign song) "out of the wilderness, out in Illinois." Back then, people still spoke of "the Illinois frontier." Lincoln came from where people were grappling with nature, subduing it, fulfilling their (and the nation's) manifest destiny in work.

As Diggins notes, American literature reflects—and reinforces—this national yearning for private space in which to work out one's personal destiny. James Fenimore Cooper in the forest, Herman Melville at sea, Mark Twain on the Mississippi, Henry David Thoreau by his pond, all expressed an American—a Jeffersonian—faith in virtue developed without dependence on political engagement, or even on "society."

Few people in contemporary America have even an inkling of what that cowboy from Manhattan, Teddy Roosevelt, called "the iron desolation" of the Great Plains. What Willa Cather, the novelist from Red Cloud, Nebraska, called "the inconceivable silence of the plains" is indeed inconceivable to most modern Americans who are enveloped by the cacophony of metropolitan living. Time was when an American leatherstocking could—and would—pack up and head west when he could hear the sound of his nearest neighbor's ax. No more. Now we need to work on our neighborliness, and come to terms with living in close proximity to one another.

The continent that our Republic spans is certainly not densely populated by Old World standards. But, then, those have never been our standards. And because so many Americans now live in close contact—social and economic—with other Americans, there seems to be a kind of national claustrophobia. It is making people increasingly surly. Intellectually and emotionally we are all Jefferson's children. And we are feeling cramped. We are speaking the aggressive language of rights and asserting myriad rights against one another.

We are now much in need of a translation of Jeffersonian philosophy for our urban situation. We need a new vernacular, not only, or even primarily, of politics, but also of civil society—that is, of all those intermediary and voluntary associations that leaven life and mediate between the individual and the state. A Jeffersonianism for our times would speak to the problem of defining, and valuing, and attaining personal independence "downtown," in the city, far from the frontier and farms where the original idea of the independent American was defined.

It is serendipitous that as we commemorate the 250th anniversary of Jefferson's birth, we also can take note of the 100th anniversary of a seminal essay. Presented in 1893 at the American Historical Association, it was Frederick Jackson Turner's "The Significance of the Frontier in American History."

Three years earlier the Bureau of the Census had declared the frontier closed. Turner considered that declaration momentous, and potentially ominous. He believed that American democratic values—nothing less than what was best in the nation's character—had been shaped by the availability of western lands. So what would become of us now, our saving spaces being exhausted?

Turner said, "In the spirit of a pioneer's 'house raising' "—voluntary cooperation in the private realm—"lives the salvation of the Republic." What would become of an America in which pioneering was a thing of the past?

Prior to the American founding, the pedigree of republican institutions had been traced back to ancient ideas. But Turner, drawing on and deepening the Jeffersonian tradition, was intimating a new declaration of independence from the Old World; he was attempting to ground American republicanism quite literally on the ground, in the vastness of the American land.

Turner's "geographical" understanding of American history was squarely in the Jeffersonian tradition. But his paper was delivered in a distinctly un-Jeffersonian setting, one that would have given Jefferson an anxiety attack, if not vertigo.

When Turner addressed the American Historical Association, the meeting was in Chicago, drawn there by the great Columbian Exposition. That Exposition had opened in October 1892 to commemorate the 400th anniversary of the coming of Columbus, and to celebrate in its exhibitions of technological and industrial marvels the triumph of the will of man over the resistant material of nature in the New World.

It was at the Chicago Exposition, in the Gallery of Machines, that Henry Adams said he felt himself knocked prostrate, "his historical neck broken by the sudden eruption of forces totally new." It was because of new forces surging through society that, early in the 20th century, many thoughtful Americans (Herbert Croly for one; Walter Lippmann for another) thought Jeffersonian individualism was no longer an answer to American problems, but rather had become the problem.

The problem, they thought, had two facets: One was the weakness of government. The challenge was to strengthen the state so that it could tame the surging energies of industrialism. The other facet of the problem was to temper American individualism so that a spirit of community could flourish. For these ends, the state has been expanding through most of this century.

The 20th century has been the century of the state. Government has grown everywhere. However, as this weary century wends to a close, there is a fresh receptivity to the core conviction of Jeffersonianism, a fresh appreciation of the primacy of the private sphere of life.

Jefferson focuses our attention on the task of building a society that nurtures individuals to self-sufficiency, including independence of politics. Now more than ever we need to be focused on that task of nurturing, because the related forces of urbanization and statism are exerting a powerful pull toward an enervating dependency. It is a dependency on large economic entities, and on government, for security. Ultimately, it is dependency on—an addiction to—security as the highest aim of life. This addiction produces, over time, a timid, fearful, debased people, erecting barriers against a competitive world, and expressing an entitlement mentality, insisting that they are entitled to government protection from uncertainty. That is an entitlement with a steep moral cost. Government that acknowledges such an entitlement becomes a bland Leviathan, a soft, kindly meant but ultimately corrupting statism, a statism of benighted benevolence.

The Washington that Jefferson fled has, in our time, become an agency of dependency. So a sensible first step would be to restore the wrecked equilibrium of our federal system. From Jefferson's era until well into this century, political debate in Washington about what Washington should do about this or that began with examination of the question of whether Washington should do *anything*—whether the federal government was constitutionally entitled to act.

Some people will say that the constitutional question is firmly closed. They will say that the "living document" has "evolved" and for many decades now has been consistently construed to emancipate the federal government from any serious restraint on its latitude for action. That is, alas, true. By construing the Constitution in a way that enables the federal government to act everywhere, we have taught Americans to think that it is natural and right for the federal government to take custody of every problem, to organize the provision of every need, to satisfy every want.

I know an accomplished fact when I see one; I can face facts of constitutional construction even when I regret them. But what I am recommending is not a constitutional but a prudential inhibition on the central government. After all, it is not as though the federal government today has excess resources of energy, intelligence and money. It is not as though the federal government is conspicuously successful at all its undertakings.

So, it would be an act of fidelity to Jeffersonianism to revive the idea of states' rights—and states' responsibilities. Now, I know some people wince when you hear the phrase "states' rights." I understand. Let me tell you a story.

Shelby Foote, in the second volume of his magisterial three-volume history of the Civil War, recounts a story concerning a Virginian, General George Thomas, who served in the Union Army. Immediately after the bloody assault on Missionary Ridge in the battle of Chattanooga, General Thomas discerned an attractive spot for a military cemetery, and put a detail to work on the project. The chaplain in charge asked Thomas if the dead were to be buried in plots assigned to the states their units represented, as was done at Gettysburg, where Lincoln had briefly spoken at a cemetery dedication a few weeks earlier. General Thomas lowered his head in thought, then shook it decisively. Making a tumbling gesture with both hands, he said, "No, no; mix 'em up. I'm tired of states' rights."

Today Americans old enough to remember America's great domestic conflicts over race relations in the 1940s, '50s and '60s may well say, as Thomas did, that they want to hear no more about states' rights. But it is well to remember that an idea should not be discredited merely by the fact that it has been put to ignoble uses. (The history of Christianity, and of other great religions, is instructive in this regard.)

It is also well to remember that in 1800, when our country still had not spilled westward over the Alleghenies, Jefferson wrote: "Our country is too large to have all its affairs directed by a single government." So let us send more political power back to where Jefferson thought it belonged, to the state and local—very local—levels. Even more important, let us get politics to the periphery of American life, where Jefferson wanted it.

To do so we will have to resist and reverse powerful tendencies in modern history, tendencies that tend to recur. Indeed, the mind of the West has long been haunted by the fear that history is, or tends to be—and will be if we are not careful—cyclical. The fear is that powerful forces, even the very logic of social development, propels societies into cycles of decay and—if societies are resourceful—regeneration. But decay is more probable than regeneration.

Although America's Founders were firm believers that history *could* be linear—that progress is possible—they knew that progress was not inevitable. And some of them had anxieties that have an astonishingly modern ring.

In December 1819, John Adams, an old adversary who had become a friendly correspondent, wrote the following to Jefferson:

> Will you tell me how to prevent riches from being the effects of temperance and industry? Will you tell me how to prevent riches from producing luxury? Will you tell me how to prevent luxury from producing effeminacy, intoxication, extravagance, vice and folly?

What was worrying Adams, and Jefferson, too, has come to be known in our day as the "cultural contradiction of capitalism." The worry is that capitalism, by its very success, by its prodigious productivity, undermines the social and moral prerequisites for its continued success. The worry is that capitalism requires thrift, discipline, industriousness and deferral of gratifications; but capitalism by its prodigal success in making Americans a people of plenty may be subverting those very virtues, making us soft and self-indulgent.

Just as there can be a "cultural contradiction of capitalism," so, too, there can be a political contradiction of democracy. It is this: The very responsiveness of democratic government to the popular will can corrupt the popular will. The more that government tries to satisfy the appetites of particular groups, the more appetites are inflamed, and the more groups organize to make their demands felt. So the very virtues that democracy presupposes—individualism, self-restraint and self-reliance—are subverted, over time, by the very solicitousness of democratic government. That subversion is in a very advanced stage today in the city Jefferson left for good 184 years ago.

We have not been properly mindful of Jefferson's warnings about the tendency of government to swell; and the tendency of the central government in a federal system to absorb other governments' responsibilities and rights; and the tendency of politics to permeate life, constricting the private sphere of life. But these tendencies are only that—only tendencies, not inevitabilities. So let us resolve to honor Jefferson by resisting the increasing dependencies in our urban society, dependencies on government and politics. We Americans are a relentlessly forward-looking people, but let us learn to live looking back over our shoulders, back to Jefferson for guidance.

Among the most moving passages in American literature is a familiar one that echoes with what can be called Jeffersonian melancholy. It is the ending of F. Scott Fitzgerald's *The Great Gatsby*. The narrator, Nick Carraway, is standing at night on a lawn on the Long Island shore. He says:

> And as the moon rose higher the inessential houses began to melt away until gradually I became aware of the old island here that flowered once for Dutch sailors' eyes—a fresh green breast of the new world. Its vanished trees, the trees that had made way for Gatsby's house, had once pandered in whispers to the last and greatest of all human dreams; for a transitory enchanted moment man must have held his breath in the presence of this continent, compelled into an aesthetic contemplation he neither understood nor desired, face to face for the last time in history with something commensurate to his capacity for wonder.

I call this Jeffersonian because it recalls the immense promise implicit in America's space. It is melancholy because it suggests that the great dream, that of being worthy of the promise, was transitory, and has passed. But it need not be so.

Jefferson's generation came many generations after the Dutch sailors' eyes first fell on our continent, but Jefferson's generation, too, held its breath, feeling it had assumed a responsibility as large as the continent. In our time the sense of freshness is gone. The houses and the cities—these human handprints on the land—are not insubstantial and will not melt away. But we should not want them to. These most un-Jeffersonian things—our cities—can be made more civilized if we rededicate ourselves to the most Jeffersonian of values, personal independence, beginning with education and finding fruition in work. The Jeffersonian legacy can live downtown.

For just one more moment let us rejoin Nick Carraway on Gatsby's lawn by the Long Island shore. His mind is on what he calls "that vast obscurity beyond the city, where the dark fields of the republic rolled on under the night." Fitzgerald's masterpiece concludes with these words: "So we beat on, boats against the current, borne back ceaselessly into the past."

The past has us in its grip. But that is our good fortune because Thomas Jefferson is a large component of our usable past. So let us beat against the current, the modern current of statism and dependency that, if unresisted, will bear us farther and farther away from Jefferson's still vital vision of our Republic.

Reprinted from The Public Interest, *Summer 1993*

A Trickle-Down Culture

Shortly after seven A.M. one day, driving through rural South Carolina, Edwin Delattre, dean of Boston University's School of Education, saw something that was both "a breathtaking picture of hope" and a dismaying reminder of "what dreadfully diminished signs of civility I look for." What he saw by the side of the road were brightly clad black schoolchildren, with backpacks, the older children attentive to the younger, heading for schools not marred by litter, graffiti, barbed wire, chains on the door or uniformed police.

Delattre was driving away from the cities of Florida, the state with the highest crime and violent crime rates, where most criminals serve only one-third of their sentences, and the phrase "juvenile career criminal" no longer shocks. The contrast between rural South Carolina and urban Florida stirred in Delattre anxieties as old as the Republic, anxieties about the compatibility of cities and self-government. But Delattre has darker anxieties than those Jefferson had about what he considered the link between the habits of rural hardihood and the virtues requisite for democracy—independence, self-control. The sociology of virtue is more problematic now than in Jefferson's day because our society is saturated by promptings to degeneracy.

Driving north, Delattre had paused in Milledgeville, Georgia, to honor the memory of the writer Flannery O'Connor, whose words provided his theme when he later addressed a colloquium back in Boston. She wrote: "You have to push as hard as the age that pushes against you." Delattre is a philosopher who has immersed himself in the realities of police work. He knows that the age pushes young people into predation not merely with grinding material impoverishment, but also with toxic ideas.

The age that pushes hard against unformed youth is not something that has just befallen us. We made it; are making it. Much of it comes from the top down, a trickle-down culture that begins with the idea that the good life consists in satisfying every impulse. Many intellectuals have helped supplant the moral categories essential to civilized living, replacing them with a watery vocabulary of "lifestyles" and "values" and "self-esteem." And now there is the idea of "victimization" which comes with a style of disputation: Criticism is met by ad hominem charges that all critics are "phobic" or sociopolitically "centric." Discourse is smothered beneath the presumption that an opponent's motives are obvious and obviously contemptible. One result of this is that people despair of affecting behavior with deliberative reasoning, and resort increasingly to litigation, political power, violence or the threat of it.

When a 12-year-old boy turns without a word and shoots dead a seven-year-old girl because she "dis'd" him by standing on his shadow, he is pushed by the age. He possesses a prickly sensitivity about his self-esteem and is incapable of distinguishing an action from a motive. What made this impulsive child? This age that celebrates unchecked impulses.

We are, Delattre believes, losing the timeless struggle between Socrates and Homer. It is the struggle between philosophy and power, between reason and passion. It is the struggle between, on the one hand, the quest for truth, justice and the improvement of the soul and, on the other hand, the lust for riches and glory, and the condoning of rash and remorseless assaults. Homeric passions were worthy of epic poetry—"Sing, Goddess, the rage of Achilles, murderous, doomed." Today's stunted, twisted notions of heroism are written in graffiti spray-painted on public walls, and in the pounding lyrics of rap music.

The age has obliterated human magnificence by linking a banality with a non sequitur—the observation that everyone has flaws, and the conclusion that therefore no one merits emulation. Having denied the possibility of human excellence, we also have, Delattre says, "obliterated the reality of human depravity by the doctrine of the moral equivalence of all putative 'lifestyles.'" The idea is abroad that there is no moral heritage worth "imposing" on children, respect for whom requires that their selection of "values" be regarded as a mere matter of taste. Delattre believes this is why so many students never criticize a proposition by saying, "I believe your view is mistaken for the following reasons." Instead, they give autobiographical reports such as, "I'm not comfortable with that." Students regard such reports about their "feelings" as final and no more in need of justification than the assertion "I don't like brussels sprouts."

Society has a seamlessness that we disregard at our peril. Academics who blithely assert that "everything is political"—for example, whether, or how, to read Emily Dickinson—are postulating that all decisions are motivated by the desire to acquire power for advantage over others. This idea, common on campuses, expresses, Delattre says, "the ethos and the mentality of the gang reaching deeply into our age, far beyond the most obvious forms of barbarity in the streets."

Furthermore, if "everything is political," emotional impoverishment is inevitable because love is impossible, selflessness being unimaginable. Hence sex cannot be expected to transcend biology and egoism. And so there are "nonjudgmental" sex education programs that communicate the judgment that healthy sexuality is separable from love and its preparedness to sacrifice. And there are 1.2 million illegitimate births in a year.

Delattre does not despair, not quite. Regarding the inner-city culture of predation, he does say that it is next to impossible to make responsible citizens from young people who have ingrained habits of violent criminality: "Predators, like the rest of us, like the habits they acquire." But hope dies hard and his thoughts recur to the cheerful young South Carolinians he saw by the dawn's early light. They had the look of wholesome products of attentive parents who are pushing against the age. Having spent much time on our meanest streets, Delattre has adjusted his manner of hoping: "Even though adulthood has forever worn away my youthful confidence that where there is life there is hope, I feel hopeful still whenever I see anything better than the worst." What small signs of civility we do seize upon.

December 13, 1993

Nature and the Male Sex

Uh oh. There is bad news on the nature-vs.-nurture front. The perennial argument is about what matters most in human affairs, that which nature does in making us or that which society does in nurturing us. Today's bulletin is: Stress nature, its importance—and its incompetence. Nature blundered badly in designing males.

If James Q. Wilson is right, and memory runneth not to when he was not, the problem is that males are not naturally suited to civilization. So society must evolve institutional restraints and correctives to make men more civilized than they tend to be. Liberals must rethink plans for social perfection through social reforms. But conservatives, too, are discomfited: Social policy does not promise perfection but it is tremendously important in staving off trouble, so government's role is inescapably ambitious.

In an American Enterprise Institute lecture on "Human Nature and Social Progress," UCLA's Wilson, president of the American Political Science Association, says that much of "the underclass problem arises from the incomplete and increasingly more difficult task of socializing some males." Humans are social animals requiring much formative support and guidance from society. But male and female humans differ substantially in the extent to which they need, and are inclined to contribute to, child care, fidelity to a single mate and peaceful relations with others. In all societies, says Wilson, men are more likely than women to play roughly, drive recklessly, fight and assault. Those behavioral differences, which appear early in life, have a biological basis in neurochemical stuff like testosterone. Socialization must contend against biology.

Many male traits, such as aggressiveness and hyperactivity, were useful many millennia ago when there were woolly mammoths to be hunted, or during the Thirty Years' War. But those traits are ruinous in today's cities. Aggression is no longer an adaptive trait in bureaucratized societies that require conformity to many norms, and technical competence more than boldness and physical prowess. Life in large cities has weakened, to the point of disappearance, civilizing ties of kinship and such institutions as churches, political parties, trade unions and fraternal organizations. Cities bring young males into close contact with strangers, multiplying opportunities for aggression.

The 19th century coped with the consequences of industrialism and urbanization by what is now derided as "Victorian morality," including the idea of the "gentleman." The aspiration was in the word—gentling. The idea involved such seemingly, but not really, minor matters as table manners and sportsmanship. Alas, the modern age is concerned with "personality" rather than character.

Character is rigid, elitist, moralistic. Personality is spontaneous, democratic. Elites abandoned the ethic of character, an ethic that encouraged and even enforced right conduct. The abandonment coincided with two epochal events, the great migration of Southern rural blacks to Northern cities and the creation of a welfare state that made survival not dependent on work or charity. Today, many entry-level jobs have left cities but prosperity has enabled young men to deal in drugs and guns. We have reproduced the historic conditions for a warrior class: separation of economic activity from family maintenance; children reared apart from fathers; wealth subject to predation; male status determined by combat and sexual conquest.

The problems of the underclass, particularly male joblessness and illegitimate births, have been unresponsive to social policies. The policies have mistakenly presumed that the problems arise from perverse incentives government can adjust or obstacles government can abolish. But, says Wilson, if mere incentives were the problem, low-income blacks would not be displaced from day labor by low-income Latinos; black-owned businesses would not be replaced by Korean-owned businesses in the same neighborhoods; low-income white women would become welfare recipients at the same rate as low-income black women; the average young black male would not be 10 times more likely to commit murder than a young white male.

Our society clings to its belief in the healing powers of better incentives and fewer barriers to individual striving. The alternative belief, that the problem is cultural (habits, mores, customs), is dismaying: It is harder to change culture than to change incentives and barriers. And faith in incentives is linked to an assumption central to our politics— that people are good at pursuing their own interests. Today's underclass is mostly black but includes only a tiny minority of blacks. Most blacks are on the ladder of upward mobility. The underclass is a group that has not benefited from our society's generally successful strategies for habituation of human beings through the do's and don'ts of daily life.

Wilson suggests two concrete measures—better security, and boarding schools for fatherless children. Take back the streets. Begin by reinstitutionalizing the mentally ill, who communicate an infectious, demoralizing ambience of disorder. "Neighborhood standards may be set by mothers," Wilson says, "but they are enforced by fathers." Not by absent fathers. Wilson advocates public and private policing to give the poor something like the protection the rich give themselves in gated suburban communities and guarded high-rises. He suggests the military tactic of "perimeter control"—blockade some streets, put checkpoints at some intersections and all public housing to disarm the armed. The boarding schools should aim to send students to colleges or apprenticeship programs. Critics will say: The schools will engage in moral, political, religious or ethnocentric indoctrination. Wilson says, "I certainly hope so." Do it, but do it wisely.

Government now toils under a crushing weight of rules, set-asides, quotas, citizens' councils, impact statements and general rights-mongering. It can do almost nothing, and probably nothing as decisive as Wilson wants done. (You conservatives who hate government should be happy. Are you?) Still, the best hope is for policies that will help produce more orderly and employable males. As Wilson says, "We do know how to wage a war on idleness, idleness that is the breeding ground of selfishness and the arena for pointless masculine display."

June 17, 1991

Hoops in a Challenging Environment

CHICAGO—"Take your hat off."

The way Gil Walker says that to the young man—softly, politely—it is more a reminder than an order. But when Walker speaks, many young men hear the voice of the commissioner. His rule against hats in the gym expresses both universal etiquette and Chicago prudence. Styles of hats and ways of wearing them often are trademarks of gangs, and that world stays outside, on the dark streets.

It is midnight. Do you know where your sons are? If you live on Chicago's dangerous West Side and if your sons are 18 to 25 years old and if they, and you, are lucky, they are dribbling a basketball up court, executing a pick-and-roll. They are off the street and out of trouble and, at the end of the night, around one A.M., they will be picking up some pointers about getting on with life off the court.

Walker, a sinewy 41-year-old black man, works for the Chicago Housing Authority, as Commissioner of the Midnight Basketball League. His will (and $90,000—about what it costs to incarcerate three men for one year) is the driving force behind 16 ten-man teams. And he is a scarce commodity in the lives of many of the young men: He is a male authority figure who is always there, 'round about midnight.

Walker was an Army brat whose travels took him from an Indiana boyhood to Japan, to college in Texas, to semipro basketball in Mexico, to this cramped boys-club gym where the air is thick with the sounds of the city game—the slap-slap-slap of basketballs and the squeak-squeak-squeak of sneakers.

The young men who play do not need to be taught much basketball, although this night there is on hand someone who could join Walker in teaching—Andre Wakefield, formerly of the Phoenix Suns. He is a product of this neighborhood, which also has furnished two members of the NBA champion Detroit Pistons—Mark Aguirre and Isiah Thomas.

"Basketball is our national sport," says Walker of black Americans. "I never met a black man who would admit he couldn't play." But of many young men who play in his league, Walker says, "No one ever sat down and taught them some things."

"Hold out your fingernails," he will tell new players. "If the nails are dirty, something else is dirty, and you're not putting my clean uniform on a dirty body." The league has uniforms, warm-ups, a player draft, an All-Star game, an awards banquet, championship rings. The scoring and league standings appear in the *Sun-Times*. Coaches get $500. For the season. And responsibility for washing the uniforms.

To be eligible for all this a player must attend practice once a week and must be a "successful individual," which Walker defines simply: "anyone taking care of a family." There is a discussion at the end of each game, at which the players get "the gospel according to Gil Walker." It begins with basketball but ends with talk about "manhood." For example, he will say:

"How many babies you got?"

"Four."

"How many are you taking care of? Tell me their teachers' names. You don't know? What kind of man are you?"

Post-game topics include how to look for a job, how to get along with co-workers, how to deal with "a boss who is on your case."

About 80 percent of the players come from "the projects." If Chicago's public housing were a city, it would be Illinois's second largest. Before the league began, gangs—there are more than 100 in the city, with about 30,000 members—were the only structure many of these young men knew. Participation in the league for some is the only source of pride, and not just for players. One mother calls it "the first time I ever had a chance to cheer for my son."

Amidst today's urban tragedy of social regression stand some extraordinary people. There are women, such as high school principals, carving enclaves from the enveloping chaos. There are men like Walker who see the grace and discipline and self-taught skills of ghetto basketball players and see something more, an unmined lode of all sorts of talents.

Basketball is a game for big, fast men in a confined space, a game of controlled—sometimes—contact. There is a fine line between legitimate contact and a foul (a city playground saying is: "No autopsy, no foul"). And in some neighborhoods, there is a fine line between a foul and a *casus belli*.

Skeptics told Walker: Give these guys uniforms, you'll make matters worse—create new gangs. Walker mixes members of rival gangs on teams and gets away with it. He remembers the night the gym lights went out. For seven minutes. His urban reflex was to get his back against a wall and wait for the worst. But for seven miraculous minutes no one moved. Then the lights, and the game, went on.

By such small victories are cities reclaimed.

October 18, 1990

Darnell Gets a Gun

Ms. Derlesher Edwards of Chicago paid $55 for a handgun and 100 rounds of ammunition because she overheard men in the small family restaurant she owns saying, "This is an easy place to stick up." Her son Darnell took the gun from her purse and put it in his school gym bag because a classmate who had stolen his candy bars said that if Darnell didn't give him more candy he would shoot him. Darnell told some classmates he had the gun, word reached school authorities and they confiscated it.

Darnell is six.

And so it goes in a nation with more gun dealers than gas stations, a nation in which, according to a new government report, firearms cause more deaths among those 15 to 24 than all natural causes combined.

In an article in *The American Scholar*, "Defining Deviancy Down," Senator Pat Moynihan writes that in the span of just one generation deviant behavior has soared to levels Americans recoil from acknowledging. So the nation has been redefining deviancy to exempt much conduct previously stigmatized, and has been relaxing the standard of what are considered "normal" levels of deviant behavior, levels that would have been intolerable by standards obtaining not long ago.

A sign of "normalizing": In 1990, according to the Justice Department, Americans reported only 38 percent of all crimes and only 48 percent of violent crimes. Such behavior is a shrug of despair.

Another sign is this *New York Times* subhead on a story about a teacher shot on the way to class: STRUCK IN THE SHOULDER IN THE YEAR'S FIRST SHOOTING INSIDE A SCHOOL. Just the first. More to come.

When the crime level, no matter how high it is or how rapidly it is rising, is "normalized," society is saying it has no expectation of improvement, and hence makes no insistence on even trying. In 1929, Moynihan notes, Chicago's Saint Valentine's Day massacre shocked the nation. Four gangsters machine-gunned seven gangsters. Nowadays it is not unusual in many cities—it is "normal"—to have such carnage on a "normal" weekend. Raymond Kelly, New York City's police commissioner, read Moynihan's article and wrote a splendid speech urging "a new intolerance." Noting that on Valentine's Day 1993 there were 12 homicides in his city—six in one Bronx apartment—Kelly said:

> The fight against crime in America, like that against Soviet domination, is now essentially a fight for freedom. Fearing crime, or becoming one of its victims, is to lose a fair measure of freedom. . . . Society's increasing tolerance of crime and antisocial behavior in general is abetting our own enslavement. The erosion of freedom caused by crime is so pervasive that we are in danger of failing to notice it at all.

He notices with disgust the parked cars with signs in their windows saying NO RADIO. These signs are attempts to communicate in conciliatory terms with thieves, saying: Break into someone else's car, there's no loot in mine. Such signs, says Kelly, are "flags of urban surrender."

Noting that there were 50 million guns in private hands in 1950, and that the number has doubled every 20 years to at least 200 million, and that most are handguns, Kelly argues for national registration of all handguns. Such registration would produce "a trail of ownership" and "an interesting trail of civil liability, as well, for persons who sold or disposed of their guns illegally or just recklessly."

Kelly also urges more "community policing," putting many thousands more officers on visible neighborhood beats. Which brings us back to Darnell's mother.

She lives in a city where Steve Johnson of the *Chicago Tribune* recently interviewed a man sentenced to six months of court supervision for carrying a small pistol—for self-defense, he said. The man plans to buy another gun and carry it illegally after his supervision ends. He told Johnson: "We have a saying on the street. We'd rather the police catch us with it than the other guys catch us without it."

So speaks a resident of Darnell's mother's city, where in 1982 Cook County Hospital's trauma unit treated "only" 500 persons who had been shot, and "only" 5 percent of them had been hit by more than one bullet. In 1991 the unit treated about 1,000 gunshot victims and 25 percent had absorbed more than one bullet.

Desperation drove Darnell's mother to buy a gun because she calculated, not unreasonably, that she could not count on the protection of the police. Until the calculus is changed for people like her, trapped in violent neighborhoods, the gun lobby can plausibly argue that gun control will merely disarm the innocent. So gun control and "community policing"—call it saturation policing—should be indissolubly coupled.

March 28, 1993

Escape Velocity:
The Physics of Childhood

CAMBRIDGE, MASSACHUSETTS—Dr. T. Berry Brazelton is from Texas—central Texas—and sounds it. But he lives hard by Harvard Yard, on a street with a fine New England name—Hawthorne Street—in a clapboard house painted a mustardy yellow popular in New England.

He is from a region fond of gregariousness, but is married to a Lowell. She remembers walking, when a young girl, with her father, a Boston Brahmin, who did not acknowledge a cousin when they passed. When she asked why, her father explained: "He knows that I know him." Brazelton put his foot down when she wanted to cut their wedding cake using her family's ancestral sword that had been used in the Civil War against the side on which his ancestors fought.

Brazelton, now 70, knows the enduring nature of America's regional and cultural differences. Perhaps that has equipped him for what has become his calling, that of calling attention to the differences that Americans least like to contemplate—those of class.

He is a pediatrician at Harvard Medical School and Children's Hospital Medical Center in Boston, and he is a member of the National Commission on Children, which will issue its report this week. In assessing the condition of America's children, the report cannot avoid the subject of class.

Brazelton's interest in class has made him a physicist of childhood. Physicists refer to the "escape velocity" of particles circling in an orbit. Some particles spin, or outside intervention causes them to spin, free from the prison of orbit onto their own long trajectory. Society's challenge is to give poor children outward velocity from the orbit that imprisons them.

Brazelton believes that the propensity of a child to flourish is established very early. The crucial variable is the child's expectation that the world will be consistently interested, supportive and encouraging.

Absence of the propensity to flourish can be "read" in the behavioral language of even a nine-month-old. Doctors, says Brazelton, must be taught to read that language in such simple activities as elementary play with blocks. The grim message of some play is that the babies expect to fail for the rest of their lives.

Handed two blocks, a baby that is at ease in the world—a baby probably already accustomed to the praise of interested adults—will manipulate the blocks vigorously, dropping one to see who retrieves it, and looking bright-eyed at any observing adult, expecting praise. A baby who expects to fail will have a more limited repertory of play—limited, Brazelton says, "by the realization that no one will care."

Poor children sense and acquire the helplessness of their parents—or, more likely, of a single parent. In 1991, 29.5 percent of all American babies were born to single women, up from 18 percent in 1980. Sixty-eight percent of all black babies were born to single women. The figure for whites was 22 percent. Single women are 50 percent more likely than married women to have low-birth-weight babies. Such babies have reduced chances of a healthy life.

In these numbers there is a strong correlation with class: Single mothers are more apt to be poor.

We now know how, using early intervention, to raise, by age three, the IQ of infants as much as 13 points. That can be the difference between social competence and failure. Such an increase in IQ points can be achieved even in infants whose neurological systems have been disorganized by the mother's ingestion of alcohol or other damaging drugs.

The brute fact is that the best predictor of a baby's prospects is socioeconomic status. And in the 1980s, among children the chance of being poor rose from 16.4 to 19.6 percent, while among senior citizens it fell from 15.2 to 11.4 percent.

Poverty is a public health problem and treatment must begin with the new family, often just a mother and child. Parents (or parent) and baby must be treated as a single patient, medically and socially. But, says Brazelton, there are three impediments to this. One is fiscal, one cultural and one pertains to the sociology of his profession.

Early intervention in dysfunctional families is labor-intensive and hence expensive. It also is intrusive, and violates a cultural value—the self-sufficiency of the family unit. Furthermore, the medical profession is increasingly science-intensive and specialized. It is neglecting the art of imparting "escape velocity" through the practice of medicine as a "family friendly" art.

So for starters, Brazelton's message is: Physicians, heal yourselves.

June 23, 1991

The "9/91" Problem

CHICAGO—Ken Van Spankeren has gray streaks in his beard and strong opinions in his head, both the result of sixteen years as principal of Orr High School, where he is attacking the "9/91" problem of American education.

Only 9 percent of the hours lived by young Americans between birth and their 18th birthdays are spent in schools, and the other 91 percent often subverts what schools do. This subversion occurs amid the distractions of affluent suburbs, but it especially occurs where Orr is.

Orr is three miles and a world west of Michigan Avenue's glittering Magnificent Mile, surrounded by a jumble of storefronts offering chicken wings, check cashing and elemental Christianity, and a jungle of unemployment, gang violence and drug dealing. Orr, serving five square miles of this troubled city, reflects the biggest problem bedeviling inner-city education—family disintegration.

Seventy-five percent of Orr's students (who are 92 percent black, 8 percent Hispanic) live in poverty; 85 percent come from homes without fathers. They began falling behind most American children before kindergarten: They were not read to or even talked to enough, or played with or taken to zoos and libraries. (A visitor's question, "Are libraries within walking distance?" is considered quaint. There is no "walking distance" across turf contested by gangs.)

So some Orr students come to school early—fourteen years early. There is an infant-stimulation program for some six-week-olds. A few of them are children of the school's 90 or so unwed mothers, whose average age is 15 and who take classes in parenting. There also is child care for some neighborhood three- to five-year-olds who, because they enter a decade early, will someday present Orr with fewer remediation problems.

Classes begin at eight A.M. but tutoring begins at 7:15 A.M. and on Tuesdays, Wednesdays and Thursdays dropout-prevention instruction continues until nine P.M. A math teacher arrives at six A.M. to teach chess to children who never saw a set at home. The teacher's team recently won a city title.

With assistance from Continental Bank, Orr is bearing Chicago's burdens. But can schools do that and also educate?

Chester Finn, author of *We Must Take Charge* and formulator of the

"9/91" problem, rightly argues that many schools spread themselves too thin and education becomes thin gruel. Every American passes through school at an impressionable age, so there is a perennial temptation to use schools for various ameliorative purposes—combatting AIDS and drugs, promoting racial harmony and environmental awareness and animal rights and so on. These purposes often compete with learning.

Many schools unwisely choose to do peripheral things in the name of social reform. Van Spankeren says he lacks the luxury of choice. Problems of the streets and homes are central, not peripheral, to urban schools' missions.

Van Spankeren prefers teachers from the inner city, who understand that students start unreceptive to learning and cannot be taught by having them open a text, read a chapter and answer questions. "Urban kids," he says, "don't learn that way."

But a danger is that educators will become too preoccupied with devising enticements to learning (for example, teaching math and English through "entrepreneurship" projects, such as Orr's student-run catering business). If so, many inner-city students will be shunted onto an educational sidetrack that takes them away from society's mainstream opportunities that require competent reading and expository writing.

Orr's better students read Ernest Hemingway, Carson McCullers, Richard Wright, Maya Angelou. They particularly enjoy *Hamlet.* All reading is done in class. Teachers assume homework cannot be done by most students, who have family responsibilities, or jobs, or both, and whose homes are unquiet and may not even contain a table at which to work.

Most of Orr's most successful students are girls. The best boys face peer pressure not to "act white." But the best male students tend to be athletes: If you can get your wrist over a basketball rim, you can be a bit bookish.

When Van Spankeren arrived 16 years ago, Orr was too similar to the surrounding streets. Radios blared, caps and earrings were worn as gang indicators and drug dealers, pimps and gang members roamed the halls. Today the radios are gone; hats and earrings are removed at the front door; no one enters without an ID card; no one leaves the building during the school day.

This is one way to tame an asphalt jungle: one school building at a time.

June 9, 1991

"Medicine" for "724 Children"

BOSTON—Herewith an understated introduction to the practice of pediatrics in the inner city: "The young child's attempts to master the age-appropriate fears of monsters under the bed are severely undermined when the child needs to sleep under the bed to dodge real bullets or attempt to screen out the violent fights of his or her caregivers."

That is from a recent article in *The Journal of the American Medical Association*, which reported a survey of elementary-school-age children in New Orleans: 90 percent had witnessed violence; 70 percent had seen a weapon used; 40 percent had seen a corpse. An estimated 10 to 20 percent of Los Angeles homicides are witnessed by children. And a study at Boston City Hospital found 10 percent of the children treated in the pediatric primary-care clinic have witnessed a shooting or stabbing before they are six, half at home, half in the streets.

BCH has been serving Boston since 1864, when Sherman was burning Atlanta. Today there are war conditions, and war effects, in many urban neighborhoods. A recent study found similar posttraumatic stress disorders in children in war-torn Mozambique, Cambodia, the West Bank—and Chicago. The disorders include inability to concentrate, persistent sleep disturbance, flashbacks, sudden startling and hypervigilance, nihilistic and fatalistic orientation toward the future, leading to increased risk taking. To be a witness to violence is to be a victim of violence.

Small wonder that Boston has its share of what are known, in the grim argot of today's cities, as "724 children"—children kept at home, indoors, seven days a week, 24 hours a day, because of the epidemic of violence. Some of the fortunate ones come into contact with the doctors and social workers at BCH, a hard-used hospital that gives new meaning to the phrase "family medicine." Children are patients but families, such as they may be, are treated.

BCH's youngest patients often ask why the adults in their lives—parents, teachers, police—can't keep them safe. BCH physicians and social workers—a commingled group—regard as a treatable health problem the consequences of traumatically learning at an early age that the world is dangerous and unpredictable. A pervasive sense of danger, according to BCH doctors, causes people to make decisions that seem inexplicable to people more safely situated. For example, some women who are HIV-infected will still purposely get pregnant even though there is a 20 to 30 percent risk of having an infected child. Doctors say those odds do not seem so daunting when considered against the odds of being shot, raped, mugged. . . . Besides, for the HIV-infected mother, childbirth is an affirmation of normality, of the fact that life goes on. Similarly, for a young inner-city male who sees death before 20 as common on the streets, a baby as an heir is an attractive idea.

A child who learns early to fear the world is apt to lose his or her natural proclivity for exploration of the world. A "724 child" may need to be taught how to participate in normal socializing play that other children learn naturally when growing up where civil peace prevails. Because we are apt to parent as we are parented, many unwed mothers or others from the culture of poverty need to be taught—and are movingly eager to learn—about talking, playing and reading with children. So BCH doctors have given children 9,000 books. Reading together can be therapy for families under the stress of crowding in apartments where children are kept on beds to prevent them from crawling on floors flecked with fragments of lead paint.

A BCH doctor notes that it is common to hear grandmothers living in poverty say of young children, "They're smart when they're little. They get dumb when they get older." There is a sad wisdom behind such statements. The children of the poor are apt to be developmentally on a par with middle-class children until, say, two. Then apparent cognitive deterioration, relative to other children—actually, failure to attain potential—is apt to become noticeable. This is a result of various traumas and emotional and cognitive deprivations. It also can reflect the withering of, or the failure to articulate, parental expectations. This deterioration is neither necessary nor irreversible, but preventing it requires intense, unremitting one-on-one contact whereby a person with the coping skills necessary for flourishing in an urban setting imparts such skills to someone who lacks them. "We know how to do this," says a BCH doctor. "It is fixable. It is just not a quick fix."

It doubtless seems anomalous, and may be in some ways inefficient, for so many social services to be dispensed through the urban health care system. But an inner-city hospital often is, for its poorest patients, the point of entry into the system of social services. So BCH's staff find themselves arranging with the employers of patients for time off for hospital visits; or dispensing basic nutritional counseling; or encouraging families to talk about everything from goals to heroes; or suggesting strategies of urban prudence.

This last, especially, can be urgent for health: An inner-city person who becomes a victim of violence has a 40 percent chance of becoming a victim again. This not only because of where he or she lives, but because of an inability to step away from the "bad vibes" of someone else's ugly intent; or because of an inability to get angry—which is normal—without acting out the anger, action being the articulateness of the streets; or because a victim often looks like a victim. Social workers here say that of the appalling numbers of children carrying weapons to school most are not aggressive but frightened. (According to a 1990 survey by the Centers for Disease Control, one of every five high school students had carried a weapon and one in 20 had carried a gun in a 30-day period.) And many of the aggressive ones have been so desensitized by urban life that they feel alive only when enjoying a "rep" (reputation), something most quickly acquired by instilling fear.

So BCH's staff does a lot that is not, strictly speaking, medicine. "But," says one doctor, "it's *all* health." Says another, "This is not like trauma surgery, where you leap in, stop someone's bleeding and are a hero in an instant." Yes, but what BCH does is much more than medicine, and does much for the dignity of doctoring, and although it does not deal in instantaneous drama, it has its own heroism.

March 22, 1993

The Eventful Life of the 75th Precinct

BROOKLYN—This is a report from a battlefield, not in the Middle East but one of the many in our midst.

To get to the 75th precinct from police headquarters in lower Manhattan, you take the Brooklyn Bridge, the engineering marvel of the 19th century. It was built in the full flush of American optimism after the guns of the Civil War fell silent, back when Brooklyn was a separate city, the nation's third largest, and building bridges symbolized the knitting-together of a nation that had been bloodily divided.

Today the trip takes you into the most shocking division in America, not the perennial division between rich and poor, but between the two Americas where gunfire is, and is not, part of the ambience of normal life. The 75th is beyond the imagining of most Americans, who haven't the foggiest idea of the dangers and affronts which many of their fellow citizens experience daily.

Even Pat Carroll, 49, almost seems to have a hard time believing it, and he has lived in the city all his life and today is the commanding officer of the 75th. He sits behind one of those government-issue metal desks. He faces, across his cramped and cluttered office, a map of a sort no police officer faced in 1965 and no layman can easily fathom. It is covered with green and red circles. They denote places in his precinct—reds are indoors, greens outdoors—where drugs are routinely sold.

The layman's instinct is: What are you waiting for? Go get 'em! But the layman has not had the bailing-the-ocean fatigue that comes from sending minor drug dealers into the criminal-justice system, only to see them replaced on the street corners even before the system spews them back onto the streets.

"Arrests aren't the answer," Carroll says, "but we can't not do that. It gives the community heart." But the community, he says, is not convinced when better arrest statistics are announced to a background staccato of gunfire.

There are in the 75th about 32 arrests a day, two-thirds of them drug-related. Arrest numbers could be tripled, given enough officers, courts, prison cells. But in a city that is financially on the rocks and emotionally on the ropes, police work requires an endless series of cold judgments, apportioning contracting human resources to an expanding problem.

The 75th ranks second in the city in 911 radio runs, and an officer is injured almost every day, often in scuffles in domestic disputes. But such disputes are hardly the worst of the pandemic violence.

"When I was growing up," Carroll recalls, "if there was a fight, you might get punched in the nose, or someone might swing a garrison belt. Nowadays someone says, 'He dis'd me' "—showed disrespect—"and guns come out." Today's weapons of choice are semiautomatics with clips holding from nine to 25 rounds. "Twenty-five years ago," he says, "you made a gun collar [arrest], it was a big to-do." In 1990, there were 1,194 gun arrests in the 75th.

When today's 49-year-old policeman was a rookie in the 1960s, robbery was the crime that defined a neighborhood at risk. Nowadays the crime is drug dealing, with accompanying gunfire.

Of course, robbery is rampant because drug habits must be fed. (If you must steal $20 worth of property to raise $5 from a fence, then a $100-a-day habit requires $400 worth of stolen stuff.) Much of the gunfire is connected with routine practices of the drug trade—claiming territory, punishing people who do not fulfill contracts.

Carroll, whose son and daughter are cops, has a master's degree in urban affairs and a quarter of a century of on-the-street education, all of which tells him this: Police will be overwhelmed until the rest of government gets on with its jobs of enacting gun controls, providing drug treatment and treating the seedbed of most crime, the dysfunctional families that send forth violent young men.

Furthermore, Carroll is convinced, as so many cops are, that society's forces for order are no match for today's popular culture. You do not talk long with cops before they mention movies which are desensitizing young people by glorifying casual brutality.

You say cops should leave sociology to the social scientists? Cops lead lives rich in instructive anecdotes, enough anecdotes to justify generalizations. Cops know that business is booming here for companies offering armed escorts and selling bulletproof vests for children.

There may be a New World Order being built beyond our shores. At home, there is an accelerating failure to (in the Constitution's words) insure domestic tranquility.

February 10, 1991

From *Scarlet Street* to the Mean Streets

NEW YORK—In 1945, this city's movie censor banned *Scarlet Street*, starring Edward G. Robinson, because the ending was so shocking: A murderer remained at large. Today, in New York's enlightenment, there is no censorship. You can see any movie you can make it to through the mean streets.

In 1945, there were 292 homicides here. In 1990, there were about 2,200. In 1945, there were 1,417 armed robberies reported. In 1990, there were about 100,000, one every five minutes, and today robbery is underreported by citizens accustomed to mayhem (such as 390 car thefts a day) as a commonplace of urban life.

A 1945 poll revealed that 90 percent of New Yorkers considered themselves happy. Today, 60 percent say they plan to be living elsewhere in five years, and crime is the primary cause of flight.

Such numbers trickle across the aircraft-carrier-sized desk of Police Commissioner Lee P. Brown. Long ago that desk belonged to a peripatetic commissioner who rarely sat still behind it: Commissioner Teddy Roosevelt's midnight rambles on the city's wild side made him a rising star. Brown, a large black man with three advanced degrees, is both praised and faulted for his phlegmatic manner.

He came here from Houston, a city with 1.7 million people spread over 600 square miles. New York has 8 million in 319 square miles. New York's per-capita crime statistics are not the nation's worst (for example, Washington's homicide rate is two-and-a-half times that of New York), but crime seems worse here because the density gives this city the nation's highest irritability quotient. Many New Yorkers are quick on the trigger, literally. In 1960, handguns were used in 19 percent of homicides. Today, they are used in approximately 70 percent. Until 1969, more killings were by knives.

For more than a generation, the fundamental act of American fun—watching television—has involved, for the average viewer, seeing 150 acts of violence and 15 murders a week. Is it really amazing that life seems to have been cheapened? Brown is not amazed.

On the other hand, it has been plausibly argued that Americans are not so much more violent than other people; they are only more armed. The argument is that you are more apt to see a fight in a British pub than in an American bar, but the British fight culminates in punches, the American fight in gunfire.

Brown is both proud of and appalled by the confiscation of 17,000 guns in 1990. But that is like damming a river with a Popsicle stick. There is a river of guns coming north from states (particularly Virginia, Texas, Georgia and Florida) where gun restrictions are derisory. In 1989, 80 percent of those arrested for serious crimes had drugs in their systems. Drug disputes help generate this fact: The typical homicide victim is a young black male killed by a young black male he knew. (Only about 10 percent of homicide victims are non-Hispanic whites.)

Drugs, like guns, are a tide against which no single city or state can erect a dike. But Brown, the calm at the eye of this city's storm about crime, does know what he can do: He can deploy more cops more usefully than in the recent past.

In medicine, much sophisticated research has resulted in proving that grandmother was right. The key to health is rest, exercise and nutrition. So, too, police science has lumbered laboriously to the conclusion that grandfather's generation knew a thing or two.

The newfangled notion of "community policing" is essentially the oldfangled notion that more police should get out of their cars and back on a beat. There, they can deal not just reactively with crime, but proactively with the disorders—loitering, poorly parented children, panhandling, anxiety that drives people indoors. These are early indices of neighborhood decay.

All that stands between the theory and the practice of such sensible policing is the residue of 1960s and 1970s liberalism, which considers it fascist for police to buttress bourgeois society's norms of good behavior.

Commissioner Teddy Roosevelt went prowling in the wee small hours with Jacob Riis, the journalist who wrote *How the Other Half Lives*. Like the patrician Roosevelt, Brown, the product of a blue-collar family, is concerned with the social incubation of crime. When Brown was a boy, the family dinner table was where his parents "looked me in the eye to see if I had done something wrong." Now, he says, if many young men eat with their families at all, it is cafeteria style.

Brown knows that the key to fighting crime—primarily a product of young men—is in things that grandmother and grandfather took for granted.

February 14, 1991

Policing Chicago's "Up South"

This is *not* a column about the potential U.S. involvement in policing ethnic enclaves in Bosnia.

CHICAGO—When Nature assembled, from a lot of good material, Leroy O'Shield, Nature had a policeman in mind. Thick-armed and barrel-chested, with close-cropped hair and a salt-and-pepper mustache, Commander O'Shield's visage expresses, in quick succession, stolid authority, intense curiosity and knowledge of life as it actually is lived. An African-American, he has the demeanor of someone who has seen many discouraging things without becoming discouraged.

However, when, 26 years ago, O'Shield, who is now 50, decided to become a cop, he did not have anything like today's 15th Police District in mind. Located in Chicago's Far West Side, it is 90,000 people in 3.2 square miles of what sociologists call a "challenging urban environment" and the rest of us call a bad neighborhood. It is not the sort of place you would want to stroll at night or raise children anytime, but many decent people must do the latter and would like to be able to do the former. O'Shield and his 242 officers want to help by using "community policing."

His recurring word is "proactive," the antonym of "reactive." It means police not controlled by 911 calls for help. Such calls are, in a sense, always too late—too late for preventive policing and the informal social controls that can prevent disorder. Police, says O'Shield, can be quite efficient at arresting criminals without reducing crime. This is because the drug epidemic has swamped the revolving-door criminal justice system—courts, prisons, probation. That system, he says tersely, is "no deterrent."

But what can prevent the crumbling of the thin, brittle crust of civilization when the culture itself is assaulting that crust? O'Shield says one of Chicago's most violent weekends followed the showing on national television of *Boyz N the Hood*, the movie about Los Angeles gangs. There was a rash of drive-by shootings and some young men arrested for the shootings said they "just wanted to see what it was like." After the Los Angeles riots, California's Governor Pete Wilson said "everybody in America" should see that movie because of its portrayal of a strong, caring father. O'Shield wishes he saw more such fathers in his district, where most young males come from homes without fathers, and most have been arrested for something before they are 21. But O'Shield calls the movie a "training film" for crime and says the message young men get from it (and from others, such as *New Jack City*) is "the mystique of being tough." O'Shield goes to such movies so he can know "what to expect" on the streets.

O'Shield and his officers would be forgiven for surrendering to fatalism and despair—for feeling that their task is akin to painting the Golden Gate Bridge, a task that never ends. He notes that when he became a policeman, police and teachers were like parents—they were sources of authority. Drug abuse was aberrant and stigmatized behavior even in rough neighborhoods. Today, he says, police work must include—indeed, must begin by—working with all community groups to reestablish the "informal social controls" of community mores.

He has two master's degrees, in criminal justice and corrections. His conversation is salted with matter-of-fact and to-the-point references to scholarly works, citing authors and publication dates. He cites one study showing that young police officers' cynicism rises, on a scale of zero to 100, from zero to 60 in their first three years. He recommends community policing for police morale as well as community morale, because it gives officers the inspiriting sense of taking the initiative.

It is not arcane. It is commonsense adaptation to the fact that most crime is committed by a few people in a few places. So: Find out who and where they are. Have a police presence throughout the community establishing relationships with merchants in their stores, with the elderly on their stoops, with young people in gymnasiums.

Chicago's West Side has been called "Up South" because so many residents came from Mississippi and Arkansas. In 25 years the area has suffered white flight and black flight. The white working class fled the black working class, which in turn fled the crime and drugs that came as the manufacturing jobs left for South Carolina, South Korea and south of the border. Social and physical disorder and fear of crime precede, and breed, crime. But disorder and fear can be driven back by bite-size efforts to bring people out of their homes into nonthreatening streets.

Even a dash of beauty can be a bulwark against the menacing sense of encroaching chaos. So community groups plant trees and flowers, and the city provides paint for covering graffiti. When the bureaucrats were slow to give permission for boarding up some abandoned buildings that had become drug markets, community groups bought plywood and notified the police that they were not waiting for permission, and the police looked the other way.

Today we seem to spend a lot of time proving with sophisticated research that earlier generations knew a thing or two. Such as: Befriend a cop walking the beat. Community policing can be as elemental as shoe leather. Asked how many more officers he needs, O'Shield says words rarely uttered in government: "I have enough." Enough, that is, if the community becomes engaged; if noncoercive social measures regain control of the children and hence of the streets; if drug treatment becomes available on demand, and made mandatory for the people involved in the drug-related crime that is 90 percent of the 15th District's crime. O'Shield stresses that the gangs that run the drug business constitute highly organized crime: "They meet just as we do." But he and community activists are meeting not just to plan to catch dealers but to prevent people from becoming customers.

The embattled enclave that is the 15th District will eventually be much better because the community is energized by involvement with O'Shield's extraordinarily patient and determined officers. Of course, "eventually" might come a lot sooner to embattled ethnic enclaves throughout urban America if we did not also police Bosnian enclaves, but this column is not about that.

May 17, 1993

Nietzsche in City Hall

LOS ANGELES—This city, transformed in a generation from a shimmering symbol of possibilities to a dark portent, now has a new mayor, Richard Riordan, 63, a nominal Republican whose problems begin with the civic culture itself.

When Mayor Tom Bradley was elected in 1973, 674,555 people voted. Since then the city has grown by almost that many, but this year only 598,436 voted. A city where 40 percent of all households have unlisted telephone numbers is experiencing a great withdrawal from public life, including public schools. It is a withdrawal into gated neighborhoods, or just indoors, or to suburbs. Why? Begin with fear.

In 1970 vehicular accidents killed more than twice as many people as gunshot homicides. In 1991 gunshots killed more than vehicular accidents did. In a recent five-year period there was a legal handgun sale for every 19 residents of Los Angeles County. Illegal sales fuel the arms race. Says Riordan, old businesses are leaving, new businesses will not locate in combat zones, tourists are going elsewhere and children do not learn in an insecure environment.

But the ratio of police to citizens, one to 500, is the nation's lowest. In Los Angeles's low-density sprawl, there are 15 officers per square mile compared with 89 in New York. Law enforcement as a percentage of city spending has declined substantially while city budgets have doubled every eight years.

Riordan won a majority of voters earning $20,000 to $40,000, including many entrepreneurial immigrants—Latinos and Asians—whose work ethic causes them to revolt against what they see as a welfare ethic. The defining datum of the current crisis is this: The number of jobs in America and the number of inner-city unemployed both grew rapidly during the 1970s and 1980s. (Yes, many jobs left inner-city neighborhoods, but waves of immigrants have traveled up to 10,000 miles to fill entry-level jobs.)

The contraction of defense industries need not be a calamity. In the 18 months after V-J Day in 1945 Los Angeles lost 232,000 of 300,000 defense jobs. But in the immediate postwar years one in eight of the nation's new jobs was created in the Los Angeles area, which still is the nation's largest manufacturing area.

The greatest service Riordan, a venture capitalist, could render would be to make the city government less harmful. Scores of permits and many months are required to get a business started; it is increasingly difficult to get a business to thrive in this high-tax and regulation-saturated environment.

The education system is not furnishing a competent workforce. The unified school district, covering 708 square miles and all or part of 28 cities and serving a polyglot population asserting scores of bilingual entitlements, should be broken up. Riordan, a Catholic philanthropist with an admirable record of involvement with inner-city education, says Catholic schools are getting much better results than public schools at less than one-third the cost.

Yet he opposes the November referendum to create a voucher program to empower parents to choose any school, public or private. He says that would devastate the public school system. What more can be said against that system, or for the referendum?

Riordan speaks matter-of-factly about "triage," the need to "forget rehabilitating certain groups" because the "cost-per-success is too high." High costs are at every hand. For example, if, as a governor's report says, one in eight California babies is born with drugs in its blood, imagine the ratio in Los Angeles.

With whimsical precision, Riordan says that in government "vision and ideas" count for 2.7 percent and "implementation" counts for "97.3 percent, more or less." His is a familiar tone of voice, heard from Henry Ford to Ross Perot. It is the brisk can-do impatience of the capitalist determined to make government more "businesslike." Business people are apt to believe that political power can be as frictionless as money movements—that governmental processes can flow like money in a market.

When Riordan speaks ingenuously of restoring the city's "lost will," skeptics may wonder: What have we here, Nietzsche going to city hall? But as Kevin Starr, the leading historian of Southern California, writes, "Los Angeles envisioned itself, then materialized that vision through sheer force of will."

This implausible city was planted in a semiarid basin by the historic hubris of willful people—first railroad tycoons, then agriculture and energy and real estate and entertainment go-getters. It has always been many factions involved in one large act of defiance—first of nature, then of all precedents of urban development. Riordan's government cannot solve many problems, other than those it creates, but he can get the city government out of the way of the energies that still teem in this basin.

July 1, 1993

Zwosgh? Wbyilk.

BALTIMORE—Yhod id od vopy Tgodhv hdaslibe ap ep—mypwahd. Zwosgh? Wbyilk.

Imagine seeing such written static wherever you look. That is how the world looks to illiterate adults.

Perhaps you have been approached in a supermarket by a shopper who asks you to read a label or identify a product, explaining that he left his glasses at home. Perhaps he did. But perhaps he is one of the millions of Americans who cannot read and he is practicing the survival skills that such people develop as they navigate through our word-saturated society.

But here, in what calls itself "the city that reads," there are places where people who have the everyday courage to cope with their illiteracy can come for help when they summon the final courage to confess their disadvantage. For example, in one of the thousands of row houses that meander up the gently rolling hills that undulate away from the harbor, there is the Ripken Learning Center, funded in part by a

$250,000 gift from Cal Ripken, the Orioles' shortstop, and his wife Kelly.

The fact that it is a pleasant place, staffed with helpful people and friendly machines, does not diminish the admiration one feels for the people who come here seeking help. Illiteracy is apt to involve a deficit of self-esteem, a quality needed by those who reenter an academic setting where they have failed before.

It is easier to imagine, and to simulate, such physical limitations as deafness, blindness or paralysis than to imagine or simulate a mental limitation. That is one reason why adult illiteracy is a particularly poignant affliction: Empathy is in short supply.

Furthermore, a special embarrassment often accompanies the problem. And the afflicted portion of the population is virtually invisible.

But nonreading adults also are an alarmingly large portion of urban populations. Many urban school systems practice the cruel kindness of "social promotions," churning out high school graduates with reading skills as low as a second-grade level. In this city, with a high school drop-out rate approaching 50 percent, 200,000 adults—46 percent of the population over 16—have not completed high school.

About a third of Baltimore residents above age 16 are unable fully to comprehend a front-page news story. Such limitations are calamitous in old manufacturing cities, such as this one, where many smokestacks have gone cold and opportunity lies in the word-driven service sector.

Anyone without a high school diploma probably has some significant reading difficulty—significant in the sense that his or her life chances are seriously limited. As are the chances of his or her children. Illiteracy is a communicable affliction. An illiterate adult cannot help a child with homework—cannot even be counted on to administer a child's prescription medicine safely. (The label says four pills. But all at once?)

The object of adult literacy programs is not to get students reading *Moby Dick* but rather to enable them to read *Green Eggs and Ham* to their children, and to read for themselves classified job ads. As the crumbling of inner-city education, and inner-city families, makes the problem of illiteracy larger, changes in the commonplace experiences of life make illiteracy more of an affliction.

A few generations ago, shopping required no literacy. You asked a grocer or drygoods clerk for a particular quantity of flour, sugar and other unpackaged goods. Nowadays, a supermarket is an arena of self-help. For most of us, that is the pleasure of the places. They are cornucopias of pleasant choices, choices triggered by packaging that employs verbal cues. For the illiterate, shopping must be part of a seamless web of tension and unpleasantness.

Imagine the strength of character that led the man who could not read, but who was vice president of his union here at Bethlehem Steel, to come for literacy help after he retired. What drew him on to learn? Perhaps this:

The abilities to see, hear or walk, although important constituents of happiness, are not, like the abilities to read and write, integral to our understanding of what it means to be a person. Human beings are language-users, enveloped by the fabric of language. In earlier ages a person could function reasonably well, and feel fulfilled, merely being able to participate in the spoken conversation of the community. No more.

So public and private literacy assistance of the sort Baltimore offers is an enhancement of the individual's humanity. Quite a gift.

March 26, 1992

"God don't make junk."

BALTIMORE—South of the Patapsco River, across from the glistening Inner Harbor, sprawls Cherry Hill, a neighborhood where, 50 years ago, public housing was built for white steelworkers who came to the city during the Second World War. Today the housing, much the worse for wear, is inhabited mostly by fragments of families that are poor and black.

It is an ocean of distress for adults and anger for children. Mark Shriver and his colleagues in The Choice Program are determined, with youth's noble disregard for daunting evidence, to drain the ocean.

Choice is a low-budget, high-energy, labor-intensive, cost-effective program run by young adults willing to spend a year or more supervising troubled youths in this city's most troubled neighborhoods. The staff, divided into teams, is on call 24 hours a day, logging 200 miles a week on the wheezing cars they use to track and contact—three to five times a day, 365 days a year—the children assigned to them by public agencies.

Early each morning the staff gathers to pool information on the barely-on-the-rails lives of the young people Choice adheres to like a bandage. Choice's aims and methods are simple. The aim is to keep the children, ages 10 to 17, swaddled in attention. The method is, in basket-ball parlance, a full-court press.

The information is swapped briskly. One staff member is away, accompanying a child to court. One was "DR'd" (disciplinary removal) from school yesterday and will spend a day at Choice headquarters receiving tutoring rather than spending the day on the streets or watching television. One Choice staffer, a slight young white woman from Texas, wearing a tailored suit, black pumps and glasses, reports that the previous night one of her young people did not check in so she went out after him. Choice workers make it a point to know girlfriends, boyfriends and hang-outs. She found her young man loitering in a park. She required him to be home in 15 minutes. He is 17 and weighs 235 pounds. He did as required.

"Required"? Choice workers have almost no sanction except their moral authority, but they have lots of that because they are lavish with life's most precious commodity: time. "They respect you," says one of Shriver's recruits, "from seeing you so much."

When Shriver makes recruiting visits to campuses, he loses about half the interested people in the first interview when he explains the hours (60 to 70 a week, with eight days off a year) and pay ($17,500). About half of the remaining half are lost when they take their first drive with a Choice worker "tracking" kids.

John Kane, 23, a Holy Cross graduate like Shriver, relishes the work because he is "living all the problems we read about." All the problems flow, he says, from three failures: "No values taught, no limits set, no consequences given." In the argot of Choice, "consequence" can be a verb, as in: "Darnell is missing school, so consequence him."

When the morning meeting ends Kane and his colleagues fan out to schools, making sure they know where their kids are. Often school officials do not need to be asked. As Kane enters the office, someone calls out, "Antoinne's fine . . . Raymond is here."

When the Choice children are not in school they are apt to be on the ragged edge of trouble, so the Choice staffers, not long gone from the comforts of middle-class homes and elite campuses, go searching down dangerous streets and into sour-smelling hallways.

Cherry Hill schools are plastered with posters addressing elemental subjects: "A baby costs $474 a month. How much change do you have in your pockets?" Choice encourages cost-benefit thinking. Baltimore spends between $40,000 and $60,000 to incarcerate a troubled child for a year. Choice requires just $6,100 in public and private money to monitor a child.

Today parents who would rather do something other than parent, assuage their guilt and disguise their neglect by saying they give their children "quality time." I have never heard a child ask for quality rather than quantity. Choice's indefatigable young adults are supplemental and sometimes surrogate parents for "their" children. These children are fortunate only—but this is a lot—in getting from Choice both quantity and quality. This is a truth of parenting: Quality is apt to be a function of, not an alternative to, quantity.

For the children of Choice, the neighborhood is their world. Many of them have traveled the mile and a half to the Inner Harbor only two or three times in their circumscribed lives. If their lives attain equilibrium, credit Shriver's credo, which is on a poster in Shriver's office. The poster is of a small black child and these words: "God made me. God don't make junk."

March 29, 1992

PART 3

The Culture

Parenting Against the Culture

There is nothing more painful to me at this stage in my life than to walk down the street and hear footsteps and start thinking about robbery—then look around and see somebody white and feel relieved.
—*Jesse Jackson*

This was the year that America looked in the mirror and blanched. This year the political system moved gingerly toward confronting the question of how public policy can nurture, or injure, character. The "person of the year," emblematic of the dominating public concern, might be a young black male dressed in the regalia of the gang and rap music cultures. And the intellectual event of the year was the publication of James Q. Wilson's *The Moral Sense*.

It has become the conventional wisdom that there is no knowledge, only opinion, about morality, and that human beings have no nature other than their capacity to acquire culture. Wilson's warning is: We must be careful of what we think we are, lest we become that. By "scavenging" (his word) in various sciences, particularly evolutionary biology and cultural anthropology, he concludes that cultural diversity, although vast, is not the whole story.

Human nature is not infinitely plastic; we cannot be socialized to accept anything. We do not recoil from Auschwitz only because our culture has so disposed us. And the fact that so much about America nowadays, from random savagery to scabrous entertainment, is shocking is evidence for, not against, the moral sense, which is what is shocked.

The development of conscience has been much studied—Jean Piaget's many hours watching Swiss children playing marbles; studies of altruism in the Holocaust; studies of twins, including those separated at infancy. The studies have produced powerful empirical evidence of a moral sense that is a component of a universal human nature.

A moral sense is the most plausible explanation of much of our behavior. Statecraft always is soulcraft, for better or worse, so the political challenge is to encourage the flourishing of a culture that nurtures rather than weakens the promptings of the moral sense.

Inside every person there is (in Konrad Lorenz's phrase) a "parliament of instincts." The moral sense, says Wilson, is among the calmer passions; it needs help against its wilder rivals. We have selfish inter-

111

ests, but also the capacity—and inclination—to judge disinterestedly, even of our own actions.

Wilson asks: Could mankind survive if parents had to have the skill, perseverance and good luck sufficient to teach every rule of right conduct the same way they teach multiplication tables? Right conduct is so important that the tendency to it must be rapidly acquired, which suggests that children are biologically disposed to imitate behavior and learn the underlying rules by observation.

Children are intuitive moralists, equipped by nature for making distinctions and rendering judgments. Instincts founded in nature are developed in the family, strengthened by daily habits—particularly in work—and reinforced by fears of punishment and social ostracism. We acquire virtues as we acquire crafts, by the practice of them. Above all, the family transforms a child's natural sociability into a moral sense.

Most of the things likely to produce enduring happiness—education, employment, stable families—require us to forgo immediate pleasures. What happens when that discipline fails? Look around. Crime used to respond to material circumstances, declining with economic growth. Now it responds to cultural circumstances, to the diminished legitimacy of what are derisively described as "middle-class values"—thrift, industriousness, deferral of gratification.

All parents are parenting against today's culture. But for disadvantaged black parents, and particularly for unmarried mothers, the lack of support from the culture is especially damaging. This is so regardless of how many (mostly white) intellectuals blandly embrace single-parent households as "alternative family systems."

"Familial and kin networks," Wilson writes, "are the essential arenas in which sociability becomes sympathy, and self-interest is transferred . . . into duty and fair play." A child's moral sense is at risk in a cold, erratic, disorderly family. Wilson reports that white parents spend, on average, 10 hours per week less time with their children than in 1960, and the decline in parental investment in children has been even steeper among black parents. This, which partly a product of family disintegration—absent fathers—is disastrous for young males, who differ from females in temperament, particularly regarding aggressiveness.

Boys are harder to socialize. In modern society, aggressiveness is no longer an adaptive trait. Civilization is partly an attempt to restrain male aggressiveness, or turn it into appropriate channels. The failure of families, and work experiences, to perform that shaping function has many consequences, including Jesse Jackson's words quoted above.

America's unending cultural war about national self-definition once concerned slavery, temperance, religion. Today it turns on illegitimacy, crime and entertainment. These will be the central subjects of political argument for the foreseeable future, and Wilson is the foremost explorer of this dark and bloody ground.

December 16, 1993

"Mind-forg'd Manacles" from the Sixties

Liberals and conservatives currently have retrospective mentalities, liberals reacting to the 1980s, conservatives to the 1960s. The difference demonstrates a double paradox of today's politics: Conservatism is the more radical, meaning thorough, critique of contemporary America. And one kind of conservatism—call it cultural conservatism—is almost as critical of another variant of conservatism as it is of liberalism.

The liberal complaint about the 1980s concerns economics—income disparities, "unfair" top tax rates and other matters more easily altered than the cultural tendencies that are the subject of the conservative critique of the lingering legacy of the 1960s. This critique is elaborated in a new book about the decade that was so formative to many people now in power.

The book is *The Dream and the Nightmare: The Sixties' Legacy to the Underclass* by Myron Magnet, an editor of *Fortune* and fellow of the Manhattan Institute. His theme is that the aspects of the 1960s about which that decade's celebrators are most pleased—a new notion of "personal liberation" fused to a political agenda, and an adversary stance toward many social institutions and values—have been ruinous to society's most marginal members.

Most of the people the census counts as poor do not stay poor long. But the underclass is defined less by its poverty than by its behavior and the cultural messages from which, Magnet believes, the behavior springs.

Magnet's analysis begins where conservatism should, with a sense of society's fragility. It is not, he notes, "natural," meaning spontaneous, for people to restrain their aggression, patiently nurture offspring in marriage, exercise foresight, calculate rationally, defer gratification, toil with discipline.

Fragility? New Yorkers who can remember when they could safely converse on park benches after dark now read of a city high school that has a "grieving room" where students mourn slain classmates.

Why, Magnet asks, did so many indices of social pathology—crime, illegitimacy, dropping out of school, drug abuse, welfare dependency—suddenly and simultaneously go wrong in the late 1960s and early

1970s? One answer, he says, is that just when the successes of the civil rights movement were removing barriers to opportunities, the values and character traits that enable people to seize opportunities—industriousness, sobriety, thrift, self-discipline, deferral of gratification—were being subverted by cultural ridicule, welfare generosity and judicial leniency.

Society, which should be a crucible for forming character, was becoming replete with what have been termed "incentives to fail." Today the cultural inheritance indispensable for familial responsibility and social competence is not being transmitted to the people who are, primarily for that reason, mired in an intergenerational transmission of poverty.

The Have-Nots, says Magnet, have been incapacitated for upward mobility by the Sixties' culture of the Haves, which tells the Have-Nots that they are crippled by victimization, in need of therapeutic preferences, and that their self-destructive behavior is a natural expression of a history of oppression. Such ideas are what William Blake called "mind-forg'd manacles."

The success of recent immigrants demonstrates, Magnet says, that "cultural values make economic opportunities." Perhaps one reason these immigrants have an easier time grasping the first rungs on the ladder of social striving is that they, with strong family and ethnic community support systems, do not hear the messages of the deforming culture.

Makers of social policy try to avoid cultural questions, preferring the soothing premise that the underclass lacks only the goods and services that government can deliver—cash, jobs, housing, whatever. But Magnet argues that poverty is more a cultural than an economic phenomenon, produced by a poverty of "inner resources." In this poverty, the cultural elite is implicated.

Since the 1960s such central institutions as the law, universities, public schools and the welfare and mental health systems have been permeated with 1960s values. Often the changes have been driven by a perverse premise—that the social order is an infringement on freedom rather than freedom's foundation.

Magnet's argument is not only with liberals but also with conservatives who discount the primacy of cultural factors. Such conservatives believe cheerfully that all people are rational economic calculators and therefore behavioral change and economic transformation require only a rearrangement of incentives—lower taxes, enterprise zones and so on. Such conservatives resemble liberals in believing that human beings are no more complicated than corn or alfalfa—they flourish or languish according to the sufficiency or insufficiency of a few physical, material factors.

To read Magnet is to realize that the conservative critique of contemporary America is the more—indeed, the only—radical critique just now. Placed alongside Magnet's comprehensive dissent from prevailing cultural premises, the complaints of liberalism—that "fairness" requires an upward nudge of taxation; that budget priorities should be fiddled this way or that—seem trivial and complacent.

But, then, if Magnet is correct, liberals should be complacent. The decade that formed them—the 1960s—formed much of the society we have.

March 21, 1993

The Condom Crusade

The Gadarene descent of society was slightly slowed recently in an unlikely place, New York City. A state court struck down a particularly offensive facet of that city's condom crusade.

Some parents from Staten Island, the sensible borough that is trying to secede from the city, challenged the "condom availability" component of the school system's AIDS "education" program. They objected not to AIDS education but to the fact that the program contained neither a requirement for prior parental consent, nor even a provision for parents to make their children ineligible for school-dispensed condoms.

The court sided with the parents. It said condom distribution is not a "health education" but a "health service" program, and hence under state law requires some parental consent. More important, the court held that the condom program without parental consent violates the parents' constitutional rights, specifically 14th Amendment due process rights construed to concern the rearing of their children.

The court stressed that condoms are distributed not in clinics away from schools, but in schools, where attendance is compulsory. There is, the court said, no compelling need for schools to act *in loco parentis* in this sensitive area, creating an environment where children "will be permitted, even encouraged" to obtain contraceptive devices, and advised about uses that may be contrary to their parents' fervent beliefs. The court stressed that the parents' complaint was not just that their children were exposed to particular ideas, but that "the school offers the means for students to engage in sexual activity."

Condom distribution is the latest chapter in a long story of cultural clashes as old as American schooling. The Supreme Court recognized the liberty interest of parents in directing the rearing and education of their children in 1923, overturning a Nebraska statute prohibiting the teaching, even in private schools, of foreign languages to children before the ninth grade.

The desire of Nebraska, and other states with comparable wartime laws, was to foster American homogeneity, especially by preventing the teaching of German. The Court said this did not justify overriding more fundamental values. In 1925 the Court, saying that "the child is not the mere creature of the state," held that Oregon's law compelling children between ages eight and 16 to attend public schools unreasonably interfered with parental discretion regarding private education.

What New York's court had no judicial occasion to say last month, but what nonetheless needs saying, is suggested by something the court did note. It noted that when schools distribute condoms they are not making available items that are hard to come by, now that condoms are prominently displayed in drug and other stores and cost about a third as much as a slice of pizza. So what motives drive the condom crusade?

New York City's condom distribution program was instituted solely with reference to AIDS, rather than as a response to the epidemic of teenage pregnancies. The program is defended with reference to reports that although New York has only 3 percent of the nation's teenagers, they account for 20 percent of reported cases of adolescent AIDS. However, those numbers do not reveal how much of this results from heterosexual intercourse and how much from needles shared during intravenous drug abuse, or other forms of transmission.

The transmission of AIDS through heterosexual intercourse is not nearly the primary means of transmission. That fact, and the fact that the condom crusade's rationale is exclusively about AIDS rather than illegitimacy, and the fact that the crusade radiates aggressive disdain for parental sovereignty—all this validates a suspicion: The condom distribution program, although justified solely with reference to disease prevention, actually is a tactic of ideological dissemination. It facilitates the campaign to "democratize" the public's perception of AIDS, a political program advanced behind such slogans as "AIDS does not discriminate" and "AIDS is an equal opportunity disease."

This campaign, misleading about the demographics and mechanics of the epidemic, has had the intended effect of making AIDS a spectacularly privileged disease. That is, AIDS receives a share of research resources disproportionate relative to the resources allocated to diseases more costly in lives and less optional, meaning less driven by behaviors known to be risky.

It is difficult to doubt that the public school condom crusade, imposed without provisions for parental consent, appeals to some proponents precisely because it derogates parental authority and expands that of government. These are twin components of a political agenda.

The agenda is to assert equal legitimacy for all "lifestyles" or "preferences," and to reduce personal responsibility, under a therapeutic state, for the consequences of choices. In short, this is the 1960s coloring the 1990s.

January 6, 1994

The Injurious Signals Schools Send

In the 1970s conservatives said about forced busing: At least it will increase demand for private education. It did. Today conservatives can take similar cold comfort from the plight of School District 24 in the borough of Queens, New York City.

The district's school board has been suspended by school chancellor Joseph Fernandez, who is the sort of bureaucrat-bully who may yet shatter America's valuable but perishable support for public education. The board refuses to implement the "multicultural" curriculum Fernandez's staff wrote to indoctrinate children with particular attitudes about, among other things, homosexuality. The bibliography of the "Children of the Rainbow" curriculum recommends for first-graders (preschoolers must make do with a gay and lesbian coloring book) books such as *Daddy's Roommate* and *Heather Has Two Mommies* and *Gloria Goes to Gay Pride*.

In *Gloria Goes to Gay Pride*, one of Gloria's mothers explains the Gay Pride Parade: "Some women love women, some men love men, and some women and men love each other. That's why we march in the parade—so everyone can have a choice." Remember that word: "choice."

Proponents of the curriculum say it teaches "tolerance," but they blur the distinction between tolerance and societal indifference. The curriculum constitutes "consciousness-raising," a euphemism for propaganda asserting the moral equivalence of heterosexual and homosexual "lifestyles."

The curriculum's supporters say it promotes "respect" and "appreciation" of gays and lesbians, just as it does for racial and gender differences. But the question of what constitutes sensible policy about sexual orientation is more complex than the question of what is sensible policy regarding racial and gender differences. Race and gender are genetically determined, not the result of choices. But postnatal events, including choices, influence sexuality.

School Board 24 is confronting this dilemma of social policy: We should combat irrational prejudice about and injustice toward homosexuals, and affirm their human dignity. But we should not communicate societal indifference, thereby weakening social promptings toward heterosexuality.

This dilemma is addressed by E. L. Pattullo in "Straight Talk About Gays" in the current *Commentary*. Pattullo, formerly associate chairman of Harvard's department of psychology, argues that the movement to abolish all societal distinctions between heterosexual and homosexual relationships is problematic because there is reason to think "that a very substantial number of people are born with the potential to live either straight or gay lives"—to "grow in either direction."

Much is unknown about the genesis of homosexuality. There may be both prenatal and postnatal determinants of sexual orientation. But surely the social environment, including schooling, sends shaping messages.

Pattullo agrees that sexual orientation must result from "a chain of events so complex that we are unaware of having made a choice." But it is "possible that substantial numbers of youngsters do have the capacity to 'choose' in the same sense they 'choose' the character that will mark them as adults—that is, through a sustained, lengthy process of considered and unconsidered behaviors. Though we acknowledge some influences—social and biological—beyond their control, we do not accept the idea that people of bad character had no choice. Further, we are concerned to maintain a social climate that will steer them in the direction of the good."

There should be similar steering toward heterosexuality. Decency toward homosexuals is compatible with social policies (regarding a range of issues, from the adoption of children to school curricula) that avoid communicating societal indifference or moral equivalence to children of unformed sexuality.

Pattullo says, "We dare not risk failing to give children clear, repeated signals as to society's preference" for heterosexual families. *Daddy's Roommate* (which says, "Being gay is just one more kind of love") and *Heather Has Two Mommies* (which says, "Heather's favorite number is two. She has two arms, two legs, two eyes, two ears, two hands . . . two mommies: Mama Jane and Mama Kate") send injurious signals.

Regarding the entangled issue of AIDS education, references to anal intercourse have been deleted from fifth-grade instruction but retained for the sixth grade, and lessons on condom usage come in the fourth grade. Such Solomonic compromises are the mark of Fernandez's "moderation."

The poorest preschoolers in New York have a lower rate of immunization against measles, tuberculosis and other diseases than children in Mexico and Uganda. But if these New York children survive, the city that cannot immunize them will give them an HIV-AIDS curriculum (for kindergarten through sixth grade) that will at least enrich their vocabularies. The curriculum's glossary includes: "Dental dam—a piece of latex that can be placed over the vulva during oral sex to protect against transmission of viruses that may be present in vaginal fluids, or over the anus during anilingus (oral sex involving the anus)."

I wonder: Are New York's sixth-graders as well informed about history and geography and poetry as they are about it being (this from their AIDS curriculum) "wise to use latex condoms with a contraceptive foam or cream containing a chemical, nonoxynol-9 . . ."?

December 6, 1992

A PC Doctrine: PC Does Not Exist

On campuses there is a new tenet in the catechism of "political correctness," the enforced orthodoxy of leftism. The new tenet of political correctness is that political correctness does not exist.

However, if you dare to question this nonexistence, if you doubt aloud that free expression is uninhibited, you may be harassed on campus, even driven from town, as was Professor Alan Gribben, more about whom anon.

The *Chronicle of Higher Education* recently reported the founding of "Teachers for a Democratic Culture," an organization of academics that "denies that left-wing students and academics are squelching dissent on college campuses." That is "misinformation" and "distortion" from "right-wing ideologies." Oh.

The *Chronicle* of one week earlier had reported from Tempe, Arizona: "In what has been called 'a classic instance of political correctness,' a speech by a Mexican-American woman who served in the Reagan administration has been canceled at Arizona State University because of student opposition."

Linda Chavez was invited to speak about her new book, *Out of the Barrio*, on Hispanic-American politics and assimilation. She was disinvited because the director of the lecture series had not realized that (these are the director's words) Chavez's "stand on the issue of bilingualism" is "so controversial among minority students."

A spokesman for the university insisted that Chavez had not been disinvited because she had not really been invited, a contract not having been issued. But a contract had been issued. And the letter disinviting Chavez used the word "cancel": "The Minority Coalition has requested that we cancel this engagement and bring other speakers whose views are more in line with their politics."

ASU's president urged that she be invited back. She has been, in the politically correct manner—not to give a speech but to debate. When politically incorrect people are invited to speak, they often are supposed to speak in tandem with a corrective person.

The University of Northern Colorado withdrew its invitation to Chavez to give the commencement address. UNC declared that the invitation had been intended to show "sensitivity to cultural diversity" but now seemed "grossly insensitive." UNC promised she would be invited back to be part of a forum.

Invitations to her have been withdrawn from Rutgers' Camden, New Jersey, campus and the Stony Brook campus of the State University of New York. No one can say at how many colleges considerations of political correctness prevent any invitation from being issued.

The *Chronicle* page that reported ASU's treatment of Chavez also reports this: "Some professors are planning ways to counter charges that universities have become centers of left-wing indoctrination." Faculty and students at the University of Michigan are planning a conference the title of which refutes the point of the conference: "The 'PC' Frame-up: What's Behind the Attack." The title leaves no doubt that this conference disputing the reality of political correctness will be politically correct.

Lynne Cheney, chairman of the National Endowment for the Humanities, recently cataloged some costs of political correctness. A Harvard historian has quit teaching a course on immigration rather than endure more accusations of racism. He found that to defend himself from such smears he would have to record all his classes and conversations with students. A Michigan professor stopped teaching a particular class rather than endure charges of "racial insensitivity" when he had students read the portions of Malcolm X's autobiography in which Malcolm describes himself as a pimp and a thief.

Six University of Minnesota professors were charged with sexual harassment. Their offenses included, says Cheney, "not greeting a student in a friendly enough manner, for example. Not teaching in a sensitive enough way. Not having read a certain novel." Cheney says these charges were eventually dropped but not until the professors had suffered substantial expenses and pain.

Alan Gribben has fared worse.

In the early 1970s he was a student radical at Berkeley. For 17 years he taught English at the University of Texas at Austin. But this Mark Twain scholar ran afoul of political correctness when he voted against a master's-level program in Third World and minority literature (he favored a doctoral-level program). He was denounced as a racist. (His wife is Chinese-American.)

Then when material with a pronounced left-wing slant was made required reading for a required course in English composition, Gribben protested this subordination of instruction to political indoctrination. He was shunned by colleagues, avoided by graduate students, effectively expelled from the life of the department, denounced as a racist at a campus rally. He received hate mail and anonymous phone calls.

He now teaches at Auburn University's campus in Montgomery, Alabama. You can contact him to tell him that political correctness has never existed.

October 20, 1991

Consciousness-raising on Campuses

At the University of Texas at Austin, as on campuses across the country, freshmen are hooking up their stereos and buckling down to the business of learning what they should have learned in high school—particularly English composition. Thousands of young Texans will take English 306, the only required course on composition. The simmering controversy about that course illustrates the political tensions that complicate, dilute and sometimes defeat higher education today.

Last summer an attempt was made to give a uniform political topic and text to all sections of E306. It was decided that all sections would read *Racism and Sexism*, an anthology of writings with a pronounced left-wing slant.

The text explains that a nonwhite "may discriminate against white people or even hate them," but cannot be called "racist." The book's editor, a New Jersey sociologist, sends her students to make "class analysis of shopping malls." "They go to a boutiquey mall and a mall for the masses. I have them count how many public toilets are in each, and bring back samples of the toilet paper. It makes class distinctions visible."

After some faculty members protested the subordination of instruction to political indoctrination, that text was dropped and the decision about recasting E306 was postponed until next year. But the pressure is on for political content, thinly disguised under some antiseptic course title such as "Writing About Difference—Race and Gender."

Such skirmishes in the curricula wars occur because campuses have become refuges for radicals who want universities to be as thoroughly politicized as they are. Like broken records stashed in the nation's attic in 1968, these politicized professors say:

America is oppressive, imposing subservience on various victim groups. The culture is permeated with racism, sexism, heterosexism, classism (oppression of the working class), so the first task of universities is "consciousness-raising." This is done with "diversity education," which often is an attempt to produce intellectual uniformity by promulgating political orthodoxy.

Such "value clarification" aims at the moral reformation of young people who are presumed to be burdened with "false consciousness" as a result of being raised within the "hegemony" of America's "self-perpetuating power structure." The universities' imprimatur is implicitly bestowed on a particular view of American history, a political agenda, and specific groups deemed authoritative regarding race, sex, class, etc.

This orthodoxy is reinforced—and enforced—by codes of conduct called "anti-harassment" codes, under which designated groups of victims are protected from whatever they decide offends them. To cure the offensiveness of others, therapists and thought police are proliferating on campuses, conducting "racial awareness seminars" and other "sensitivity training."

These moral tutors have a professional interest in the exacerbation of group tensions, to which university administrations contribute by allowing, even encouraging, the Balkanization of campus life. This is done by encouraging group identities—black dorms, women's centers, gay studies, etc.

The status of victim is coveted as a source of moral dignity and political power, so nerves are rubbed raw by the competitive cultivation of grievances. The more brittle campus relations become, the more aggressive moral therapy becomes, making matters worse.

The attempt to pump E306 full of politics is a manifestation of a notion common on campuses: Every academic activity must have an ameliorative dimension, reforming society and assuaging this or that group's grievance. From that idea, it is but a short step down the slippery slope to this idea: All education, all culture, is political, so it should be explicitly so. And any academic purpose is secondary to political consciousness-raising. The classroom is an "arena of struggle" and teaching should be grounded in the understanding that even teaching English composition is a political activity.

Recently a teacher's description of a freshman composition course at a major American university said that writing skills should be learned "in connection to social and political contexts" so "all of the readings I have selected focus on Latin America, with the emphasis on the U.S. government's usually detrimental role in Latin American politics . . . damning commentary on the real meaning of U.S. ideology . . . responsibility for 'our' government's often brutal treatment of . . ." And so on.

This, remember, for a course on composition. But, then, the teacher is candid about sacrificing writing skills to indoctrination: "Lots of reading. . . . Consequently, I will assign considerable [*sic*] less writing than one would normally expect."

On other campuses, writing requirements are reduced to the mere writing of a journal, a virtually standardless exercise in "self-expression" that "empowers" students. This is regarded as political liberation because rules of grammar and elements of style are "political" stratagems reinforcing the class structure to the disadvantage of the underclass, which has its own rich and authentic modes of expression from the streets.

So it goes on many campuses. The troubles at Texas are, as yet, mild. But the trajectory is visible: down. So is the destination: political indoctrination supplanting education.

September 16, 1990

Literary Politics

The Modern Language Association's opposition to the nomination of Carol Iannone to the National Council on the Humanities is not quite sufficient reason for supporting her. But MLA hostility is nearly necessary for creating confidence in anyone proposed for a position of cultural importance. The President nominated Iannone at the behest of the chairman of the National Endowment for the Humanities, Lynne Cheney, to whom the Council tenders advice. The MLA, composed mostly of professors of literature and languages, is shocked—shocked!—that people suspect it of political motives. Oh? The MLA is saturated with the ideology that politics permeates everything. The unvarnished truth is that the MLA's sniffy complaint amounts to this: Iannone is not "one of us." Her writings confirm that virtue.

She teaches at NYU and is vice president of the National Association of Scholars, a burgeoning organization resisting the politicization of higher education. She is a trenchant critic of the watery Marxism that has gone to earth in the MLA and elsewhere on campuses. Academic Marxists deny the autonomy of culture, explaining it as a "reflection" of other forces, thereby draining culture of its dignity. The reduction of the study of literature to sociology, and of sociology to mere ideological assertion, has a central tenet: All literature is, whether writers are conscious of it or not, political.

Writers, say the academics Iannone refutes, are captives of the conditioning of their class, sex, race. All literature on which canonical status is conferred represents the disguised or unexamined assumptions and interests of the dominant class, sex, race. Hence culture is oppressive and a literary canon is an instrument of domination. This ideology radically devalues authors and elevates the ideologists—the critics—as indispensable decoders of literature, all of which is, by definition, irreducibly political.

Shakespeare's *Tempest* reflects the imperialist rape of the Third World. Emily Dickinson's poetic references to peas and flower buds are encoded messages of feminist rage, exulting clitoral masturbation to protest the prison of patriarchal sex roles. Jane Austen's supposed serenity masks boiling fury about male domination, expressed in the nastiness of minor characters who are "really" not minor. In *Wuthering Heights*, Emily Brontë, a subtle subversive, has Catherine bitten by a *male* bulldog. Melville's white whale? Probably a penis. Grab a harpoon!

The supplanting of esthetic by political responses to literature makes literature primarily interesting as a mere index of who had power and whom the powerful victimized. For example, feminist literary criticism is presented as a political act, liberating women writers from the oppression of "patriarchal literary standards." Thus does criticism dovetail with the political agenda of victimology. The agenda is the proliferation of groups nursing grievances and demanding entitlements. The multiplication of grievances is (if radicals will pardon the expression) the core curriculum of universities that are transformed into political instruments. That curriculum aims at delegitimizing Western civilization by discrediting the books and ideas that gave birth to it.

Iannone criticizes the "eruption of group politics in literature," noting that many scholarly activities, from the shaping of curricula to the bestowing of academic awards, have become instruments of racial, ethnic and sexual reparations for Western civilization's sins. The left's agenda does liberate, in this perverse way: It emancipates literature from the burden of esthetic standards. All such standards are defined as merely sublimated assertions of power by society's dominant group. So all critics and authors from particular victim groups should be held only to the political standards of their group. Administration of these, and of the resulting racial and sexual spoils system in the academy, "requires" group politics: Under the spreading chestnut tree, I tenure you and you tenure me.

As esthetic judgments are politicized, political judgments are estheticized: The striking of poses and the enjoyment of catharsis are central in the theater of victimization in academic life. All this, although infantile, is not trivial. By "deconstructing," or politically decoding, or otherwise attacking the meaning of literary works, critics strip literature of its authority. Criticism displaces literature and critics displace authors as bestowers of meaning.

It might seem odd, even quixotic, that today's tenured radicals have congregated in literature departments, where the practical consequences of theory are obscure. Obscure, but not negligible. As James Atlas writes, the transmission of the culture that unites, even defines, America—transmission through knowledge of literature and history—is faltering. The result is collective amnesia and deculturation. That prefigures social disintegration, which is the political goal of the victim revolution that is sweeping campuses.

The fight over Iannone's nomination is particularly important precisely because you have not hitherto heard of it or her. The fight is paradigmatic of the many small skirmishes that rarely rise to public attention but cumulatively condition the nation's cultural, and then political, life. In this low-visibility, high-intensity war, Lynne Cheney is secretary of domestic defense. The foreign adversaries her husband, Dick, must keep at bay are less dangerous, in the long run, than the domestic forces with which she must deal. Those forces are fighting against the conservation of the common culture that is the nation's social cement. She, even more than a Supreme Court justice, deals with constitutional things. The real Constitution, which truly constitutes America, is the national mind as shaped by the intellectual legacy that gave rise to the Constitution and all the habits, mores, customs and ideas that sustain it.

There has been a historic reversal: Many of the most enlightened defenders of our cultural patrimony are now out in the "practical" world, including government, and many philistines are in the academies shaping tomorrow's elites, and hence tomorrow's governance. That is why Lynne Cheney and Carol Iannone matter more than do most of the things that get the public's attention.

April 22, 1991

Commencement at Duke

Commencement address delivered at Duke University, May 12, 1991.

Commencement speakers often say, somberly, that graduates are bidding good-bye to campus tranquility and entering the real world's turbulence. But lately some of society's stresses have come to campuses, including this one. Duke's Class of 1991 can be forgiven for feeling that, in recent years, the ivory tower has been topped by battlements. So deservedly great is Duke's stature, its disputes resonate far beyond its broad lawns. Indeed, there is, in several senses, a national interest in the great debate, in which Duke partakes, concerning academic policies.

So today I want to tread, gingerly, onto that contested ground. I do so respectfully. I am respectful of this magnificent institution, which has earned its eminence. And I am respectful of the complexity of the academic disputes that have, of late, enlivened life at Duke and elsewhere.

The adjective "academic" is often used as a dismissive synonym for "inconsequential," as in the phrase "the point is of only academic interest." And it is often said that the bitterness of academic politics is inversely proportional to the stakes—that what happens on campuses does not much matter "out there" in the "real" world. But history is the history of mind; you are what you read; ideas have consequences—indeed, only ideas have lasting consequences. Therefore, the quality of our national life reflects, after a short lag, the quality of thinking on campuses.

Conditions on some campuses call to mind the tombstone in a rural English churchyard, which contains the simple six-word epitaph: "I told you I was sick." Duke is not sick. The vigor of its arguments suggests not anemia but robustness. Indeed, it has been your good fortune, you of the Class of 1991, to be present here for arguments that clarify the nature not only of the academic enterprise but also of the American experiment.

Every sermonette, such as mine here, should pick some cogent thought to construe. My text today comes from a great giver of advice, the poet Robert Frost, who once said: "Don't join too many gangs. Join few if any. Join the United States and join the family—but not much in between unless a college."

That advice, like the man who proffered it, is quintessentially American. It is very American in its general injunction in favor of individualism and against excessive joining—against defining oneself too much by group affiliations. But it also is especially American in its inclusion of an institution of higher education, along with family and nation, in a trinity of essential allegiances.

Why did Frost do that? Because universities are entrusted with nothing less than a task central to America's identity and success. Theirs is the task of transmitting the best of the West—the culture of our civilization—to successive generations who will lead America, the most successful expression of that civilization.

We are, as Lincoln said at Gettysburg, a nation dedicated to a proposition. There is a high idea-content to American citizenship. It is a complicated business, being an American. We are all like Jay Gatsby—made up, by ourselves. But we are not made up of randomly aggregated moral and intellectual materials. Rather, we are made up of moral and intellectual resources that have been winnowed by time and must be husbanded by universities.

By decisions about what schools should do—about what we should study and read—we define our polity. This is why America's primary and secondary schools have always been cockpits of religious and ethnic conflicts.

What is now occurring on campuses is an episode in the unending American drama of adjusting the rights of the individual and the rights of the community. Individuals have a broad right to study and teach what they wish—up to a point. (I shall return to that four-word phrase—"up to a point.") That point is set, in part, by the community's right to perpetuate itself.

Lincoln said: "A house divided against itself cannot stand." It is equally true that a society unaware of itself—with no consensus about its premises and purposes—cannot endure. In Lincoln's day, a collision of two clear and diametrically opposed premises nearly proved fatal to America. Today there is a potentially fatal idea in circulation. It is the idea that there should not be in this pluralistic society any core culture passed on from generation to generation.

To those who say we are threatened by a suffocating "hegemony" of Western civilization's classic works, I say: If only that were the problem! The real danger is not cultural hegemony but cultural amnesia, and the concomitant Balkanization of the life of the mind.

I just used a verb derived from a proper noun, the verb "to Balkanize." That verb was born of the sorrows of the Balkan nations. The First World War, and hence most of this century's horrors, began in the Balkans, where fragmentation was contagious.

Today there is ample evidence of the Balkanization of America's intellectual life. This Balkanization begins with the assertion that any syllabus composed of traditional classics of Western civilization will "underrepresent" certain groups—racial, sexual, ethnic or class-based groups.

Well, are the great works of Western civilization primarily products of social elites? Yes, of course—for many reasons, including the fact that these works come to us from centuries where literacy itself was an elite attainment. But it is fallacious to argue that therefore these works perpetuate an oppressiveness that allegedly is the essence of Western civilization.

Some people who fancy themselves intellectually emancipated—who think themselves liberated from what they call a stultifying cultural inheritance—are, in fact, far from free. They actually reside in "the clean, well-lit prison of one idea." Today's imprisoning idea is philosophically primitive and empirically insupportable. It is that any humanities text merely "reflects" its social context and thus should be read as a political document.

Too often the meaning of the crucial word "reflects" disappears in a mist of imprecision. Usually the assertion that a text "reflects" its context is either trivially true or flagrantly false. It is trivially true if it means only that the text, like its author, stands in some relation to the setting in which the author wrote. But it is false if it means that any text should be construed politically, with politics understood crudely as mere power relations of domination and subordination in the era in which the author wrote.

Such thinking causes the study of literature to become a subdivision of political history and to be studied as sociology. This reduction of the arts to social sciences is reverse alchemy—turning gold into lead.

This is the result of the imprisoning idea that the nature of everything, from intellectual works to political acts, is determined by race, gender and class. Alas, any single idea purporting to be a universal explanation, a comprehensive simplifier of social complexities, requires its adherents to be simple, and makes them so. Today's dubious idea also makes its adherents condescending—and worse.

It is condescending and deeply antidemocratic when intellectuals consign blacks, or women, or ethnics, or the working class, or whomever, to confining categories, asserting that they can be fully understood as mere "reflections" of their race, sex or class, and that members of those groups have the limited "consciousness" supposedly characteristic of those groups.

The root of this mischief is the assertion—the semantic fiat—that everything is political. If the word "political" is promiscuously used to describe any choice or judgment involving values, then "political" becomes a classification that does not classify. One cannot say it too emphatically: Not all value judgments are political judgments.

It is not a political judgment that certain works have contributed mightily to the making of our civilization and hence must be known if we are to know ourselves. It is not a political judgment that certain books have demonstrated the power, down the generations, to instruct us in history, irony, wit, tragedy, pathos and delight. Education is an apprenticeship in those civilized—and civilizing—passions and understandings, and not all texts are equal as teachers.

We must husband our highest praise, as Karl Marx did. Marx celebrated the art of Greek antiquity, not because it had a proletarian origin—it did not—but because it met—indeed, set—standards that transcend any particular class or culture.

The legacy of Western thought is a mind capable of comprehending and valuing other cultures while avoiding the nihilism that says all cultures are incommensurable and hence all of equal merit.

Sensible people rejoice at any chance to study another culture's Rousseau or Cervantes or Dickens. But education is too serious a matter to become a game of let's pretend, a ritual of pretending that enduring works of the humanities are evenly distributed throughout the world's cultures.

We want to be able imaginatively to enter, and to empathize with, other cultures. But we must live in our own. And our own is being injured by some academic developments that impede understanding.

We see on campuses the baneful habit of joining what Robert Frost would have considered "too many gangs"—and the wrong sorts of gangs. We see the spread of intellectual gerrymandering, carving up curricula into protected enclaves for racial, sexual and ethnic groups. Often this is done on the condescending premise that members of these groups have only a watery individuality—that they have only derivative identities, derived from membership in victim groups.

The premise of this analysis is that Western civilization has a disreputable record consisting primarily of oppression and exploitation—that Western civilization has been prolific only at producing victims.

That idea leads, in turn, to the patronizing notion that members of a victim group are disadvantaged unless taught by members of their own group and unless they study works by group members. Otherwise (or so the theory goes) members of the group will lack self-esteem, an attribute which is presumed to be a precondition for, not a result of, achievement. This sort of thinking promotes envy, resentment, suspicion, aggression, self-absorption and, ultimately, separatism.

It is a crashing non sequitur to say that because America is becoming more diverse, university curricula must be Balkanized. Actually, America's increasing diversity increases the importance of universities as transmitters of the cultural legacy that defines and preserves national unity.

Some policies advanced today in the name of "diversity" might better be associated with a less agreeable word—"fragmentation."

Some policies instituted in the name of "multiculturalism" are not celebrations of the pluralism from which American unity is woven. Some of these policies are capitulations: They involve withdrawal from the challenge of finding, and teaching, common ground on which Americans can stand together—not the little patches of fenced-off turf for aggrieved groups, but the common ground of citizenship in the nation, which is one of the good gangs of which Robert Frost spoke.

Many of today's Balkanizing policies are products of a desire to show sensitivity to the feelings of particular groups. Sensitivity is a good thing. But, remember: The four most important words in political discourse are "up to a point." Armies, police, taxation, even freedom and equality are good only "up to a point."

In the context of today's campus disputes, sensitivity, too, is good— up to a point. What is not good is the notion that sensitivity about one's own opinions generates for oneself an entitlement not to be disagreed with or otherwise offended. Or that the only way to prove one's sensitivity is by subscribing to a particular political agenda.

Some critics complain that a traditional curriculum built around the canon of great works of the Western mind necessarily reinforces authority and docile acceptance of existing arrangements. But these critics, some of whom fancy themselves radicals, could take lessons in real radicalism from many of the writers of those classic works.

Virtually every subsequent radicalism was anticipated in Plato's inquiries. No person more radical than Machiavelli ever put pen to paper—Machiavelli, whose *The Prince* became the handbook for modern masterless men and women who are obedient only to rules they write for themselves.

Four years after *The Prince* was written, Martin Luther nailed his 95 theses to a church door, asserting the primacy of private judgment— conscience. There is a golden thread of magnificent radicalism connecting that white German theologian to his namesake, the black American minister—a thread connecting Luther's 95 theses and Dr. King's "Letter from Birmingham Jail."

Do not try to tell the deposed tyrants of Eastern Europe that the study of the central figures of American civilization inculcates subordination to the status quo. Europe's recent revolutions against tyranny were fueled by the words of American presidents, particularly the third and 16th, Jefferson and Lincoln.

There is today a warmhearted idea that every academic activity must contribute to the reforming of society by assuaging this or that group's grievances. This idea leads to fracturing the community into antagonistic groups; to the drowning of individuality in group thinking; to the competitive cultivation of group grievances; to the subordination of education to political indoctrination. In short, some good intentions produce bad educations.

Today's complacent judgment that American education is healthier than it seems is akin to Mark Twain's jest that Wagner's music is better than it sounds. Eight years ago a national commission stated, "For the first time in the history of our country, the education skills of one generation will not surpass, will not equal, will not even approach those of their parents." This disaster is, I think, partly a result of too much educational energy being invested in the pursuit of social goals, which, though arguably worthy, are undoubtedly peripheral to the main mission of schools.

Fortunately, we need not deplore the education that has been given to the portion of this generation that is privileged to be graduating from Duke. Embarrassing though the fact may be, it is a fact that you, the Class of '91, who may consider the word "elitist" an epithet, are, this day, certifiably of the elite. But let me assuage any uneasiness you may feel. Elitism—meaning a disproportionate role in government and society by small groups—is inevitable. The question for any society is not whether elites shall rule, but which elites shall rule. The problem for any democracy is to achieve consent to rule by suitable elites.

To produce suitable elites, universities need leaders with the confidence of Benjamin Jowett, who for many years was head of Oxford's Balliol College. Once when Jowett submitted a matter to a vote of Balliol's dons and was displeased with the result, he announced, "The vote is twenty-two to two. I see we are deadlocked."

Jowett, like many great university statesmen, understood that a university cannot be a democracy, all sail and no anchor, blown about by gusts of opinion and fashion. It must be anchored in the convictions of intellectual leaders who are confident of their authority because they know they stand on the shoulders of giants—those great thinkers of whose legacy today's teachers are custodians and transmitters.

On March 4, 1861, with the fabric of America unraveling around him, Lincoln delivered his First Inaugural Address. In one of the most felicitous phrases in American rhetoric, he held out the hope that Americans would be summoned back to friendship by "the mystic chords of memory."

It is always thus: America is always dependent on its collective memory. And universities are keepers of that flame. Arguments about university curricula are not narrowly, crudely political, but they are, in an important sense, constitutional arguments: They concern how the American mind shall be constituted. And in a democracy, mind is all that ultimately matters, because everything rests on the shiftable sands of opinion.

That is why democracies are in permanent danger; and why it is prudent to be pessimistic—not fatalistic, not resigned to the worst, but pessimistic, alert to the dangers. The moral of the human story is that things go wrong more often than they go right because there are so many more ways to go wrong. Truths increase arithmetically; but errors increase exponentially. Most new ideas are false; hence most "improvements" make matters worse. That is why wise people are wary of intellectual fads and are respectful of the received greatness which, in academic context, is called the canon.

The nice part about being a pessimist is that you are constantly being either proven right or pleasantly surprised. Duke is one of life's pleasant surprises. As you have been passing through Duke, Duke has been passing through a fiery furnace of debate, and it, like you, is, like steel, stronger for having been tempered by the heat. That is why I predict special success for the Class of 1991 and continued greatness for Duke.

My life around politics has taught me the hazards of making predictions. When I was at Oxford thirty years ago, the university press published volume three of Isaac Deutscher's biography of Trotsky, and the student Marxist Association had for Deutscher a party, which I infiltrated. There I heard Deutscher say—quite solemnly—this about Trotsky: "Proof of Trotsky's farsightedness is that none of his predictions have come true yet." Recurring predictions about the final ruin of America's universities have not come true yet and, I wager, never will.

Reprinted from The American Scholar, *Autumn 1991*

Commencement at the College of William and Mary

Commencement address delivered at the College of William and Mary, May 15, 1994.

Brevity is not only the soul of wit, it is, on occasions such as this, plain politeness. And it is prudent. I am the last impediment standing between you and the world that is, you are sure and I hope, to be your oyster. I do not want to be trampled in a stampede, so I shall confine my remarks to a subject of manageable scope.

My subject is the nature of knowledge and the nature of our nation. This may seem like a subject sufficiently broad to consume this afternoon and many more, but fear not. I know the rules of academic ceremonies such as this.

I am, or at least I once was, what used to be called a "faculty brat." Which is to say, I am a child of a professor—of philosophy, retired, at the University of Illinois. Worse still, obedient to the current practice of ruthless full disclosure, I confess to being a former professor—of political philosophy, at Michigan State University and the University of Toronto. I mention this part of my checkered past diffidently because in recent decades the public has come to look askance at the academic community. The public's suspicion is that campuses have become incubators of intellectual strangeness, and worse.

I well remember an evening in 1976 when I saw how much of a problem the professoriate had. That night in 1976 was when Pat Moynihan, late of the Harvard faculty, won the Democratic nomination to run against the incumbent U.S. senator from New York, James Buckley. Over at Buckley headquarters Jim said he looked forward to running against *Professor* Moynihan, and he was sure *Professor* Moynihan would run the kind of high-level campaign one could expect from a Harvard *professor*. A few minutes later, back at Moynihan headquarters Pat met the press. A reporter informed him that Jim Buckley was referring to him as "*Professor* Moynihan." Pat drew himself up to his full, considerable height and said with mock austerity, "Ah, the mudslinging has begun."

Pat Moynihan was being droll. But beneath his wit there lurked a sobering point: Something had caused a dark lowering cloud of suspicion to gather over the academic community. Today the cloud is larger and darker.

Is the educated, temperate public right to wonder about the temperateness of many educators? Is it reasonable to wonder whether many educators are remaining faithful to their traditional mission? That mission is the conservation, enlargement and transmission of the ideas, understandings and values on which a society such as ours—a society based on persuasion and consent—depends.

I believe the educated public *is* rightly worried. The problem is that a particular cluster of ideas, and a concomitant sensibility, have gained currency in some academic circles. If the ideas are not identified, understood and refuted, they can seep like slow, cumulative poisons into the larger society, with large and lasting consequences in our politics, our governance and our traditions of civility.

The ideas advance under the banner of "postmodernism." That is a faith with many factions, but it claims to have had one founding prophet. His name was Nietzsche. He proclaimed the words that postmodernists have made their core tenet. His words were: "There are not facts, but only interpretations."

Now, Nietzsche is here conscripted as a prophet without his permission. In fact, regarding Nietzsche the postmodernists are guilty of philosopher-abuse. They are saying something silly: Nietzsche was not. He was not asserting, as postmodernists do, a kind of epistemological despair arising from a radical indeterminacy about reality. Rather, he was making a sober epistemological point. It was that facts are never only facts, naked and pristine and self-evident and immediately apprehended by all minds in the same way in all circumstances and contexts. Rather, he said knowledge is conditioned in complex ways by the contexts in which what we call facts are encountered, and by mental processes, not all of them conscious mental moves, that can be called interpretations.

The postmodernists' bowdlerizing of Nietzsche distills to a simple, and simple-minded, assertion. It is that because the acquisition of knowledge is not a simple process of infallible immediacy, there can be no knowledge in any meaningful sense. Therefore, we are utterly emancipated from rules of reasoning and may substitute willfulness for rationality. All interpretations are let loose to play in a theater of unrestrained semantic egalitarianism.

Note that postmodernism has an almost comically unpromising beginning in its misunderstanding of Nietzsche. Postmodernism is erected on the rickety scaffolding of what is less a paradox than an absurdity. It is the assertion that it is a fact that there are no facts. Unfortunately, the fact that something is absurd does not mean it is inconsequential. Indeed, much of modern history is a sad story of absurdities that managed to become cloaked with power.

Postmodernism is all about the wielding of power, because it is not—it cannot be—about anything other than power. It has no content other than the assertion that the content of any proposition, any book or any mind is arbitrary, or the result of race or ethnicity or sex or class, and deserves no more respect than any other content of any proposition, book or mind.

It may seem to sensible people that I must be caricaturing this idea of postmodernism, or exaggerating its prevalence. As evidence to the contrary, consider a pamphlet issued by the American Council of Learned Societies. The pamphlet baldly asserts that "the most powerful modern philosophies and theories" are "demonstrating" that "claims of disinterest, objectivity and universality are not to be trusted, and themselves tend to reflect local historical conditions." The phrase "local historical conditions" is generally understood to mean "power relations."

Now, "the most powerful modern philosophies and theories" demonstrate no such thing. Nevertheless the crux of postmodernism is the postulate that any supposedly disinterested deliberation actually is merely self-interest disguised. And, postmodernists say, it is a duty of "realists" to "unmask" the "power relationships" and "power struggles" that are the reality beneath every pretense of reasoned persuasion.

Concerning these ideas, let us not mince words. The ideas are profoundly dangerous. They subvert our civilization by denying that truth is found by conscientious attempts accurately to portray a reality that exists independently of our perceptions or attitudes or other attributes such as race, ethnicity, sex or class. Once that foundation of realism is denied, the foundation of a society based on persuasion crumbles. It crumbles because all arguments necessarily become ad hominem; they become arguments about the characteristics of the person presenting a thought, not about the thought.

Once a society abandons its belief in facts and truths, and its belief in standards for distinguishing facts and truths from fictions and falsehoods; once intellectuals say, "We are all Nietzscheans now, and there are no facts, only interpretations"; once this occurs, then, as Professor John Searle says, "it seems arbitrary and elitist to think that some theories are simply true and others false, and that some cultures have produced more important cultural products than others."

Searle, a philosopher at the University of California at Berkeley, knows what follows from the postmodernist fallacies. If there are no standards rooted in reason, if there are only preferences and appetites arising from group "solidarity" and interests, then there can be no education as education has traditionally been understood.

For example, until recently it was believed that, Searle says, "the study of the great classics of literature gave the reader insights into human nature and the human condition in general." But nowadays many intellectuals consider it arrogant folly to speak of "classics" or "great works." Indeed, as Searle says, many people avoid the word "works," preferring to speak merely of "texts." That word has the "leveling implication that one text is as much a text as another." Therefore the works of, say, Walt Whitman or Walt Disney are all, and equally, texts.

Clearly some of the ideas of postmodernism, by infusing academic life with politics and frivolity, subvert the function of, and dissipate the social support for, colleges and universities. And when the relationship of such institutions to the surrounding and sustaining society becomes problematic, those institutions swiftly learn a painful lesson about the perishable nature of prestige.

A few years ago I stood with a friend, a teacher at Brasenose College, Oxford, looking out from his study window at those "dreaming spires" of the University. My friend, worried about the decreasing public support for that University, said: "This is the prettiest view in Oxford. Hence the prettiest view in the south of England. Hence the prettiest view in Europe. Hence the prettiest view in the world. And yet," my friend continued, "the time may come when young people and scholars will no longer beat a path to our many doors." "Remember," he said, "three centuries ago everyone wanted to go to the University of Padua."

Who in a future shaped by the postmodern sensibility will want to attend any college or university steeped in the idea that "there are not facts, but only interpretations"? What society will devote scarce resources to the support of institutions that regard intellectual life as a sublimated—a barely sublimated—power struggle over competing political agendas of racial, ethnic or sexual groups asserting solidarity against one another?

I ask these warning questions as an admiring friend of academic life. I write a syndicated newspaper column; I write a column for a national weekly news magazine; I appear each week on a network television news program. Yet no matter how much journalism I do—newspaper, magazine and broadcast—the more certain I am that a fourth mode of communication matters more than those three. It is books I have in mind. And books are the business of colleges and universities.

Or should be. Unfortunately, we are witnessing, on campuses and throughout society, the displacement of books and all they embody—a culture of reason and persuasion—by politics. And it is politics of a peculiar and unwholesome kind, called "identity politics." The premise of such politics is that the individual is decisively shaped, and irrevocably defined, not by conscious choices but by accidents. The premise is that people are defined not by convictions arrived at by processes of reason and persuasion, but by accidents of birth and socialization—by their race, ethnicity, sex or class. The theory is that we *are* whatever our group is, and that we necessarily think and act according to the circumscribed mental makeup of the group's interests. This theory is starkly incompatible with, and subversive of, the premises of American democracy.

More and more intellectuals are receptive to the idea that all politics is, or should be, "identity politics," and that all intellectual life is really politics. The idea is that intellectual life may be unconscious politics, but it is politics nonetheless—a struggle of power, for power—and should become conscious politics. Furthermore, we are told it is simple honesty to get the struggle aboveboard, front and center, by calling every intellectual distinction and dispute what it is—a political move in a power game.

We see such thoughts institutionalized in our politics, in the doctrine of "categorical representation." That doctrine holds that people can be properly represented, and their values can be truly understood and empathized with, only by people who are from the same "category" of people—women by women, African-Americans by African-Americans, Hispanics by Hispanics, homosexuals by homosexuals, and so on. This doctrine fuels the fracturing of the American community into mutually suspicious and truculent factions, each proclaiming itself irremediably at odds with—ever incomprehensible to—all persons who are not members of that faction.

Often nowadays we hear a question posed that is not really a question. It is an oblique assertion of what the ostensible questioner considers a self-evident truth. The question is: Should we not all respect and honor one another's differences? The gravamen of the "question" invariably is that differences of race, ethnicity and sexuality all should be "respected" and "honored."

I disagree. Why should respect and honor accrue to accidents of birth? Given that they are accidents, what, precisely, is there to honor? Surely, respect is owed to, and honor should flow to, *individuals,* for their attainments of intellectual or moral excellence, not merely because of any membership in any group.

Professor Searle draws the correct, and dismaying, conclusion about the idea of organizing society around, and basing politics on, "respect" for group "differences." If identity politics is valid, then "it is no longer one of the purposes of education . . . to enable the student to develop an identity as a member of a larger human intellectual culture." If the premise of identity politics is true, then the idea on which America rests is false. If the premise of identity politics is true, then there is in no meaningful sense a universal human nature, and there are no general standards of intellectual discourse, and no possible ethic of ennobling disputation, no process of civil persuasion toward friendly consent, no source of legitimacy other than power, and we all live immersed in our groups (they once were called tribes), warily watching all other groups across the chasms of our "differences."

No sensible person wants to live in such a society. Therefore all sensible people should be worried.

I am *temperamentally* inclined to worry. That is why I am a conservative. Proper conservatives subscribe to the "Ohio in 1895 Theory of History"—so named, by me, because of this: In 1895 there were just two automobiles in Ohio—and they collided. Conservatives expect trouble and are rarely disappointed. They understand the universal application of the Buttered-Side Down Law, which is: The chance of the bread falling buttered-side down is directly proportional to the cost of the carpet.

Still, even discounting the conservative propensity for worrying, reasonable people of all persuasions, conservatives and liberals alike, should see that there is a clear and present danger in the sprouting of "identity politics" in the social soil fertilized by postmodernism. The result of such politics can eventually be the Balkanization of our nation.

Note the word "Balkanization." What that term derives from is much in the news just now. A geographical expression has become a political pathology. And if you want to see the world that the postmodernist sensibility could make, look abroad.

If you want to see what happens when all differences immediately become power struggles and nothing but power struggles, look at the Balkans. There "identity politics" is practiced with the ruthlessness that comes with the belief that there can be no other kind of politics—no disinterested politics of ideas and persuasion. When groups assume that they are locked in their mutually unintelligible differences, you get the nasty and brutish state of nature that Hobbes depicted. Odd, is it not, how the postmodern sensibility seems suited to, and conducive to, a world of premodern tribalism.

A society steeped in the postmodern sensibility will have an uneasy conscience about teaching certain great truths, values or works because it will wonder: Who are we—who is anyone—to say that anything is greater than anything else? And a postmodernist community cannot long remain a community. It will lose the confidence necessary for the transmission of precious things—tested ideas and values—held in common.

This subject is endlessly fascinating. However, a speaker should never use the word "endless" when addressing a restive audience. Every such speaker should remember the story of White Sox manager Jeff Torborg's trip to the mound to remove pitcher Jim Kern. Kern told Torborg he wasn't tired. Torborg said, "I know, Jim, but the outfielders are."

I am not tired, but you have every right to be tired of me holding up your just reward for four years well spent at this splendid college which has prepared you well for success in our magnificent nation.

Our nation is, I passionately believe, the finest organized expression of the Western rationalist tradition, the tradition that is the soul of what we call Western civilization. I do not so describe our nation because it always behaves reasonably. Rather, I do so because our nation incarnates steady confidence in the capacity of people to guide themselves by deliberation.

Three hundred and one years ago this institution embarked upon its great work. That work involves conserving and conceiving and refining and transmitting the ideas and understandings that nourish freedom. This institution's early work helped to give rise to this Republic that remains the most important thing that ever happened in all of mankind's quest for the good life. Many people around the world remain unconvinced of, even hostile to, the meaning of our Republic. Therefore William and Mary's work for freedom is far from done. Neither is yours, Class of 1994, as you bear this college's high standards into the world.

But, you will doubtless be delighted to learn, my work, for today, *is* done. Thank you for letting me do it.

May 15, 1994

Television Teaching Violence

An Indiana school board had to issue an advisory to children, who had been crawling into storm drains, that there were no Teenage Mutant Ninja Turtles down there. To understand why this was necessary is to understand one of the causes of America's epidemic of violence.

And the path to understanding that Indiana advisory can begin in a remote Canadian community that in 1973 (signal reception problems having been overcome) was due to acquire television. Social scientists seized the opportunity to investigate the effects of television on this community's children, using for comparison two similar towns that had long had television.

Before television was belatedly introduced, they monitored rates of inappropriate physical aggression among 45 first- and second-graders. After two years of television, the rate increased 160 percent, in both boys and girls, and in both those who were aggressive to begin with and those who were not. The rate in the two communities that had had television for years did not change.

Other researchers studied third-, fourth- and fifth-grade boys in two Indian communities in northern Manitoba. One got television in 1973, the other in 1977. The aggressiveness of boys in the first community increased immediately, in the second it increased four years later.

A study from 1960 to 1981 of 875 children in a semirural American county (controlled for baseline aggressiveness, intelligence and socioeconomic status) found that among persons subsequently convicted of crimes, the more television they had watched by age eight, the more serious their subsequent crimes. A "second-generation effect" was that the more television a parent had watched as a child, the more severely that parent punished children.

Seven U.S. and Canadian studies establish correlations between prolonged childhood exposure to television and a proclivity for physical aggressiveness that extends from preadolescence into adulthood. All this is reported in *The Public Interest* quarterly by Brandon S. Centerwall, an epidemiologist at the University of Washington.

He used a historical oddity—because of disagreement between Afrikaner- and English-speaking South Africans, that nation had no television prior to 1975—to study the effect of television on violence rates in the prosperous industrial society of white South Africans.

He studied homicide rates among white South Africans, white Americans and all Canadians. From 1945 to 1974 the white homicide rate in the United States increased 93 percent; in Canada, 92 percent; in South Africa, the white homicide rate declined 7 percent.

Neither economic growth, civil unrest, age distribution, urbanization, alcohol consumption, capital punishment nor the availability of firearms explains the 10-to-15-year span between the introduction of television and the doubling of the homicide rate in the United States and Canada—or the similar lag in South Africa after 1975. Furthermore, Centerwall believes that the introduction of television helps explain different rates of homicide growth for American whites and minorities.

White households began acquiring television sets in large numbers approximately five years before minority households. White homicide rates began increasing in 1958. A parallel increase in minority homicide rates began four years later.

A 14-month-old infant can adopt behavior it has seen on television. Because young children are unable to distinguish fact from fantasy, they regard television as information about how the world works. (Hence the need for the Indiana school board's advisory.) And, Centerwall says, in the world as television presents it, violence is ubiquitous, exciting, charismatic and effective:

In later life, serious violence is most likely to erupt at moments of severe stress—and it is precisely at such moments that adolescents and adults are most likely to revert to their earliest, most visceral sense of the role of violence in society and in personal behavior. Much of this sense will have come from television.

So what can be done? Centerwall believes that violence is a public health problem deserving measures as practical as nutrition, immunization and bicycle helmet programs. He suggests requiring all television sets to be manufactured with locking devices by which parents can control children's access to a set or to particular channels. But such devices presuppose the sorts of parents who would not need them: parents alert to the dangerous degradation of taste and behavior by entertainment saturated with violence.

Wiser parents are the only hope because, as Centerwall understands, there is no hope for cooperation from the television industry. It exists to draw audiences for advertisers. Desensitized Americans are attracted by ever stronger doses of ever more graphic violence. A decline of one percent of advertising revenues would cut the television industry's revenues a quarter of a billion dollars.

So as Centerwall says, it is as idle to expect television to help combat the epidemic of violence that is derivative from violent entertainment as it is to expect the tobacco industry to help combat the epidemic of lung cancer that is a comparable sign of that industry's sickening health.

April 8, 1993

The Stab of Racial Doubt

Shelby Steele has icy loathing for the Penn State program that pays black students for improving their grades—$580 for improvement from C to C+, for example. It is, says Steele, "kindness that kills," a corrupting incentive for blacks to "hustle their victimization," pocketing cash for mediocre grades that would embarrass many whites. Steele asks: "What better way to drive home the nail of inferiority?"How do such perverse entitlements—"more a yoke than a spur"—happen? It is a long story, still being written.

In 1965, speaking at a black university (Howard), President Johnson said: "You do not take a person who, for years, has been hobbled by chains and liberate him, bring him up to the starting line of a race and then say, 'You're free to compete with others,' and justly believe that you have been fair." Such thinking was, and is, the source of racial entitlements. But, says Steele, it deflected emphasis from black to white responsibility. Blacks as individuals were invisible. Blacks were visualized as a mass of victims ("hobbled") to be "taken" toward progress by white patrons. Where, asks Steele, is the black challenge?

Steele is a challenge to blacks. He teaches English at San Jose State. He is black. His writings on race are the most powerful since Martin Luther King's "Letter from Birmingham Jail." However, the stark moral clarity of King's era has, because of King's victories, been replaced by daunting ambiguities. Fortunately, Steele combines the literary sensibility of novelist Ralph Ellison with the analytic acuteness of America's most profound black man, Frederick Douglass. So if you read no other book this autumn, well, shame on you, but make it Steele's *The Content of Our Character: A New Vision of Race in America.*

Discussion of race has become boringly choreographed. Black leaders demand racial entitlements; whites concede racial expertise to such leaders but are befuddled by those leaders' insistence that racism is of undiminished virulence. Steele begins with a bleak paradox: Most blacks are by many measures farther behind whites than before civil rights laws radically expanded opportunities. If conditions have worsened as racism has receded, "then much of the problem must be of our own making." It has been made by the cultivation and exploitation of victim status.

In the 1960s "black power" demands in the context of white guilt gave blacks a political stake in being perceived in a tableau of victimization. But that posture produces an acid of doubt that leaks back into the inner lives of blacks, corroding their confidence in their ability to use expanded opportunities. Individual demoralization is the price paid for collective entitlements for blacks-as-victims.

What Steele calls the "harangue-flagellation ritual" between blacks and whites has left a legacy of blacks addicted to indiscriminate complaining to enhance claims of victimization. This often leads to "a new class of super-victims who can feel the pea of victimization under twenty mattresses." Another legacy is white guilt expressed in black entitlements. Steele calls this the guilt of self-preoccupation rather than the guilt of genuine concern. For whites such entitlements are "the public relations of good intentions. For blacks they are a distraction from the toil of racial development. The entitlement trap transforms whites into paternalists and keeps blacks dependent on the kindness of white strangers and on replenishing the white guilt that generates entitlements. Such guilt is not an infinitely renewable resource. When it is depleted, what then?

Steele is particularly struck by something he sees on campuses, "a flight from opportunity that racism cannot explain." It is a result of "integration shock," the shock "of being suddenly accountable on strictly personal terms."

Although the vast majority of black students come from middle-class families, on largely white campuses blacks are five times more likely to drop out than whites. (Black colleges have only 16 percent of all black students but 37 percent of all black graduates.) Even six years after admission to college only about 26 percent of blacks graduate. Blacks have the highest dropout rates and lowest grades of any group in universities. This is in spite of—perhaps in part because of—the network of institutional solicitousness: black studies departments, black dorms, and so on.

The current resegregation of campus life reflects what Steele calls "the impulse to carve our segregated comfort zones that protect us more from our own doubt than from whites." Blacks, he says, are more oppressed by doubt than by racism. The barriers to black progress are as much psychological as social and economic. Those doubts and barriers are made worse by leadership addicted to wringing power from victimization. Blacks often arrive on campuses unsure whether they have been admitted on merit or because of some dispensation that denigrates, in advance, any achievement. This sharpens what Steele calls "the stab of racial doubt." In the new vogue for the appellation "African-American" Steele sees a "reaching for pride through nomenclature," another sign of despair about gaining pride from real advancement.

All Americans, but particularly black Americans, are paying a terrible price for the apostasy of today's civil rights leaders from the original premise of the civil rights movement. The premise was that race must not be a source of advantage or disadvantage. Defining black identity in terms of exaggerated victimization buys racial entitlements, but at the price of demoralization.

The catechism of victimization suffocates individuality and censors distinctive voices. But not Steele's voice, which sounds the theme of Ellison's *Invisible Man*: "Our task is that of making ourselves individuals." It is a theme that has found voices in every generation, as in 1848:

> What we, the colored people, want is *character*, and this nobody can give us. It is a thing we must get for ourselves. . . . It is gained by toil—hard toil. Neither the sympathy nor the generosity of our friends can give it to us. . . . It is attainable; but we must attain it, and attain it each for himself. I cannot for you, and you cannot for me.

Still as true as when Frederick Douglass wrote it. Time winnows away all but the best writings. Steele's writings will last, to be read by generations as distant in time from him as he is from Douglass, whose worthy successor Steele is.

September 24, 1990

The Journey Up from Guilt

Some developments that may seem as different as chalk and cheese actually are part of a single change: The middle class has begun giving up guilt. This moral movement, still gathering strength, is apparent in such disparate phenomena as California's primary and the career of Margaret Thatcher. And to any American making the journey up from guilt, there must be an amusing obtuseness in this headline from *The Chronicle of Higher Education*:

RACIAL TENSIONS CONTINUE TO ERUPT ON CAMPUSES
DESPITE EFFORTS TO PROMOTE CULTURAL DIVERSITY

"Despite"? Try "because of." A multitude of sins are committed, and excused, in the service of "diversity." They include reverse discrimination, quotas and other "race (or sex or sexual-preference)–conscious remedies" used to advance political agendas of guilt-mongering groups. Indoctrination, dolled up as regular college classes, is tamped into students to nurture "sensitivity" to the feelings of this or that group. Censorship of speech is inflicted to enforce sensitivity to the various victims of "historical injustices."

To the surprise of no sensible person, and the shock of academia, all this has the predictable effect of worsening relations between groups. It encourages individuals to adopt group identities and group thinking. And some campus tensions reflect the fact that many people are now resisting being conscripted into the role of the guilty. The rhetoric of collective guilt has worn out its welcome.

Kenneth Minogue, a British philosopher, believes that the repudiation of collective guilt marks a historic cultural turning. Collective guilt has long been a familiar idiom of contemporary politics. Many middle-class people have been brought to see self-vilification as a duty and a sign of cultivated sensitivity. But they are weary of being on what Minogue calls a moral treadmill, unable to avoid guilt even by leading blameless lives because guilt arises from membership in a guilty society. They are encouraged to suffer a debilitating sense of responsibility for all social ills. This is, as Minogue says, an irrationality that involves, among other fallacies, the idea that we can be omnipotent over all problems.

A grievance industry, specializing in rituals of complaint, produces a pseudopolitics of foot stamping. Society is retribalized into prickly, shin-kicking "communities." That term, says Minogue, is a misnomer, as in the phrase "the homosexual community." This usage implies that communities are especially homogeneous groups, defined in terms of a single trait. Proliferating communities of victimhood assert their own histories and value systems to go with their grievances. They nominate pantheons of heroes (hence anthologies of "gay poets" and exhibits of "feminist artists"). Universities are Balkanized by the multiplication of black studies, women's studies, homosexual studies, and so on. These "disciplines" (another misnomer—they often are exempt from discipline) are produced by the guilt-based politics of acquiring the coveted status of victim.

New doctrines are minted to multiply society's collective transgressions, and victim groups, retroactively. For example, Minogue says, radical feminism licenses an academic cottage industry devoted to reading history as a record of men's injuries to women. Any modern state, says Minogue, can be analyzed (and delegitimized) as a product of historic injustices, each demanding reparations. Such demands dominate political agendas; they are psychological taxes levied by professional victims against nonvictims who have inherited guilt. Politics, says Minogue, becomes a melodrama about the redemption of a sinful society, particularly the middle class.

But today important voices dissent from the doctrines of collective guilt. Thatcher denounces the "bourgeois guilt" that people are pressured to feel because they are better off than some others. Thatcherism is, among other things, a doctrine of psychological liberation from pangs of conscience about material accomplishments. Inculcation of such pangs has been high on socialism's agenda. Minogue believes another woman played a part in emancipating the West from the culture of guilt: Jeane Kirkpatrick talked back to the United Nations, that diffuser of gaseous guilt. Reagan and Thatcher signaled wholesome impatience with ersatz guilt by withdrawing from the United Nations' most egregious guilt factory, UNESCO.

Dianne Feinstein won California's Democratic gubernatorial primary, propelled by her stand—horrifying to guilt-drenched liberal Democrats—in favor of capital punishment. She is, whether she knows it or not, a third woman advancing, and advancing because of, the repudiation of guilt. The subject of punishment cuts to the quick of any policy. It touches people's confidence in the justice of their social arrangements and the correctness of the doctrine of personal responsibility for behavior. Support for capital punishment is shorthand for this sentiment: Crime is not caused by society; culpability resides in guilty individuals, not flawed institutions.

In the 1960s America's prison population declined from 212,000 to under 200,000, although crime rates rose. By 1975 the prison population had risen to nearly 240,000, but crime rates had risen much faster. Then because of altered attitudes of thousands of decision makers in the criminal justice system, reflecting the civic culture, the prison population began to rise rapidly. It rose to 315,000 in 1980 and to more than 600,000 today, even though the rise in crime was slower in the dozen years after 1976 than in the dozen years before. It tripled in part because cultural liberalism was waning. America felt more confident about punishing because it felt less collective guilt for crime.

Freudian social theory holds that guilt produces civic virtue by inhibiting the pursuit of private interests. The rhetoric of "compassion" that fueled the growth of swollen welfare states was partly a product of the culture of guilt. Then in the 1970s, from the Third World (one vast victim, according to "progressive" guilt instructors), came the oil shocks that disrupted economic growth and demonstrated that welfare-state entitlements—codified compassion—grow more surely than the economies that must pay for them. This provoked Western publics to reconsider where to draw the line demarcating social and individual responsibilities. This, too, is part of growing up from the politics of guilt.

June 18, 1990

Our Expanding Menu of Rights

In Eden Prairie, Minnesota, Cheltzie Hentz has triggered local, state and even federal investigations of her charge that her right to freedom from sexual harassment has been violated. She is seven. Her alleged harassers—boys on the school bus—use, she says, "naughty language." Cheltzie is, the *Los Angeles Times* reports, the youngest person ever to provoke a harassment inquiry by the U.S. Department of Education. The co-president of the local parent-teacher organization says, "This is not sexual harassment. Children at this age don't have a concept of sexual harassment." Sure they do. They get it in school. Cheltzie's school district teaches, from kindergarten on, a sexual harassment curriculum. And the state recently awarded a young woman $15,000 because Duluth officials were not vigorous enough in responding to sexual graffiti on a restroom wall.

Nowadays the news is full of examples of the expansion of freedom by the multiplication of rights.

A Miami judge has struck a mother lode of hitherto undiscovered rights. Seems homeless people have a right to "safe zones" where they can sleep, cook, eat, defecate and do other things the judge calls "harmless" and "inoffensive" involuntary and life-sustaining acts. He says antivagrancy laws and some other measures by which the community tries to maintain order violate the homeless people's rights to equal protection, due process and freedom from cruel and unusual punishments.

New York's highest court recently minted a new right, ruling that Domingo Antommarchi was improperly convicted because he was not present when the judge spoke with some potential jurors during jury selection. *The New York Times* reports:

> It was not good enough, the court ruled, that Mr. Antommarchi's lawyer was present, and it did not matter that Mr. Antommarchi never asked to be included in the conferences near the judge's bench. Mr. Antommarchi, who was sitting a few feet away in the courtroom, had a constitutional right both to hear the discussions and to see the facial expressions and demeanors of the potential jurors, the court said.

This new right may result in overturning thousands of criminal convictions, including those in the Central Park jogger attack, the Happy Land Social Club fire that killed 87 and the subway knifing that killed a Utah tourist. And what of the community's interest in safety? It is only that, a mere "interest," not a right, and so must yield.

Small wonder life is stressful nowadays. However, people have expanding rights to compensation for stress. *The Wall Street Journal* reports that Florida has recognized a right to disability benefits for a woman who complained of mental stress from working alongside "large black males." The *Journal* also reports:

> In California, lawyers prowl outside factories after layoffs have been announced trying to recruit stress cases. Workers only have to claim that 10 percent of their anxiety is job-related to collect benefits. One L.A. clinic even offers the workers' comp equivalent of frequent flyer miles—a free trip to Las Vegas for anybody who visited the clinic 30 times in three months.

A Duxbury, Massachusetts, fireman savagely clubbed his wife, fracturing her skull, severing an ear and leaving her partially deaf. A judge decided the clubber had been temporarily insane and acquitted him. But the fire department fired him. Big mistake. David Frum reports in *Forbes* magazine that the clubber filed a complaint and seven years of litigation produced a ruling from the Massachusetts Commission Against Discrimination: The clubber was a victim of "handicap discrimination" because his aberrant behavior wasn't his fault. The commission ordered him rehired and paid $200,000 plus 12 percent interest for back pay and emotional distress (which he had a right not to suffer).

The drug violation—his seventh—that earned Yankee pitcher Steve Howe a "lifetime" ban from baseball? Not his fault. An arbitrator says Howe has a right to play because his cocaine use is somehow a result of hyperactivity.

A 17-year-old Maryland girl tried out for the football team. If school authorities had prevented her, or perhaps had even tried to dissuade her, her rights would have been violated and she could have sued. In the first scrimmage she was hurt. She is suing the school district for $1.5 million on the ground that no one told her "of the potential risks of serious and disabling injury inherent in the sport."

The Wall Street Journal reports that a student is suing Princeton because of injuries received from high-voltage machinery when he climbed onto the roof of a railroad shuttle that serves a station owned by the university. Brown University spent two years and upward of $50,000 fending off a suit by a young woman who sought $700,000 because she hurt her arm on a broken soap dish while showering in a dormitory with her boyfriend. (A janitor says the dish was intact before she got into the shower.)

In the 1960s the cry of student liberation was "no more *in loco parentis!*"—colleges should not take the place of parents in supervising students' comportment. Today the demand is for the right of anyone to do anything he or she pleases, and the right to be compensated for any unpleasant consequences. According to today's entitlement mentality, this is just a facet of the general right to risk-free life. Thus the University of Alaska at Fairbanks was ordered to pay $50,000 to a man injured when he and a woman slid down a snowy hill on an inner tube and hit a tree. The woman died. The court held that the school's warning signs, which the two ignored, were insufficient. (Perhaps the ignoring of them proved the insufficiency?) The case on behalf of the woman's estate is pending.

A man paralyzed while playing football for Texas Christian University in 1974 is claiming a right to workers' compensation—retroactive and ongoing—because he says college athletes are like employees. The Supreme Court is being asked to decide whether a prisoner's right to be free from cruel and unusual punishment is violated if he is denied a smoke-free environment. And . . .

Sorry, no more space for other examples of America's expanding menu of rights. Only room for one question. Feel freer? Me neither.

December 14, 1992

Anita Hill's Tangled Web

One of them lied. Anita Hill's charges were as detailed as Clarence Thomas's denials were categorical. Now comes a book, *The Real Anita Hill* by David Brock, that dismantles the myth that Hill is a conservative Republican who was driven from Washington by sexual harassment. Brock assembles an avalanche of evidence that Hill lied—about her career and her relations with Thomas.

What a tangled web we weave when first we practice to deceive. Hill, who wanted to make her harassment charges against Thomas anonymously, and then confidentially, was pulled into the public arena when her written statement to the Senate was leaked by her anti-Thomas allies. But her misadventure began weeks earlier, when her friend Susan Hoerchner told Senate staffers that while living in Washington in the spring of 1981 she had been told in a telephone conversation with Hill that Hill was being sexually harassed at work by Thomas. But that was six months before Hill went to work for Thomas and 10 months before the alleged harassment began—at which point Hoerchner was living in California. When, during an interview with Senate staff, Hoerchner realized her contradiction, she quickly huddled with a lawyer representing Hill, then changed her story: She could not remember when or where she had the telephone conversation.

In the spring of 1981 Hill was working, and failing, at a Washington law firm. Asked about her departure from the firm, she testified under oath: "It was never suggested to me at the firm that I should leave the law firm in any way." A senior member of the firm swore in an affidavit that Hill was told that the low caliber of her work made it "in her best interests" to seek employment elsewhere. (Judiciary Committee Democrats blocked a Republican request to settle the conflict by subpoenaing the firm's records.) Thomas hired Hill at the Education Department, where several people remember her claiming to have been harassed at the law firm. Could those claims have been made to mask her professional failure?

Two people purported to corroborate Hill's claim to have been harassed by her "supervisor" after she followed Thomas to the Equal Employment Opportunity Commission in 1982. But they did not testify that she had named Thomas. And "supervisor" would have been an odd way for an assistant to refer to the chairman of a federal agency. One of her several supervisors at the EEOC had a reputation as a harasser.

Thomas's personal reputation was impeccable until autumn 1991, when Hill made her embroidered charges. (She swore that her testimony contained more lurid details than her FBI interview because the two agents had not asked for all details. Both agents disputed her.) By 1991 Thomas had been the subject of five FBI checks and the hostile scrutiny of four Senate confirmations. No one other than Hill has challenged Thomas's testimony concerning his comportment toward her. No one could be found to testify to ever having seen her exhibit the demeanor of a harassment victim. No one who had worked with the two of them on a daily basis testified to believing her.

Most harassers have a pattern of harassment. (So far 23 women have accused Senator Packwood.) Not one of the scores of women Thomas has worked with supported Hill's portrayal of Thomas. Most harassment victims avoid their harassers. Hill testified that she only once drove home with Thomas, who lived nearby. But a co-worker testified that Hill told him she did so several times and hoped for a more personal relationship with Thomas. Hill said she followed Thomas when he moved from Education to the EEOC because she thought that was necessary to stay employed. But she, a Yale graduate, had signed a document asserting that she had "career tenure." And a co-worker testified to telling Hill that she could keep her job at Education. Hill swore that she did not know who would be replacing Thomas. Thomas's replacement swore that she knew and that he offered her the same job she had under Thomas.

Telephone logs show that after she moved to Oklahoma she called Thomas many times. First she said the logs were "garbage." Then she said she was only returning calls from him. Then she conceded initiating some. She said one was "following up" another professor's letter inviting Thomas to lecture. But that "follow-up" call was made three months before the letter was sent. She testified that a law dean asked her to drive Thomas to the Tulsa airport. The dean said Hill called the night before to ask if she could drive Thomas so she could show him her new car.

At the EEOC she irritated co-workers by trying to assert a special relationship with Thomas. Brock presents much evidence that she left the EEOC, and Washington, bitter with Thomas because of increasing hostility to his conservatism and because she was not given an appointment for which Thomas did not consider her competent. At the University of Oklahoma, Brock reports, she has been prominent in the shrill but conventional campus leftism of racial and sexual politics. Reporters rummaged in Thomas's garbage in search of damaging information; scrutiny of Hill was and has been less searching. *The New York Times* reported that even "her closest friends" know little of her political views. *The Washington Post* reported those views to be essentially like Thomas's. Accurate reports of her political and personal conflicts with Thomas would have suggested a motive for mendacity.

To believe that Hill told the truth you must believe that dozens of people, with no common or even apparent motive to lie, did so. Brock's book will be persuasive to minds not sealed by the caulking of ideology. If Hill is a "victim," it is not of sexual harassment or (in language she has used from a lecture podium) "the powerlessness of women" in "our misogynist society." Rather, she may be a victim of the system of racial preferences that put her on a track too fast for her abilities, that taught her to think of herself as a victim and made her fluent in the rhetoric of victimization.

Thomas's ordeal was a manifestation of the politics of character assassination, whereby political differences become occasions for moral assault. It worked against Bork. It almost worked against Thomas. Perhaps the unmasking of Hill will give the practitioners of such politics pause.

April 19, 1993

Fornication vs. "Free Exercise"

The latest twist in the trivialization of the "civil rights" agenda began in Massachusetts when two brothers, Paul and Ronald Desilets of Turners Falls, refused to rent an apartment to a young woman who said she would be sharing it with her "live-in boyfriend." Both Desilets are devout Catholics who believe that renting to an unmarried cohabiting couple would compromise their faith by making them complicit in fornication.

An old law still on the Massachusetts books makes fornication a crime (punishable by three months in jail or a $30 fine). But a recent state civil rights law forbids discrimination on the basis of all the usual things, including "marital status."

Now, the law against fornication—sexual intercourse between people not married to each other—may seem quaint in an age when there are no longer enough forests to produce sufficient wood for all the stocks that would be needed to punish all the sinners who have violated the law. But even if you believe that a law not enforced loses its validity, Massachusetts courts believe such laws remain permissible expressions of public values.

The Desilets say enforcement of the antidiscrimination statute against them, in favor of the unmarried couple, would infringe their constitutional right to the "free exercise" of religion. The state, with the awful literalness of the fanatic, says: The antidiscrimination law is the law. The Desilets respond: Read the wretched thing. It forbids discrimination on the basis of a particular "status." But it is *conduct* we are objecting to.

They are willing to rent to people of all faiths and pigmentations, single, married or divorced. But it is, they say, a bit thick for the state to pretend that it has a more compelling interest in helping unmarried cohabiting couples find apartments than in protecting the First Amendment freedom of people to practice their religion.

It is, the Desilets say, passing strange for the state to argue that they forfeit their right to the free exercise of religion just because the state says their understanding of their religious duties conflicts with a state regulation in a commercial context. It is particularly strange because Massachusetts's constitution stipulates such vigorous protection of religious belief and behavior.

It says no person shall be "hurt, molested or restrained, in his person, liberty or estate, for worshipping God in the manner and season most agreeable to the dictates of his own conscience; or for his religious profession or sentiments; provided he doth not disturb the public peace." The state, acting on the contemporary liberal notion that more important than what people do is that whatever they do should be compulsory, suggests anarchy may ensue if the Desilets are not broken to the saddle of the state.

The state suggests that this case concerns mere commercial behavior, and that the protection of "free exercise of religion" extends only to rituals and services. The Desilets believe the exercise of their religion must involve striving to be obedient to God in every aspect of their lives.

The Desilets' opponents, in their ardor for a court order compelling the Desilets to disregard their faith, have even tried the argument that protecting the Desilets' free exercise of religion, as they understand it, would violate the constitutional prohibition of the "establishment of religion." That argument would make meaningless the protection of "free exercise."

The Desilets are not trying to force their religious beliefs on anyone. The state is trying to force contemporary sexual values on them. And as to the state's suggestion that the Desilets' refusal to rent to the unmarried couple constitutes a "disturbance of the peace," the state should take two aspirins and a nap until the dizziness passes.

The Desilets cite a passage from the new book *The Culture of Disbe-*

lief: How American Law and Politics Trivialize Religious Devotion by Stephen Carter of Yale Law School:

> In our sensible zeal to keep religion from dominating our politics, we have created a political and legal culture that presses the religiously faithful to be other than themselves, to act publicly, and sometimes privately as well, as though their faith does not matter to them.

The protection of the free exercise of religion expresses a political philosophy: Government should behave with humility and restraint because its proper reach is limited by superior values. But Massachusetts, once a cradle of American liberty, is behaving as badly as some of its earliest residents did, with the Puritans' bullying disrespect for the individual's rightful sphere of privacy.

March 13, 1994

The Swedish Bikini Team Parachutes into Court

For connoisseurs of the amusements that American litigiousness produces, it doesn't get any better than this.

For, it seems, centuries Stroh Brewery, maker of Old Milwaukee beer, has run television commercials featuring males out fishing, hiking and generally bonding and, come sundown, drinking that beer and sighing, "It doesn't get any better than this." But in recent ads, just after that line is sighed, the Swedish Bikini Team arrives by raft or parachute or whatever, and not dressed for high tea.

Trouble is, five female employees at Stroh's St. Paul, Minnesota, brewery have done something as American as buying a six-pack. They have gotten a lawyer and gone to court, charging that the commercials produce, encourage and condone (three distinctly different things) sexual harassment, discrimination and assault in their workplace. Each employee is seeking monetary damages for numerous verbal and physical offenses detailed for the court.

Now, pity the people who must make beer commercials. Most beers taste pretty much alike. Furthermore, the target audience consists of young males who drink too much of the stuff, thereby proving that getting their attention requires messages more glandular than rational.

Let us, as lawyers say, stipulate something: the Stroh's ads (which the company says are supposed to be parodies) are offensive and incompatible with America's evolving sensibilities (although perhaps not the sensibilities of the less-evolved target audience). The question is: Do we want courts scrutinizing commercials for evidence of causal connections with bad behavior already legally proscribed?

Commercial speech enjoys less First Amendment protection than most other speech, but it usually is protected if it is truthful and not misleading. However, the women's lawyer, Lori Peterson, is undeterred by the radicalism of asking government, in effect, to punish commercials that have never been found obscene, indecent, illegal in purpose or harmful to the audience. Her argument is that the harm eventually done to women is caused by the debasement of some men who see the commercials.

One supporter of the suit, law professor Ronald K. L. Collins of Catholic University in Washington, D.C., says the commercials are part of "the infrastructure of sexism," so they should be treated as legally equivalent to the behavior they allegedly foment. Certainly this suit, asserting causal connections between speech broadcast into living rooms and behavior in workplaces, is potentially the thin end of an enormous wedge.

If successful, it could give rise to a censorship regime from which only one good would flow: If courts undertook to extirpate from advertising anything that anybody considers part of the "infrastructure of sexism," courts would have no time for other mischief.

Peterson says, "Just as a kid looks to its parents as to what is appropriate behavior in the home, so does the employee look to the employer as to what behavior is acceptable in the workplace." Leave aside the quaint paternalism of Peterson's view of the American working man (and, for that matter, the American kid). But note the logic of the argument: Even speeches by corporate executives might be considered causes of bad behavior arising from a bad workplace environment.

"Imagine," says Peterson, "our collective horror at seeing black men drop out of the sky to serve white men beer, tap-dance and shine shoes for them. . . . Why is this scenario seen as horrible but similar caricatures of women (with oversized chests and undersized minds) still accepted?"

Her argument is that the racist commercial would arise from a legacy of slavery and would result in continued racial disadvantage, and that the Swedish Bikini Team commercials similarly have antecedents and results involving stereotypes associated with injurious social treatment. But she is postulating something that cannot be demonstrated, a direct causal connection between broadcast stimuli (the commercials) and subsequent behavior by particular people.

The basic point, lost in the rush to litigate, is this: Sexual abuse of the sort the women allege violates clear, enforceable laws. The attack on the commercials is a gratuitous reach for a "consciousness-raising" judicial fiat to impose preferences and tastes by claiming them as rights.

Recently a federal judge in New York said something germane to this contretemps. He made a plaintiff pay $60,000 in legal fees to the defendant, a school district she had sued. She had charged that her son was kept out of an honor society as retaliation for her family's criticism of his school, thereby violating the family's First Amendment rights. The judge said:

> Our federal court system is being brought into ridicule and our Constitution is being debased by persons who proclaim themselves to be its strongest supporters: civil rights advocates and attorneys purportedly working in the public interest. By attempting to elevate mere personal desires into constitutional rights and claiming denial of their civil rights whenever their desires are not realized, these persons are demeaning the essential rights and procedures that protect us all.

It doesn't get any better than that.

December 1, 1991

The Tangle of Egos and Rules

In literature as in life, lawyers are swarming like locusts. The hit movie made from John Grisham's novel *The Firm* (Tom Cruise's first movie since he played a lawyer in *A Few Good Men*) is about nasty lawyers working for the mob and portrays the government (run by and for lawyers) as not much nicer. Grisham, a lawyer-novelist who today has the second best-selling hardback and the first, third and fourth best-selling paperbacks, has sold 25 million books in 18 months. Lawyer-novelist Scott Turow's *Pleading Guilty*, his third lawyer novel (following *Presumed Innocent* and the even better *The Burden of Proof*), is fourth on the hardback list. Why this fascination with lawyers? The reasons are related to the reasons why there are so many lawyers.

Modern society's complexity makes people feel maddeningly dependent on others for elemental social needs. Society's density has them aggressively jostling one another, throwing elbows—and litigation—for social advantage. As traditional sources of social norms—families, schools, churches—weaken, law seeps into the vacuum. As laws, regulations, rules, contracts, mediations, arbitrations and negotiations multiply, so do lawyers. Antipathy toward lawyers expresses resentment of the need to rely on people without whose arcane skills (and vocabularies) we frequently cannot function. Doctors, too, are like this, but most patients still feel that doctors generally are on their side and are providing something they need, whereas lawyers seem increasingly parasitic.

Disdain for Congress is related to Congress's reputation as a nest of lawyers displaying their profession's skill at making work for itself. Modern government, indiscriminately meddlesome, invites—indeed incites—people to hire lawyers to bend public power for private advantage. Potential losers from this process defensively hire countervailing lawyers.

The Cold War's end has been hell for spy novelists, but lawyer novels satisfy an unslaked thirst for tales of conspiracies and shadiness. Many Americans believe that what is apparent about society is a mere façade; they want to see society's hidden gears and pulleys, and the people— mostly lawyers—who work them. "To me," says the comedian Jerry Seinfeld, "a lawyer is basically the person that knows the rules of the country. We're all throwing the dice, playing the game, moving our pieces around the board, but if there is a problem the lawyer is the only person who has read the inside of the top of the box." Many Americans suspect that lawyers wrote the inside of the top of the box for their benefit.

In *The Firm* a lawyer says of tax law, "It's a game. We teach the rich how to play it so they can *stay* rich—and the IRS keeps changing the rules so we can *keep* getting rich *teaching* them." A flat and simple tax is the nightmare of the parasite lawyer-lobbyist class, which today is purring contentedly about the new administration. And contemporary liberalism, which in the name of "compassion" has made the status of "victim" lucrative, multiples "rights" and prompts belief in a "right" to be compensated, by someone, for all of life's many misfortunes or disappointments.

Turow thinks his novels have found a large readership because "the law remains our one universally recognized repository of values." About this he is, I think, exactly wrong. People may once have believed that, but his novels are superb in part because, truthfully and without cynicism, they subvert that soothing belief. Perhaps the emotional equilibrium of some people is served by faith that law has routinized justice. Some people, having rejected traditional faiths in transcendent sources of salvation, seek from the lush growth of laws the comforting illusion of a moral economy in the world, guaranteeing that good is rewarded and evil is punished. It is not mere coincidence that the twilight of the gods has brought the dawn of the age of lawyers. They are custodians of the arrangements that are supposed to keep chaos in check. Law purports to put a structure of order, even reason, into life.

But for Turow's fictional lawyers, life often is the experience of moral vertigo and the law is a labyrinth of ambiguities. As one of his most complex and sympathetic characters, Alejandro (Sandy) Stern, says, "The toil of man in society! The rushing about, the telephone calls, the small breaks of light in the tangle of egos and rules." Turow's demystifying novels convey how many and wide are the fissures through which proof, truth and justice can leak away in trials and other legal processes. Such processes often are less akin to the tidiness of engineering than to the gropings of premodern medicine. A Turow character says:

> Come into the teeming city, with so many souls screaming, I want, I need, where most social planning amounts to figuring out how to keep them all at bay—come and try to imagine the ways that vast unruly community can be kept in touch with the deeper aspirations of humankind for the overall improvement of the species, the good of the many and the rights of the few. That I always figured was the task of the law, and it makes high-energy physics look like a game show.

Turow's novels are not mere entertainments. They transcend their genre; they are literature that will last. American literature, from Cooper in his forests to Melville on the oceans to Twain on the river, is rich with regrets about society pressing in on the individual. But we are still much in need of a literature that looks contemporary society in the face, sees it steadily and sees it whole, and does not despair about the dignity of the individual, the efficacy of choice or the sphere of freedom. Turow's novels of the law convey a sense of society's weight and thickness, but they also suggest that life is lived largely in the gaps in the fabric of the law that is stretched thinly over the tumultuousness of humanity.

The cadences of Turow's prose as well as the substance of his stories are as urban as the sound of a jazz saxophone at two A.M. He has been admiringly compared to Theodore Dreiser, another novelist fascinated by Chicago's raw energy. If Chicagoan Turow's Kindle County isn't Cook County, Illinois, it is close enough. It is acquiring a reality as a convincing moral landscape comparable to that of Faulkner's Yoknapatawpha County.

July 26, 1993

Sheldon Hackney's Conversation

Sheldon Hackney hears America talking and is dismayed. He thinks the talk is inexpert and unorganized and needs federal help. Hackney, who heads the National Endowment for the Humanities, wants Washington to organize a "national conversation" about pluralism. The NEH was created pursuant to LBJ's promise that Washington would transform America into a great society. That transformation still has a way to go, but perhaps Hackney's "conversation" is the missing ingredient of greatness.

The NEH says the conversation—perhaps it should be The Conversation—will discuss really big topics, such as "What holds us together?" and "What do we value?" It will be "designed to engage a significant proportion of the American people" in discussions about diversity. Would, say, 10 percent be a "significant" portion? Hackney says, "This conversation will be a failure if it doesn't include everybody."

Of course for more than two centuries Americans have been talking, without NEH guidance, about the topics Hackney suggests for The Conversation. Jeffersonians against Hamiltonians, Jacksonians against Whigs, slaveholders and secessionists against their critics, people convinced that the nation's identity was implicated in decisions about immigration, antitrust, public schools, prohibition, integration—conversations about basic values have been unceasing. So skeptics may wonder why this common and spontaneous activity needs to become an elaborate federal program, one (in the NEH's words) "conducted directly" or "funded" or otherwise encouraged by the NEH, with "focus groups" to "scientifically" examine questions concerning pluralism, "pilot citizens groups" to "experiment" with "approaches to discussing" pluralism, "promotional tours," and so on.

However, subsidizing talk about diversity today is akin to subsidizing crabgrass: The problem is a surplus, not a shortage. Another problem about today's pandemic talk about diversity is that academics often are the most emphatic talkers. Hackney is a former professor and university president, and academics will be prominent among the orchestrators of The Conversation. That is not reassuring.

On campuses everywhere there are programs to promote "diversity" and "multiculturalism" and to encourage the "identity politics" of groups that define themselves by race, ethnicity and sex. Not surprisingly, these tend to become grievance groups fighting for room in which to cultivate their separateness and competing for high rank among victims deserving recompense. Rhetoric is especially shrill and relations are especially rancorous on campuses where "sensitivity" experts have rubbed nerves raw. Intruding the government and federally subsidized academics as supervisors of our conversations could make matters worse. Perhaps it would be wiser for Americans to spend less time pondering their group identities and destinies and instead to get on with their individual lives. Just a thought.

Hackney says "state humanities councils have already started people talking to each other about who we are as a nation and what holds us together." Note the "started." Is he serious? Americans have been talking about such things since the Mayflower Compact was signed. But perhaps people like Hackney think nothing really serious happens until government gets involved and makes the activity into a budget item. Some prickly people may detect an aroma of condescension in the notion that the nation's talk about serious subjects cannot proceed adequately without federal guidance. They may even see paternalism in the fact that when, last month, the NEH gathered some scholars in Chicago to begin planning The Conversation, the meeting was closed to the public.

And if The Conversation is to be implemented by a federal agency, should it be an agency headed by the man whose last job, as president of the University of Pennsylvania, involved several debacles at the expense of free speech? There was a famous prosecution of a student for allegedly violating Penn's speech code, and a famous nonprosecution of those who destroyed an entire edition of the campus newspaper. The destroyers were black and they had found a conservative columnist insensitive, and Hackney says he is "basically a free-expression absolutist," which he presumably is except when he isn't.

He is worried about the civility of conversation about divisive issues, but he may be too pessimistic about that because he has been so long among academics, who are not now known for their measured discussion of social issues. He also is worried that The Conversation may "fail." However, it is hard to see how it can fail, because he says "the conversation needs to go where the American people take it." Given that wherever it goes it should go, it can already be declared a resounding success. He is similarly serene about criticism of The Conversation because criticism is, conveniently, proof of the virtue of the idea. He says the criticism is "wonderful" because "it indicates that there's something here." This is a perfectly bulletproof federal program: Criticism vindicates it.

Hackney says America's deepest problems reflect confusion about values, confusion The Conversation is to correct. But when he talks about what is perhaps the gravest problem, family disintegration, Hackney the moralist becomes a materialist, ascribing the problem primarily to economic factors. He recently said: "The President has been talking ... about values, deterioration of the family, of the loss of the work ethic, and he says that family structure has been eroding for 30 years. I think that's probably right ... and that's because of various forces. ... the economy is a big one, the fact that growth has not been very robust in the last 15 years, and individual income, family income, has been stagnant," so in many families both parents work.

But the problem is families without two parents. And notice how Hackney scampers away from the fact that the rapid deterioration of the family began 30 years ago, when such social pathologies as illegitimacy and welfare dependency began to explode. Instead, Hackney locates the problem in a period defined by the economic policies of two Republican presidents. Some people will suspect Hackney is tailoring his conversation to suit political sensibilities. But perhaps Hackney will do better when conducting The Conversation for our betterment.

April 18, 1994

Pork for the Articulate

The selection of Jane Alexander to be chairman of the National Endowment for the Arts was itself a work of art, of sorts. Of course nowadays almost anything may, without serious challenge, be said to be a work of art. But more about that problem anon.

After a hearing that lasted barely an hour, the Senate confirmed Alexander with a unanimous swoon. Her confirmation process proved that chivalry is not dead and that she, although an altogether modern woman, knows the usefulness of male gallantry, reactionary though it may be in theory. The mostly male Senate asked her no searching questions about the problematic business of spending $175 million a year to shape public sensibilities. The men vibrated like tuning forks to her words about how the arts are—necessarily?—"life enhancing." She said she has a vision that "every man, woman and child find the song in his or her heart."

Clearly she has mastered the arts-speak that passes for, and suffices for, argument on behalf of the NEA. It is a sugary patois that calls to mind Joseph Epstein on Carl Sandburg's poetry: "Clichés run through his verse like calories through cheesecake." But Alexander also has the poise and presence of a fine professional actress, and she has a gifted political bureaucrat's knack for assembling coalitions and for blurring distinctions.

The NEA was created in 1965, at the high tide of the Great Society hubris about the competence of government, when Congress, lashed on by Lyndon Johnson, was a cornucopia. Convinced that Washington had mastered the management of the economy and eliminated business cycles, the political class assumed that henceforth the—definite article "the"—political problem would be the pleasant one of deciding how to dispense a gusher of revenues. Today, in a rather different fiscal environment but in a nice office high in the Old Post Office on Pennsylvania Avenue, Alexander presides over one of the most secure federal spending programs. It is instructive to note why it is that.

Alexander correctly says that it is a mistake to focus attention entirely on what she delicately describes as the NEA's involvement with "controversial" art. The NEA was born just as the last remnants of consensus about the nature of art and its public purposes was dying. By 1972 the NEA was funding, for example, *Dinner Party*, a triangular table with 39 place settings of vaginas on dinner plates.

The NEA scatters its support broadly, to many groups that enjoy considerable latitude in melding money from various sources. So NEA money often is, in effect, laundered en route to facilitating dubious undertakings. The NEA then tries to exercise what is known in Washington as "plausible deniability." Nevertheless, NEA money was involved in the "performance artist" who inserted a speculum into her vagina and invited members of the audience onstage to view her cervix with a flashlight. The NEA funded a Chicago film project that was advertised with a poster announcing "Sister Serpents Fuck a Fetus." The theme was: "For all you folks who consider a fetus more valuable than a woman, have a fetus cook for you, have a fetus affair, go to a fetus house to ease your sexual frustration." Recently NEA funds went to three Wyoming artists for an exhibit—if that is the *mot juste*—of 70 cows inscribed (painted; why not branded?) with a feminist's thoughts. Well, not everyone has the same song in his or her heart.

Such sophomoric attempts to shock the bourgeoisie confirm Paul Valéry's axiom that "everything changes but the avant-garde." But, to repeat, Alexander is right that "controversial" art should not monopolize the attention given to the NEA. She correctly says that most of what the NEA does is popular. She does not say, but it is the case that, it is particularly with the political class.

She notes that government subsidizes scientific research and development and she says the arts deserve equal treatment. But suppose government wants to cause the production of, say, a large-scale scientific instrument that private market forces would not produce—say, a space telescope. Government knows how to assemble relevant experts, to measure their progress, and to know when the goal has been reached. Baptists and atheists, liberals and conservatives, can collaborate. Now, try to develop an analogy with arts projects.

Arguing that the arts "always have been subsidized," she elides a lot of distinctions, such as those between state subventions and private patronage. She even notes, in justification of the NEA, that without the help of his brother Theo, Vincent Van Gogh "would have drifted into obscurity." She also is gifted at the Washington art of arguing that her programs pay for themselves.

In a recent speech in Indiana, Pennsylvania, she sounded like a member of Congress, reciting the blessings the NEA has bestowed on western Pennsylvania. It brought the Ballet Hispánico and the Pittsburgh Ballet to Johnstown, enabled the American Theater Arts for Youth to perform in Indiana and Ford City, helped the Indiana Arts Council (the NEA is just the top of an enormous pyramid of government involvement in the arts) to hire a director. The NEA supported a playhouse in Ebensburg, and the Johnstown symphony, and the Southern Alleghenies Museum of Art in Loretto, and gave $800,000 last year to support the state Council on the Arts, and so on. She asserted that Pittsburgh's tax revenues from the arts have doubled since 1990, and she vaguely associated the arts with the creation of 6,300 permanent new jobs "projected" by the end of the decade. She said the arts in Pittsburgh are outdrawing that city's professional baseball, football and hockey teams combined. She did not explain why, if Pittsburgh's arts are so popular, they need federal subsidies.

With an earnestness that seems entirely ingenuous, she tells of her travels, marveling that everywhere she is greeted by outpourings of gratitude. That is no doubt true, but hardly a marvel. Repeatedly she says, "I can't tell you how many people came up to me and said how glad they are. . . ." Yes, of course. But only in Washington do people believe that expressions of gratitude fully justify the federal activity of getting one group to pay for another group's pleasures. No wonder Washington's political class has clasped Alexander to its breast as one of its own.

In Washington the best defense is a brazen offense. She thumpingly asserts that the NEA is "probably the most successful agency in the federal government." Its success is, she says, "unparalleled." Well. If a government agency exists to encourage, say, the production of corn or electric power or highways or housing, it is a relatively straightforward task to formulate standards for measuring the agency's success or failure. But the NEA cannot help but be a huge success. Using money to do the summoning, the NEA summons "art" from the vasty deep, and lots of stuff called "art" comes forth. The summoner is not particular about what can be called art. (Which can cause problems. In the Netherlands the government has long been committed to subsidizing the production of art and to avoiding any undemocratic standards of quality. As a result the government has a huge storage problem of "art" it cannot even give away.)

Alexander stresses the NEA's role in "leveraging" money from the private sector. She says NEA grants generate an elevenfold return in private money. That may be a mixed blessing. Some NEA grants give a patina of legitimacy to foolishness, or worse, and enable highly political and lightly talented organizations to milk support from well-meaning but uninformed people in the private sector.

There was a time when the question of what constitutes serious art was answered by patrons and the educated public, perhaps influenced by philosophers. Today the very question "Is it art?" is considered at best an impertinence and at worst a precursor of "censorship," understood as a refusal to subsidize. Today art is whatever the "arts community" says it is, and membership in that community involves no exacting entrance requirements. (This is a familiar Washington rhetorical trope: "You are a *lobby*, we are a *community*.") Increasingly, the "arts community" is characterized by strident insistence that any attempt to distinguish the serious from the philistine in art is bad because it is both elitist and populist. It is impermissibly elitist because it assumes that a few are more talented than most. Yet it is impermissibly populist because it implies that the arts ought at least to try to be marginally popular—that they generally should pay for themselves by attracting audiences, rather than by attracting government grants.

Alexander hopes people will "look to the NEA for a vision for the arts in the 21st century." But given what is known about both the behavior of government and the history of art, it is passing strange to suppose that a government bureaucracy is suited to the business of such vision-making. Alexander speaks of the arts as being often "prophetic." A similar bromide of arts-speak is that art should discomfort, provoke, disturb, etc. This conceit gives an arts bureaucracy a bias toward novelty, the political and "the new." This means a tilt against standards of taste because, as a character says in Alan Bennett's play *Forty Years On*, "Standards are always out of date. That is what makes them standards."

The NEA says that "peer review" of proposed projects ensures proper standards and rigor in the disbursement of subventions. But as we have seen, the screening process often is, to say no more, porous.

Besides, would "the arts community" agree to a system whereby defense contracts were approved by "peer review" panels composed of defense contractors? Of course defense contractors comprise a lobby, not a "community."

Trouble attends government subsidies for the arts everywhere. New York City, which faces a yawning budget gap, shells out $87.3 million a year to 431 arts groups. An aide to the new mayor speculates that "there's a lot of stuff going on because it's clubhouse-type political handouts." Good guess. *The New York Times* reports that plans to increase—yes, increase—support for the city's premier arts institutions, "possibly" by cutting support for lesser ones, "was met with anger and trepidation" by politicians and "members of the arts community."

Any plan for supporting only the best is reflexively denounced as "elitist." That epithet comes awkwardly from the directors of museums and dance troupes and other things that claim to deserve subsidies because they have scant popular support. But this is the residual argument for public television in an era of rapidly proliferating cable choices: Some programming should be subsidized precisely because it cannot earn an audience sufficient to make it commercially viable. Finally, it is said that refusal to subsidize the most marginal art is a sin against "diversity."

However, the basic truth is that arts subsidies exist because the political market is working the way it often does in a democracy. Subsidized arts are pork for the articulate, for people nimble and noisy in presenting their employment or entertainment as an entitlement. So the subsidies are secure, as is the right of every man, woman and child to have federal support in finding the song in his or her heart.

January 10, 1994

The Most Arrogant Lobby

Reading that playwright Jon Baitz, recipient of a $15,000 grant from the National Endowment for the Arts, is making two donations of $7,500 to two institutions recently denied NEA grants for exhibits of what *The New York Times* primly calls "sexually explicit material," you may think: What a swell fellow Baitz is, putting his money where his mouth is.

But is it really his money that is funding his morality skit? Baitz proudly says he is giving away "my own funds, not the Endowment's."

Please. Baitz is a clever enough hustler to bilk the government but is not clever enough to make such sophistry succeed. Money is fungible. He is, in effect, giving his grant away, thereby contemptuously overturning three decisions of a government funding agency (the decisions to fund him and not to fund the two institutions he now funds).

An NEA spokesperson, who was born to be a bureaucrat, responded to Baitz's moral grandstanding with this fatuity: "We are delighted anytime someone in the private sector wants to support the arts."

By his gesture, with which he is awfully pleased, Baitz proved that he in no way needed the $15,000, which was given "to support activities which contribute to your creative development"—research, travel, whatever. How did they do it, Eugene O'Neill and Tennessee Williams and the rest who wrote plays before the NEA was concocted to irrigate "creative development" with federal cash?

In a letter to the NEA reeking of self-congratulation, Baitz says his money-shuffle saves him from being "complicit" in the "cultural sacking of this country" by conservatives. What lacerated the conscience that Baitz is now hawking in public was the decision by the NEA's acting director to veto two $10,000 grants to two universities for art exhibits, grants an NEA peer review panel approved. (In cultural matters "peer review" is regarded as sacred, as it would not be in the awarding of, say, defense contracts. There it would be considered mutual back-scratching.)

Some of the art that the NEA has declined to subsidize depicts castration, floating body parts, small photos of body parts and huge sperm. One painting is titled *Genital Wallpaper.* A sympathetic exegesis of this stuff says: "It uses fragmented sculptural body parts to express a sense of alienation and isolation that is very much part of what people are experiencing in our country."

The Washington Post, disapproving the NEA veto, notes archly that "depictions of genitalia" are "not exactly an unheard-of element" in great art, such as that of "Michelangelo and Bernini." Now there's a question the *Post* can dispatch a critic to consider: Has the NEA veto injured an actual or potential Michelangelo or Bernini? (Critic, pay particular attention to the sculpture *Milk,* made of wax, paper towels and baby bottle nipples.)

Actually, the question of artistic merit is, by the logic of critics of the NEA veto, impermissible because it involves government in making decisions about art's powers and purposes. You might think that the argument for subsidizing art must be that the art serves some social good. But when the NEA starts distinguishing between art that does and does not so serve, up rise cries of "censorship."

Surely art that has no power of social improvement has no claim on public resources. But when government tries to base funding decisions on relevant criteria, moral exhibitionists like Baitz begin to prance and pirouette.

Artists—or, in the precious language they prefer, the "arts community"—are the most preposterously arrogant lobby in an era infested with lobbyists demanding entitlements. In fact, it is theoretically impossible to demand a more expansive entitlement than the "arts community" demands—public funds for no defined public purpose.

Because the NEA will not fund stuff like *Genital Wallpaper* (saying it is "unlikely to have the long-term artistic significance necessary to merit Endowment funding"), some in the "arts community" are refusing to request NEA grants. They say the NEA is morally unfit to give them public money, so they are pulling back the tin cup they have held out. This is supposed to punish conservatives. Ouch.

In his letter praising himself, Baitz, who has made moral preening something of an art form, says that his NEA grant mortifies him because it means he is insufficiently offensive to the "psychosexual hysterics" and "cultural carpetbaggers" now rampant in America. He compares his plight to that of an artist praised by the Vichy government of Nazi-occupied France. He says America is an "anguished" country sinking (you may not have noticed) into bland "grayness."

Baitz, who pulls his snout from the public trough only to lecture the public on its moral inferiority to him, should be told that it is impolite to talk with one's mouth full.

June 7, 1992

This Golden Age of Art

The deep waters of the art world are yet again being roiled by the great Latrine Debate.

Next month a three-hole privy seat from an old Long Island outhouse will be auctioned as fine art, or perhaps just as an artifact, because one, and perhaps two, famous painters painted it—or, at any rate, put paint on it—as part of the merriment of a 1954 croquet party. The question is, is it art?

Willem de Kooning was an "abstract expressionist artist"—never mind the oxymoron—who painted the toilet seat. Perhaps he had the help of his roommate, Jackson Pollock, another abstract expressionist. A connoisseur of de Kooning says, "As soon as I saw it I knew it was of his hand." But even the cognoscenti can't be sure about the contribution of Pollock, he of the famous canvases of dribs and drabs.

The New York Times, speaking *ex cathedra,* announces, "The seat is executed in a style typical of the two masters." The space between the three holes has undulating black stripes of various thickness and texture. The *Times* says "the stripes culminate in thick, angry globs of black paint characteristic of Pollock."

What makes a glob angry rather than, say, serene or reverent or whimsical? Let those decide who bid at the auction. De Kooning and Pollock paintings fetch millions, but is this toilet seat art or a mere artifact? Millions of dollars may turn on the distinction. Or, more likely, dollars will make the distinction. If millions are bid, that will settle it: It's art.

Before the croquet party was over, de Kooning tore off two of the latrine covers and gave them to a friend. Years later, after the Latrine Debate began, the friend returned them. Did the return of the seats restore the art to perfection? Or was tearing them off part of de Kooning's act of creation? We are in deep water indeed.

Years ago, someone who was present at the creation said "it was done as a joke" for the croquet party and should not be treated as art. But what gave that person, Mrs. de Kooning, the right to rule that something isn't art? I mean, is this still a democracy or what?

The point of abstract art is democracy, understood as populism, egalitarianism and anti-intellectualism. Abstract art is immediately and equally "understandable" by everyone, there being nothing whatever to understand about stripes and splotches.

But the worm of elitism has entered the fruit. As art became more empty, art critics became more wordy. Critics constituted themselves into an indispensable clerisy. No one could understand abstract art until critics had infused it with "meaning." For example: "Pollock's strength lies in the emphatic surfaces of his pictures, which it is his concern to maintain and intensify in all that thick, fuliginous flatness. . . ."

The democratization of art means "one person, one artist." When anyone says anything is art, who is to say otherwise? So an "earth artist" stretches a curtain across a Colorado valley. A "conceptualist" spends 16 days on the Trans-Siberian Railway placing a different slate beneath his feet each day, then burns his notes and smushes the ashes on the slates, which are then exhibited. A "postminimalist" artist exhibits a live pig in a cage. An aspiring artist—who needs to aspire?—receives college credit for spending a weekend in a gym locker and calls this "a duration-confinement body-piece."

Of course modern art can misfire. A "kinetic sculpture"—a bucket of fireworks atop the Brooklyn Bridge—had a faulty fuse. An artist's pride and joy—a bathtub specked with plaster—was mistakenly used to cool beer for a party in the museum displaying the tub. At another gallery a janitor cleaned up a pile of bricks that was actually a display.

Recently your tax dollars have been at work subsidizing (it's all right; America has no more pressing needs) "performance artists" like the one whose art consists of political diatribes which she punctuated by smearing her chest with chocolate to symbolize excrement (and the beastliness of men to women). Such stuff is supposed to shock the bourgeoisie but the bourgeoisie keeps opening its wallet, thereby proving that the purest philistinism is fear of being called a philistine.

In 1917 Marcel Duchamp anonymously submitted to a gallery a urinal for display. The narrow-minded gallery rejected it but, says *The New York Times,* "It is now widely thought to be art, a paradigm of Duchamp's lifelong attempt to subvert traditions." Oh. Then Robespierre was an artist and the Russian Revolution was a whopping act of art.

Today many artists, short on talent but long on shrewdness, have stopped trying to shock the bourgeoisie and have turned instead to milking it. Hence government funds for "performance art" and auctions of painted privies.

A decade ago, Robert Hughes, a strong, sane voice about the art scene, noted that American art schools were graduating more people every five years than lived in Florence when Michelangelo and Raphael did, and that New York City had more galleries than bakeries. We must be living in a golden age of art.

January 19, 1992

Giving Paranoia a Bad Name

Oliver Stone's movie *JFK* will give paranoia a bad name and should give us all pause. Viewing his travesty about the Kennedy assassination makes one wonder what Stone would have thought about the century's most consequential assassination.

On June 28, 1914, six young men were poised in Sarajevo, Bosnia, to throw bombs at the car of Archduke Franz Ferdinand. Five of them, intimidated by the crowds or unwilling to hurt the archduke's wife, did nothing. However, one asked a policeman which car was the archduke's, the policeman identified it and the boy threw his bomb, which bounced off the archduke's car and exploded under the following car.

One of the others, Gavrilo Princip, went off disconsolately for coffee at a corner café, where he loitered. Later, the Archduke, going to a museum, decided to visit the people injured by the bomb. His driver, confused about the route to the hospital, stopped in front of the café where the astonished Princip sat. Princip leapt up and shot the Archduke and his wife, thereby lighting Europe's fuse.

Stone's portrayal of this would be: Like, wow, what a complex conspiracy brought the victim to the assassin's cleverly contrived coffee break. The driver was not confused, the first bomb "miss" was a ruse, the policeman was in on the plot, and there must have been hundreds of others, too. Who was behind it all? Well, who benefited? Munitions makers—merchants of death.

That is the message of Stone's celluloid diatribe. Much of America's establishment conspired to kill Kennedy because he loved peace and "they" wanted war. Strange that a society so sick allowed such a saint to be president at all, but this is cartoon history by Stone, who is 45 going on eight.

In his three-hour lie, Stone falsifies so much he may be an intellectual sociopath, indifferent to truth. Or perhaps he is just another propagandist frozen in the 1960s like a fly in amber, combining moral arrogance with historical ignorance.

He is a specimen of 1960s arrested development, the result of the self-absorption encouraged by all the rubbish written about his generation being so unprecedentedly moral, idealistic, caring, etc. He is one of those "activists" who have been so busy trying to make history they have not learned any.

Of America's two other assassinations of the 1960s—of Robert Kennedy and Martin Luther King—Stone says, "There's no doubt that these three killings are linked, and it worked. That's what's amazing. They pulled it off." Ah, yes: "they." Who are "they" who used Sirhan Sirhan and James Earl Ray as well as Lee Harvey Oswald for their purposes?

They are, he says, "a moving, fluid thing, a series of forces at play." Can he be a tad more specific? OK. They are "a parallel covert government." They are merchants of death, omnipresent, omnipowerful—but unable to stop Stone from unmasking them. Amazing indeed.

History teaches that as a conspiracy increases in size arithmetically, the chances of it unraveling increase exponentially. Yet Stone asserts that a conspiracy of many thousands (involving the FBI, the CIA, the armed forces, the Secret Service, the Mafia, the doctors who performed the autopsy, Earl Warren and the other members of his commission, the press and many others) succeeded until, 28 years later, there came a hero: Stone.

Back in Stone's formative years—those 1960s he loves so ardently—members of the John Birch Society thought President Eisenhower had been a Communist. Intellectually, Stone is on all fours with his mirror images, the Birchers, who, like Stone, thought Earl Warren was a traitor. Stone and they are part of a long fringe tradition, the paranoid style in American politics, a style ravenous for conspiracy theories.

Why is actor Kevin Costner lending himself to this libel of America? Is he invincibly ignorant or just banally venal? Nothing else can explain his willingness to portray as a hero Jim Garrison, who, as New Orleans' district attorney, staged an assassination "investigation" that involved recklessness, cruelty, abuse of power, publicity-mongering and dishonesty, all on a scale that strongly suggested lunacy leavened by cynicism.

After covering the assassination story for 28 years, the journalist who knows most about it is *The Washington Post*'s George Lardner. He documents Stone "stomping on presumptions of innocence, cooking up fake admissions, ignoring contrary evidence, and giving a conspiratorial tone to inconsequential facets of the tragedy that were explained long ago." Stone himself should have played Garrison.

Every viewer will have his or her favorite Stone fabrication. Mine is either the assertion that U.S. troops from Germany were airborne over America as part of the plot, or the assertion that President Johnson reversed a Kennedy order about Vietnam that in fact Johnson approved four days after the assassination, or the assertion that the CIA had stories about Oswald's arrest in some foreign papers almost at the moment he was arrested.

The through-the-looking-glass premise of this movie is: Proof of the vastness of the conspiracy is that no one can prove it exists. Stone's pose is that he loves America and the truth equally. That is true.

JFK is an act of execrable history and contemptible citizenship by a man of technical skill, scant education and negligible conscience.

December 26, 1991

The cult of ethnicity produces what Schlesinger calls a culture of self-pity and victimization. There is a "contagion of inflammable sensitivities" which makes the bonds of national identity brittle. It is instructive that this, perhaps the most serious counterrevolution ever mounted against the American Revolution, comes from the left. The stakes are high because, as Schlesinger says, "history is to the nation rather as memory is to the individual."

July 14, 1991

"History with the Politics Left Out"

The two most important months in Washington's history were June 1790 and June 1987. In June 1790, Jefferson and Hamilton met in Manhattan and agreed: Jefferson would support Hamilton's plan for national assumption of states' debts, Hamilton would support Jefferson's plan for moving the capital south from New York. In June 1987, Bea Kristol moved here from New York with her husband, Irving.

He is a one-man critical mass, whose move symbolized the movement of the nation's center of intellectual gravity from New York and to the right. She is a distinguished historian who writes under the name Gertrude Himmelfarb.

In this year's Jefferson Lecture, the 20th sponsored annually by The National Endowment for the Humanities, she delivered a timely rebuke to those historians who jeopardize our political future by devaluing the politics of the past. The devaluation is done in the name of "democratic" values against "elitism." But it deprives mankind of elevating truths about individual greatness. Himmelfarb's point is pertinent to this city today because the style of history she deplores demoralizes nations and makes leadership difficult.

The title of her lecture, "Of Heroes, Villains and Valets," comes from Hegel's amplification of the dictum that "no man is a hero to his valet." Hegel said, "No man is a hero to his valet not because the former is no hero, but because the latter is a valet."

Schoolmasters, said Hegel, delight in demonstrating that Alexander the Great and Julius Caesar were motivated by base passions, therefore their deeds were not heroic, and therefore the schoolmasters are superior to their subjects. Himmelfarb says Hegel's schoolmasters are today's professors, particularly practitioners of the "new history."

These historians believe that "elitist" varieties of history—those focusing on political, diplomatic and intellectual events—condescend to the common people. Such historians think democratic values make it mandatory to explain the past with reference not to the extraordinary actions and ideas of a few, but rather to the ordinary activities of the many.

Thus one of them says—I'm not making this up—"Mickey Mouse may in fact be more important to an understanding of the 1930s than Franklin Roosevelt." Not only elites but elitist themes—great ideas and books from great minds—are moved to the margin of the human story. In their place is put history written to fit the mentality of historians mesmerized by race, gender and class, today's trinity of obsessions that supposedly explain human behavior and history's past.

But, says Himmelfarb, "history from below" or "history with the politics left out" is itself the real condescension to common people. It denies that ordinary people have any ideas, motives or interests other than those of their ordinary lives. If race, gender and class are the categories that decipher historical determinism, then the new history must disabuse ordinary people of their understanding of their past.

Ordinary people think princes and presidents and villains—Louis XIV, FDR, Hitler—have been event-making individuals. But in the hands of the new history, such individuals become mere "reflections" of deeper forces deciphered by the new clerisy—the historians.

It is particularly perverse that such writing of history flourishes at the end of a century so shaped by event-makers—Hitler, Stalin, Mao, Churchill, Roosevelt, De Gaulle. But implausibility is a price the new historians gladly pay for ideological correctness that (not coincidentally) enhances their status.

The new historians are like "deconstructionist" literary critics who displace authors, explaining what the particular authors were "really" doing when they wrote—whether the authors knew it or not. The new history elevates the historian to the role—half priest, half artist—of explaining history's meaning to the masses who obdurately persist in thinking that politics matter.

If political events are mere "epiphenomena," then politics loses its history-shaping grandeur, and ordinary people lose the dignity that attaches to those who participate in the human pageant through self-government. If, as the new historians insist, social "structures" and impersonal "forces" make history, both individuality and freedom are discounted.

When historians deny that a preeminent few may have disproportionate impact on the destinies of the many, the historians also deny the people's ability to rise above determinism and modify their fate. Thus does the new historians' anti-elitism breed fatalism and pessimism about the very possibility of leadership.

This style of history abolishes man as a political animal who uses reason and responds to rhetoric to seek fulfillment in civic life. If you discount the importance of individuals and their utterances—choices, and the rhetoric that justifies and elicits support for them—you discount the importance, and perhaps even the possibility, of real democracy.

To a country dismayed by the valet-soul of today's politics and servile state, Himmelfarb says: A grander future requires better history books. They teach us how to think about ourselves and our polity and hence they are pregnant with our future.

May 2, 1991

Zachary Taylor's Unquiet Dust

The dust of America's 12th president has been disturbed in a Louisville, Kentucky, tomb. A coroner and a forensic anthropologist are seeking to still or confirm speculation that Zachary Taylor, not Lincoln, was the first president assassinated. Whatever is learned in this investigation will serve human happiness by underscoring the lovely contingency of history.

If Taylor was deliberately poisoned, the foul deed most likely was done by Southerners angry about his opposition to expansion of slavery. If so, the plotters fell victim to the vagaries of things. They may have saved the Union by making more likely the failure of the South's eventual resort to arms.

Taylor's condition in his final days was consistent with arsenic poisoning. If that occurred, traces of arsenic will be detectable in bits of hair, fingernails, bones and other tissues. However, findings must be analyzed in light of the fact that there often was arsenic in embalming fluids.

What happened on Thursday, July 4, 1850? What usually happens on July Fourth, only more so. There was much speechifying. The country did not yet have major league baseball or MTV to entertain it. Rhetoric was popular entertainment. And that day, in 1850, the cornerstone of the Washington Monument was being laid, with the President on hand.

It was a typical high-summer day in 19th-century Washington—sunny, hot, humid and dangerous. Humidity is natural to this river town, and was even worse then, before the draining of the marsh that lay, breeding mosquitoes, where the Tidal Basin and Jefferson Memorial now are.

The danger arose from the nature of mid-19th-century urban life, the abundance of horses and animals in the midst of human population, the absence of sanitation measures and of scientific understanding that soon would produce public health advances concerning housing and food handling.

Orators did rattle on in those days, so Taylor broiled in the sun for several hours, refreshing himself with ice water, chilled buttermilk and cherries and perhaps other fruits and vegetables. Washingtonians had been told to avoid such things because the country was experiencing epidemics of Asiatic cholera.

That night Taylor was uncomfortable. The next day he worked a bit, but by Saturday his family was alarmed. An army surgeon diagnosed "cholera morbus," an elastic 19th-century term denoting a variety of intestinal ailments. He died on July 9.

"Old Rough and Ready," as his troops affectionately called him, was the hero of the battle of Buena Vista in 1847. He was a Southerner who owned 140 slaves, but he was a strong-willed military nationalist who said he would personally take the field and hang secessionists.

Furthermore, he opposed the expansion of slavery. He said that if Congress passed the Wilmot Proviso, banning slavery in territories acquired from Mexico, he would sign it. Congress never passed it. If Taylor had lived, might it have?

When he died he was on the verge of sending to Congress a message demanding immediate admission of California and New Mexico as free states and settlement of a New Mexico–Texas border dispute in favor of the former.

Now, it is conceivable that had he lived, he might have cowed secessionists into permanent peaceableness. But it is much more likely he would have provoked secessionists, bringing on bloodshed.

Daniel Webster said at the time: "If General Taylor had lived, we should have had a civil war." If so, we would have had it before another decade of growth of the North's strength through industrialism and immigration, and before the birth of a new political party that found a nation-saving leader in a former Illinois congressman who had opposed the war that had made Taylor a hero and hence president.

History is a rich weave of many threads. Many of them, if pulled out, could cause a radical unraveling, setting the past in motion as a foaming sea of exhilarating contingencies.

For more than a century we have been plied and belabored by various historicisms purporting to prove what happened had to happen, that history is a dry story of the ineluctable working of vast impersonal forces unfolding according to iron laws of social evolution. People, the historicists say, are mere corks bobbing on powerful currents. This demoralizing doctrine denies the possibility, ultimately, of meaningful self-government, for individuals or nations.

That is why either way the Louisville investigation turns out—blame unsanitary cherries or blame unscrupulous opponents—Taylor's death tantalizes. It gives a glimpse of an always inspiriting prospect— possibilities, paths not taken. Things could have been different; choices and chance cannot be scrubbed from the human story; we are not corks; we matter.

The fate of a president 141 July Fourths ago whispers in our ear: "The river of history could have cut a different canyon."

June 20, 1991

The Monsoon of Our History

At the battle of Shiloh, a wounded Union soldier was told to leave his rifle and go to the rear. He soon returned, saying, "Gimme another gun. This blame fight ain't got any rear." Neither did the war.

It was fought in 10,000 places, this monsoon of our history. And now for five nights, *The Civil War* is magnificently encompassed on public television. If better use has ever been made of television, I have not seen it and do not expect to see better until Ken Burns turns his prodigious talents to his next project.

He is the filmmaker five of whose 37 years went into the making of this masterpiece of national memory. Our *Iliad* has found its Homer: He has made accessible and vivid for everyone the pain and poetry and meaning of the event that is the hinge of our history.

The Civil War is the largest event in human history. A large claim, that, but defensible, on five grounds.

At issue, and not just for this country, were the two polarities of political possibility: self-government and slavery. The war catalyzed the world's noblest political career, Lincoln's. The war (in Walt Whitman's phrase) "condensed a nationality": It completed the American founding, settling questions unanswered in 1789. It transformed the foremost democracy into a nation of such philosophic clarity and political unity that, in the next century, it could save the world from several tyrannies akin to slavery.

For more than a century this argument has raged: What caused the war? Was it an "irrepressible conflict"? What, at its core, was it about? About 15 minutes into Burns's 11-hour series, you learn—you *see*—the answer.

You see a 19th-century photograph, black-and-white of course, of a black man's back. It is hideously covered with scars left by a lash. Burns's camera does not dwell; the narrative does not even mention what we have briefly seen. Burns knows how to blend passion and delicacy: Reticence can be its own emphasis.

The Civil War was the prototype of the great engine of change—social, cultural, scientific—in the modern world. It was the first modern war, waged, in the end (in Georgia and South Carolina, by Sherman), against civilians, and won by the side best at mobilizing an industrial base.

The First World War, from the wounds of which the Western world is only just now recovering, was prefigured in the trenches at Petersburg, Virginia. The firepower that killed 7,000 in 20 minutes at Cold Harbor, Virginia, was an anticipation of the Somme.

Two days' fighting at Shiloh killed more Americans than all previous American wars. September 17, 1862—Antietam—is still the bloodiest day in American history. Two percent of the American population died in the war. And then there were the survivors of the first great modern war and the last great war before modern medicine: In 1866, one-fifth of the state of Mississippi's revenues were spent on artificial limbs.

Was it worth it? Yes. When the war began, one in seven Americans was owned by another American.

Less than 1 percent of the North's population was black, but by the end of the war 10 percent of the Union forces were black. One of them was a handsome boy named Jackson, about 12. Burns's camera pans slowly up an old photograph, up past the bare feet, ragged trousers, shredded shirt of "Contraband Jackson." (Contrabands were slaves who escaped to Union lines.) Then the camera pans up another photograph, up over boots, fine trousers, past a drum and snappy blouse, to the face of . . . Drummer Jackson.

Burns's film of the battlefields today, and the old photographs, are "framed" by ambient sounds—hoofbeats, cannon, musketry, steamboat whistles. The birds you hear are the kind that called at the times and places of battles. The camera moves, sometimes at a canter, down roads and over ridges.

And the pictures are exquisitely married to words, astonishingly rich 19th-century English usage, not only from leaders but from the letters and diaries of soldiers and citizens. The first episode includes a love letter of unbearable beauty, written on the eve of the first Battle of Bull Run by a soldier who was to die there.

The war was haunted by eerie occurrences.

Wesley Culp was born on Culp's Hill in Gettysburg. As a teenager, he took to wandering, wound up in Virginia. Came the war, he enlisted. He died a few yards from the house in which he was born, on Culp's Hill.

Because the first Battle of Bull Run put soldiers in his kitchen,

Wilmer McLean moved deep into Virginia to escape the war. He settled in Appomattox. The war ended in his living room.

That was the way of the war with "no rear." That is why it resonates so, and why Burns, by enriching our understanding, enriches our citizenship.

September 20, 1990

PART 4

Issues and Choices

The Unintended Consequences of Unpalatable Choices

Perhaps the 1969 encounter on the helicopter was a meeting of the different political sensibilities of Harvard and the University of Chicago.

Pat Moynihan, President Nixon's domestic policy adviser, with a Harvard man's confidence in the efficacy of government, had just returned from prompting the French government to smash the "French connection" by which most heroin destined for America was refined from Turkish opium in Marseilles. Moynihan's companion on the helicopter to Camp David was Labor Secretary George Shultz from the University of Chicago, home of flinty realism about the power of strong appetites to create markets in spite of the disapproval of governments.

Moynihan happily told Shultz about his achievement in France. "Good," said Shultz with deflating dryness. "No, really," said Moynihan, "this is a *big* event." "Good," said Shultz, again not interrupting his paperwork to feign excitement.

"I suppose," ventured Moynihan, "you think that so long as there is a demand for drugs, there will continue to be a supply."

"You know," Shultz replied, "there's hope for you yet."

Moynihan recalls this in his essay "Iatrogenic Government" in the *American Scholar* quarterly. (Iatrogenic: "induced inadvertently by a physician or his treatment.") It is a timely story of the unintended consequences of unpalatable choices, and of choices more unpalatable than public policy might have made them.

In 1969 Moynihan recognized the drug epidemic as yet another instance of "the central experience of modern society," the disruption of society by technology. The environment is injured by technology; populations are displaced by technology; drivers and pedestrians are maimed by technology; cities are choked by technologies. And cities are terrorized by the crime generated by the traffic in drugs that are products of technology.

Products, to be precise, of 19th-century German organic chemists. They produced morphine, a medicine that begat a monster. From it came a distillation that made users feel *"heroisch"*—hence the name "heroin." From opium to morphine to heroin; from coca to cocaine to crack: We have climbed the technological ladder before, from wine to beer to brandy and gin.

Distilled alcohol became a scourge of the 18th century when the Renaissance invention of distillation met the abundance of grain produced by the agricultural revolution. The public health calamity of cheap gin was an important reason why London's population growth stagnated between 1700 and 1750.

The second law passed by the first U.S. Congress imposed a tariff on Jamaican rum to encourage consumption of American whiskey. Not much encouragement was needed. Americans commonly drank whiskey at breakfast and on through the day. Laborers digging the Erie Canal were given a quart of Monongahela whiskey a day, issued in eight four-ounce portions beginning at six A.M.

People thought this was healthy. (Not long ago people thought cocaine was a nonaddictive refresher.) But social learning occurred regarding alcohol. By the end of the 19th century the temperance movement had reduced per capita alcohol consumption two-thirds. Then came Prohibition, a public health success (alcohol-related illnesses declined dramatically) but with a high social cost in criminality.

And today? Given current chemical technology—note this qualification—drug policy requires a choice between two nasty outcomes, a broad public health problem resulting from legalization or a more localized but devastating crime problem, particularly among vulnerable inner-city populations. We have chosen the latter.

However, we persist in pretending that we can make a "cleaner" choice—interdiction of supply, bolstered by executions of drug "kingpins." But a nation with long coastlines and open borders—and skies—cannot "interdict" a compact substance that is sucked north by a $100 billion demand. (America's demand for cocaine can be supplied from 96 square miles of Latin America—a patch the size of Milwaukee.) Interdiction may raise drug prices somewhat, but raising the price of a highly pleasurable and highly addictive substance may raise the rate of the crimes committed to procure the substance.

Moynihan says that "federal drug policy"—iatrogenic government—"is responsible for a degree of social regression for which there does not appear to be any equivalent in our history." Today more Americans are imprisoned for drug offenses than for property crimes. However, Moynihan says, the "failure" of our drug policy is the success of our strategy to avoid the public health calamity that certainly would result from legalization.

But we may be living with the consequences of another kind of failure. By now, given how much we know about brain chemistry, we probably should have a technological response to the destructive forces unleashed by 19th-century chemistry. Government support should have provided the resources (and prestige; that matters in science) for research to discover chemical compounds that block or reverse the pleasure- and addiction-producing effects of drugs. Is it too much to ask that this be taken as seriously by medical researchers as AIDS is?

Moynihan believes that, given the setting of the drug problem amidst the collapse of family structure in the inner city ("to use an epidemiological analogy, we have a famine-weakened population attacked by a fierce new virus"), only a neutralizing chemical technology can do much good. But pending fulfillment of that hope, there is one other, drawn from humanity's encounter with alcohol: Given experience, the species learns, adapts, behaves more sensibly.

June 27, 1993

Pricing Life

"Who," asked Senate Majority Leader George Mitchell when questioned about the cost of clean-air legislation, "can calculate the dollar value of a child's health and life?" Well now. Whose child, mine or yours?

We calculate the value of loved ones and strangers differently. Parents will pay more to educate their children than they would be willing to have government pay, in taxes, for all children. Government does not legislate for "a" child.

Mitchell's question was rhetorical, and his point is not just that such a calculation is complex. Rather, his implication is that attaching monetary values to such moral values is morally dubious, even repellent. However, policymakers do that constantly. They do not advertise that fact; they often do not admit it even to themselves. But it is sometimes—not always—well to dwell upon it.

Let us stipulate that the clean-air compromise to which the Bush administration has subscribed is sensible. Its cost to industry (to be passed along in various ways) would be about $21 billion. That may be, as some say, a bargain, purchasing health care savings and preventing much lost productivity as a result of pollution-related illness and premature death. That may be so, but two things must be said.

First, we have seen this movie before. Washington is always awash with programs "certain" to pay for themselves, programs that will not really cost what they seem to cost. A jobs program will "pay for itself" in increased tax revenues and decreased welfare payments; a tax cut will be self-financing because wondrously stimulative; health savings will exceed the costs of this or that environmental program.

Second, one thing is certain: The $21 billion spent for cleaner air cannot be spent on other things. Many environmentalists argue that health and longevity are values so valuable that no alternative augmentations of social welfare can be weighed against them. Like all extremisms, this could produce perverse outcomes.

It is obviously preposterous to say that any incremental improvement in health, however marginal, is worth any cost to, say, economic vitality, however severe. Economic vitality produces jobs, wealth and other satisfactions; economic vitality underwrites government, the arts and sciences, including sciences pertaining to health. It is crude biological materialism to assert that health and longevity are values superior to all others.

But even if one grants that premise, policymakers face morally difficult trade-offs. Comparative returns on health must be considered. The $21 billion spent on cleaner air is $21 billion that cannot be spent on immunization, infant mortality, care for poor pregnant women. If we really believe that health and longevity are values immune from cost-benefit scrutiny, we should, for starters (on an endless list), limit automobile speeds to 35 mph and ban left turns.

Last week, a bipartisan commission voted 8–7 to recommend providing health insurance and long-term care to all in need. It would cost business $20 billion and government $66 billion. Because the government has inadequate resources (of revenues, and of the will to increase them), the commission's proposal is being dismissed as a mere audit of needs it would be nice to fill. An additional 70¢ tax on a gallon of gasoline (raising the price, in real terms, to what it was in 1980) would pay for it. But no elected official is going to say that such a gasoline tax, or some other equivalent revenue-raiser, is morally obligatory lest we be guilty of putting a dollar value on health and life.

Policies concerning health take odd caroms. The use of automobile safety belts is good, but because of it there are fewer dead drivers and passengers, so there are fewer organs available for transplants. Smoking is a health catastrophe, but an end of smoking would be a blow to Social Security and private pensions: Their actuarial assumptions count on millions of smokers dying before they collect much, or any, of their entitlements. Antipollution technologies required on cars since 1980 have raised car prices, thereby encouraging many people to continue driving older cars. Pre-1980 cars are one-third of those now operating and they produce 86 percent of automotive pollution.

Environmentalism is a worthy concern. But it is one among many, and attaching the adjective "environmental" to legislation and demonstrating a health benefit from the legislation does not give it irresistible momentum for enactment.

The idea that "life is priceless" comes under the category of useful nonsense. It is useful to talk that way, thereby inclining our minds to place high value on life, precisely because we constantly must act in ways that cause that value to be bruised and compromised by competing values.

March 8, 1990

Al Gore's Evangelism

Someone retrieved Kipling's poem "Recessional" (the one about "dominion over palm and pine" and "lesser breeds without the Law") from the wastebasket where Kipling had tossed it. Whether that someone did literature a favor is debatable. Clearly Al Gore's book *Earth in the Balance* is wastebasket-worthy.

The senator says our civilization is a "dysfunctional family." He favors a "wrenching transformation of society," altering "the very foundation of our civilization." Some leaders have effected such changes. Moses, Jesus, Muhammad. But the U.S. government?

Gore's environmentalism is a caricature of contemporary liberalism, a compound of unfocused compassion (for the whole planet) and green guilt about "consumptionism" (a sin that Somalia and many other places would like to be more guilty of). His call to "make the rescue of the environment the central organizing principle for civilization" is embarrassing. Who wants politicians who are unaware of the comical figure they cut when announcing new "central organizing principles" for civilization?

When Gore asserts, as he recently did yet again, that "the world scientific community" is in "consensus" about global warming, he is being as cavalier about the truth as the Bush campaign has been about Clinton's tax increases. Gore knows that his former mentor at Harvard, Roger Revelle, although concerned about global warming, concluded before his death last year that "the scientific base for greenhouse warming is too uncertain to justify drastic action at this time. There is little risk in delaying policy responses."

Gore is marching with many people who not long ago were marching in the opposite direction. *New York* magazine's Christopher Byron notes that Stephen Schneider of the National Center for Atmospheric Research in Colorado is an "environmentalist for all temperatures." Today Schneider is hot about global warming; 16 years ago he was exercised about global cooling. There are a lot like him among today's panic-mongers.

Gore complains that the media, by focusing on controversy, threatens the planet by creating skepticism about the agenda for which he insists there is scientific consensus. Actually, too often skepticism (about Love Canal, acid rain, the—it turns out—nonexistent Northern Hemisphere hole in the ozone layer) is vindicated long after being portrayed in the media as a moral failing, rather than as an intellectually debatable position.

Gore, who has spent most of his life in Washington's governing circle, overflows with the certitude characteristic of that circle. He knows the future and knows exactly what it requires, which turns out to be an unprecedented expansion of government—spending, regulating, evaluating technologies, and transferring wealth abroad.

He has mastered the Washington art of arguing that his agenda won't really cost anything. You know: This or that program or regulation will make us healthier or smarter or better behaved, and therefore will make us more productive, so economic growth will increase and so will revenues, and thus everything will "pay for itself." Gore's new wrinkle on this is environmentalism-as-business-opportunity. We shall prosper by making environmentally "necessary" products. Perhaps.

The hoariest cliché in modern American politics is a "Marshall Plan" for this or that (nowadays usually "the cities"). It is being given another trot around the track by Gore's call for a "Global Marshall Plan." He is vociferous against the "hubris" of our technological civilization, but he partakes of the hubris of the government class, which, having failed at its banal but useful business down the street (schools, bridges, medical care), has an itch to go global.

Gore's particular ideas (lots of new taxes, treating the automobile as a "mortal threat" to civilization and much more) have no constituency. But what is dismaying is the way he trades in ideas, uncritically embracing extremisms that seem to justify vast expansions of his righteousness and of the power of the government he seeks to lead.

His unsmiling sense of lonely evangelism in a sinning world lacks the sense of proportion that is produced by a sense of history—and of humor. The planet is more resilient, the evidence about its stresses more mixed and the facts of environmental progress more heartening that he admits. His book, a jumble of dubious 1990s science and worse 1960s philosophy ("alienation" and all that) is a powerful reason not to elect its author to high office in the executive branch, where impressionable people will be bombarded by bad ideas in search of big budgets.

September 3, 1992

The Strange Career of Eco-Pessimism

Many confidently—even eagerly—predicted catastrophes are late in arriving. There is a lengthening list of traumas to the planet that were supposed to have happened but haven't. This is one reason to be unimpressed by the "Earth Summit" in Rio.

The Audubon Society calls that summit "the most important meeting in the history of mankind." (So much for the Council of Trent, the Congress of Vienna and the first meeting of Plato and Socrates.) But anytime agents of 160 governments gather, remember: Some Third World governments (which are most of the world's governments) are "kleptocracies." They would rather redistribute the First World's wealth than abandon the statism that is the basis of their power. Statism also is the impediment to their people's prosperity and therefore a cause of environmental injury.

Some environmentalists (usually at comfortably endowed universities in developed countries) dislike economic growth, and many environmental measures hinder it. But growth is a prerequisite for environmental improvement. The worldwide pattern is that environmental damage increases until per capita income increases to a point where people enjoy a social surplus and feel they can ask government to trade some growth for environmental healing.

So before we are stampeded into growth-inhibiting actions to combat global warming, we should recall that less than 20 years ago—not long in a planet's life—the politically correct panic concerned global cooling. Then there were "many signs pointing to the possibility that the Earth may be headed for another ice age" (*The New York Times*, August 14, 1975), moving "toward extensive Northern Hemisphere glaciations" (*Science*, December 10, 1976) and facing "continued rapid cooling of the Earth" (*Global Ecology*, 1971) and "the approach of a full-blown 10,000-year ice age" (*Science*, March 1, 1975).

It was then said that "a new ice age must now stand alongside nuclear war as a likely source of wholesale death and misery" (*International Wildlife*, July 1975) and that "the world's climatologists are agreed" that we must "prepare for the next ice age" (*Science Digest*, February 1973). *Newsweek* reported (April 28, 1975) "ominous signs" that "the Earth's climate seems to be cooling down" and meteorologists "are almost unanimous" that "the trend will reduce agricultural productivity for the rest of the century." The *Christian Science Monitor* reported (August 27, 1974) that armadillos had left Nebraska, retreating south, and heat-loving snails had retreated from Central European forests, and "the North Atlantic is cooling down about as fast as an ocean can cool," glaciers "have begun to advance" and "growing seasons in England and Scandinavia are getting shorter."

Nowadays *Newsweek*'s Gregg Easterbrook, writing in *Washington Monthly*, offers his "Law of Doomsaying": Predict catastrophe no later than 10 years hence but no sooner than five years away—soon enough to terrify but far enough off that people will forget if you are wrong. Easterbrook has not forgotten Stanford's infallibly wrong Paul Ehrlich, who in 1968 said, "The battle to feed humanity is already lost. . . . we will not be able to prevent large-scale famines in the next decade." Since 1968 world grain production has increased 60 percent. For 30 years world excess food stocks relative to consumption have grown faster than population.

In 1980 Ehrlich bet economist Julian Simon $1,000 that in a decade the prices of five resources (copper, chrome, nickel, tin and tungsten) would rise. The prices of all five fell. Ehrlich paid. And Stephen Moore of the Cato Institute reports (in *The Public Interest*) that, contrary to predictions that increased population and industrialism would produce scarcities, "by every objective measure natural resources became more, not less, plentiful in the 1980s."

Indeed, "many environmentalists now complain of the ecological damage that will occur as a result of cheap and accessible energy," Moore says. Measured in terms of the amount of time a person must work to purchase them, natural resources are, on average, 20 percent cheaper than in 1980, half as costly as in 1950 and five times less costly than in 1900.

Eco-pessimism persists, more solid than environmental science, in part because it serves a political program. Some environmentalism is a "green tree with red roots." It is the socialist dream—ascetic lives closely regulated by a vanguard of bossy visionaries—dressed up as compassion for the planet.

Various reasons for gloominess come and go (dioxin and acid rain have recently been demoted as menaces), but the supply of gloominess is remarkably constant. A recent *Science* magazine editorial, "The Attractiveness of Gloom," satirically offered a new version of Murphy's Law: "Things are worse than they can possibly be." It quotes a fictional

Dr. Noitall, who says his fellow gloommongers are handicapped by the fact that standards of living, and life expectancy, keep rising. However, he takes comfort from the fact that anxiety will remain high because "expectations always increase more rapidly than productivity."

And he contentedly anticipates "the panic that will spread through the population when they read about the epidemic of deaths through natural causes." You read about it first here.

May 31, 1992

The Politics of Nutty Numbers

To the untrained eye, it was just another of the numbing numbers by which journalism calls attention to this or that crisis: "Every year, the World Health Organization estimates, 220,000 people die from pesticide poisoning." To the trained eye of Richard McGuire, New York's Commissioner of Agriculture and Markets, that assertion in an upstate New York newspaper's editorial looked implausible.

It was. Follow McGuire as he follows the slithering number to a lesson about the strange life led by some statistics and the terrible data on which government often makes decisions.

A call from McGuire's office to the upstate editor revealed that he had received the editorial from a California newspaper syndicate service. A call there revealed that the 220,000 number was from information supporting Senator Patrick Leahy's (D-Vt.) bill to prohibit U.S. companies from exporting pesticides whose use is banned in America. Leahy was concerned about America importing foods containing residues of chemicals banned here.

Leahy's office directed McGuire to the WHO, which directed him to a WHO report. McGuire wrote to the author in Switzerland, who wrote back to say the figure of 220,000 deaths came from another WHO publication.

The author had warned readers that "reliable data on pesticide poisonings are not available and the figures given are derived from various estimates." Unfortunately, he said, quoted figures often acquire misplaced momentum because they are shorn of their tentativeness.

Here is what the WHO publication the author relied on actually said: "Of the more than 220,000 intentional and unintentional deaths from acute (pesticide) poisoning, suicides account for approximately 91 percent, occupational exposure for 6 percent and other causes, including food contamination, for 3 percent." Of the 3 percent (itself a guess), we are left to guess what portion involved food contamination.

WHO's basic message was that there were actually 20,000 deaths from unintentional pesticide poisoning in a world population of 5 billion. The numbers floated downstream, from the WHO to the Senator's office to the editorial writer's office where this was written:

> Every year, the World Health Organization estimates, 220,000 people die from pesticide poisoning; 25 million people fall victim to injury or illness. There are no reliable numbers on how many of those casualties result from exposure to unlicensed chemicals exported from this country. . . . But there is no question that the American manufacturers who continue to traffic in these poisons are a significant part of the problem.

That is, American traffickers in poisons are unquestionably a significant part of the problem, if there is a significant problem. (U.S. Food and Drug Administration tests on imported foods reveal no significant problem with chemical residues on food imports.)

The use of nutty numbers to advance political agendas may result from cynicism or from confusion born of carelessness. The result can be foolish public policies, feeding on and fed by the journalism of apocalypse.

Twenty years ago *The Public Interest* published "The Vitality of Mythical Numbers" by Max Singer, then president of the Hudson Institute. He dissected a then commonly cited number, that New York City's "100,000-plus" heroin addicts were stealing upward of $5 billion worth of property a year.

The assumptions behind the numbers were: 100,000 addicts were each spending an average of $30 a day on their habits, or $1.1 billion a year (100,000 × 365 × $30). Stolen property is fenced for about one-quarter of its value, so addicts must steal upward of $5 billion worth.

Singer was skeptical.

Most stealing by addicts then was by shoplifting and burglary. All retail sales in the city then totaled $15 billion (including cars, carpets, diamonds and other goods not susceptible to shoplifting). All losses from all forms of theft and embezzlement were about 2 percent. Even if shoplifters accounted for half of that (they don't; employees steal much more), and if all shoplifters were addicts (they aren't), the addicts' shoplifting total would be $150 million.

Burglary? Even if one-fifth of the city's 2.5 million households had been burglarized each year (they weren't), and accepting the police estimate that the average loss from a burglary was property worth $200, the burglary total ($200 × 500,000) was $100 million.

So even with inflating assumptions, the burglary and shoplifting sum was a quarter of a billion dollars' worth of property. That is not chopped liver, but it is one-twentieth of $5 billion.

Probably the "100,000-plus" number of addicts was inflated. A pertinent question about such numbers is: Whose interests are served by a numerical exaggeration? The answer often is: The people whose funding or political importance varies directly with the perceived severity of a particular problem.

Here, then, is a helpful number: two. When an advocacy group cites hair-raising numbers about the problem for which they are advocating solutions, or a bureaucracy cites such numbers about the problem its programs address (homelessness, drug abuse, teenage prostitution, whatever), divide the numbers by two.

Similarly, when the Office of Management and Budget issues deficit projections, multiply by three.

January 5, 1992

Gambling with the Nation's Character

If life is, as a poet said, a sum of habits disturbed by a few thoughts, we should think clearly about those habits we deliberately develop. Consider the rapid spread of legal gambling.

Until 1989 just two states, Nevada and New Jersey, had casino gambling. Then such gambling returned to Deadwood, South Dakota, where in 1876 Wild Bill Hickok was shot in the back while holding a poker hand. Since then 11 more states have legalized some casinos. Staid Minnesota today has more than New Jersey.

Lotteries helped to finance Jamestown, the Continental Army, Dartmouth, Harvard, Princeton and many public works. Today 32 states and the District of Columbia have government-run lotteries which in 1991 siphoned up $17 billion. Forty-seven states participate in some form of gambling.

Fifty-two Indian tribes in 17 states (so far), exploiting a Supreme Court ruling that states do not have regulatory powers over tribes, are operating casinos and bingo operations grossing $6 billion annually. States cannot tax Indian casinos, but can profit from them. For example, a Connecticut tribe—whose casino, a three-hour drive from New York City, soon will employ 10,000—has struck a bargain with their state: The tribe will give a projected $100 million annually to Connecticut as long as not even a single slot machine is legalized off the reservation. Around the nation some cities are contemplating ceding parcels of land to Indians as "reservations" where gambling would be legal and the cities would get a cut.

In Tunica County, Mississippi, America's fourth-poorest county in the 1990 Census, unemployment has been halved, largely because of a riverboat casino. (Four other states also have riverboat casinos.) It may net the county $2 million annually, a sum about the size of the county's current budget.

Five states operate keno and two others are flirting with it. Maryland hopes to raise $100 million this year from keno gambling. Maryland keno is a high-speed video lottery offering bets every five minutes on monitors in 1,800 bars and other places. Supporters of this say to critics: If you object to this windfall from the behavior of consenting adults, what taxes do you propose to use to compel a similar sum from reluctant citizens?

In 1991 gross revenues from legal gambling nationwide were $26.7 billion, more than five times the box office of the domestic movie industry. States received only 2.4 percent of their revenues from lotteries, but this sum—$7.5 billion—net was not trivial.

Are there social costs from all this? Lots, beginning with the ruinous—to health, work and families—excesses of compulsive gamblers. These are people susceptible, perhaps for psychological or even physiological reasons, to what the American Psychiatric Association calls "a disorder of impulse control."

Now, classifying such destructive behavior as a "disease" can be a tactic for attaining access to government and insurance money, and can further attenuate the notion of individual responsibility. And calling a behavior "addictive" is problematic. But research suggests that some compulsive gamblers are peculiarly prone to a "high," like a drug user's, from abnormally elevated levels of endorphins in the blood when they are excited by gambling. For such people, gambling truly is "suicide without death."

Furthermore, state-sponsored and -advertised and -hyped lotteries are exploitative. Per capita sales of lottery tickets are higher in poor inner-city neighborhoods than in suburbs, and the disparity is even larger when lottery spending in poor and affluent neighborhoods is calculated as a percentage of household income.

Michael Berberich, writing in *Notre Dame* magazine, recalls with appropriate disgust an Illinois lottery billboard in a Chicago ghetto: THIS COULD BE YOUR TICKET OUT. Thus does government peddle a spurious but tantalizing hope to people particularly vulnerable to delusive promises and ill-equipped to decipher the discouraging probabilities.

Gambling can be a benign entertainment, but it can become, for individuals and perhaps for a society, a way of attempting to evade the stern fact that (as Henry James said) "life is effort, unremittingly repeated." Gambling inflames the lust for wealth without work, weakening a perishable American belief—that the moral worth of a person is gauged not by how much money he makes but by how he makes his money.

By institutionalizing a few highly publicized bonanzas, government foments, for its benefit, mass irrationality. It also deepens "the fatalism of the multitude," the belief that life's benefits are allocated randomly.

Joseph Epstein, the essayist, notes that "to have come to America in the first place was to take a serious gamble. To advance with the country's frontier was another gamble." Nowadays, when life for most non-poor Americans is without routine risk, gambling may be a way of infusing life with stimulating uncertainty.

But by now, with a deepening dependency of individuals and governments on gambling, we are gambling with our national character, forgetting that character is destiny.

February 7, 1993

"Goals 2000," Yet Again

The other day the Senate was doing the usual, issuing imperious commands to the future, when a senator did the unusual: He said the future will not be impressed.

The Senate was debating the "Goals 2000" education bill when Pat Moynihan rose to compare two of the goals—the only quantifiable ones—to grain production quotas in the Soviet Union. The two goals are that by the year 2000 the high school graduation rate will be "at least" 90 percent, and that American students "will be first in the world in mathematics and science achievement." Said Moynihan, "That will not happen."

Other goals range from the difficult to define (all children will start school "ready to learn") to the difficult to imagine (every school "will be free of drugs and violence"). Such silliness is a bipartisan tradition. In 1984 President Reagan decreed goals for 1990 not unlike the goals President Bush offered in 1990 for 2000, some of Bush's goals being identical to President Clinton's.

Such goal-setting is progress, of sorts: Policymakers are speaking the language of cognitive outputs rather than monetary inputs. But it is not much progress because policymakers are still preoccupied with inputs.

In 1966 sociologist James Coleman and his colleagues published data from a huge survey of public schools and students. Postwar education policy had been focused where the public education lobby wanted it, on financial inputs such as per pupil spending, teachers' salaries, pupil-teacher ratios. However, Coleman's report, which Moynihan says was so "seismic" that the government considered not releasing it, concluded: "Schools are remarkably similar in the effect they have on the achievement of their pupils when the socioeconomic background of the students is taken into account."

Or as a sociologist had said to Moynihan at an academic gathering when Moynihan was an academic and Coleman was still compiling the data, "Have you heard what Coleman is finding? It's all family." That is, the best predictor of a school's performance is the quality of the homes from which the students come to school.

In 1989 a researcher reported in confirmation of Coleman that "variations in school expenditures are not systematically related to variations in student performance." And later: "Researchers have tried to identify inputs that are reliably associated with student achievement and school performance. The bottom line is, they have not found any."

Paul Barton of the Educational Testing Service estimates that about 90 percent of the differences in average proficiency among the states' schools can be explained by five factors: number of days absent from school, number of hours spent watching television, number of pages read for homework, quantity and quality of reading material in the home, the presence of two parents in the home. Now, unless the government has a plan for making those variables vary, positively and quickly, the goals about graduation rates and math and science achievements are airy puffs of legislative cotton candy.

Between 1910 and 1969 the graduation rate rose from 8.8 percent to 77.1 percent. By 1980 it had receded to 71.4. The government estimates that it was 73.8 last year. It has never been higher than 77.1. It will not be 90 in six years. In 1991 American 13-year-olds ranked 13th among 14 nations surveyed in math and 12th among 14 in science, rankings that are essentially unchanged in three decades and will not be substantially changed in six years.

Moynihan says the "official delusion" indicated by such goals may be "evidence of a dysfunction in the political world far more portentous than that in our high schools." Actually, "Goals 2000" involves less delusion than calculation, and there are three reasons for it.

First, government cannot do much, and can do next to nothing quickly, about the quality of families, other than stop making matters worse with today's welfare system, a system that would be expensive and politically risky to reform. Second, government may now use the vocabulary of outputs but it is still addicted to dispensing financial inputs and defining the dispensing as progress. Third, the Democratic Party is in alliance with, and most politicians are in fear of, the National Education Association, the public education lobby that has a huge stake in inputs like the $700 million in 1995 budget authority for "Goals 2000."

One of the legislation's goals is to "increase parental involvement." One way to do that would be to make parents active shoppers for education, using school-choice programs. But confronted with an amendment that would have authorized a small ($30 million) demonstration project empowering poor children to choose among public and private schools—the NEA's nightmare—the Senate said no. Enacting the practical is politically impossible and promising the impossible is routine politics.

February 17, 1994

The Need for National Testing

Never has the nation been safer from foreign menaces, and never before has the nation been graduating students less well educated than those of the immediately preceding generation. These facts warrant this conclusion: Today the principal threat to America is America's public-education establishment.

It tenaciously opposes national testing of primary and secondary school students. As Chester Finn of Vanderbilt says in his indispensable new book, *We Must Take Charge*, the education establishment knows that testing would shatter the public's complacency and bring demands for accountability.

Sixty-three percent of those ages 18 to 24 cannot find France on an unlabeled map (fewer than half find New York); 60 percent of 11th-graders do not know why *The Federalist* papers were written; 94 percent of 11th-graders cannot compute simple interest; in tests comparing their math and science skills with those of five foreign countries and four Canadian provinces, American 13-year-olds finish last; New York Telephone finds that 115,000 of 117,000 applicants flunk its employment exam; 80 percent of applicants flunk Motorola's exam seeking levels of seventh-grade English and fifth-grade math. Every American employer knows it is possible—indeed, common—for high school graduates to be functionally illiterate.

National testing would be a lever for moving the entire world of education. Measurable standards for cognitive learning would shape curricula and teacher education, and would provide criteria for pay differentials among teachers, and for declaring the educational bankruptcy of some schools.

Some conservatives are afraid national tests would further institutionalize the political ideology of the education establishment. Testing might be an occasion for indoctrination through politicized questioning. Furthermore, say conservatives, any movement toward a more national curriculum would make possible continent-wide mistakes.

Momentum toward national testing, and all that it entails, was imparted by the 1989 "education summit" with the president and all 50 governors at the University of Virginia—Mr. Jefferson's university. Any permeation of education by national standards does involve another departure from Jeffersonian impulses, toward those of his rival, Hamilton, that apostle of centralization and national, rather than local, consciousness.

However, many conservatives, like most Americans, are alarmed enough to put aside their traditional preference for educational localism. National testing is necessary for acquiring information about educational results that can galvanize and guide reform. Anyway, localism makes less and less sense in a nation of increasing mobility among regions, a nation flunking—as a nation—the international test of competitiveness.

The parlous condition of public education was the foremost domestic concern voiced by voters in 1990 Election Day exit polls. More than 70 percent of Americans (the figure is higher among parents) support standardized national testing, including a national high school graduation exam, keyed to a national curriculum.

Conservatives' qualms about national tests should be assuaged by the ferocity of the education establishment's opposition to such tests. That establishment wants to preserve America's unwarranted sense of well-being that is based on lax or tendentious assessments of cognitive learning. Most Americans like the illusion of living in Lake Wobegon, where "all the children are above average."

It is no coincidence that the philosophy and interests of the education establishment coincide exactly. Testing is "judgmental" and hence jars the educators' warm, "caring," empathetic, "child-centered" therapeutic ethic that nurtures "self-esteem." This produces today's toxic mixture of low expectations and grade inflation.

Testing would make possible a result-oriented assessment of education, would end today's practice of gauging the quality of education by the amount of money spent on it. Testing is necessary for a system of accountability—clearly stated goals, accurate information about progress toward them and positive and negative consequences of the information.

Thus, Finn says, national testing is a first step toward transforming America from a culture of lassitude back into a culture of achievement:

> When it comes to consumer information about outcomes, the American education system has been engaged in a massive cover-up. If the Securities and Exchange Commission allowed publicly traded corporations to conceal this much data about their profits and losses, we'd have a crisis of investor confidence—and a lot of ruinous investments.

Finn notes that few people think doctors should autonomously set health policy. Everyone knows war is too important to be left to soldiers. It is time for "civilian" control of education, the largest item in every state's budget—a $230 million enterprise at the primary and secondary levels.

Education is second only, and not by much, to defense as the nation's most expensive common provision. National testing is a step toward facing this fact: The safer the world becomes militarily, the less prepared America is to prosper in it, because knowledge matters more as military prowess matters less.

June 2, 1991

Constitutional Law at the Kitty Kat Lounge

When the women who dance at the Kitty Kat Lounge in South Bend, Indiana, are dressing, so to speak, for work, putting on, as they would rather not, pasties and G-strings, their talk may well turn to constitutional law and to laments about the retirement of Justice Brennan.

His replacement, Justice Souter, voted with the majority that, had Brennan been there, would have been a minority last week. The Supreme Court ruled, 5–4, that the First Amendment protection of free "expression" is compatible with Indiana's law prohibiting total nudity in public places.

The four dissenters (Justice White writing, joined by Marshall, Blackmun and Stevens) agreed as to why they think Indiana's law is unconstitutional. The five justices in the majority had three different reasons for the opposite conclusion. Because First Amendment law is so encrusted with the barnacles of bad decisions, all nine justices missed the main point.

An Appeals Court held that the nude dancing done at the Kitty Kat is "inherently expressive," communicating an erotic message, so Indiana's law is forbidden by Madison's amendment. But Chief Justice Rehnquist, in a plurality opinion joined by O'Connor and Kennedy, said nude dancing in barrooms is only "marginally" within even "the outer perimeters of the First Amendment." This "expressive conduct," although performed only for consenting adults, conflicts with Indiana's legitimate interest in protecting "order and morality." Most states have such laws against people appearing nude among strangers in public.

Souter stressed not Indiana's right to promote morality but its right to combat evils—the secondary effects of "adult entertainment establishments," including prostitution and other crimes. The new justice indicated that he thinks the Constitution is friendly toward nudity in ballet or serious plays. Souter said that nudity is a condition, not an activity, and that Indiana is targeting the condition, not any expressive activity. He notes that one of the women challenging Indiana was, when this case began, starring in a pornographic movie showing near the Kitty Kat without interference from Indiana.

The Supreme Court has previously said there can be "some kernel of expression" in almost every activity, if only expression of the thought that the activity should be undertaken. But Indiana is proscribing nudity, the condition, not just an erotic "message." Rehnquist said, safely, that "the appearance of people of all shapes, sizes and ages in the nude at a beach" would hardly convey eroticism but would be illegal, which proves Indiana is not stomping on expressive activity. Anyway, pasties and G-strings make the dancers' message (the justices had a videotape) only "slightly less graphic."

However, Justice White scored a palpable hit when he said: How can Rehnquist say the law is designed to protect morality but that the activity the law bans expresses no morally relevant message?

Scalia's concurring opinion came closest to a satisfactory way of sustaining Indiana's law. He said the Rehnquist opinion erred in arguing that the First Amendment is even peripherally germane. Indiana's law is not like the unconstitutional law banning flag burning. That law prohibited particular conduct precisely because of its expressive attributes.

Indiana's law would be faulty if it targeted only expressive nudity. (Scalia here conceded that the dancing is expressive, and the "expression" implicates the First Amendment.) But, said Scalia, Indiana evenhandedly prohibits nude beaches, nude hot dog vendors, even a gathering of "60,000 fully consenting adults crowded into the Hoosierdome to display their genitals."

Although it is hard to imagine John Marshall or Oliver Wendell Holmes worrying about such stuff, the decision did implicitly make a serious point: Communities as well as individuals have rights. But is it necessary for the Court to be so convoluted and oblique in reaching that conclusion?

The Kitty Kat dancers' complaint against Indiana, and now against the Court, is impeccably Reaganite: It is the cry of small business against government regulation. The dancers are, or were when the litigation began, paid commissions on drinks sold while they dance, and some say they make more money dancing nude.

Does that mean their "expressive conduct" is commercial speech, meriting only modest First Amendment protection? The Court can grasp that nettle when next (such is the Court's itch for First Amendment fine-tuning, there will be another case) the Court defines constitutional dress for almost-nude dancers.

James Madison, who was the primary author of the First Amendment, would find the Kitty Kat amazing but not more so than the notion that the First Amendment is germane to what transpires there. It is evidently impossible to get today's Court to take seriously the fact that Madison purposely wrote an amendment that protects not "expression" but speech, the use of words, an activity indispensable for reasoning and persuasion, and hence for democratic government, which is the point of the Constitution and its amendments.

June 27, 1991

Splitting Split Hairs About "Establishment of Religion"

An Everest of paper already has been piled up in the unending litigation to fend off "establishment of religion" in America. Now the Supreme Court has ruled 5–4 that even nonsectarian invocations and benedictions at public school graduations are unconstitutional. This trashing of a traditional community rite—and right—is a result of judicial obtuseness and arrogance.

Two decades ago the Court, inebriated by its ingenuity, concocted a three-part test of "establishment." This test prohibits government action that has a religious purpose, or has the primary effect of advancing or inhibiting religion, or fosters excessive entanglement of government with religion.

The test was an incitement to litigation, and soon the Court, wielding its theological micrometer, was ruling that a Hanukkah menorah in Pittsburgh was constitutional because it was near a Christmas tree but a crèche down the street was unconstitutional because, unlike a court-approved Rhode Island crèche, it did not have enough secular stuff (reindeer, snowmen, Santa's houses) to dilute sufficiently the religious "purpose." Thus were courts forced to make judgments that, a disgusted judge said, are "more commonly associated with interior decorators than with the judiciary."

Hairs were split, then split again. The Court ruled that government could help finance maps for parochial schools but not books. A critic wondered: What about atlases—books of maps?

We all wondered: Could Establishment Clause law become sillier? It now has.

Now five justices (Kennedy writing, joined by Blackmun, Stevens, O'Connor and Souter) have added a fourth test of "establishment." They have ruled that a rabbi's prayers at a Rhode Island public junior high school's graduation constituted "psychological coercion." The prayers placed "subtle and indirect public and peer pressure" on unbelievers, who, when asked to stand or "maintain a respectful silence," face "the dilemma" of protesting or appearing to participate. The justices say that the possibility that peer pressure would "coerce" someone into doing something for appearances, and someone would falsely appear to be making a religious affirmation, makes the prayers an "establishment" of religion.

Cut more trees, make more paper, summon the lawyers, prepare to litigate such questions as:

Was there unconstitutional coercion in the Pledge of Allegiance that preceded the rabbi's invocation? The Pledge mentions God. Besides, coercion to political orthodoxy—"peer pressure" to recite the Pledge—is presumably just as unconstitutional as coercion to religious orthodoxy.

Justice Scalia raises that question in his scathing dissent, joined by Rehnquist, White and Thomas. Scalia notes that three years ago, Justice Kennedy wrote that the meaning of the Establishment Clause "is to be determined by reference to historical practices and understandings." Now Kennedy, who evidently lacks any intellectual compass, finds unconstitutional a tradition as old as public school graduation ceremonies. The Court, Scalia says, has invented "a boundless, and boundlessly manipulable, test of psychological coercion." The Court's new "psycho-coercion test" of "establishment" is "as infinitely expandable as the reasons for psychotherapy itself."

Consider this: Is there not suddenly unconstitutional "psychological coercion" toward political orthodoxy in the playing of the national anthem at sporting events? Is there not "public and peer pressure" to stand respectfully? See you in court.

The Court majority, inciting litigation, says it has not addressed the question of whether praying in civic ceremonies involves unconstitutional "psychological coercion" when "mature adults" are involved. The decision surely applies to high schools as well as junior highs. And as Scalia says, high school graduation is so significant precisely because it is regarded as entry into adulthood. He wonders: "Will we soon have a jurisprudence that distinguishes between mature and immature adults?" *The Washington Post*, approving the Court's ruling, says it protects "schoolchildren." "Children" who can vote? Come to think about it, maybe the decision does not apply to high schools. Let's litigate!

The framers of the Establishment Clause sought to proscribe the imposition of religious orthodoxy, or financial support for religious institutions, by force of law backed by threats of punishment. Now, however, out of the thin possibility that maintaining respectful silence during a moment of religious observation might seem to imply some religious affirmation, the Court has made peer-pressure "coercion" into "establishment" of religion.

By the brittle logic of this ruling, graduation prayers are still permissible if school administrators announce, perhaps in graduation programs, that no one is compelled to join in prayer, and no one will be assumed to be praying if they are polite while others are praying. To such niggling is society reduced by this Court's manic fine-tuning of our "rights."

Whose rights? A Rhode Island junior high graduate has successfully asserted her right to extinguish a traditional right of American communities to express reverence. Because something the community enjoyed annoyed this young woman, communities from coast to coast must abandon traditions. According to liberal theory—individual rights are everything, community rights nothing—we are more free because of this.

Liberals can take heart. The Court still has a majority of their kind of justices, people incapable of drawing reasonable distinctions, people arguing, with Orwellian logic, that they are reducing "coercion" by stamping out cherished traditions.

June 28, 1992

Religion's Subordinate Role in
Our Republic

The Supreme Court is not obligated to tutor Americans in their nation's premises. Still, last week Justice Scalia passed up an opportunity to make the most philosophically illuminating case for a Supreme Court ruling that underscores the subordinate place of religion in the American polity.

Two Oregon men, both Native Americans, were fired from their jobs and denied unemployment benefits because they ingested the hallucinogen peyote as a traditional sacrament of the Native American Church. Oregon law bans all use of peyote, which is made from cactus. The men argued that this violated the First Amendment ban on laws "prohibiting the free exercise" of religion.

Citing precedents running back to the 1879 Court ruling affirming the constitutionality of laws banning the Mormon practice of polygamy, Scalia wrote: "We have never held that an individual's religious beliefs excuse him from compliance with an otherwise valid law prohibiting conduct that the state is free to regulate."

Oh? In 1972, the Court held that a member of the Old Order Amish religion was exempt, on free-exercise grounds, from complying with Wisconsin law requiring parents to send their children to school until age 16. Scalia's argument that this 1972 ruling is compatible with the principle he now asserts is unconvincing.

However, Scalia, joined by Chief Justice Rehnquist and Justices White, Stevens and Kennedy (O'Connor concurred in the result but not the reasoning), is correct on this point: The Court has often held that the right of free exercise does not relieve a citizen of an obligation to comply with a "valid and neutral law of general application"—a law not aimed at the promotion or restriction of religious beliefs—"on the ground that the law proscribes (or prescribes) conduct that his religion prescribes (or proscribes)." Note the word "conduct."

In addition to the polygamy ruling, Scalia cites rulings upholding laws that require, in spite of religiously motivated objections, payment of taxes, compulsory vaccination and other conduct. Scalia says free-exercise protection is not violated if the burdening of religiously motivated conduct is an "incidental effect" of a valid law.

Justice Blackmun, joined in heated dissent by Justices Brennan and Marshall, charges, plausibly, that the Court has now overturned precedents pertaining to the Constitution's religion clauses. The Court has indeed often asserted an indissoluble link between some religious conduct and belief, and has required government to satisfy exacting tests about a "compelling interest" before allowing laws to interfere with religiously motivated conduct.

Scalia should have forthrightly said that the 1972 Old Order Amish decision was mistaken. He could have invoked the support of the patron saint of libertarians—Saint Thomas. No, not Thomas Aquinas—Thomas Jefferson. To understand the philosophic pedigree of Scalia's sensible position is to understand the cool realism and secularism of the philosophy that informed the Founders.

A central purpose of America's political arrangements is the subordination of religion to the political order, meaning the primacy of democracy. The Founders, like Locke before them, wished to tame and domesticate religious passions of the sort that convulsed Europe. They aimed to do so not by establishing religion, but by establishing a commercial republic—capitalism. They aimed to submerge people's turbulent energies in self-interested pursuit of material comforts.

Hence religion is to be perfectly free as long as it is perfectly private—mere belief—but it must bend to the political will (law) as regards conduct. Thus Jefferson held that "operations of the mind" are not subject to legal coercion, but that "acts of the body" are. Mere belief, said Jefferson, in one god or 20, neither picks one's pockets nor breaks one's legs.

Jefferson's distinction rests on Locke's principle (Jefferson considered Locke one of the three greatest men who ever lived) that religion can be useful or can be disruptive, but its truth cannot be established by reason. Hence Americans would not "establish" religion. Rather, by guaranteeing free exercise of religions, they would make religions private and subordinate.

Twenty-three states and federal law exempt the religious use of peyote from prohibitions, and Scalia indicated sympathy for that policy. However, he rightly insists it is not constitutionally obligatory.

If, he says, some religious conduct is thus disadvantaged, that is an "unavoidable consequence of democratic government." At least government as Locke justified it. And, says Scalia, it "must be preferred to a system in which each conscience is a law unto itself." Locke saw that danger in religiously riven Europe.

The Founders favored religious tolerance because religious pluralism meant civil peace—order. Thus Scalia is following the Founders when he finds the limits of constitutionally required tolerance of "free exercise" in the idea that a society is "courting anarchy" when it abandons the principle stated in the 1879 ruling: "Laws are made for the government of actions." If conduct arising from belief, not just belief itself, is exempt from regulation, that would permit "every citizen to become a law unto himself."

Scalia's position is not only sound conservatism, it is constitutionally correct: It is the intent of the Founders.

April 22, 1990

Orwell in New Jersey

The most important issue has been joined. A suit filed in New Jersey by the National Organization for Women, the state American Civil Liberties Union and others claims that mothers on welfare have a constitutional right to additional payments for however many children they choose to have, in or out of wedlock. The suit argues, in effect, that the state law denying welfare increases for babies born to women already on welfare violates the Constitution's "privacy" right because it intrudes upon "the most personal of decisions: whether or not to have children." Because the law attempts to "influence" family planning and reduce rates of conception and childbirth, it burdens the welfare mothers' "fundamental rights to make decisions about family composition, conception and childbirth without undue governmental intrusion."

The conclusion is Orwellian: If government withdraws from subsidizing illegitimacy, it is being intrusive. But the suit is right about one thing. The law does involve the state in stigmatizing behavior the state "disfavors." It is about time.

Stanley Crouch, a black journalist, wants black Americans to aspire to reestablishing the civility of their community circa 1955, when teenage pregnancy "was not acceptable behavior" and "those girls became pariahs. . . . They saw that they were the ones left holding the bag and if that meant they had to abstain from sex, they did." Among policymakers a lively debate has begun concerning measures that might help to restore the stigma that until recently attached to illegitimacy. This debate, and an illegitimacy rate expected to reach 80 percent among minorities by the end of the decade, define the context in which NOW, the ACLU and other liberal groups want to make subsidized illegitimacy a fundamental constitutional right. This, too, is the context:

"We just kept finding kids under blankets," said a police officer last month when 19 children of six mothers and 17 fathers were found living in a Chicago apartment surrounded by rat droppings and dog feces and sharing a bone and bowls with a dog. "This," said a welfare worker, "is what we see all the time." Said another, "It's not uncommon." The mothers had received about $54,000 in welfare cash payments and food stamps and about $20,000 from Medicaid in the preceding year. Three of the children had just been expelled from school because their immunizations were not up to date. In some states welfare mothers who fail to keep their children immunized get their benefits cut.

The New York Times reports that a check of 1,800 of Newark's welfare recipients found that 23 percent had been listed with the same names and Social Security numbers in Manhattan at some time between 1991 and 1993. Those 425 cheats have collected more than $1 million illegally since 1991. They were caught because they were carrying welfare identity cards for both states when they were arrested for cheating on the $1 train fare into Manhattan.

Charles M. Sennott of *The Boston Globe* has reported on the extended family of Eulalia Rivera, who in 1968 came from Puerto Rico to the Boston housing project where she still lives. She has had 17 children. One died, two others are in Puerto Rico. The other 14, ranging in age from their early 20s to 48, are all on welfare. Rivera, 65, has 74 grandchildren, "virtually all of whom have come of age in the welfare system and many of whom are beginning to apply for welfare themselves," Sennott reports. Rivera's 15 great-grandchildren are a fourth welfare generation. One of Rivera's daughters, Clarabel, was arrested after the scalding of one of her six children. When asked the whereabouts of the five fathers of those children, one of Clarabel's brothers (he says he is on welfare because of a "nervous condition") said, "Oh, wow, I have no idea." At the home of another Rivera son who is on welfare because of "bad nerves," Sennott says two of Rivera's grandchildren, ages 11 and 16, sat watching MTV at 1:30 P.M. on a school day.

The Rivera family of about 100 may be costing taxpayers from $750,000 to $1 million a year. One of Rivera's daughters, who does not work because of what she calls "anxiety attacks," gets $820 a month, plus Medicaid, plus a subsidized apartment. When Sennott asked her about taxpayers' anger, she said, "Just tell them to keep paying," and slammed down the phone.

The taxpayers won't. Last week Virginia's legislature passed a measure making welfare mothers ineligible for higher benefits when they have additional children. The measure also makes welfare contingent on work by recipients, and removes recipients from the welfare rolls after two years. Virginia's action came three days after the Maryland NAACP endorsed a proposal to deny additional aid to mothers who have additional children while on welfare. The state NAACP said the existing system "tends to shelter unwed mothers and absentee fathers from the consequences of their actions." A 1992 poll by the liberal Joint Center for Political and Economic Studies found that 58 percent of blacks thought government should not increase aid when unwed mothers have more children.

Concluding that Washington is incapable of properly reforming welfare for 5 million families in 50 "very diverse states," Senator Nancy Kassebaum, the Kansas Republican, proposes "a straight swap": Washington would give the states responsibility for welfare and would assume more or even all the states' Medicaid burdens. She says trends clearly suggest "we already have lost a large part of the present generation, and we will lose even more of the next," so welfare reform "is at least as important and urgent" as health care reform. By fixing responsibility for welfare at the state level "with no federal strings attached," Kassebaum's legislation would prompt the rest of the states to do what about half of them already are doing—experiment with reform. Suddenly the nation sees that its most important problem is the conjunction of illegitimacy and welfare dependency.

March 21, 1994

Those Silhouettes of Sprinting Families

ON INTERSTATE 5, NORTH OF SAN DIEGO—If you blink you may miss them. Don't blink. They are signs of the time.

They are large yellow signs of the sort that use black silhouettes—of falling rocks, leaping deer, playing children—to warn motorists. But the silhouettes on these signs are of a running family—a father, mother and small daughter. They represent illegal immigrants who risk, and sometimes lose, their lives, sprinting through the stream of speeding vehicles to evade a government checkpoint.

Here, where the surf rumbles a few hundred yards from the traffic's roar, where the Republic runs out of room and the horizon reminds Americans of Asian nations exporting economic challenges and challenging immigrants, here two of the nation's political preoccupations fuse: immigration and the North American Free Trade Agreement.

From the moment in the 18th century when national consciousness began emerging on the thinly settled eastern fringe of this continent, the animating question of American politics has been: What kind of people do we want to be? Uniquely blessed by the burden of choice—the French, for example, do not share our sense of perpetual becoming—we now face, with immigration and NAFTA, choices that will shape who we are.

In Sacramento and Washington, legislative hoppers are piled high with proposals, from national identity cards and increased border patrols to diminished entitlements for immigrants, to slow the flow of foreigners. Some are sound; almost all deserve debate and will get it, evidence that anxiety about immigration is now discussable, rather than dismissable as xenophobic primitivism. But all such proposals pale in significance when compared with NAFTA.

What impels immigrants to risk everything crossing the freeway—or the ocean it borders? The hope of betterment—in a word, jobs. Most immigrants would prefer to pursue a productive future at home. NAFTA will help potential immigrants to prosper at home—if NAFTA can be rescued from current irrationalities of American politics.

Pat Buchanan Republicans, a small but gingery group, oppose both immigration and NAFTA, an incoherence matched within the Democratic Party. Many Democrats are queasy about acknowledging the principal incentive for immigrants—the availability of entry-level jobs in America—because many black leaders blame the disorderly lives of the inner-city underclass on the supposed unavailability of such jobs. Furthermore, freer trade means, as freedom generally does, an uncertain future, and so is threatening to the timid, including some Democratic constituencies, such as organized labor.

Fear (Buchananites are timid nationalists—a phenomenon once considered a contradiction in terms) touches the immigration issue at every turn. Does immigration increase crime? Perhaps. But would denying, say, educational entitlements to the children of illegal immigrants serve domestic tranquility?

Because governments are objects of interests and conduits of passions, such as fear, much that governments do is mistaken. But most mistakes—spending here, taxing there—are correctable. However, if this moment for liberalized trade through NAFTA is missed, there will be a spate of surrenders by the government—in the name of "compassion"—to timid interests demanding protection. And if immigration law is changed in a manner that codifies fear and hostility, America's identity will be altered.

Protection, candidate Clinton said, is just a fancy word for giving up. Giving up, that is, the nation's characteristic stance of confidence about competition and a fast unfolding future. And if immigration reform takes the form of a fearful flinching from infusions of ambitious and industrious newcomers, America will have gone far toward redefining itself as whiny and embattled.

The idea that most immigrants are drawn here by welfare entitlements misses a huge and heartening truth. What was once called "the Protestant ethic"—faith manifested in social advancement through individual striving—is coming in quantity from Catholic countries to the south.

Richard Rodriguez, an American writer of Mexican parentage, says that Tijuana, comparable in size to its neighbor, San Diego, is, in a sense, more American than San Diego. He means that Tijuana is rawer, less middle-aged, more as America used to be in its youthful boisterousness.

But America is more than an economy, more than an arena for individual striving for material betterment. It also—it primarily—is a culture and a fabric of civic traditions. Singapore booms, but is not "American."

In the flood tide of 19th-century American confidence, Walt Whitman proclaimed that America was more than a nation, it was a world. The justifiable concern about today's immigration is that America may be becoming less than a nation, a community lacking a clear cultural definition, a mere geographic expression.

Still, remember the reality represented by the silhouettes on the yellow signs. There is something unseemly about an America that is frightened by families sprinting across the freeway to get to work. Such an America has much more to worry about than those families.

August 19, 1993

The Transformation of the Nation

LOS ANGELES—"Nativism," a noun denoting some nasty history, is now an epithet distorting debate about this nation's policy regarding immigration.

Nativism, meaning irrational and mean-spirited partiality toward native-born people and hostility toward immigrants, is as old as the Republic. Before the end of the 18th century German immigrants were stigmatized as an unassimilable ethnic group because of their language and religious ardor. Religious and racial prejudice greeted, among others, Irish immigrants on the East Coast and Chinese on the West Coast.

But xenophobia and greediness—the desire to slam shut the golden door—do not explain all or even most of today's opposition to current immigration policies, particularly here. America is, as *The Economist* says, "the only first-world country that shares a 2,000-mile border with the third world . . . dirt roads up against bright lights." And the most luring lights are those of Southern California.

In the 1980s about 9 million people immigrated to the United States legally, another 2 million illegally. Today one-third of all immigrants come to California, where the population, currently 31.5 million, rose by 570,000 last year and is expected to rise another 600,000 this year. Most of the growth is from immigration from Mexico, Central America and Asia, or from births to recent immigrants.

Concern about immigration is approaching monomania in this state where the recession has approached the depths of a depression. Here, as elsewhere, immigration is discussed first, and too much, as an economic issue.

The arguments about immigration—what kind of people should come, and in what quantities—is actually two arguments. One is economic, but the more important and interesting one is cultural.

The economic argument concerns immigration's costs. Is immigration economically injurious? Or do immigrants constitute a net addition to the nation's wealth—if not immediately and in every location, at least over time and to society generally?

Resolution of this argument requires complex calculations that quantify, among many other variables, the economic value of the infusion of entrepreneurial energy from those who travel across the Pacific in search of entry-level American jobs and find them. Such industrious immigrants may, or may not, have a depressing effect on some American wages; if so, that may, or may not, make American industry more suited to an increasingly competitive global economy.

Many immigrants, particularly very new ones, cost more in welfare, health and educational services than they pay in taxes. (All immigrants pay sales taxes; many pay income taxes.) However, their economic activity—earning and spending—makes them, I believe, substantial net contributors to national wealth. (In *Fortune* magazine, Jaclyn Fierman says that 25 percent of immigrants in the 1980s had college degrees.) But that positive economic fact does not settle the argument about the net effect of, and proper policy concerning, immigration.

The cultural argument about immigration begins with this fact: Immigration at the end of this century occurs in a social context different in two crucial ways from the context at the beginning of the century.

Today immigrants are received into a welfare culture that encourages an entitlement mentality. That mentality weakens the mainspring of individual striving for upward mobility. A generous welfare state such as the United States, and California especially, can lure migrants. To the extent that the welfare culture has such enervating effects, the argument for immigration as a source of social invigoration fails.

The second difference in the context of immigration, another difference that makes problematic the tradition of liberality regarding immigration, is the weakening of the ideal of assimilation. But it is unclear the extent to which immigrants themselves are hostile to or even ambivalent about assimilation.

The anti-assimilationist impulse may emanate primarily from those native-born intellectuals who believe America is a sick, racist, sexist, exploitative, oppressive, patriarchal, etc., society into which no self-respecting person would wish to assimilate. Furthermore, say some intellectuals, "diversity" is an inherent good—the more the better because it is good to weaken a sick community's sense of community. In addition, individual "authenticity" requires adherence to ethnic identity. And ethnicity should be the basis of a civic life built around group rights and entitlements. (Here is an immigration policy: For every 10 immigrants, deport an unhappy tenured professor.)

Such homegrown intellectual fruit can poison the debate about immigration, and perhaps can spoil immigrants. Debate should begin with this premise: America is not just an economy; it is more than an arena for wealth-creation. It is a culture. The high rate of immigration since 1960, combined with the high fertility rate of immigrants relative to that of native-born Americans, is producing rapid change in the nation's ethnic and cultural balance.

Peter Brimelow, a contributing editor of *National Review* and senior editor of *Forbes*, says: "The onus should not be on the critics of current policy to explain their motives. Instead, supporters of current policy must explain why they wish to transform the American nation as it had evolved by 1965."

True. And accusations of "nativism" are not explanations.

July 29, 1993

Forty Years of Aftershocks

Forty years on, the constitutional earthquake of May 17, 1954, is still causing aftershocks. The Supreme Court's school desegregation ruling in *Brown* v. *Board of Education* was sound social policy and the correct constitutional outcome. However, the reasoning by which the Court reached that outcome, combined with the moral prestige the ruling gave the Court, has produced an era of anticonstitutional judicial policy-making, and of racial discrimination by government.

The Court held that assigning white and black children to separate schools on the basis of race violates the 14th Amendment's guarantee of equal protection of the laws. Unfortunately, the Court's ruling was insufficiently radical.

The Court waxed sociological, citing such data as the preference of some black children for white dolls, which may have been related to school segregation. And the Court cited studies—studies more problematic than the Court assumed—concerning the effects of segregation on children's abilities to learn. By resting the ruling on theories of early childhood development, the Court's rationale limited the antidiscrimination principle of the ruling to primary and secondary education.

As Robert Bork has written, making the ruling contingent on sociological findings "cheapened a great moment in constitutional law." The proper rationale for the *Brown* outcome was simply that government should not use racial classifications in making decisions.

Had the Court said that plainly in 1954—had the justices been content to apply not sociology but the sweeping legal principle that racial classifications by government are inherently violative of equal protection—much subsequent Court-produced mischief might have been avoided. Instead, before a generation had passed the Court was ordering busing—the exclusion, on the basis of race, of children from neighborhood schools and the transportation of them to more distant schools.

The *Brown* decision led directly to the 1964 Civil Rights Act, in which Congress stipulated nondiscrimination for much of public life, proscribing discrimination by government and by individuals in employment and public accommodations. Or so Congress thought. Just four years later the Court was saying otherwise.

The 1964 act defined school "desegregation" as "the assignment of students to public schools . . . without regard to their race." But in 1968 the Court held that compliance with *Brown* involved more than ending segregation, which hitherto had been understood as the government-compelled separation of the races by the law. The Court said that when all-white or all-black schools—so-called "*de facto* segregation"—still existed, government-ordered racial discrimination was required.

The phrase "*de facto* segregation" is an Orwellian oxymoron. Segregation is *de jure*—by law—or it is not segregation. Nevertheless, soon there was forced busing, involving the assignment of children to schools on the basis of race. Busing became one of the most costly failures—costly in money, ill will, educational distortion and flight from public schools—in the history of American social policy.

The tragedy of racial policy since *Brown* is that the 1964 Civil Rights Act was twisted, against legislative intent, by people whose idealism made them serene in their cynicism. As Professor Lino Graglia of the

University of Texas Law School writes, the act was seized and turned inside out by bureaucrats and judges who considered ending racial discrimination by government and businesses too modest a goal. Instead, they wanted—still want—to produce, by decrees, proportional representation by race in many institutions and activities.

Racial discrimination is any action based on race. The 1964 act forbade discrimination in employment. Yet the Court has held that the spirit of the act requires what the letter of the act forbids—that employers often must take race into account for various "affirmative action" purposes. The Court also has held that Title VII of the act does not prohibit discrimination against whites.

In *Brown* the Court held that racial discrimination stigmatizes those who are discriminated against. Post-*Brown* decisions have proven that discrimination can stigmatize its intended beneficiaries. Graglia notes that racial preferences presuppose—and teach—that this is a racist nation, that blacks cannot compete on merit, and that self-discipline, industriousness and responsibility are less important for blacks than establishing claims of victimization. This, says Graglia, is a prescription for black self-destruction and a cycle of racial hostility.

The rightness of *Brown* as social policy established in many minds the principle that it is not merely permissible for judges to make social policy, but that policy made by judges is inherently superior, morally, to policy made by elected representatives of the people. The resulting four decades of judicial activism have weakened the ethic of self-government—elected representatives exercising responsibility. But as Graglia says, morality often is a casualty of moral crusades.

May 15, 1994

The Racial Spoils System

Two recent events illustrate two axioms: Almost nothing is as important as almost everything in Washington is made to appear. And the importance of a Washington event is apt to be inversely proportional to the attention it receives.

Last week, while overwrought politicians and echoing media were deconstructing the President's maunderings about "tax revenue increases," little notice was given to another event, one of the most retrograde Supreme Court rulings ever.

The Court bestowed, prospectively, its constitutional imprimatur on virtually any racial spoils system Congress enacts. The Court effectively overturned a series of precedents that had at least limited the proliferation of what are euphemistically called "race-conscious" policies.

The Court, launching a large innovation with a slender majority, ruled 5–4 that henceforth Congress may assign special benefits to particular government-preferred minorities (to the detriment of all who do not make the "preferred" list) and Congress may do so (herewith the large innovation) without regard to any injury resulting from discrimination. Reverse discrimination is now cut loose from the pretense that it is merely a remedial measure.

During the Carter administration, the Federal Communications Commission, serving that administration's political strategy of courting the Democratic Party's most loyal constituencies, adopted reverse discrimination ("minority preference" is the preferred euphemism) policies. These gave certain minorities advantages in acquiring lucrative broadcast licenses. Later Congress mandated this.

Some injured people argued that this violated the constitutional guarantee of equal protection of the laws. Now the Court has baldly asserted, without enough real reasoning to qualify even as sophistry, this: Equal protection is not violated if the injury done by reverse discrimination serves "an important governmental objective."

If the Court adheres to this radical new principle, Congress will have a virtually illimitable right to allocate wealth and opportunity on the basis of skin pigmentation.

Hitherto, reverse discrimination has been regarded as constitutionally problematic and permissible only when narrowly tailored as a necessary remedy for past or present discrimination. Now Justice Brennan, joined by White, Marshall, Blackmun and Stevens, has held that the FCC's reverse discrimination is justified by the comparatively trivial objective of promoting broadcasting "diversity."

Never mind the patently meretricious, not to mention racist, assumption that minority ownership necessarily results in particular broadcasting content. And never mind the violence done to the First Amendment by the notion that Congress has the right to legislate what it considers the "correct" content of broadcasting—a politically stipulated mix of ideas. Justice O'Connor, joined in dissent by Rehnquist, Scalia and Kennedy, stresses the main point: This ruling is another, and huge, retreat from the Constitution's core principle, that rights inhere in individuals, not groups.

Where will the Court's vast new tolerance of racial preferences lead? No one knows—other than to an avalanche of litigation about racial classifications to promote any goal that Congress calls "important." All that shall be needed to ratify race-based government is for the Court to certify, as in this case, that the reverse discrimination is "benign."

What, you ask, are the Court's constitutional criteria of "benign"? "Constitutional"? Are you kidding? The five black-robed legislators casually overturned a line of precedents requiring strict scrutiny of racial classifications. Those precedents said racial classifications could not pass constitutional muster unless Congress tailored them narrowly for strictly remedial purposes.

Now these justices must continue to legislate their political whims, bestowing or withholding the label "benign" as the spirit moves them. They must be capricious because there can be no constitutional principle that identifies "benign" disregard of equal protection.

Thirty-six years ago, the Court declared school segregation unconstitutional because segregation stamped blacks with a "badge of inferiority." Today the Court, and the Congress whose promiscuous use of racial preferences the Court now permits, is deepening that stigma. Under "benign" reverse discrimination, blacks, particularly, are identified as permanent wards of paternalistic government, a race regarded as a perpetual child afflicted by so many pathologies that constitutional guarantees and core American values must be violated for therapeutic reasons.

The Court is now so unprincipled, and the political temptation for Congress to legislate racial spoils systems is so strong, that a strong remedy is required. Instead of amending the Constitution to protect the flag, which does not need such protection, we need an amendment to protect—to restore, really—equal protection of the laws.

The Constitution needs this 27th Amendment: "Neither Congress nor the states may classify persons on the basis of race, sex or ethnicity for the purpose of preferential treatment."

July 5, 1990

Districting by Pigmentation

North Carolina's 12th Congressional District straggles 141 miles down Interstate 85 and for most of its length is no wider than the highway. Says a state legislator, "If you drove down the interstate with both car doors open, you'd kill most of the people in the district."

The district was drawn to sweep together enough blacks to guarantee a black member of Congress if all the blacks (a slender 53 percent majority) do as the government obviously thinks they should—vote as a herd. The state drew the district under duress from Bush's Justice Department, which thought it was applying the Voting Rights Act. It is read to require the creation of many "majority minority" districts, the boundaries of which veer hither and yon, gathering in blacks or Hispanics.

Twenty percent of North Carolina voters are black. When redistricting after the 1990 census, North Carolina created one "safe" black district. Not enough, said Washington. Hence the 12th District.

Now the Supreme Court has ruled, 5–4, that the 12th District may amount to unconstitutional racial gerrymandering. Why? Perhaps whites are denied the "equal protection" right to "race-neutral" electoral processes? But the Court has never affirmed any such right, and hardly can without finding the VRA unconstitutional. Justice O'Connor's opinion (joined by Rehnquist, Scalia, Kennedy and Thomas) contains political maxims more convincing than its constitutional reasoning. It is less an argument than an esthetic recoil from a political act—District 12. O'Connor's opinion sows confusion about what is permitted, or required, by the VRA in the way of racial gerrymandering.

"It is unsettling," says O'Connor, "how closely the North Carolina plan resembles the most egregious racial gerrymanders of the past." Such as Mississippi's "shoestring" district during Reconstruction, which swept enough blacks into one narrow district along the river to leave five other districts with white majorities. Or such as Alabama's redrawing of the city borders of Tuskegee in the 1950s to turn a square city into a 28-sided entity excluding many black voters from the city. However, O'Connor feeling "unsettled" does not constitute a constitutional argument. What should unsettle her, and us, is the many "race-conscious" government actions that have brought us to monstrosities like North Carolina's 12th.

O'Connor says the bizarre shape of the 12th is "unexplainable on grounds other than race" and "reapportionment is one area in which appearances do matter." Actually, the 12th District appears compatible with the VRA, as currently construed (or misconstrued), and not incompatible with any constitutional principle of government action that the five justices affirm. They do not affirm the principle that government actions must be colorblind.

Courts have construed the VRA to mean that for blacks and Hispanics the right to vote implies some sort of right to a certain level of desired results: The Act effectively entitles blacks and Hispanics to a certain percentage of Congressional seats.

O'Connor cites former Justice Brennan's warning that "even in the pursuit of remedial objectives, an explicit policy of assignment by race may serve to stimulate our society's latent race consciousness, suggesting the utility and propriety of basing decisions on a factor that ideally bears no relationship to an individual's worth or needs." But for two decades the government, responding to the civil rights industry's lobbying for a racial spoils system (always called "remedial"), has made race consciousness not latent but conspicuous in policymaking. And the VRA obviously assumes the "utility and propriety" of basing voting decisions on skin pigmentation.

O'Connor says that a Congressional district that is obviously created solely to effectuate the perceived common interest of one racial group "reinforces the perception that members of the same racial group—regardless of their age, education, economic status, or the community in which they live—think alike, share the same political interests, and will prefer the same candidates at the polls." But the VRA promotes that "perception" as a normative rule. The five justices do not say that an act promoting that perception is unconstitutional. They say only that when redistricting is obviously driven by racial calculations, there must be the "compelling" justification of remedying past discrimination.

The Act implicitly affirms the doctrine of "categorical representation," which holds that the interests of a particular racial, ethnic or sexual group can only be understood, sympathized with, articulated and advanced by members of those groups. This doctrine threatens the core tenet of the nation's public philosophy—the principle that rights inhere in individuals, not groups. That leads to this Balkanizing proposition: Group thinking is natural and admirable.

The Court majority offers the muddy suggestion that racial gerrymandering will pass muster if the resulting districts are not too aggressively indifferent to "compactness, contiguousness, geographical boundaries or political subdivisions." Those are nice attributes of districts but are neither mandated by the Constitution nor respected by the VRA. American politics and law will continue to be disfigured by stains like the 12th District as long as we pursue the chimeric "justice" that is produced by "race-conscious remedies" for race-conscious injustices in the past.

The five justices' sensible political philosophy makes them squeamish about the VRA's promotion of particular racial results. But until the justices are prepared to find the VRA, as currently construed, unconstitutional, they, and we, will be troubled.

July 12, 1993

Sympathy for Lani Guinier

Lani Guinier deserves some sympathy. She is an academic and a liberal Democratic activist, so she probably cannot understand what the fuss was about. She probably rarely associates with people who think her ideas are strange. (After McGovern lost 49 states in 1972, a member of Manhattan's liberal literati exclaimed in bewilderment, "But everyone I know voted for him!") Many of Guinier's ideas are extreme, undemocratic and anticonstitutional. But they also are reflections or extensions of tendencies in today's academic thinking and public policy.

She believes majority rule is inherently problematic in America's incurably racist society. She favors federal imposition on state and local governments of rules that would generate results pleasing to groups she prefers. She says existing civil rights laws demand "a results-oriented inquiry, in which roughly equal outcomes, not merely an apparently fair process, are the goals." Any process is unfair if the outcomes it produces frequently disappoint Guinier's favored groups. She says "each group has a right to have its interests satisfied a fair proportion of the time." Each group, that is, among those groups that Guinier believes merit preference. She will decide what is a "fair" proportion. Her radical proposals include weighted voting, racial vetoes of majority actions and other measures to abridge or block majority rule.

Anyone shocked by Guinier's ideas has not been paying attention to developments in the culture and in public policy. We already have moved a long way toward Guinier's goal of a nation of grievance groups exploiting the coveted status as "victims" (of America's wickedness) to claim special rights and entitlements.

Guinier, believing results more important than rules, would dilute democracy in order to promote "progressive" social outcomes. Judicial activists have been lionized for doing just that. (Impatient with democratic debate about abortion policy? Get a court to discover a new "right.") Guinier believes blacks should have special rights. Well, where she works, they do. She teaches at the University of Pennsylvania, where some blacks angry about a conservative columnist destroyed virtually an entire press run of the newspaper, without any punishment.

She says that blacks who are not elected primarily by black votes are not "authentic" black leaders. "Authentic" blacks have deep roots in "the community." (Guinier, a graduate of Harvard and Yale Law, is a wealthy tenured Ivy League professor; and she is an arbitrator of black "authenticity." She suggests that a black Republican can be only "descriptively black.") She says "authentic" blacks have a "cultural and psychological view of group solidarity." But many of liberalism's advanced thinkers embrace the idea that groups are homogeneous and that groupthink is natural and good. Affirmative action policies often are justified as ways of including "minority perspectives," as though racial and ethnic groups have (or "authentic" members of these minorities have) uniform "perspectives." Such tribalism is premodern and morally retrograde but it is all the rage where Guinier comes from: academia.

An implication of her writings is that only blacks can properly represent blacks. That is the theory of "categorical representation," which holds that the interests of particular groups can be understood and articulated only by members of those groups. This idea was codified years ago in the Democratic Party's quota system for convention delegates. *The New Republic*, calling for withdrawal of the Guinier nomination, denounced her "reductionist identity politics," the premise of which is that identities, and rights, derive from group membership. But that is the idea that has produced racial "set-asides," hiring quotas and other "race-conscious remedies," including the "race norming" of test scores to prevent "disparate impacts" of employment tests. (Under race norming, scores are segmented by racial groups and an individual's scores are reported not in relation to all those taking the test, but only in relation to others in the individual's racial group. Race norming was outlawed in 1991 but the Clinton administration is promoting policies very similar.)

People like Guinier, who affix the label "civil rights" to every bit of their political agendas, have made it an empty phrase—a classification that no longer classifies. This, too, is a consequence of a "progressive" idea—"critical race theory," which is fashionable in many law schools. It holds that America is so saturated with racism that any social problem is a civil rights problem. Guinier believes the Voting Rights Act is violated by any legislative body where measures favored by certain government-approved minorities are often defeated. She purports to believe that under the Voting Rights Act as amended in 1982, such a pattern of defeats is itself proof of illegal "prejudice" that makes mandatory her "remedial" overthrow of the rules of American democracy. But it is impossible not to detect cynicism: How can she square what she (and she virtually alone) says Congress did, in 1982, with her dogma that white-majority legislatures cannot rise above America's pandemic hostility to blacks?

Speaking of cynicism, Ralph Neas, the "civil rights activist" who ran the campaign of lies and scurrilities against Robert Bork, argued on

Guinier's behalf that senators should defer to a president's personnel choices. But Neas was a leader of the successful campaign for rejection of William Lucas, Reagan's choice for the position Guinier sought, because Lucas was a particularly objectionable phenomenon—a black conservative. Still, presidents generally should get the people they want. Guinier was an exception to that rule because she aggressively misconstrues the laws she would have been responsible for enforcing.

At the end of this debacle Clinton's attorney general was still describing Guinier's nomination as "superb," Clinton was claiming that he had just that day discovered what his friend of 20 years thinks and the usual groups (the Congressional Black Caucus, feminists, etc.) were making the usual claim that Guinier is a "victim." Just another day in the "reinvention of government" by a "New Democrat." What next? Next, this lot will "fix" the economy and "reform" the health care system. Hang on.

June 14, 1993

The Military Meritocracy

In many old World War II movies an officer named Winthrop (or some such white-bread WASPy name) tells a sergeant (O'Reilly, like a cop) to get volunteers for a dangerous mission. Forward steps an ethnic salad: Kowalski, Bloomberg, Positano, Sanchez, Graff. But no blacks.

Bigotry in the war had one benefit for its victims: fewer casualties. Nearly 75 percent of blacks in service were in the Army, which by September 1944 was 8.7 percent black. Several black units saw heavy fighting. The famous 92nd Division suffered more than 3,000 casualties in Europe and received more than 12,000 decorations and citations. But most blacks were in combat support (engineers, transportation, quartermasters). Only 2.8 percent of the combat arms (infantry, artillery, cavalry, armor) were blacks.

Today the services are, to hear some critics tell it, too integrated. Blacks are a larger portion of the services than of the population, and a larger portion of enlisted personnel than of officers. Blacks are about 12 percent of the population, 20 percent of the services (33 percent of the Army, 20 of the Marines, 15 of the Navy and Air Force) and only about 7 percent of officers. Many who complain about the low number of black officers are the same people who, by stigmatizing American society, and not least the military, have discouraged blacks from making the sort of military careers that lead to commissions.

An ancillary benefit of today's war may be the further discrediting of anachronistic and blinkered black leadership. Many leaders—Jesse Jackson, Benjamin Hooks and the like—seem to believe that black power depends on portraying blacks as victims of an unrelievedly racist society. This idea has led America waist-deep into the quagmire of counting by race in order to engineer "correct" balances here, there and everywhere.

Some black leaders and their white allies have a political interest in regarding blacks, and getting blacks to regard themselves, as victims who must be wards of government, and of politicians mediating the distribution of benefits. The rickety structure of affirmative action, quotas and the rest of the racial spoils system depends on victimology— winning for certain groups the lucrative status of victim.

Understandably, the focus of blacks in Congress is on domestic policy. Only two of 55 members of the House Armed Services Committee are black and only two of 46 members of the Foreign Affairs Committee. But much of the domestic rhetoric and policy directed at blacks presupposes, and by presupposing teaches, dependency. Today's inspiriting pictures of blacks making prominent contributions to the competence of the military are, I suspect, disagreeable to those who espouse victimology.

Every black in uniform is a volunteer, which complicates the portrayal of them as victims. But Hooks, head of the NAACP, and others like him say blacks volunteer "because this nation can't provide them jobs." Never mind that military service is a dignified job. The innuendo is that blacks are impelled not at all by the spur of patriotism but only by the lash of necessity. An implication is that most blacks in the services come from the underclass.

Actually, whereas white volunteers are on average poorer and less educated than whites generally, most black volunteers have at least a high school diploma and come from working- and middle-class families. Getting into today's military—the highest caliber in American history—is harder than graduating from many high schools. Indeed, 95 percent of all Army personnel have high school diplomas, compared with 76.5 percent of the population.

Controversy about the alleged "overrepresentation" of blacks in the military comes hard on the heels of the successes of the movie *Glory* and the PBS series on the Civil War. About 188,000 Union warriors— twice as many men as Lee had at Gettysburg—were black. The 166 black regiments were more than 8 percent of the Union forces. Blacks had something to prove. A Confederate general said: "You cannot make soldiers of slaves. . . . And if slaves seem good soldiers, then our whole theory of slavery is wrong." Most black soldiers had been slaves until a few months, even days, before enlisting. Frederick Douglass said: "Once let the black man get . . . a musket on his shoulder and bullets in his pocket, and there is no power on earth which can deny that he has earned the right to citizenship."

In 1991 the only things blacks have to earn or prove in the military are what whites have to earn or prove. They are earning their pay and proving their worth—and patriotism—as individual professionals. Enough, already, of the groupthink of people who see everything through the distorting lens of race. That monomania is a civilian luxury. Military men and women are too busy making the military a model for interracial harmony, not perfect but worthy of emulation by civilians.

Just a few decades ago blacks joked that baseball was the only field in which a black man could wave a wooden club at a white man and not start a riot. Today's military is a place where blacks regularly tell a large number of whites what to do. One of the telling facets of military life is so familiar it is never thought about: uniforms. Individuality is not extinguished but people are fitted to functions. It was, after all, a soldier (Napoleon) who characterized the good society as one of "careers open to talents."

Just last year, when it seemed that peace was busting out all over faster than you could say "peace dividend," there were those who worried that the shrinking of the military would victimize blacks by shutting off careers open to their talents—careers that teach talents, too. Why is there a black chairman of the Joint Chiefs of Staff before there has been a black chairman of GE, GM, IBM or any of the other Fortune 500 corporations (all of which are pygmies compared to what Colin Powell chairs)? There are many reasons but one may be that today's military is a more severe meritocracy than most corporations.

Military life aspires to resemble professional sports in one particular—concentration on performance. At the tip-off of next weekend's NBA All-Star game there will be at least eight blacks on the court. Too many? That is a dumb question to those who understand basketball and an ugly question to those who understand America.

February 11, 1991

The New Sovereignty

Bill Clinton, his annoyance building like steam in a boiler, barely hung on to the remnants of his sangfroid. There he was, struggling to produce an administration with as many racial, sexual and ethnic flavors as bouillabaisse has ingredients. Yet he was being hectored by a monstrous regiment of women claiming he was perpetuating patriarchy, or worse (if there can be anything worse).

"Bean counters," he called the women complaining about the number of men he was picking, and he accused them of "playing quota games and math games." How tiresome of them. But how like Democrats.

Patricia Ireland of the National Organization for Women rightly says, "Expectations were set by him in the first place." He did, after all, say his administration would "look like America," thereby advertising his intention to pick fewer white males. This was an invitation to various groups to start counting beans and being ostentatiously unhappy.

Now Representative Pat Schroeder (D-Colo.) says, "His Cabinet will look like America, with men at the top. That isn't what we thought he meant." He meant: Watch my virtuoso math game. He asked for the trouble he now has.

"And if that fails, track down an Eskimo," was *The New Republic*'s tart comment on this remarkable (because nowadays it strikes so many advanced thinkers as unremarkable) sentence in a *New York Times* report on Patricia Wald asking not to be considered as attorney general: "It was unclear if Judge Wald's decision to remove her name from the list would cause Mr. Clinton to broaden the search beyond the remaining women to include some black men." *The New Republic*, noting the insult to the groups for whom this or that Cabinet appointment seems to be reserved, says this "is the old Democratic Party speaking, not the new."

Not so. The newest passion among the party's tone-setting "progressives" is for "diversity" and "multiculturalism"; for "race-specific remedies" to "discriminatory" policies that have "disparate impacts" on certain government-favored groups; for curing society's "heavily gendered" nature, and so on and on.

In 1965 President Johnson said, "We seek . . . not just equality as a right and a theory but equality as a fact and equality as a result." By the late 1960s the pursuit of equal social outcomes had the Democratic Party Balkanizing itself and eager to do likewise to the nation. The process was driven by a doctrine called "categorical representation," according to which the interests of particular groups can be properly represented only by members of that group.

With a mixture of moral posturing and elbow throwing, Democrats championed group entitlements in many places, from the delegations to their conventions, to hiring policies in the public and private sectors. But now Clinton is no longer enjoying the "politics of identity" as practiced by grievance groups exercising what Shelby Steele calls "the new sovereignty."

Sovereignty, says Steele, is increasingly bestowed by government on other institutions, on little nations within the nation—on groups organized around unassuageable grievances. On campuses, for example, such groups (blacks, women, Hispanics, Native Americans, Asians, gays, lesbians) often assert sovereignty through physical separateness in their own "studies" departments, ethnic dorms and lounges and campus centers, preferential admission and fiscal aid policies and faculty hiring quotas. The utterly predictable result is an increase of racial, ethnic and sexual divisiveness.

Sovereign fiefdoms, says Steele, have become "ends in themselves," providing careers for a "grievance-group executive class." But such careers, on campuses and in organizations jostling for government preferment, can provide careers only if the grievances are permanent. There are, Steele notes, three keys to permanency.

First, grievances must be inherent in membership in the group. It must be postulated that to be black, female, Hispanic, gay, lesbian, etc., is necessarily to be threatened, victimized and separated from the rest of America. Second, the group must make the absence of sovereignty—an insufficiency of extra-constitutional group rights—itself a grievance.

Third, the group must arrange its priorities to maximize what Steele calls its "grievance profile." For example, the NAACP makes the divisive issue of affirmative action a high priority, although that policy has little to do with the advancement of blacks and next to nothing to do with combating the problems that most threaten blacks—crime, teenage pregnancy, family disintegration. Similarly, working-class women do not write NOW's agenda.

Politicians are comfortable dealing with what Steele calls "a legalistic grievance industry" because that industry speaks the language of power and of middle-class agendas. It is, says Steele, easier to enact entitlements for, say, Hispanic college students, than it is to improve kindergartens in East Los Angeles.

Furthermore, power negotiations can be semi-secret. Quotas, set-asides and other aspects of the racial-sexual-ethnic spoils system are rarely debated in Congress or campaigns. Rather, they emerge from executive orders and agency regulations without much public scrutiny.

But as Clinton cobbles together his administration, the spotlight has illuminated the women's branch of the grievance industry playing "the quota games and math games" that the Democratic intelligentsia enjoys and that Clinton was playing when, allowing considerations of "diversity" to crowd considerations of competence, he promised, in easily decipherable code words, an administration that would "look like America."

December 27, 1992

Drive American, If You Can

Hilda Gage, a judge in Pontiac, Michigan, was moved, she says, "by a sense of patriotism and a concern for the economy," when she recently sentenced a chronic speeder, who is an automobile test driver, to drive only American cars.

Well. Can he drive a 1992 Ford Crown Victoria? It is assembled in Canada with parts from America, Japan, Mexico, Britain, Spain and Germany. Can he drive a Chevrolet Geo Metro, which is made by Suzuki and Isuzu?

Pity the poor Michigander who must enforce the rule banishing foreign cars to the back of the parking lot at one automobile plant. Where does he send a Mercury Grand Marquis, which has the same polyglot pedigree as the Crown Victoria? Where does he send a Mazda Navajo? Aside from the nameplate, it is a Ford Explorer, made by Ford in Kentucky. Let's consider Jaguars (Ford owns the company) and Saabs (GM owns 50 percent) fit only for traitors, but Toyota Corollas are made by a GM-Toyota joint venture in California. Can they park up front?

You can't tell the traitors without a scorecard, or even with one. Ford Festivas are Korean-made and Mercury Tracers are made in Mexico. Some GM cars have more Japanese components than some Japanese cars do. So what distinctions are made by the St. Louis barber who gives customers a $1 discount if they arrive in American cars? Or the Edwardsville, Illinois, gas station owner who gives a 2¢-a-gallon discount to drivers of American cars?

Toyota has sought the protection of the coach of Da Bears, Mike Ditka. (He is a product of Polish exports to America.) He has made a television ad saying, approximately, lay off the Japanese or I'll break your knees. Eight Japanese automobile companies have spent $9 billion building U.S. plants that employ 30,000 Americans and sustain several times that many jobs among suppliers. Small wonder that several states have given huge subsidies to lure such plants.

In an age when a Ford Probe is a Mazda MX-6 and a Mitsubishi Eclipse is a Plymouth Laser, what's a real patriot to do? Have a beer—domestic, please—and watch a little TV on a patriotic Zenith. Trouble is, it's made in Mexico, whereas Mitsubishi is made in Santa Ana, California, by more than 600 of the 58,000 Americans employed in manufacturing by Japanese firms in Southern California.

Forty percent of all Japanese-brand vehicles sold in America are made in America. But a tire dealer in Fremont, Ohio, won't sell tires to owners of foreign cars. That'll teach 'em.

Teach who? Teach what? Shut up and salute the flag, even it is being waved by some people whose interests are more pecuniary than patriotic.

The Congressional Automotive Caucus, composed of members from auto-producing states, has a bill to give a tax credit of up to $2,000, equal to 15 percent of the price, to buyers of American cars. This subsidy—hey, what is $10 billion among friends?—is not pleasing to U.S. car dealers, 90 percent of whom sell some foreign vehicles. The dealers are talking about—for purely patriotic reasons, of course—a tax credit to anyone trading in a car eight years old or older. (There are 74 million of them.)

But what about dirt excavators? Greece, New York, recently contemplated paying more for a John Deere than for a Japanese brand. Trouble is, the latter was made in America and the former in Japan. Time was when things were simpler.

Nonimportation is nothing new. In response to the Stamp Act (1765) and the Townshend Acts (1767) the colonists discouraged—by persuasion if possible; by publicity and ostracism if necessary; sometimes by mobs—importation of British goods.

Granted, some people were more interested in capturing markets than in defending political principles. But the striking contrast between then and now is the emphasis *back then* on elevated values.

Nonimportation was linked to moral revival, to a turning away from luxury, extravagance and dissipation and toward thrift and industry, all in the interest of liberty. Sewing bees, the wearing of homespun cloth, and avoidance of imported teas and wines were ways of linking nonimportation to virtues, and of linking Americans' virtues with America's strength and freedom.

Robert Middlekauff, in his history of the American Revolution (*The*

Glorious Cause, a volume in the *Oxford History of the United States*), emphasized that economic measures such as nonimportation were broadly viewed as means to higher ends. With nonimportation, Americans were summoned to values higher than mere commercial advantage. They were called upon "to consider what sort of people they were."

In light of today's exploitation of anti-Japanese passions, what kind of people are we?

February 9, 1992

Are We "A Nation of Cowards"?

Jeffrey Snyder's timing is either perfect or perfectly awful. Just as there seems to be a coalescing consensus that the keys to controlling violent crime are more police and fewer guns, along comes Snyder to trouble the conscience of anyone who thinks so. In his essay "A Nation of Cowards" in *The Public Interest* quarterly, he argues, with a potent blend of philosophy and fact, as follows:

> Crime is rampant because the law-abiding, each of us, condone it, excuse it, permit it, submit to it. We permit and encourage it because we do not fight back, immediately, then and there, where it happens. . . . The defect is there, in our character. We are a nation of cowards and shirkers.

Strong words, those, but not stronger than his argument, the gravamen of which is that the crime problem cannot be addressed without confronting the moral responsibility of the intended victim. Taking responsibility for one's life, family and community requires fighting back when threatened with violence. How? By possessing and mastering the means of resistance. He means an "equalizer"—a handgun. A responsible citizen, he says, "will be trained in the use of his weapon, and will defend himself when faced with lethal violence."

Before examining his argument for an armed citizenry, consider the freshest evidence of the nation's quickened concern about crime.

On Election Day voters in liberal Washington State gave emphatic (76 percent) approval to the "three strikes and you're out" initiative which mandates life imprisonment without parole for people convicted of three major felonies. California, although taxaphobic, nevertheless voted to make permanent an existing tax to provide $1.5 billion for public safety—more police and firemen. (Arson has made fire a facet of California's anxiety about crime.) Fiscally conservative Texas endorsed a $1 billion bond issue to build more prisons and mental health facilities.

The day after the elections the House of Representatives, with a familiar mixture of posturing and false advertising, passed yet another crime bill, this one purporting to subsidize the hiring of 50,000 police officers. It probably would fund fewer. The Senate promptly pumped up the money. For 40 years Congress has passed a crime bill in every two-year session, except the last one. The criminal class has not been impressed.

The day after the elections the President held a ceremony to push the bill that would require a five-day waiting period for the purchase of a gun. The attention given to this "Brady bill" seems disproportionate, given that 93 percent of the guns obtained by violent criminals are not obtained through lawful transactions that are the focus of most gun-control legislation.

More interesting, the day after the elections Senator Pat Moynihan proposed whopping tax increases on various kinds of handgun ammunition. He even favors a 10,000 percent tax on the Winchester 9mm hollow-tipped Black Talon cartridge. ("Penetrates soft tissue like a throwing star—very nasty," boasts an advertisement.) That tax would make 20 cartridges cost about $1,500. In large portions of Moynihan's New York City people are slain by stray—that's right, stray—bullets. Moynihan says: Guns do not kill people, bullets do. We have a 200-year supply of guns and a four-year supply of ammunition, so concentrate on the latter.

Snyder, an attorney in Washington, where the mayor begs for military help against crime, demurs, comprehensively. America, he says, is wrongly called an "armed society." He thinks we would be better off if it were. Most of the guns owned by law-abiding citizens are kept at home, but 87 percent of violent crimes occur outside the home. The constantly armed portion of the community consists primarily of the police and violent criminals. Multiplying the former cannot make us safe from the latter.

It is, says Snyder, foolish and craven to expect police to perform as personal bodyguards. The existence of police does not relieve individuals of all responsibility for self-protection. That judgment has both prudential and moral dimensions. Gun owners like to say, "Call for a cop, call for an ambulance and call for a pizza. See who shows up first." The Department of Justice reports that in 1991, for all crimes of violence, only 28 percent of calls to the police were responded to within five minutes. And it is now more likely that an American will be injured by violent crime than that he will be injured in an auto accident.

Feminists, says Snyder, rightly insist that rape is not about sex but about domination. What is at issue in crime is not just property but dignity. Crime, he says, always violates the victim's dignity, which can hardly be said to exist if the victim does not deem it worth fighting for. Crime is "an act of enslavement" and a personal readiness to resist it should be regarded as a prerequisite of self-respect, properly understood. He notes that "self-respect," which implies standards by which one judges oneself, has been supplanted in public discourse by the locution "self-esteem," which simply means having warm feelings about oneself. Repeating the shibboleths of the gun-control movement makes many people feel good about themselves. Snyder's argument should disturb their peace.

Much gun-control advocacy is directed against normal citizens, who are depicted as at best benighted and at worst barbaric. Gun owners are routinely characterized as uneducated, intolerant, possibly paranoid rednecks—people urgently in need of reeducation and "consciousness-raising" from the liberal agenda. In Mario Cuomo's depiction, gun owners are "hunters who drink beer, don't vote and lie to their wives about where they were all weekend." (Cuomo quickly recanted this. Gun owners do vote.) Actually, the gun-owning population is pretty much like the general population because approximately one of every two households has a gun.

Now, Snyder is right that the gun-control movement often radiates distrust of average citizens, whose supposed mental and moral deficiencies are such that "only lack of immediate access to a gun restrains them and prevents the blood from flowing in the streets." Nevertheless, it is reasonable to wonder whether a nation whose citizens cannot program their VCRs and who increasingly will not respect stoplights (surely you have noticed the increasing lawlessness of drivers) is a nation whose citizens are insufficiently dexterous and too aggressive to be safely armed.

Snyder says the idea that only the police are qualified to use firearms is akin to saying that "only concert pianists may play the piano and only professional athletes may play sports." The flaw in Snyder's analogy is that if you play the piano unskillfully, you neither kill nor wound anyone. However, Snyder has evidence more powerful than his analogy.

In 13 states citizens who wish to carry arms may do so, having met certain requirements. Consider Florida, which in 1987 enacted a concealed-carry law guaranteeing a gun permit to any resident who is at least 21, has no record of crime, mental illness or drug or alcohol abuse, and who has completed a firearms safety course. Florida's homicide rate fell following the enactment of this law, as did the rate in Oregon after the enactment of a similar law. Through June 1993, there had been 160,823 permits issued in Florida. Only 530, or 0.33 percent, of the applicants have been denied permits. This indicates that the law is serving the law-abiding. Only 16 permits, less than ⅟₁₀₀th of 1 percent, have been rescinded because of the commission, after issuance, of a crime involving a firearm.

Ninety percent of violent crimes are committed by persons not carrying handguns. This is one reason why the mere brandishing of a gun by a potential victim of violence often is a sufficient response to a would-be attacker. In most cases where a gun is used in self-defense, it is not fired. Can the average citizen be trusted to judge accurately when he or she is in jeopardy? Snyder answers that "rape, robbery and attempted murder are not typically actions rife with ambiguity or subtlety." Furthermore:

> Florida State University criminologist Gary Kleck, using surveys and other data, has determined that armed citizens defend their lives or property with firearms against criminals approximately 1 million times a year. In 98 percent of these instances, the citizen merely brandishes the weapon or fires a warning shot. Only in 2 percent of the cases do citizens actually shoot their assailants. In defending themselves with their firearms, armed citizens kill 2,000 to 3,000 criminals each year, three times the number killed by the police. A nationwide study by Don Kates, the constitutional lawyer and criminologist, found that only 2 percent of civilian shootings involved an innocent person mistakenly identified as a criminal. The "error rate" for the police, however, was 11 percent, over five times as high.

Concerning what we may call "the running-of-red-lights syndrome" in contemporary America, I put the point to Snyder and he fired back a fax:

> Regarding your observation about our society's general level of aggressiveness and disregard for rules, you may wish to consider Robert Heinlein's famous dictum that "An armed society is a polite society." Knowing that one's fellow citizens are armed, greater care is naturally taken not to give offense. The proposition is, of course, difficult to prove, but you can find some support for it in English literature. Observe the polite formality with which strangers address each other in inns in, for example, Fielding's *Tom Jones* or (with comedic exaggeration) in Dickens's *Pickwick Papers*. While no doubt attributable in part to England's class structure and the education received by the aristocracy, I would hesitate to say that it had nothing to do with the fact that gentlemen generally were armed.

Or as is famously said in American literature, by the hero of Owen Wister's *The Virginian*, "When you call me that, *smile!*" Such was politeness in the armed society of 19th-century Wyoming.

Finally, there is the matter of the Second Amendment. This Republic's Founders constitutionalized, which means they made fundamental, the right to possess firearms, and they did not do so unreflectively. They placed that right second in the Bill of Rights, yielding precedence only to rights pertaining to speech, worship and association, and they did that for philosophically serious reasons. The philosophy of classical republicanism recognizes a crucial relationship between personal liberty and possession of arms by a people prepared to use them. Snyder believes that the Second Amendment is as much a product of this philosophy as of the Revolutionary War experience or the exigencies of frontier life: "To own firearms is to affirm that freedom is not a gift from government. . . . As the Founding Fathers knew well, a government that does not trust its honest, law-abiding, taxpaying citizens with the means of self-defense is not itself worthy of trust."

Yes, and yet . . . no society can be called successful where violence is so prevalent and random that lawful citizens must go about prepared to dispense violence in self-defense. No one wants to live, raise children and grow old in such a society. But government is constituted to provide, first and foremost, domestic tranquility sufficient to make unnecessary the sort of personal measures that Snyder recommends. If such measures are becoming necessary, do not blame Snyder.

Snyder writes that the "association of personal disarmament with civilized behavior is one of the great unexamined beliefs of our time." Not anymore it isn't. His searching examination of it may not compel your assent—I remain unpersuaded—but it must shake some soothing assumptions regarding crime and civic responsibilities. I am among those whom Snyder faults, civilly but firmly, for insufficient rigor in reasoning about these matters. I find being reproved by him a bracing experience because it enlarges my understanding while subtracting from my certainties. I salute him and thank him.

November 15, 1993

Should Death Again Be Public Theater?

SAN FRANCISCO—State-inflicted death used to be public theater with didactic purposes, and may be again if KQED, the public television station here, wins its suit asserting a right to film executions.

Reporters have always attended California executions. A press sketch was made of the most recent one, in 1967. But before KQED filed suit, prison policy was changed to require reporters to be empty-handed (no note or sketch pads, tape recorders or cameras). After the suit was filed, the rules were revised again to ban all reporters from any executions.

This comprehensive ban may protect San Quentin's warden against KQED's original contention that he was unconstitutionally discriminating against graphic journalism because of its content. However, the ban opens him to another charge: He is unconstitutionally infringing the newsgathering right by abolishing a historic access to a government function, without serving a compelling government interest.

The First Amendment is not a blanket freedom-of-information act. The constitutional newsgathering freedom means the media can go where the public can, but enjoys no superior right of access. Courts have recently protected press access to particular government functions when there is a history of openness and when openness would facilitate the function. Journalists claim no right to witness, say, Federal Reserve meetings or Supreme Court conferences. But executions are scripted rituals, not deliberative processes. Every other aspect of California's criminal justice system—trials, parole and clemency hearings, press conferences by condemned prisoners—can be televised.

The warden's real concerns, for the dignity of the occasion and for society's sensibilities, are serious. Solemnity should surround any person's death, and televised deaths might further coarsen American life.

There has not been a public execution since 1937 (a hanging in Galena, Missouri). At the time the Constitution was adopted, public executions were morality pageants, featuring civil and clerical orators, designed to buttress order and celebrate justice. But by the 1830s authorities, alarmed by "animal feelings" aroused by public executions, were moving executions behind prison walls, inviting representatives of the proliferating penny newspapers to be society's surrogate witnesses.

KQED says television conveys an "immediacy and reality" that is lost when events are "filtered through a reporter and conveyed only in words." It would be more accurate (and less obnoxious to writers) to say pictures have unique saliency and increasing importance in a decreasingly literate society. (California's Department of Education estimates that one in four California adults is functionally illiterate.) No camera can make capital punishment more troubling than Orwell ("A Hanging," just six pages long) and Camus ("Reflections on the Guillotine") did while working "only in words." Still, KQED could argue that Orwell and Camus are rarities and public understanding should not depend on literary genius being common in journalism.

It is dismaying but undeniable: Most Americans get most of their information, such as it is, from television. But televised executions would transmit peculiar "information," and for a problematic purpose. Information is normally valued as nourishment for reason. Many advocates of televised executions hope the horrifying sight would stir passions, particularly revulsion.

Attempts to proscribe capital punishment as unconstitutionally "cruel and unusual" have foundered on two facts: The Founders did not consider it so (the Constitution assumed its use) and society's "evolving standards of decency" have not made it so. Society's elected representatives continue to enact capital punishment.

KQED says it would not exercise a right to broadcast an execution live, nor would it even videotape it without the permission of the condemned. But although a court can affirm the journalistic right KQED asserts, it cannot mandate KQED's scrupulousness. Whether broadcast executions would be in bad taste or excite prurient interests are editorial concerns beyond the proper purview of government.

Televised executions might accelerate the desensitization of America. However, much death has been seen on American television: foreign executions (of the Ceausescus; a Saudi beheading), the Zapruder film of President's Kennedy's exploding skull, Robert Kennedy bleeding onto a hotel kitchen floor, the explosion of the shuttle *Challenger*, Hank Gathers's death on a basketball court. Would tape of an execution be more lacerating to the public's sensibilities than the tape of Los Angeles police beating a motorist nearly to death?

There have been 143 executions since capital punishment was resumed in 1977. They have lost their novelty, hence much of their news value: A recent Texas execution (by lethal injection) did not even draw the permitted number of reporters. Perhaps this distresses those who support capital punishment for its deterrent power. If KQED prevails, publicity will be ample, at least for a while.

However, the dynamics of the public mind, and hence the consequences of a KQED victory, are unpredictable. Perhaps the unfiltered face of a coolly inflicted death would annihilate public support for capital punishment. But perhaps society values capital punishment because of its horribleness, from which flows society's cathartic vengeance. All that is certain is that the constitutionality of capital punishment is linked to the public's values, which are malleable.

May 12, 1991

If This Is a "Cramped" Role for Government . . .

At Hyde Park, where he placed a single red rose on FDR's grave, President Clinton lamented that for 12 years Republican presidents tried "to cramp the role of government." His implication was that now government will be unleashed. Well.

His displeasure should have been directed also at the Founders, who designed the system of separation of powers—of checks and balances, of limited and enumerated powers—designed, in part, to cramp government's role. And during the 12 "cramping" Republican years, virtually no government programs were terminated, most programs grew, federal civilian employment rose (even during the darkest years of the Reagan Terror—1981–89—it rose 216,000), and federal outlays rose from $591 billion to $1.5 trillion.

The grandiosity of Clinton's plans for government growth can be gauged by the fact that he considers this a record of a "cramped" role for government. And remember, government's growth and cost are vastly understated by mere budget totals.

There are also all the compliance costs of such measures as (to take just three from the Bush era) the amendments to the Clean Air Act, the Americans with Disabilities Act and the 1991 Civil Rights Act. The Clinton administration already has contributed additional compliance costs to the burden of doing business: The Family and Medical Leave Act.

A recent study by Republicans on the Joint Economic Committee of Congress concluded that just since 1988, new regulations, including a 27 percent increase in the minimum wage since 1990 (with another increase planned), raised per worker costs for small businesses at least 33 percent.

It is difficult to calculate, even to the nearest $100 billion, the annual costs of all regulations. However, $400 billion—a sum larger than the federal deficit—is a conservative estimate. To be sure, some social benefits do come from regulations. But who believes we would choose to purchase all those benefits if their real prices were prominently fixed to them?

And then there are the costs of the purely pernicious "diversity" regulations, as enforced by a government unfortunately not noticeably cramped during the 12 Republican years. In a stunning article in the February 15 issue of *Forbes* magazine, Peter Brimelow and Leslie Spencer report on the sacrifice of merit hiring to quotas, and other consequences of this country's exquisitely misnamed "equal employment laws." The cost of all this—a huge hidden tax—may already have depressed the gross domestic product by four percentage points—approximately what we spend on the entire public school system.

Today American business is infested with affirmative action officers. These private sector bureaucrats are busy implementing racial and sexual discrimination (discriminatory laws) on behalf of various government-approved minorities (and one majority—women) known as "protected classes." The object is to produce a "balanced" workforce.

Corporations with federal contracts of more than $50,000—hundreds of thousands of corporations—must spend billions of dollars developing affirmative action plans for achieving payrolls that reflect the composition of the qualified workforce. All American employers with more than 15 employees come under the Equal Employment Opportunity Commission's Uniform Guidelines on Employee Selection Procedures and can be sued if their workforce "balance" strikes someone as "wrong." Brimelow and Spencer report this hair-curling testimony from Thomas Maggiore, a Phoenix restaurateur:

> In 1987 EEOC's local field office wrote me a letter saying they had reason to believe I didn't have enough women "food servers" and "busers." No woman had complained against me. So the EEOC advertised in the local paper to tell women whose job applications we had rejected—or even women who had just thought of applying—that they could be entitled to damages. Twenty-seven women became plaintiffs in a lawsuit against me. The EEOC interviewed me for hours to find out what kind of person I was. . . . I supplied them with hundreds of pounds of paper. I had to hire someone full-time for a year just to respond to EEOC demands. Six months ago I finally settled. I agreed to pay $150,000 in damages, and as jobs open up, to hire the women on the EEOC's list. . . . I have to advertise twice a year even if I have no openings, just to add possible female employees to my files. I also had to hire an EEOC-approved person to teach my staff how not to discriminate. I employ 12 food servers in these two restaurants. Gross sales, around $2 million. How much did it all cost me? Cash outlay, about $400,000.

Maggiore's ordeal is but one of many comparable outrages that occurred during the 12 years when Republicans had government on what Clinton considers too short a leash. Imagine, if you can, how much more omnipresent, officious, intrusive, bullying and expensive government will be now that it is staffed and directed by people who, like the President, think government's role has been too "cramped."

February 25, 1993

An "Excess of the 1980s" Speaks His Mind

At the Cato Institute, a libertarian think tank in Washington, D.C., a recent lecturer drolly introduced himself in language fashionable in Clinton's Washington: "I am an excess of the 1980s."

He is T. J. Rodgers, president and CEO of Cypress Semiconductor, which he founded 10 years ago with one used computer and no other employee. He is one of those who, in Clinton's words, "profited most from the uneven prosperity of the last decade." (A question: What would "even" prosperity look like?)

Today he is wealthy, but forgive him that sin. His company, which has paid $60 million in taxes, has created 1,500 jobs for employees who have paid $150 million in taxes. They all own Cypress stock, which has generated today's market value of $500 million for shareholders.

"Venture experts," he says, "are wrong more often than they are right. But surely they are right more often than Washington would be." If that thought is sensible, the proposed National Competitiveness Act (H.R. 820) is not.

It would get government deeply into business as a venture capitalist, providing loans to, and buying preferred stock in, venture companies. This capital allocation would be done by the Commerce Department, currently run by Ron Brown, the former lobbyist and head of the Democratic National Committee. H.R. 820 could be a political slush fund for compliant companies.

If so, it might achieve the nearly impossible—making the Commerce Department's record even worse than it is. More than half the almost $1.2 billion lent by Commerce in the last two decades is in default. In the 1970s the Economic Development Administration at Commerce lent $471 million, of which just $60 million has been recovered. And what is the penalty for such failure in Washington? A reward, such as H.R. 820's fresh infusion of taxpayers' dollars. Do you wonder why there is so much failure in Washington?

Representative Chris Cox (R-Calif.) notes that H.R. 820 would add more than $1 billion to the deficit in 1995. It would do so by authorizing the government to buy 20 percent of the equity capital in venture firms and to guarantee the dividends on preferred stock. "I suppose, therefore," Cox says with tart irony, "it is fitting that this bill is called the National Competitiveness Act, because it will give most private firms the opportunity to compete with government-subsidized securities."

Or perhaps H.R. 820 should be titled The Wesley Mouch Memorial Bill. "This whole plan," says Cox, "reeks of special-interest favoritism and make-work waste for bureaucrats. Anyone who has read Ayn Rand's *Atlas Shrugged* will see frightening similarities between this statist scheme and the disastrous projects of the novel's arch bureaucrat, Wesley Mouch."

But Cox's preferred title for H.R. 820 is The Jurassic Park Act because it will squander money cloning "new industrial dinosaurs." The bill's premise is that Commerce bureaucrats and political operatives make better investment decisions than do authentic venture capitalists and authentic investors when putting their own money at risk.

But when private investors guess wrong, the market liquidates their mistakes. When government capital-allocators guess wrong (as they are bound to do much more often than private investors, whose calculations are not colored by politics), the government just relabels its mistakes as "jobs programs" and pours in more money to keep them afloat.

Cox quotes Don Valentine, a venture capitalist who helped launch a number of venture companies, including Apple Computer: "To Washington I say, please do not help us. The world of technology is complex, fast-changing and unstructured. It thrives best when individuals are left alone to be different, creative and disobedient. Go help all the people who know how pork works and who want to be taken care of. But please do not help us."

Of course Cox and others have argued in vain. The Democratic-controlled House passed H.R. 820, not to enhance competitiveness but to concentrate yet more power in Washington, further permeating American economic life with the inefficiencies of politics.

Consider. Clinton wants to raise the top tax rate on the wealthy, who do a disproportionate share of the nation's investing; and he wants to impose a 10 percent surcharge on those who have the most to invest; and he wants to increase the corporate rate; and he wants to keep high the capital gains tax rate that punishes people who increase the value of an enterprise. And yet he has the brass to say H.R. 820 is "wise," presumably because venture capital formation is inadequate. H.R. 820 is a paradigm of government fattening itself by pretending to cure problems it causes.

So, which do you prefer, T. J. Rodgers, the self-described "excess of the 1980s," or H.R. 820, a sample of the excesses of the 1990s?

June 10, 1993

A Speck of Government Immortality

By small as much as by large actions the government defines itself. It recently did so regarding the Civilian Marksmanship Program, a little—$2.5 million annually—speck of government immortality.

The program began 90 years ago, after the Spanish-American War alerted the military to the fact that many recruits drawn from an increasingly urbanized society were lousy shots. So the program was created to encourage shooting clubs and marksmanship competitions.

This year Representative Carolyn Maloney (D-N.Y.) asked the House to kill the program, noting that the Army, according to the General Accounting Office, cannot identify "any training or mobilization reliance" for the program that gives away 40 million rounds of ammunition and other supplies annually. The program, she said, is just a subsidy of a hobby and she added sarcastically—and unwisely, considering her colleagues' receptivity to bad ideas—"Why do we not have government-subsidized fishing trips?"

But Representative Paul Gillmor (R-Ohio) defended the program, saying that most U.S. Olympic shooters in 1992 had benefited from it. And Representative Bill Brewster (D-Okla.) said it is cheap compared with other youth programs. And Representative Randy Cunningham (R-Calif.) said it is an anti-crime program teaching the safe handling of firearms and getting "kids off the streets." (More than half the participants in the program are over 26 years old.) He added that Maloney had refused to vote to cut even 5 percent from the National Endowment for the Arts, "a total boondoggle." And Gerald Solomon (R-N.Y.), announcing himself almost too angry to speak, said he votes constantly for benefits like mass transit subsidies for Maloney's New York City constituents, so she is an ingrate for opposing "a vital, vital program" benefiting his rural shooters. And Representative Harold Volkmer (D-Mo.) invited everyone to his district to see the benefits of federally funded Boy Scout BB gun competitions.

And so it went, silliness (the NEA, mass transit subsidies) invoked to justify reciprocal silliness, until the House voted 242–190 to preserve the program. Having acted to ensure that there will be no ammunition shortage in America, the legislators could return to rationalizing the recent tax increase with reference to the budget "crisis," and they could get on with the "reinvention of government."

In the Senate, the story was similar when Senator Frank Lautenberg (D-N.J.) proposed ending "the absolute outrage" of "the freebie firearms program." This drew upon him enfilading fire from the likes of Senator Larry Craig (R-Idaho), who was eager to refute the idea that 1993 is all that unlike 1903. He said, "I know that many of us would argue today that times have changed, but . . ." Craig proved his point—not that the military is still running short of straight shooters, but that times have not changed in Congress, where no program is too anachronistic to command a majority.

Senator Conrad Burns, a Republican, struck a judicious tone: "Like every Montanan, I want to cut wasteful spending. But . . ." The Senate's 67 votes to preserve the turn-of-the-century program came from liberals and conservatives because, like most of what goes on in Congress, the argument had nothing to do with any idea other than this one: Any program with a constituency should be preserved.

The government, which becomes more broadly despised as it becomes more comprehensively solicitous, no longer has even a residual sense of the great tradition of constitutional reasoning about what is and what is not a proper federal undertaking. The brief, weak threat to the Civilian Marksmanship Program was important not because it was newsworthy, but because it wasn't. The episode is worth contemplating not because it was unusual, but because it exemplifies what our career political class considers a productive use of its time and our money.

And the survival of this small program is germane to two debates about large matters, term limits and a constitutional amendment to require a balanced budget.

Ask yourself this: Is it not probable that legislators serving under term limits—people not making every decision with an eye to making their incumbency as perpetual as every federal program is—would be more likely, at least occasionally, to terminate a few of the more ludicrous spending programs?

And when, a few weeks hence, Congress considers the constitutional amendment to require a balanced budget and a supermajority to raise taxes, opponents in the political class will solemnly warn that the amendment would dangerously diminish Congress's "flexibility." Ask yourself: What could be more inflexible than that class of political careerists who cannot terminate even a relic of the Spanish-American War?

November 3, 1993

Coercion Pollution

Remember?

Around the curve
Lickety-split
Lovely car
Wasn't it

Roadside doggerel, sponsored by Burma Shave, was part of the fun of automobile travel long ago, when the world was young and the reforming spirit occasionally took a day off.

Nowadays, as America approaches perfection, the fine-tuners of life have returned their attention to this Republic's remaining billboards. Here comes another of Washington's morality plays—playlets, really—pitting "activists" against an industry, the former fighting for beauty, the latter for profit.

But the billboard industry has two things to be said for it. It is defending an important right, and it is not as insufferably noble as its adversaries.

Bills now pending in Congress would amend the 1965 Highway Beautification Act which provides compensation for owners required to dismantle billboards. In 1965 there were 1.1 million signs along the Federal Interstate and Primary Highway systems. Since then more than 700,000 have come down.

But dismantlings slowed drastically in the 1980s when federal appropriations for compensation became scarce. And in 1978 the outdoor advertising industry got the 1965 act amended to require state and local compensation for signs banned by changes in local zoning ordinances.

The new attack on billboards, tailored to this era of fiscal austerity, has one objectionable feature. It would allow state and local governments to ban billboards without paying compensation. Instead they could merely allow a grace period of amortization for owners to recoup in rentals a sum equal to construction costs.

Billboards are often referred to as "visual pollution" and "sensory litter." A *Boston Globe* editorial calls the billboard an "unsightly nuisance." Why a sign telling travelers that there is a cheap motel a mile ahead is a "nuisance" to anyone is unclear. Perhaps people who feel that way do not operate or stay at the kind of low-cost motels that get most of their business from millions of nonaffluent travelers who get their information about inexpensive accommodations from roadside signs. But, still, are these signs a "nuisance"?

Let us stipulate that all of us sensitive people would rather see trees than signs. Now, if we are quite done preening about our exquisite taste and delicate sensibilities, can we spare a moment for thoughts about justice and the Constitution? At issue are the Fifth Amendment provisions of the Bill of Rights that say people shall not be deprived of property without due process and just compensation.

The billboard industry says the substitution of amortization for compensation is slow-motion confiscation, and the industry has a point. Imagine "amortizing" private homes for highway purposes, without compensation.

No one disputes the legitimacy of using government power to regulate signs. But the Constitution is not trivial, even when it inconveniences something as nobly named as Scenic America, the lead organization in the anti-billboard coalition of environmental groups.

It is disingenuous to dress up the proposed legislation in Jeffersonian language about "restoring local control." States already have the power to regulate, even ban billboards, with just compensation. The question is, shall constitutional values be disregarded because Americans would prefer not to pay the price—compensation—of an improvement they desire?

In this era of $400 billion deficits, Americans are adept at making others (the voiceless and voteless generations to come) pay a significant portion of the price of today's choices. Taking the property of billboard owners, and diminishing the value of the property of people who rent land for billboards, and doing this without proper compensation, fits today's political morality: Enjoy the benefit, make others pay.

Critics say billboards are "parasites" and "free riders," benefiting from highways but not contributing to their construction and maintenance. If so, that problem could be addressed by taxing them more heavily. On the other hand, people who live near high-density highways suffer inconveniences for which rental income from signs on their land can be partial compensation.

Americans seem increasingly irritable and aggressive toward one another. Privacy—the right to be let alone—is under increasing pressure. On campuses speech is increasingly regulated in the name of a new entitlement—the right of hypersensitive people to pass through life without being annoyed by the thoughts of others. And now comes an intensified attempt to abridge some people's property rights in order to spare other people, often passersby, something they consider a "nuisance" because it is "unsightly."

Some of those who are eager to get visual "litter" and "pollution" out of sight are unwilling to pay a fair price for property taken or devalued. They can fairly be suspected of relishing the prospect of wielding power over others. Call this "coercion pollution." It is a growing problem in the social environment.

May 9, 1991

"Taxi!"

The world, a wit has said, is divided into two kinds of people, those who divide the world into two kinds of people and those who do not. I say: The world is divided between those who do and those who do not understand that activist, interventionist, regulating, subsidizing government is generally a servant of the strong and entrenched against the weak and aspiring.

Consider the cases of the Houston jitney operator and of the four men trying to launch the Quick Pick Cabs taxi company in Denver.

Alfredo Santos, 40, drove a cab in Houston until he became one of those disturbers of the status quo, a man with a new idea. He would run jitney services, particularly in the city's poorer neighborhoods.

Jitneys are small vehicles, usually automobiles or vans, that transport people along designated routes for fixed fares, usually higher than bus fares but lower than taxi fares. Jitneys often serve remote or low-density neighborhoods, or poor neighborhoods where automobiles may be luxuries, taxis are expensive and reluctant to visit, and municipal bus service does not meet all transportation needs.

Trouble is, Houston has a 69-year-old law proscribing jitneys. It was passed in 1924 to protect the electric streetcar company. The streetcars charged a flat rate regardless of distances traveled, so long-distance travelers were subsidized by short-distance travelers, who became customers for jitneys. In Houston, as in many other cities, the jitneys' revenues exceeded the streetcars' lost revenues, indicating that jitneys also attracted customers from taxis, and pedestrians.

Houston's streetcar company sought protection and, being strong, got it, partly because most jitney operators were black and primarily served blacks. This pattern of protection occurred in many cities, but in some cities illegal jitney services still flourish.

In 1989 some libertarian lawyers, now functioning in Washington as the Institute for Justice, filed suit on Santos's behalf and as part of a concerted strategy to resuscitate judicial protection of economic liberty.

They charged that the anti-jitney law violated Santos's constitutional rights, including his 14th Amendment rights to due process and equal protection of the laws, and to the full privileges and immunities of citizenship.

The Institute concedes (not cheerfully) that government has broad powers to regulate economic activity. But the Institute seeks enlightened application of judicial rulings that regulation must be reasonably related to the legitimate promotion of the public welfare. The Institute wants to narrow judicial deference toward government regulation that is anticompetitive both in intent and effect.

Santos is a civil rights litigant who seeks no quota or set-aside or other entitlement. He only seeks opportunity and he is still waiting for a judge to rule on his claim. Perhaps the Institute's four Denver clients will get more expeditious consideration of their attempt to crack Denver's government-sustained taxi oligopoly.

The four men—an African-American and three immigrants from Africa—are frustrated by their experience working for the three existing companies, are eager to experience the satisfactions of entrepreneurship, and are determined to bring better taxi service to Denver's poorer neighborhoods. They want to start a taxi company. Trouble is, since 1947 Colorado's Public Utilities Commission has rejected every new application for a license to launch a competitor to the existing companies.

The taxi industry in America grew without significant regulation until the 1930s. Then the combination of rising industrial unemployment and falling car prices brought many new drivers into the industry. Soon there came a wave of regulations restricting entry into the field. The regulations were largely a result (according to the Federal Trade Commission) of pressure from public transit firms and established taxi fleets.

Today most cities have a fixed number of taxi licenses, or a fixed ratio of licenses to population (all-wise government knows just the right numbers), or require, as in Denver, a showing of "public convenience and necessity" to win a license. Such regulations often are perfunctorily rationalized as relevant to safety, but their clear aim is to protect economic entities powerful enough to hire lobbyists.

In 1974 a federal study concluded that regulations restricting entry into the taxi business, and restricting price competition, cost customers $800 million annually, and that removal of such anticompetitive measures would create 38,000 entry-level jobs. Nineteen years later, both numbers must be even larger.

When the four Denver men went before the PUC, two of the three existing taxi firms opposing them shared the same lawyer. The four men were bombarded by burdensome interrogatives from lawyers. (For example, what was their five-year advertising plan?) Then their application was denied. So the Institute is bringing the 14th Amendment into play.

The world is divided into two kinds of people, those who want to prosper by competing, and those who want to prosper by getting government to cripple their competitors. America is divided between genuine entrepreneurs and those persons whose entrepreneurship consists of turning government into a dispenser of privilege and injustice.

February 4, 1993

Grassroots Tyranny

Imagine living in your own house in close confinement with hostile strangers whom your state government prevents you from evicting. Imagine this for seven years. Jerrold and Ellen Ziman and their two children did not imagine this nightmare, they lived it. Theirs is a cautionary story of a growing phenomenon—grassroots tyranny.

In February 1984, the Zimans purchased a town house in Manhattan's Greenwich Village, planning to restore it as a single-family home. The house had been configured for seven rental units, three of which were occupied and covered by the state's rent control law, an "emergency" and "temporary" program enacted during wartime, in 1943, and still on the books.

But in June 1984, New York changed the rent control rules, making it extremely difficult to evict anyone, and impossible to do so without years of expensive wandering in bureaucratic wastelands. So the Zimans camped for years in two rooms of "their" house, finding drug paraphernalia left by tenants or by those to whom the tenants gave keys to the house.

The government-dictated rent did not even cover the Zimans' maintenance expenses. They acquired full possession of their house only after rent control—and $100,000 spent fighting it—had reduced them to a "hardship" exemption from the restrictions on the right of owners to evict unwanted tenants.

Their case, which suggests the interminable and impenetrable Jarndyce and Jarndyce case in Dickens's *Bleak House* (perhaps filtered through Kafka), is an example of what is referred to in the title of Clint Bolick's new book, *Grassroots Tyranny*. Bolick is a combative litigator determined to convince fellow conservatives that "conservative judicial activism" is neither an oxymoron nor a bad idea.

Conservatism, defining itself in reaction to the federal government's aggrandizement under the New Deal and Great Society, has often endorsed virtually unbounded powers for state and local governments, to counter centralization of power in Washington. But Bolick notes that "in today's society a zoning commissioner or a tax assessor can have far greater impact on personal liberties than the president."

America has more than 82,000 units of government—not even counting state and local regulatory boards—below the federal level. The federal government has "only" 2 million civilian employees; lower government has 500,000 elected officials and 13 million employees.

State and local governments, subservient to strong local interests, commit myriad injustices, such as ludicrous licensing requirements that restrict entry into professions, for the benefit of those already in the professions. For example, the Kansas Cosmetology Board recently decreed that Monique Landers, a 15-year-old African-American honored as one of the nation's five Outstanding High School Entrepreneurs, must close her $100-a-month business braiding and washing hair in Wichita. The board, acting at the behest of hair salons and cosmetology schools, says she must either go to cosmetology school and get a license, or go to jail.

The Framers of the Constitution would not be surprised about the many such outrages Bolick documents, or by the fact that today's gravest attacks on free speech occur in small communities susceptible to tyranny in a small sphere—on college campuses. The Framers, acutely interested in the sociology of liberty, understood that small communities are particularly vulnerable to domination by overbearing majorities.

The Framers also understood that stable, tyrannical majorities can best be prevented by the multiplication of minority interests, so the majority at any moment will be just a transitory coalition of minorities. Hence Madison favored an "extensive republic," and Jefferson made the Louisiana Purchase to guarantee a sphere sufficient for a healthy multiplicity of factions.

Federalism expresses a constitutional preference for decentralized power. However, Bolick, whose book is subtitled *The Limits of Federalism*, argues that "the Framers were not concerned primarily with favoring one type of government over another, but with limiting the power of government, regardless of its source." They had been appalled by the excesses of local majoritarianism, such as debt relief by the overturning of contracts, under the Articles of Confederation. They were sentimental about nothing, least of all the virtues of government below the federal level.

Too many conservatives, Bolick argues, dogmatically celebrate "states' rights" and local autonomy as ends in themselves, rather than as instrumental to the protection of individual liberty. Bolick is one of a cadre of conservatives eager for courts to use the Ninth Amendment ("The enumeration in the Constitution, of certain rights, shall not be construed to deny or disparage others retained by the people") as a context for construing the entire Constitution, and particularly to block state and local acts of majoritarian tyranny, violating economic liberty and property rights.

Today the Zimans are suing New York, arguing that the years during which they were denied enjoyment of their house constituted a "taking" of property for which the Fifth Amendment ("... nor shall private property be taken for public use without just compensation") requires restitution. They have joined the counterrevolution against infringements of economic liberty and abridgement of property rights—the crucial privacy rights—by local government leviathans. And conservatives everywhere are rethinking the relative values of majoritarianism and individual liberty, federalism and judicial activism.

July 15, 1993

Colorado's Testiness

DENVER—You cannot fling a brick in this city without hitting a water lawyer, which strikes some people as a good reason for brick-flinging. Some people here say (some of them through clenched teeth) that 90 percent of the West's water lawyers practice in Colorado. However, no one here says "Poor California!," parched though it is.

California has a drought but also has some Colorado water. And Coloradans are ahead of downstream Californians in making hard decisions—and having them made for them—about the West's limiting resource.

Last December one such decision determined that the Two Forks dam, discussed and planned intermittently for 50 years, will not be built. Cheesman Canyon 50 miles south of here, a favorite of fishermen, floaters and backpackers, will not be inundated by 359 billion gallons of river water behind a dam 615 feet tall.

The result has been a scramble by communities and other interests to see what water rights are for sale. That depends on prices, which depend on—well, that depends. Decisions, essentially political, must be made about what the West is going to be. They will affect the rest of us, not only when we vacation but also when we buy food.

Less than a century ago much of the territory west of the Mississippi was designated on many maps as "The Great American Desert." Water, or the scarcity of it, made the West what it is—inhabitable and productive, or not.

To understand Colorado's testiness, understand geography. Colorado is the only state that has no rivers flowing into it from elsewhere. Eight—the Platte, Rio Grande, Arkansas, Yampa, White, Dolores, San Juan and Colorado—rise here and flow out. Some of the Colorado reaches California.

Water is a peculiar sort of resource. It falls from the sky or gathers underground. It flows down from mountains and through many jurisdictions. Water has been a reason for bloodshed for as long as mankind has been fighting, and the American West has had its share of water wars.

Today we are civilized as all get out, so we litigate rather than fight. Sorting out the property rights to this precious fluid (more precious, over time, than oil) made Westerners unusually litigious even for Americans. It also made them highly political and uncomfortably wedded to the federal government. The federal government owns much of the West (79 percent of Nevada, Idaho 61, Utah 60, Oregon 52, Wyoming 47, California 45, Arizona 45, Colorado 30, New Mexico 33, Montana 30). And the West's fate has been bound up with the Bureau of Reclamation.

But now another, much newer federal agency matters, too. The Environmental Protection Agency sealed the fate of the Two Forks dam, thereby probably putting an end to the era of the big dams that made the modern West. The animating value of that era—economic development—collides everywhere with other values, including environmental preservation.

The species whose habitats are threatened include not just trout but suburbanites. Many people moved to Colorado to enjoy the environmental assets that their moving here has jeopardized. Some would like to close Colorado's door. They can slow its growth. One way to do that is to turn the water tap until local governments find it difficult to authorize more sewer hookups.

Denver does not need more water for itself, and the surrounding satellite communities are not yet in dire straits. However, Two Forks dam would have facilitated continuing urbanization of the front range of the Rockies, from Fort Collins to Pueblo.

Residential and commercial development requires water, but agriculture requires much more of it: 90 percent of Colorado's water goes for irrigation and other agricultural purposes. Furthermore, fly fishing and other recreational uses of water are now big business (tourism is a $5.6 billion chunk of Colorado's economy) as well as recreation for the natives.

Americans, a people of plenty, are loath to learn this lesson: Scarcity can be an improving experience. Just as recessions wring inefficiencies from the economy, increased competition for a scarce resource encourages economic rationality.

Water has flowed into current uses because it has been cheap relative to economic returns from using it. It has been cheap not only because it has been plentiful but because it has been allocated politically rather than economically—by legislation and litigation rather than by auction, meaning markets.

Americans are more ready to praise markets than to surrender their destinies to them. Economic rationality is just one value among many. Water will increasingly force the West to make, as no other region must, semi-socialist choices. It must choose between government policies that will plan different futures.

So henceforth the West's wide open spaces, home to rugged individualists, will ring with political rhetoric. Westerners are condemned to a grand argument about the collective decisions that will allocate the scarce resource on which everything depends.

March 28, 1991

The Neighborhoods of AIDS

A reasonable surmise is that, about 50 years ago, in east and central Africa, some hunters and their families who ate monkeys became infected with a low-virulence (and for a long time quiescent) progenitor of what is now known to be the virus that causes AIDS. Thus on the continent where the human race may have begun, there began an epidemic.

Its dynamics have now led some researchers to an encouraging conclusion: In America, the disease is largely concentrated in perhaps 30 neighborhoods nationwide. Change behavior in those places and the epidemic will recede.

When Dr. Stephen C. Joseph was practicing medicine in central Africa in the early 1970s, he saw many cases of undiagnosed wasting syndromes, progressive infections and bizarre malignancies. By 1981, five gay men in Los Angeles had similar afflictions. By 1986, when Joseph became commissioner of health in New York City, he knew what was happening, and why.

As he writes in his harrowing book, *Dragon Within the Gates: The Once and Future AIDS Epidemic*, an epidemic requires not only a microbe but also an appropriate social context. AIDS found two contexts in New York City. "The artistic, cultural and fashion enterprises which are particularly important to New York's world standing and economy," writes Joseph, "have traditionally included large numbers of gay men." Then in the late 1980s there came a great epidemiologic shift, away from gay white males and toward minority heterosexuals—needle-sharing intravenous drug abusers and their sexual partners.

AIDS has been particularly disconcerting because the nation had come to believe that it was no longer vulnerable to mass infectious disease. But modernity actually abetted the epidemic. In Uganda and Tanzania it was spread by roadside prostitutes whose clients were truckers and soldiers traveling on the modern road system. Africa has been increasingly integrated into the world flow of transportation, commerce, tourism and traveling students. This is a century of global interconnections, so pandemics—infectious diseases spread globally—are now more possible than ever.

Furthermore, AIDS, like lung cancer, coronary artery disease and motor vehicle accidents, is a characteristic 20th-century epidemic: It is closely related to current behavior. Related, in fact, to voluntary, conscious and intimate behavior, that involving sex and drugs. And much of the high-risk behavior is highly concentrated in a few small areas.

Last Sunday Gina Kolata, a science writer for *The New York Times*, reported that some experts now believe that the AIDS epidemic in America "can be all but stamped out," without a vaccine or wonder drug. The strategy would involve concentrating on prevention of risky behavior that is particularly prevalent in 25 to 30 neighborhoods nationwide, in such cities as New York, Miami, Los Angeles, San Francisco, Houston, Newark and Camden, New Jersey. However, Kolata says, among the measures public health officials want to concentrate in those neighborhoods are some that many conservatives oppose, including free distribution of clean hypodermic needles, many more drug treatment programs and explicit sex education "adapted to the language and mores of affected neighborhoods."

However, the political impediments to rational AIDS policies involve much more than just conservatism. AIDS in America has been associated with stigmatized and illegal behavior, and has been concentrated among marginalized groups—homosexuals and inner-city poor—that feel vulnerable to oppression. So there has been a concerted effort to "democratize" the disease. The politically correct message has been that everyone is vulnerable—"AIDS does not discriminate." And there has been resistance to targeting the risky behavior of particular groups.

Such behavior is resurgent. Two days before the *Times* carried Kolata's article it carried another story under this headline: IN THE AGE OF AIDS, SEX CLUBS PROLIFERATE AGAIN. The city now has about 50 such clubs, a majority catering to gay men. Patrons can have anonymous sex with multiple partners. One club even advertises "HIV Positive Night" to attract people already infected.

Joseph struggled to get such establishments closed in the 1980s, when there were 200 new AIDS cases reported in the city each month. Today 500 new cases are reported each month. But the city government, perhaps weary of doing battle with gay groups and civil liberties lawyers, now professes to hope that the clubs can be made a net plus for public health by being encouraged or required to distribute condoms and employ monitors to supervise sexual activity. As though people patronize such places in order to be supervised.

The primary public health task in an epidemic is to protect the uninfected. Until there is an arsenal of AIDS medicines, the epidemic will remain less a medical challenge than a test of political will. "AIDS," writes Joseph, "is the first major public health issue in this century for which political values rather than health requirements set the agenda." If we are serious, that will stop. And so, perhaps, will the epidemic.

March 14, 1993

The Trajectory of an Epidemic

At Barnes Hospital in St. Louis in 1919 a doctor summoned some medical students to an autopsy, saying the patient's disease was so rare that most of the students would never see it again. It was lung cancer.

That story, from Dr. John A. Meyer's article "Cigarette Century" in the December *American Heritage*, illuminates like a lightning flash this fact: Much—probably most—of America's hideously costly health care crisis is caused by unwise behavior associated with eating, drinking, driving, sex, alcohol, drugs, violence and, especially, smoking. Therefore, focusing on wellness—on preventing rather than curing illness—will reduce the waste inherent in disease-oriented, hospital-centered, high-tech medicine. The history of the connection between cigarettes and lung cancer illustrates the fallacy of associating health with the delivery of medicine.

One of those 1919 medical students later wrote that he did not see another case of lung cancer until 1936. Then in six months he saw nine cases. By the 1930s advances in immunology and public health measures (sanitation, food handling, etc.) were reducing the incidence of infectious diseases. But the nation was about to experience an epidemic of behaviorally driven disease.

The lung cancer epidemic can be said to have sprung from the 1881 invention of a cigarette-making machine. Prior to that, commercial manufacturing of cigarettes was, Meyer says, a cottage industry. But by 1888 North Carolina's James Buchanan Duke (whose fortune endowed the university) was selling nearly a billion cigarettes annually. Next, war, the shaper of our century, worked its transforming force. Duke's company and the National Cigarette Service Committee distributed cigarettes free to soldiers in France during World War I. So important were cigarettes thought to be to morale, General Pershing demanded priority shipment for them.

Between 1910 and 1919, U.S. cigarette production increased 633 percent, from 10 billion to almost 70 billion annually. Meyer notes that O. Henry's meticulously observed short stories, written at the turn of the century, almost never mention cigarettes, but the expatriates—men and women—in Hemingway's *The Sun Also Rises* (1926) smoke constantly. By the 1930s physicians were struggling with the consequences of the new, "emancipated" behavior.

In 1930 the lung cancer death rate among men was less than 5 per 100,000 per year. By the 1950s, after another war, in which cigarettes were sold for a nickel a pack and were distributed free in forward areas and were included with K rations, the death rate among men was more than 20 per 100,000. Today it is more than 70 per 100,000, women's lung cancer rates are soaring and lung cancer is far and away America's leading cause of cancer death.

We have come a long way from the early days of television, when the sponsor of anchorman John Cameron Swayze's *The Camel News Caravan* required him to have a lit cigarette constantly visible. The aggressiveness of today's antismoking campaigns is attested, paradoxically, by a "smoker's rights" movement trying to protect from employment discrimination those persons who only smoke away from the job.

The American Cancer Society is testing the tolerance of the magazine industry, which last year got $264.4 million—4 percent of its revenue—from tobacco advertising. Some magazines may refuse to run ACS advertisements that say "Smoking promotes zoo breath" or "More Americans die each year from illness related to smoking than from heroin, crack, homicide, car accidents, fires and AIDS combined." (A current idiocy: The loud, abrasive entertainer Denis Leary, who harangues MTV's young viewers about the dangers of crack, smokes while haranguing.)

The social disaster of the smoking addiction illustrates why behavior modification, especially education, is the key to cost-containment regarding health. And journalism can help, as *The Washington Post*'s Jay Mathews deftly demonstrated in his reporting on the Liggett company's campaign to revive the Chesterfield brand of cigarettes, a brand which has not been advertised for decades.

Launched 80 years ago, Chesterfield flourished when smoking was most glamorous, from the 1930s into the 1950s, when the "Chesterfield Girl" was a television fixture. Today 50 million addicted Americans still pay $26 billion for almost half a trillion cigarettes each year, so if Chesterfield wins one-half of 1 percent of the market (2.4 billion cigarettes), it will be a success.

To achieve that, Liggett is merchandizing Chesterfields with a $50 million advertising campaign featuring soft, 1930s-style photography. Mathews reported that—and this, too:

> Janet Sackman, who was the Chesterfield Girl on *The Perry Como Show* in the late 1940s, said she was not impressed. She speaks with difficulty because of surgery for both throat and lung cancer, which she blames on 33 years of smoking urged by a Chesterfield executive who thought she would look more authentic. "People who smoke ought to take a look at me," she said.

And at the trajectory of the epidemic from 1919 until now.

December 24, 1992

The Clintons' Lethal Paternalism

The debate about the Clintons' health care plan is, literally, a matter of life and death. If anything like that plan becomes law, there will be much unnecessary premature death and other suffering. The plan would reduce the quantity and quality of health care and medical technologies by vastly expanding government's coercive role. To see why support for the plan plummets as analysis of it proceeds, see the analysis in *The New Republic* by Elizabeth McCaughey of the Manhattan Institute.

The plan authorizes seven presidential appointees, the National Health Board, to guess the nation's health care needs and decree how much the nation may spend meeting them. Everyone would be locked into one system of low-budget health plans picked by the government. Fifteen presidential appointees, the National Quality Management Council, not you and your doctor, would define the "medically necessary" and "appropriate" care a doctor could give you. There would be 15-year jail terms for people driven to bribery for care they feel they need but the government does not deem "necessary."

Government would define a minimum level of care and herd people in particular regions into dependence on the lowest-cost organization able to deliver that level. Doctors would be driven into organizations in which they would be punished financially for giving more treatment than the organizations' budget targets permit. The primary care physician assigned to you would be, McCaughey notes, a gatekeeper with an incentive to limit your access to specialists and high-tech medicine. The premise of the Clintons' plan is not just that government knows best, but that government knows everything relevant, including how many specialists there should be—no more than 45 percent of all doctors. McCaughey says many medical students will be told that the specialties they prefer are closed, or closed to them because they are not the right race or ethnicity. Yes, the plan subordinates medical values to "diversity."

To further suppress, through rationing, consumption of other than low-budget, low-tech medicine, the plan would empower a presidential appointee (the secretary of HHS) to control the price of any new drug. Control would be based on the development cost and profitability of each drug, rather than a company's full range of drug development outlays. But for every drug that becomes profitable, 1,000 do not. Thus the Clintons' plan would certainly suppress research that might spare millions of persons some of the ravages of AIDS, Alzheimer's, breast and ovarian cancer and other diseases.

The Clintons' plan's subtractions from public health and personal freedom would be preposterous prices to pay even to give insurance to 38 million uninsured Americans. But the actual number of chronically uninsured—those uninsured involuntarily and for prolonged periods—is only about 6 million, less than 3 percent of the population, and they are not denied medical care. Indeed, per capita spending on them is 60 percent of per capita expenditures on the insured pre-Medicare population, according to Irwin Stelzer.

Writing in *Commentary*, Stelzer refutes the notion that we must be spending "too much" on health care because other nations spend less, or because we spend more than we used to, or because the results are not commensurate with the expenditures. Yes, other nations spend smaller percentages of GDP on health care. But when did, say, Japanese living standards (Japanese doctors see an average of 49 patients a day for an average of five minutes per visit) become America's aspiration? Canada? There are 1.4 million Canadians queuing for care and 45 percent of those awaiting surgery say they are in pain. America spends twice as much per student on higher education than the average for 24 industrial nations. Stelzer wonders: How many professors endorsing the

Clintons' "global budgets" to limit health care spending would favor capping professors' salaries?

American values are one reason health costs are high. About 30 percent are incurred in the last six months of patients' lives. American behavior—violence, diet, unsafe sex, drug abuse, teenage illegitimacy (severely underweight babies cost an average of $158,000 in care)—produces health costs that cannot be blamed on inefficiencies in the system.

The Clintons' "projection" that without their plan health care spending, currently 14 percent of GDP, will reach 26 percent by 2030 is akin to the government's projection—remember?—of oil at $100 per barrel. Market forces—new discoveries, conservation, alternative fuels—refuted the hysterics who trumpeted the "energy crisis" as an excuse for expanding governmental command of the economy. Government is even less competent to anticipate the future of medicine.

Health care cost 5 percent of GDP in 1960. All in favor of spending at 1960 levels signify by saying let's do without bypass operations (300,000 this year), CAT and PETT scans, MRIs, endoscopes and other diagnostic technologies, laser microsurgery and all the other capabilities that have come with increased costs.

Roy Porter, a medical historian, limns the astonishing acceleration of medical advance in our lifetimes. Since the 1930s sulfa drugs and antibiotics have made childbirth safe for mother and child. In 1940 penicillin was still being tested on mice, and pneumonia, meningitis and comparable infections were frequently fatal. The 1950s produced polio vaccines, psychotropic drugs for mental illnesses and medicines for biochemical abnormalities. Pediatric cardiology leapt forward as did, in the 1960s, organ transplants. Treating prostate cancer with hormones and arthritis with cortisone, deciphering the role of slow viruses in chronic diseases of the central nervous system—these and many more marvels constitute a therapeutic revolution in a half century.

All this success is driven by a subtle symbiosis among complex, mature professions and institutions. It is horrifying to think of these life-enhancing jewels of our civilization coming under the control of political bureaucracies. The Clintons' plan presents the face of paternalistic liberalism, of government that is bullying because it is arrogant, and arrogant because it does not know what it does not know. It is unlovely and, literally, lethal.

February 7, 1994

Well, Then, How Many Hispanics *Should* There Be in Thoracic Surgery?

Having stormed, in the name of *Les Misérables*, the ramparts of Republican reaction, Democrats, who call themselves "the party of compassion," now have produced a budget that slashes assistance to poor people for home heating, but cuts nary a nickel from the National Endowment for the Arts, an agency paradigmatic of government's solicitude for the already comfortable. Welcome to the revolution. Moral ostentation was liberalism's delight during the fallow years when Republicans were in power and homeless people were in the streets illustrating the "uncaring" nature of Republicans. But in the liberal party's budget the big winner is the Justice Department, primarily because of funding to put more police on the streets where homeless people still are. No wonder many liberals are uneasy and the administration's leading liberal, Hillary Rodham Clinton, is quite cross.

Television has been aswarm with ads she considers frightfully unfair criticisms of her health care plan. The ads actually are mild—a prototypical couple saying gosh we don't need costly new bureaucracies to fix health care. "Propaganda!" cries Mrs. Clinton's husband. But if he and she want to see real mendacity, they should see the ad purporting to be a neutral presentation of facts.

It is sponsored by the League of Women Voters, whose agenda is liberal, and the Kaiser Family Fund, a liberal foundation. The Kaiser family name is on Kaiser Permanente, a huge HMO of the sort the Clintons' plan would favor. The ad says, "84 percent of Americans who lack health insurance are in families that work hard and pay taxes, but don't get health insurance on the job. That's eight out of ten of us, and that's a fact." No, that's not. Note the pronoun "us." The implied antecedent is the American population, all of us. But the "us" really refers to the approximately one in seven of us who at any moment lacks insurance (some briefly, between jobs, some others voluntarily, because they choose to run the risk).

The administration's slipperiness in portraying a "crisis" and the plan to solve it has been accompanied by vituperativeness when the slipperiness is revealed, as it has been by, among others, Elizabeth McCaughey of the Manhattan Institute, writing in *The New Republic*. A few weeks ago her withering analysis of the Clintons' plan, complete with meticulous page references to the 1,364-page bill, documented the fact that the plan would give government comprehensive control over individuals' personal medical care. The White House shrilly accused her of a "blatant lie" and of being "deliberately misleading." When *The New Republic* challenged the White House to send forth someone, anyone, to debate McCaughey, the White House refused—wisely, considering McCaughey's shredding, in the current *New Republic*, of the White House's written response to her first article.

For example, the White House called "ridiculous" her contention that the bill involves racial quotas in medical training. She directs readers to page 515 of the bill. A new bureaucracy that would determine the number of training positions in each teaching hospital would also calculate the percentage of trainees at each teaching hospital "who are members of racial or ethnic minority groups" and which groups are "underrepresented in the field of medicine generally and in the various medical specialties." Too few Hispanics in thoracic surgery? Government will fix that, too.

Confronted with McCaughey's scholarly precision and tone (she is a constitutional historian with a Columbia University Ph.D.), and with other criticism, administration spokespersons, and especially Mrs. Clinton, have unsheathed a 1960s style of discourse, treating political differences as occasions for moral assaults. Doctors, pharmaceutical companies, insurers and the rest of the private sector—it is "rife with fraud, waste and abuse," says Mrs. Clinton—are guilty of greed. It remains to be seen whether Mrs. Clinton's role in Whitewater and related matters disqualifies her as America's moral auditor. However, her moral certitude is commensurate with her intellectual confidence.

Having spent her adult life lawyering and politicking, she now stipulates, among many other medical things, the proper ratio of primary care doctors to specialists. She says: "The American people did not stand on the street corners and say, 'Give us more thoracic surgeons.' " But neither did they ask politicians and their spouses to lay down the law about such matters. When a health insurance agent asked Mrs. Clinton what would happen to her job under the Clintons' plan, Mrs. Clinton replied, "I'm assuming anyone as obviously brilliant as you could find something else to market." Obviously another of Mrs. Clinton's assumptions is that she and her friends have a right to rearrange other people's lives.

Replying to a question concerning whether the plan's "employer mandates"—payroll taxes—might injure small businesses, which are most of America's business, she sniffed, "I can't go out and save every undercapitalized entrepreneur in America." No one is asking her to come "out" and "save" them, but she should refrain from injuring businesses that would not be "undercapitalized" if the Clintons' plan did not confiscate part of their capital.

The Congressional Budget Office last week issued a ruling that one Democratic senator welcomes because "it means we don't have to lie." It refuted the Clintons' preposterous contention that their plan is merely a privately funded reorganization of private programs, not a new government program, and so the costs should not show up in the federal budget. The CBO said the Clintons' plan is a new entitlement program—larger than Social Security—in which "federal law . . . would determine the benefits and premiums." The CBO said the revenue stream raised from employers by the compulsion of the government's sovereign power must appear, like taxes, in the budget as government receipts.

By making untenable the Clintons' pretense that their plan involves no broad new tax, the CBO protected the budget's ability to function as a record of the portion of the private economy that is taken to fund government programs. The White House lobbied furiously to dissuade the CBO from stating the obvious, which the White House rightly considers potentially ruinous.

February 21, 1994

Facing the Skull Beneath the Skin of Life

There is a large laguna in the nation's current conversation about medical matters. Unless we talk about something we flinch from facing—death—we will aggravate some problems of modern medicine, for two reasons. Enormous costs are incurred in the final months of patients' lives. And society's stance toward death shapes its stance toward life. Unless we think more clearly than modern medical prowess inclines us to think about dying, we shall not understand something strange.

At a moment when medicine has brought us blessings beyond our grandparents' dreams, a sour aroma of disappointment surrounds the healing arts. Indeed, the medical and political professions are now akin: The more omniprovident government is, the lower it sinks in public esteem and the more impatient, demanding and crabby its beneficiaries become. Roy Porter, medical historian, says medicine is suffering a malaise that is partly "the price of progress and its attendant unrealistic expectations."

Medicine has become a prisoner of its success. As the Western world becomes healthier, it craves more medicine until, Porter says, medicine's mandate becomes muddled. "Medical maximization" becomes a patient's right and a doctor's duty. "Anxieties and interventions spiral upwards in a double helix" as "medicine-mongering" leads to "gung-ho, 'can-do, must-do' technological perfectibilism: everyone has *something* wrong with them, everyone can be cured." But there is a law of diminishing returns in medicine, pointing to an ignominious destiny—medicine bestowing meager increments of unenjoyed life, the result of disproportionate investments of resources, comparable to athletes taking steroids to shave milliseconds from sprint records.

The subject of medicine is deeply, even metaphysically, disturbing because it reminds us that death is coming and could come with the next tick of the clock. Furthermore, progress regarding medicine's timeless aspirations—longer life, better health—has whetted appetites for unlimited progress toward retarding senescence and preserving youthfulness. Concerning such yearnings, Sherwin B. Nuland says, briskly: Too bad. Medicine has a job to do, but nature does too, and will do it, medicine be damned. Nature's job is to send us packing so that subsequent generations can flourish. And medicine that does not respect limits set by nature can make death unnecessarily unpleasant, and can distort life too.

Nuland is a surgeon and a surgical writer—precise, incisive, unsentimental. In his harrowing new book, *How We Die: Reflections on Life's Final Chapter*, he says that life's final flickerings are, more often than not, messy and agonizing and devoid of dignity. Life is dappled with periods of pain, but in dying there often is only the affliction. And medicine—or, more exactly, the wrong kind of doctoring—can make matters worse.

Eighty-five percent of the aging population will succumb to one of seven ailments—atherosclerosis, hypertension, adult-onset diabetes, obesity, Alzheimer's and other dementias, cancer and decreased resistance to infections. Nuland's purpose in "trooping some of the army of the horsemen of death across the field of our vision" is to "demythologize the process of dying." He does. Do not pick up his book at bedtime. Its unsparing detail about the incremental debilitation of our tissues and organs is almost assaultive. Did you know—do you want to know—that in every decade after age 50 your brain loses 2 percent of its weight? Nuland's explanation of a heart attack is enough to cause one, but his description of one is less searing than what he has to say about AIDS.

He pummels his readers with their mortality in order to get them to face the skull beneath the skin of life. In the Western world in less than

100 years the life expectancy of a child at birth has more than doubled. This has incited the hope that there is no species-determined limit to life span. But Nuland believes there are "natural, inherent limits. When those limits are reached, the taper of life, even in the absence of any specific disease or accident, simply sputters out." And a good thing that is, says Nuland, noting that, in medicine and elsewhere, two world views are in tension. One view recognizes nature's inexorable tides. The other believes that science's task is to throw all available resources into resisting those tides, even though those tides, by constantly renewing the species, stabilize our social environment and make possible civilization's progress.

Every doctor who understands, as Nuland does, that medicine is an art as well as a science is apt also to be a moralist who understands that medicine's fight against illness can be fierce without being disproportionate. An obsession with longevity distracts us from our duty to live well. Acceptance of death is a prerequisite for rising above concern for mere bodily continuance. Biology confirms what philosophy teaches: We are social creatures whose lives point beyond themselves, toward children. Children, says Leon Kass, another philosophical doctor, are "life's answer to mortality, and their presence in one's home is a constant reminder that one no longer belongs to the frontier generation."

Mortality gives life symmetry, and an urgency about getting on with good works. But accepting limits goes against the grain of medicine, which Nuland calls the "most egocentric of professions" and "the one most likely to attract people with high personal anxieties about dying." Medicine is especially susceptible to modern science's "fantasy of controlling nature." Medicine, he says, has lost the humility proper in the presence of nature's power. That fact is related to this one: Today 80 percent of Americans die in hospitals, too often tangled in webs of wires and tubes in intensive care units which are, Nuland says, "the purest form of our society's denial of the naturalness, and even the necessity, of death."

"Between the lines of this book," he says in his epilogue, "lies an unspoken plea for the resurrection of the family doctor. Each of us needs a guide who knows *us* as well as he knows the pathways by which we can approach death. . . . At such times, it is not the kindness of strangers we need, but the understanding of a longtime medical friend." Health care reformers, please note.

March 7, 1994

PART 5

Politics

The Winding Road to the Reagan Years

An Address to the Reagan Forum, the Ronald Reagan Library, Simi Valley, California, February 28, 1994

Edward Gibbon, historian and wit, was dryly funny even in his footnotes, such as this one concerning giraffes: "... the tallest, the most gentle, and the most useless of the large quadrupeds. This singular animal, a native only of the interior parts of Africa, has not been seen in Europe since the revival of letters."

Was it mere coincidence? Or did the quickening of Europe's intellectual life actually cause the departure of the giraffes? Did they have an aversion to learning? Gibbon was being playful with the *post hoc ergo propter hoc* fallacy: The rooster crows and then the sun rises, therefore the crowing causes the sunrise. Political argument often involves the use of such fallacies. The process of claiming praise or assigning blame for problems solved, or aggravated, involves sorting out causal connections from the welter of variables in the complex churning of our continental society—no easy task.

The basic rule by which credit and blame are apportioned in politics is this: If you are standing there when something good happens, you get to take the credit. Politicians praising themselves are not under oath. And as a Chicago politician once said, let us not "cast asparagus." But let us assess the Reagan years.

The 1980 election was the third of three history-shaping events in a span of just 25 months. The first was the election on October 16, 1978, of Pope John Paul II. The second event was the election on May 3, 1979, that made Margaret Thatcher Britain's prime minister. Together, these three events presaged a kind of (forgive me, Californians) earthquake that would bring down walls, literally as well as figuratively. The spark that lit the fuse that led to the blowing up of the Berlin Wall on November 9, 1989, was lit in June 1979, when the Pope visited his native Poland. The result was national incandescence. The Thatcher and Reagan eras also were episodes of national revival. Consider the economic results of Reaganism.

The stagflation of the late 1970s did much to produce the Reagan presidency. Nowadays economic distress moves America to the right, not the left. When the economy falters, many Americans become particularly alert to the deleterious effects of government's redistributionist measures and regulations—effects on savings, investment, entrepreneurship and industriousness. The 1970s moved America to the right for the 1980s. And what do the 1990s tell us of the results?

In 1994 in Western Europe the unemployment rate is expected to be about 12 percent, almost double that of the United States. This is an extraordinary reversal of fortunes. In the 1960s and 1970s the U.S. employment rate was twice that of Western Europe's. What happened? The 1980s happened. The U.S. unemployment rate has fallen to half that of Western Europe's even as the U.S. labor force has been growing twice as fast as Western Europe's. The key to America's success has been job creation—19 million in the Reagan years, which is about 19 million more than Europe's net job creation in those years. There were 93 consecutive months of economic growth, a peacetime record. The economy grew by one-third during the Reagan years, as though we had added to our economy another economy the size of West Germany's. By the time President Reagan left office the deficit, as a percentage of GDP, had been declining for six years. What is rightly referred to as "the Reagan defense buildup" is wrongly thought to have continued throughout his administration. In fact, the final budget he submitted called for the sixth consecutive real (inflation-adjusted) decline in defense spending.

In the so-called "decade of greed" Americans gave more to charity—more as a percentage of their wealth—than ever before, and did so in spite of the fact that the reduction of marginal tax rates sharply reduced the incentives for giving. The "decade of greed" can more accurately be called the "decade of industriousness" because more Americans worked harder than ever before, producing more wealth than was produced ever before.

But the boom of the 1980s was unsettling to many people. While the U.S. economy added those 19 million jobs, Fortune 500 corporations shrank by 4 million jobs, and went from 58 percent of industrial output to 42 percent. Rapid change generates stress, and thus generates supporters for a liberal party that equates any discomfort with "victimization" and "unfairness." The Democratic Party proclaims itself the "party of compassion." Compassion means the prevention or amelioration of pain. Change can be painful. So a party that flaunts its compassion will be disposed against economic dynamism.

Michael Barone, author of *Our Country: The Shaping of America from Roosevelt to Reagan*, notes that the Democratic Party is tugged in two directions by competing concerns with growth and equity. Growth often seems to that party less urgent than "fairness" as defined by government and produced by political intervention in market allocations of wealth and opportunity. The Democratic Party of President Cleveland concentrated on growth: laissez-faire at home, free trade, hard money, low taxes, balanced budgets. Woodrow Wilson, embracing some of the Populists' and Progressives' agenda for equity through government action, produced the income tax, the Federal Trade Commission and antitrust legislation. FDR's first priority was to reignite growth in an imploding economy that had shrunk 50 percent. Only later, with less popular support, did he emphasize equity measures to redistribute the wealth of "economic royalists."

The Second World War, and pent-up consumer demand after the war, produced the growth that produced the revenue that financed government programs (such as the G.I. bill and FHA mortgages) that facilitated equity. But as Barone notes, equity was then understood as upward mobility for people who adopted socially useful behavior (going to school, starting families). And since the mid-1960s Democrats have handicapped growth by applying to all policy questions "the test of equity," as defined by whatever ideology is ascendant in the party at the moment.

Democrats, says Barone, opposed decontrol of oil prices, claiming the poor would suffer. But oil prices fell. Democrats favored bureaucratic delivery of education and other services because bureaucracies serve everyone equally. Badly, perhaps, but equally. Democrats reviled Reagan's tax cuts because the rich benefited. Never mind that most people did, too, from growth with low inflation. While Republicans were winning three presidential elections, Democrats were crunching numbers to prove that everyone was becoming worse off, as measured by the Democrats' (not the voters') definitions of "fairness." Is this or that group better off than it was? Or than it would have been if things had stayed as they were (which things never do)? Or relative to this or that group? Such microquestions should yield to a few macrofacts.

The Democratic Party used to stress job creation and low inflation. Until Carter's double-digit inflation, Democrats were vocal about inflation being a cruel tax on the poor, who devote a high proportion of their income to consumption. Indisputably, Reagan's tax cuts coincided with sharply declining inflation and prodigious job creation. In the 1980s population increased 10 percent but the number of Americans employed increased 20 percent. Labor force participation reached 66 percent, a record level exceeding even that of World War II.

Democrats respond to these numbers with three complaints. They say many of the new jobs are low-skill and not "meaningful." In fact, the Bureau of Labor Statistics reports that high-skill jobs have increased much faster than low-skill jobs. Second, Democrats say income distribution has become less equal. But this started in the mid-1970s and slowed when the nation's longest peacetime expansion began in 1983. Furthermore, income distribution is driven increasingly not by tax policies but by education disparities that determine economic destinies in a knowledge-based economy. Third, Democrats say the tax cuts unleashed gluttonous consumption, underinvestment and the demise of manufacturing. But manufacturing today is about the same percentage of GDP as 20 years ago.

The tax cuts of August 1981 were echoes of June 1978, when Californians passed Proposition 13, slashing property taxes. By the late 1970s, taxes were a big issue because of the—how soon we forget—biggest issue: inflation. It produced "bracket creep," floating taxpayers into higher brackets. This produced revenues Democrats needed so they could continue the game of giving periodic tax cuts and counting on inflation silently to erase them. However, after the 1980 election, Democrats joined the tax-cutting consensus.

By the time the crucial congressional vote on the Reagan tax cuts came in August 1981, the choice was between Reagan's cuts and the Democrats' quite similar cuts. So similar were the two plans, Reagan belatedly embraced indexation of the tax code. Hence he could say in his address to the nation: If you are only going to live two more years, the Democrats' bill is better.

Reagan's tax cuts served a general strategy for governing: Stimulate the economy and let growth dampen demands for government preferences for particular groups. Not long ago, Democrats understood the wisdom of this. Barone notes that the last time Democrats won an impressive presidential victory, in 1964, was *before* LBJ passed the Great Society legislation. His 1964 landslide followed two large legislative achievements—a civil rights bill that banned quotas, and a tax cut.

The Democratic Party is still trying to regain the strength it had in the early 1960s, before the Great Society legislative program, an episode of overreaching and underachieving, cracked public confidence in the competence of government. That confidence grew during, and because of, the Second World War. But by the end of the 1960s the Democratic Party, the party of assertive government, was, like the government, in crisis.

In 1970 two moderate Democrats published a book to warn their party of a precipice ahead. In *The Real Majority* Richard Scammon and Ben Wattenberg warned that "social issues" such as crime were acquiring a saliency comparable to economic concerns, and that the phrase "law and order" should not be disdained by liberals as racist "code words."

In February 1968, on the eve of the first of five Republican victories in six presidential elections, a Gallup poll asked: "Is there any area around here—that is, within a mile—where you would be afraid to walk alone at night?" The "yes" response was: men 19 percent, women

50 percent. Scammon and Wattenberg saw the social dynamite: Half of America's husbands had wives afraid to go out at night. In 1992—11 federal crime bills later—the "yes" response to Gallup's question was: men 28 percent, women 59 percent.

According to Scammon and Wattenberg the average voter was then saying he did not expect politicians to solve all such problems, "But I do expect that any politician I vote for will be on my side." One function of the Reagan presidency was to reassure many Americans—many of whom were "Reagan Democrats"—that the government was not an adversary determined to "raise their consciousness"—and raise their children, too.

An irony of the Reagan years is that the man who ran against Washington, who proclaimed that government often is the problem for which it pretends to be the solution, this man did much to restore, or at least slow the erosion of, confidence in government. Remember, as the 1970s drew to a close the air was thick with somber warnings from sober people who thought the United States had become "ungovernable." The symptom of "ungovernability" was inflation, which was produced by government. Because of inflation, the currency itself was failing as a store of value. Inflation made core virtues of our civilization—thrift, deferral of gratification—seem foolish. A theory widely held in 1980 was that inflation was a disease of democracy and that no democracy could cure it. That is another theory killed by a fact—the fact that America stopped inflation.

There are additional useful comparisons between the late 1970s and the early 1990s, comparisons that suggest the significance of the 1980s. Consider the recent trajectory of the military, which was in crisis just 15 years ago, with the opposite trajectories of many domestic institutions. The military changed its thinking, behavior and, often, its personnel. It achieved results and prestige. But Michael Barone, author of the 1992 *Almanac of American Politics*, says:

> The public sector institutions of which liberals have had custody for the last 20 years—the public schools, central city bureaucracies, university governance—have performed poorly. The people in charge of them have a million excuses: they have a poor quality of students or constituents, they don't have enough money, they must do things according to certain rules and regulations because of internal institutional imperatives. These are the same excuses the military made 15 or 20 years ago. . . . The leaders of liberal public sector institutions are continuing to make excuses. . . .

And to make indictments. Two indictments of the Reagan years illustrate the distinctive moralism of liberalism. The indictments concern consumption and taxation. The charge is that during the Reagan years there was too much of the former and not enough of the latter. Well.

First, some thoughts about consumption and its critics. Someone once said Times Square is beautiful if you can't read. The person who said that meant that the gaudy neon and other advertisements would be nice if they were not advertisements. That person was a snob. (Really. He was Oscar Wilde.) He considered the desires of the masses necessarily vulgar.

Another visitor from abroad had a keener understanding. When Boris Yeltsin returned to Russia from America in 1989 he said that to understand America, "at least 100 million Soviets must pass through the American school of supermarkets." He exclaimed, "Their supermarkets have 30,000 food items. You can't imagine it. It makes people feel secure."

Bull's-eye. Yeltsin saw the connection between material values and political values. Possession is not a trivial thing, be it possession of a house that provides privacy, of a car that confers mobility, of clothes that express individuality, of the ability to undertake travel that broadens. Consumption is not peripheral, let alone inimical to, the personal fulfillment that is a goal of life and hence of politics. However, as long as a high level of consumption has been possible, some moralists have treated it as problematic.

Michael Schudson, a sociologist, identifies five forms of disapproval. Two are imports from Europe. The socialist criticism is that consumerism rests on exploitation of workers and, if they are allowed to participate in it, it enervates them, sapping their ardor for social transformation. The aristocratic criticism of consumerism is an esthetic of snobbery: Mass tastes are necessarily low. Three other criticisms of consumerism are homegrown. The Puritan version faults consumption as a distraction from spirituality. The Quaker version condemns the multiplication of commodities as an offense against simplicity. The republican criticism is that the absorption of individuals in private satisfactions saps civic virtue.

Contemporary liberalism's hostility toward our "consumer culture" is an amalgam. There is Puritanism in liberal guise, as when Jimmy Carter said many Americans "worship" consumption and do not know that "consuming things does not satisfy our longing for meaning." There is the vanity of intellectuals with small cars and large egos and the arrogant conviction that they are the rightful auditors of the masses' choices. Finally, there is liberalism's variant of the socialist idea of exploitation: Advertising is villainous. Advertising, liberal critics say, is today's ubiquitous instrument of social control. It is necessary to sustain capitalism once "natural" appetites are sated. Absent advertising to manufacture "artificial" consumer demands, the system would stagnate.

The liberal critique of consumer society, which stresses the power of advertising, portrays Americans as manipulable dolts. But the people get that message and are not amused. The transformation of liberalism into a doctrine of condescension can be dated from the rapturous reception that liberals gave John Kenneth Galbraith's *The Affluent Society* in 1958. That book portrayed Americans as passive lumps, children manipulated by manufacturers who manufacture both products and appetites for them. It pictured Americans as in need of wise governors acting *in loco parentis*. Liberals volunteered for that role.

The idea that today's prosperity was brought into being by something bogus (advertising) and is bad in effect (the "worship" of misplaced "meaning" that Carter lamented) produced an unappealing agenda and an undemocratic process for pursuing it. Litigation came to be preferred to legislation as courts rather than Congress became the liberals' preferred instruments of social change. After all, if the people are debased in their tastes, and barely rational in their decision-making, then institutions that are representative of the people should for that very reason be avoided. Liberalism became a style of disdain, portraying America as vulgar, sick, racist, sexist, imperialist and so on. Liberalism began hectoring Americans, telling them that many of their desires (for big cars, for neighborhood schools, for plenty of police and many other things) did not deserve respect.

Contempt for consumer culture is generally an affectation of comfortable people addicted to the pleasures of condescension. And there is a large dollop of condescension in the enthusiasm some people have for taxation. They believe governments spend money more sensibly than individuals do. It was said that Gladstone desired the people to be prosperous only so they could pay more taxes. Some liberals seem to think like that.

Liberalism developed when liberty was threatened by the forces of order—the state, or an established church. Today people feel more threatened by disorder. Modern American liberalism developed to redress a perceived imbalance between supposedly anemic government and the surging power of entities and forces in industrial society— banks, corporations, railroads, "the trusts," business cycles. But especially now that (since October 1991) government jobs outnumber manufacturing jobs in America, few people believe there is an insufficiency of government.

Furthermore, over the last 30 years America's political center has shifted, to the disadvantage of liberalism. Watergate and Vietnam caused an erosion of confidence in the motives of government. The internationalization of economic life has weakened the power of governments. The mobility of money and businesses inhibits governments because wealth can flee from currencies that are threatened by inflation, or from jurisdictions where growth is slow or government is meddlesome. Hence liberal parties, whose promises depend on strong activist government, are decreasingly plausible. Furthermore, long recessions and slow growth increase individual anxiety and decrease social solidarity, thereby weakening society's support for collective actions through government.

The weakening of social solidarity, and the erosion of confidence in government, have made the issue of taxation paramount. During the Second World War an Irving Berlin lyric was:

You see those bombers in the sky—
Rockefeller helped to build them,
So did I—

In war, Americans were shoulder-to-shoulder. Today they are at daggers drawn, ready to fight the government, especially about taxation. But hostility to taxation is a venerable tradition.

In 1294 the Dean of St. Paul's was the sort of fellow Ronald Reagan could respect. The Dean knew how to lodge a tax protest. When Edward I summoned the senior clergy to his presence and demanded half their revenues, the good Dean dropped dead on the spot.

Until this century Americans were not permanently saddled with an income tax, or the government growth that the income tax can irrigate. But by the first decade of this century there were well-advanced changes—in the government's revenue base and the government's appetite for action—that would soon produce the income tax. By the end of the 1880s there was intense pressure to reduce tariffs, then the largest source of federal revenue. And because this country was by then an industrial power, it was importing primarily raw materials which were subject to lower tariffs than finished goods. Thus revenues were falling. Furthermore, federal land sales, another source of revenue, were declining.

But spending was increasing, especially for the Navy, which by 1905 received 20 percent of the federal budget. And Congress, acquiring a taste for redistributing income, substantially increased pensions for veterans, a lobby then as potent as the elderly are today.

In 1894 the government ran the first deficit since the Civil War and enacted a short-lived income tax. It was declared unconstitutional in 1895. In 1913 the Constitution was amended and Congress enacted another income tax: 1 percent on income between $3,000 and $20,000, with a 6 percent surcharge on higher incomes. Only 1 percent of Americans paid anything. Then the war came. By 1919 the top rate was 77 percent, and the minimum taxable income was lowered to $1,000.

The foundation of the modern state—the mechanism for raising vast revenues—was in place. The mere existence of the mechanism altered America's political culture by quickening the itch of the political class to provide benefits to client groups who were convinced that they would be net winners from income transfers. This hastened the growth of the politics of envy (clothed in the language of "fairness"). Such politics is practiced by a political class offering an ever-expanding menu of popular benefits that ostensibly will be paid for by unpopular minorities ("the rich," "corporations").

Today a willingness to spend other people's money to please one's own constituents is taken to be the measure of a politician's moral stature. Here conservatism's dissent is loud and clear.

Modern conservatism began in Edmund Burke's splendid recoil from the French Revolution, not only from the terror but also from the Revolution's assault on privacy in the name of civic claims. Conservatism has always been defined by its insistence on limits to the claims of the public sector. Contemporary American conservatism was born in reaction to the New Deal and subsequent enlargements of the state. This conservatism objects to conscription of the individual into collective undertakings. Taxation can become such conscription.

Now, some people say a preoccupation with taxes is, if not reprehensible, certainly not morally serious, because taxes are merely material concerns. That is pernicious nonsense. It is dangerous to our inheritance of freedom and hence not only to our wealth but also to our spiritual health. Here is why.

A great constant of American history is this question: How much government do we want? From that question, subsidiary questions must be unpacked. Such as: What do we want that only government can do or give, or that government can do or give much better than other institutions can? What price, in taxes or diminished freedom, are we willing to pay for these things? Today we are paying an exorbitant price.

In the winter 1994 issue of *The Public Interest* quarterly, Laurence Kotlikoff, a Boston University economist, and Jagadeesh Gokhale, an economist with the Federal Reserve Bank of Cleveland, wrote: "Americans born at the turn of this century paid just over a fifth of their lifetime incomes to the government. Those born at the beginning of the next century are likely to pay well over half their lifetime net incomes to the government."

But the policies that would produce that baneful result will not just happen to us, like the weather. What we need now are leaders who have Ronald Reagan's insouciant disrespect for bogus inevitabilities. We need to recapture the sense of possibilities that America had when it was born. It has been said that America was born claiming perfection and promising progress. It was born on the farm and moved to town, leaving behind the Jeffersonian vision.

The Louisiana Purchase, and restrictions on expansion of slavery, were supposed to guarantee a vast inland empire of small farmers perpetually renewing the young Republic's yeoman virtues of independence and self-sufficiency. But two aspects of 19th-century America—huge tracts of land to be cultivated, and a labor shortage—spurred the mechanization of agriculture. This increased production, and also increased price fluctuations and debts. Farmers saw their economic, political and social standing decline. Their independence and self-sufficiency were, by other names, loneliness and vulnerability forced upon them by bad roads and bad communications and cycles of overproduction, declining prices, failure and foreclosure.

I stress the problems of farmers to underscore a point: Big, activist government in America was *not* initially a response to urban industrialism. Forty years before the New Deal, rural populism was America's first powerful political movement to insist that the federal government has broad ameliorative responsibilities. Government responded with rural free delivery, rural electrification, paved roads (as late as the 1920s, most of South Dakota was untravelable during rainy springs), regulation of railroads and grain elevators, and the then radical policy of commodity price parity—an economic entitlement, a harbinger of the welfare state.

Historians argue heatedly about whether consensus or conflict is the dominant feature of American history. Actually, there is consensus about the cultural values of capitalist individualism; *and* there also is constant conflict between economic interests. Furthermore, although economic conflicts occur in a context of consensus about capitalist values, the economic conflicts often reinforce disagreement about other political values.

Consider the Republican Party which, like the Republic, got to the present from several directions. The Republican Party was the great "nationalizing" force and the architect of modern energetic government.

America's Founders learned (from John Locke, among others) that government exists for the modest purpose of protecting liberty, understood primarily as freedom from government. But the Republican Party's commitment to minimalist government did not survive the first Republican presidency. As the Civil War changed from a war to restore the Union as it had been, to a crusade for "a new birth of freedom," the federal government came to be regarded differently. It was seen less as a threat to freedom and more as a provider and enlarger of freedom.

The proximate cause of this changed perception was the Emancipation Proclamation, which was made possible by the Union victory at Antietam. So let us say that John Locke died at Antietam.

Before the Civil War the federal government had been barely visible to most Americans. By the end of the war the federal civilian bureaucracy was 53,000 strong. By then the federal government was the nation's largest employer and the Republican Party was determined to use it, vigorously. The war inaugurated a Republican era. Reconstruction in the South, and government-driven economic development in the North and West, reflected a redefinition of American freedom as something served by government power. As Eric Foner writes in his history of Reconstruction, the Emancipation Proclamation clothed federal power with moral purpose and a new class put that power to the service of what that class considered moral: its interest in economic growth.

The war stimulated industry, from railroads to meatpacking to clothing, and after the war, the Republican Party became the instrument of a commercial class demanding activist government to keep the growth going. Republican administrations provided tariffs, a national paper currency and banking system, public debt and encouragement of immigration. The Homestead Act and Land Grant College Act spread agricultural and other remunerative knowledge. Land grants and bond issues promoted railroads and other "internal improvements." War was waged against Indians who were slow to recognize the romance of railroading on their lands.

The 19th century may have been a century of "individualism" but it also was a century of tariffs, subsidies, monopoly grants to canals and railroad companies. Ten percent of the public domain was given in land grants to finance the transcontinental railroads. The Union Pacific alone was given 4,845,977 acres of Nebraska—one-tenth of the state—including every other section along its right of way for 24 miles on each side of the track.

Until well into the 20th century, writes Michael Barone, Republicans were "the national, activist, even busybody party." Democrats, professing Jeffersonian defense of localisms, respected regional mores, "from segregation in the South to the saloon in the North." In the 1920s and '30s some Republicans—Robert La Follette, George Norris, Fiorello La Guardia—were among the strongest congressional advocates of government policies of nationalization and redistribution. And remember, it was a Republican administration—Eisenhower's—that undertook the simultaneous construction of two of the most ambitious modern public works, the St. Lawrence Seaway and the Interstate Highway System.

So Republicans, with their heritage of activism, cannot be altogether scandalized by the fact that since 1929 government expenditures (federal, state and local) have grown four times as fast as GDP and federal

expenditures have grown seven times as fast. In 1929 private investment was five times larger than the federal budget; in 1991 it was about
half as large. Again, big government was born during an era of Republican domination, 1870–1932, before there was a federal welfare state
(other than pensions for Civil War veterans). In just 26 basically Republican years, 1887–1913, there came the Interstate Commerce Commission, the Sherman Antitrust Act, the Food and Drug Administration, the
Federal Trade Commission, the Federal Reserve System and the federal
income tax.

By the beginning of the 20th century a majority of Americans felt that
government needed strengthening because it seemed anemic compared
to the institutions and problems of industrial capitalism. However, on
the eve of the 21st century, an American majority believes that government is overdeveloped, decreasingly competent and increasingly costly
to freedom.

I had reason to brood about this when, not long ago, I drove north
from Washington to a city that claims to have been the nation's first
capital—York, Pennsylvania. There one can usefully meditate about
why Americans are so dismayed about the federal government.

The Continental Congress came to York when it fled Philadelphia in
1777, the grim year that the British, noting the three sevens, called "the
year of three gallows." On November 15 the Congress approved the Articles of Confederation, the nation's first constitution. Desperately
struggling to throw off a tyranny and determined not to create a new
one, the authors of the Articles created only a wisp of a government.
The constitution adopted in York created a government too limited to
establish the necessary priority of national over state citizenship. But
the second Constitution, the one written 70 miles east of York 10 years
later, created what has become today's swollen government, a government operating with no limits on incontinent spending and regulating.

The Constitution we now have empowers Congress to make any laws
"necessary and proper" to promoting the "general welfare." "Necessary" is now construed broadly to mean "helpful," and anything helpful
is deemed proper. So today we have an utterly unleashed and frenzied
Congress. It is funding bike paths, fish farms, the production of mohair,
the study of the Hatfield-McCoy feud and thousands of other trivialities
pleasing to factions in 435 congressional districts.

Today Congress is broadly despised because it is so comprehensively
solicitous of its despisers. It tries to do too much, usually at the behest
of factions among the despisers. It does thousands of little things, but
does few of the important things adequately—things like budgeting and
providing domestic tranquility.

Until well into this century, the federal budget reflected a particular understanding of the Constitution. The budget dealt with a few fundamental undertakings—defense, revenue collection, public works that neither the private sector nor lower governments were able to provide. Today the budget reflects the federal government's unlimited notion of its purview and competence—its eagerness to promote prosperity, fine-tune "fairness," administer "compassion," nurture the arts and sciences, and so on—everything, everywhere.

For about 150 years after the Founding, political controversies at the federal level were apt to begin with debate about constitutional principle—whether the federal government's enumerated powers entitled it to act in a particular field. Only after that was settled was there debate about the proper policy for that field. Today almost nobody in either the legislative or executive branch believes that there is any subject, any sphere, from which the federal government is constitutionally excluded. However, the eclipse of that idea does not mean that prudence should not do what constitutional principle once did—restrain the federal government's itch to be active everywhere, an itch that is discrediting the federal government and making a mockery of federalism.

We have strayed far from sound principles. But let us not despair—conservatives least of all. History has come our way. As a British socialist recently said, "Every contemporary democratic society is capitalist." Today, for the first time in two centuries, the left has nothing coherent, let alone militant, to say about the problem framed by the first great critic of the left, Edmund Burke—the problem of distinguishing between "what the state ought to take upon itself to direct by the public wisdom, and what it ought to leave, with as little interference as possible, to individual discretion."

Marx thought communism would be the final stage in mankind's passage from feudalism through capitalism and then socialism, to the end of history. Actually, communism was the rebirth of feudalism's melding of economic and political life. Today the pressure for the expansion of politics into the economic sphere is mounting in many places. The acceleration of technological change, and intensified competition in the global economy, are provoking reactions against freedom even in societies which have much experience with the stresses that freedom occasions. The reflex of flinching, of seeking to freeze the status quo, poses a large challenge to contemporary politics. The challenge is to make freedom palatable for those who, with reason, find it threatening.

Democratic governments are nowadays held responsible for any process that produces casualties, as economic dynamism invariably does. Furthermore, as capitalism makes nations increasingly wealthy, those nations become decreasingly tolerant of the discomforts of change. They crave stability. Therefore, the coming of capitalism to underdeveloped countries, by making them more productive and generating competitive pressures on developed nations, diminishes those developed nations' support for liberal trade policies. So we should listen to the warning from Chris Patten, governor of Hong Kong:

> A Martian visitor traveling from the mud and disease of Tudor London via the tepee settlements of North America to the Ming mandarinate of 16th-century Beijing would have guessed without a millisecond's hesitation that China would lead the world for centuries to come. Where Europe was made up of warring cities and domains, China had an efficient government to preside over a sprawling but united country. China knew the power of the pen and the sword; it had invented both printing and gunpowder. It had invented the compass, too, and had sent a huge navy halfway around the world. No one could touch China for plenitude of civilized living; no one could match its inventiveness and industrial might. But it did not work out like that. The Martian got it wrong. The Middle Kingdom retreated behind its great wall, and history told a different tale.

We, who have seen the Berlin Wall fall, must not retreat behind the wall of government protection from change. The security promised by government is actually a chimera. "Security" is today the theme of the first Democratic president elected since the 1970s. And pursuant to the sound advice that one should perform an unpleasant duty each day to stay in moral trim, I herewith will say something nice—sort of—about the liberalism now ascendant in Washington. What I say is: It could be worse.

Consider this irony: The great achievement of 20th-century liberalism is the welfare state which, because of the ravenous appetite of its entitlement programs for revenues, is now the principal impediment to contemporary liberalism's goal of activist government. Half the federal budget is now devoured by entitlement programs—government on automatic pilot. The entitlement programs' transfer payments go disproportionately to the elderly—pensions and medical care—so this portion of the budget will swell as the population ages. (Seventy-six million baby boomers—those born between 1946, the year of Bill Clinton's birth, and 1964—are heading for senior citizen status.) Another 15 percent of the budget goes to pay interest on the national debt. That leaves only one-third of the budget for defense and discretionary domestic spending. So, what is left for the political left?

To be on the left is to believe this: The goal of politics is to capture state power in order to force egalitarian social change. But the American left cannot cope with the American middle. The middle class has most of the nation's money and has no desire to pay more taxes. So the government will, over time, become a transfer payment pump, a great gray source of stipends for familiar entitlement programs. The federal government that Clinton and like-minded liberals see as an "agent of change" may soon be a device defined by inertia—entitlements, interest payments, defense and not much else.

Already the government is almost immobilized by its thousands of threads of commitments. This presents a striking contrast with the nimbleness of government at the dawn of modern liberalism. On day two of FDR's famous first 100 days he ordered a national bank holiday. On day five Congress passed his banking bill almost unanimously. On day seven, in spite of a revolt by 90 Democrats, the House passed his bill cutting veterans' benefits and federal employees' pay. On day 12 he submitted a farm bill that presaged many of the subsequent follies of federal agriculture programs. The House passed it on day 18. On day 17 he had proposed the Civilian Conservation Corps. It became law three weeks later. On day 36 he proposed the Tennessee Valley Authority. He signed it into law on day 76. On November 2, 1933, FDR was given the proposal for a Civil Works Administration to employ people on such public works as street repair and digging sewers. By November 23, 800,000 people were employed; five weeks later, 4.25 million—8 percent of the nation's labor force. Today it might take months just to negotiate the racial set-asides for such a program.

The governmental activism of the 1930s, Ronald Reagan's formative years, may or may not have been on balance wise, but at least the activism was driven by something dire—the Depression. Imagine: One day in May 1934 a dust storm stretching from Texas to Canada and soaring 15,000 feet blew east. Dust settled on FDR's desk and on ships hundreds of miles out on the Atlantic. By December, two of every five South Dakotans were on relief—the nation's highest percentage. In July 1935 the grasshoppers returned.

The government activism of the 1960s, the years of Ronald Reagan's political ascent in opposition to that activism, was driven by the self-interest and hubris of the government. By then, government itself—the governing class—had become the largest interest group, lobbying itself for the enlargement of itself. The shining creations of governmental activism of the 1960s, unlike those of the 1930s, had few glittering consequences because they were not produced by the sort of broad, powerful political forces that produced, say, Social Security and unemployment insurance. What, then, produced much of the activism of the 1960s? The same force that is producing the activism of the 1990s—a class of professional reformers.

Bred to life in the public sector, the private sector is as foreign to many of them as Mongolia. Their careers do not just depend on the extension of state power, their careers *are* that extension. They believe that they, being experts, know best. And the fact that there is not much public demand for most of the activism that the experts want is itself proof of the need for the activism. And it is proof of the expertise of the experts who discern the need. They think people need to become wards of government experts precisely because people do not understand what the experts understand, starting with the indispensability of the experts.

Consider O'Sullivan's First Law (authored by John O'Sullivan, editor of *National Review*): "All organizations that are not actively right-wing will over time become left-wing." O'Sullivan has in mind organizations like the American Civil Liberties Union, the Ford Foundation, the Episcopal Church. People who run such organizations tend to disdain business, making money, private property, even the current arrangement of society. But O'Sullivan's law holds for U.S. administrations: Those not conservative by principle become statist and hyperactive by innate momentum. They are staffed by people who have no principled reason for resisting government's natural tendency to expand. Indeed, they are in the public sector because they think it is wiser and more moral than the private sector.

And there is another inherent disadvantage under which conservatism operates. Conservative ideas, says Pete du Pont, are harder to sell than liberal ideas because the costs, or risks, of conservative ideas often are immediate and obvious, whereas the benefits may be delayed and indirect. For example, a capital gains rate reduction may increase the deficit and make some rich people richer, "but," says du Pont, "the benefit of a stronger economy arrives on a different train, an unknown track and with an uncertain schedule."

Conservatism has both rhetorical and fiscal strategies for containing the growth of government power. One strategy is to peel away government's authority by flaying it rhetorically as an incestuous jumble of corrupt elites incapable of empathy with ordinary people and incompetent at government's basic tasks—budgeting, educating, maintaining public works. Conservatism preaches that intervention in economic and social relations does not merely propitiate interest groups, it creates them. Some of them organize to defend benefits that were bestowed without having been requested. This is supply-side government, whereby government supplies a program, thereby increasing the supply of groups making demands.

Interest groups, drawn to Washington like flies to manure, resist revitalizing federalism by devolving responsibilities to states. Such devolution would inconvenience interest groups. They prefer "one-stop shopping" (the phrase is from Michael Horowitz of the Manhattan Institute) in Washington to shopping in 50 capitals.

There is a sense in which conservatism, as a criticism of the concentration of power in a large central government, is the natural inheritor of the American impulse called "populism." This is so because the modern state is inherently unfair. It is so because it is susceptible to manipulation by well-heeled and well-connected interests. But caution is in order when identifying conservatism with populism.

"Populism" is by now another word pounded to mush by careless usage. The most successful populist of this half-century was a Democrat: George Wallace. He shaped the vocabulary, and hence the agenda, of national politics. He could give today's Democratic populists a lesson in Washington bashing. Remember his 1968 promise to toss the pointy-headed bureaucrats' briefcases into the Potomac? But today's Democrats are implausible Washington-bashers. Their party is primarily responsible for Washington's swollenness and hubris.

Populists are people who adore "the people," so populists must be swell people, right? Not necessarily. Populism has a chip on its shoulder and self-pity in its heart. Its fuel is resentment, usually of some conspiracy from afar by an alien elite. Populism often has been xenophobic, racist, nativist, anti-Semitic and paranoid. Still, real populism, that of the late 19th century, did have the dignity of moral seriousness about the country's core values in an era of wrenching social change.

Americans still are, and ever will be, arguing about the tension between freedom and equality, interestedness and virtue. History never halts. Who would want it to? Certainly not the cheerful President who, believing in the fecundity of freedom, sought the presidency in 1980 so he could push the fast-forward button on history. The sense of an acceleration of events during the eight Reagan years was no accident. But the acceleration seems to have unhinged the understanding of those who are supposed to make sense of current events—the journalists.

After a quarter of a century in Washington, I know that journalists, who fancy themselves paladins of "the public's right to know," are themselves often the last to know. That is, they are the last to know the deeper currents running in our culture. This is largely because Washington journalists are so thoroughly marinated in that city's political culture. They like it. That is why they are what, and where, they are. And that is why they will be the last to understand the good done by conservatives in the 1980s, when the old principles were revitalized, with the result that the future, at home and abroad, looks more beckoning.

More than five years have passed since the January day when the helicopter carrying the President and Mrs. Reagan rose from the Capitol plaza, flew a farewell circle around the Washington Monument and headed for Andrews Air Force Base and a flight back to California. They can be confident of the judgment of history about their years in Washington. History, said a wit (a witty historian, in fact, Phillip Gudella), repeats itself, and historians repeat each other. So do journalists as they dash off their first rough drafts of history. Subsequent drafts are apt to be wiser. There is no such thing as a final draft of the history of anything. However, the balanced judgment that will, I wager, be struck by judicious historians will be kind to the Reagan years and respectful to the man by whose name those years will forever be known.

February 28, 1994

The Coming of Congressional Government

Two weekends ago, when the government was under the Gramm-Rudman guillotine, the President traveled back to Washington from Camp David by car—not even a limousine—rather than helicopter, to affirm frugality. This Carteresque gesture began a week during which Bush stepped from his car onto a bunch of political banana skins strewn by himself. On Monday he said X about taxes. On Tuesday some Republican senators told him he really thought not-X, and he agreed. Asked on Wednesday (before Thursday's several staggers) whether he could clarify his position he said, "Let Congress clear it up." Those were portentous words.

Because of Bush's limitations as a leader he is losing a perennial constitutional argument: Who comes closest to having a mandate to rule, the President or Congress? Bush's pratfalls last week underscored the evanescence of presidential power. Bush is a case study of why, more often than not, presidents lack mandates and Congress has, if not a mandate, the next best thing: supremacy.

Bush contributed to the restoration of the American norm—congressional government—by the way he campaigned. Today he is augmenting congressional ascendancy by governing in a manner that illustrates this: Most presidents lack the skill or will to make the presidency more than subservient. And now Robert A. Dahl, emeritus professor at Yale, has published (in *Political Science Quarterly*) an essay, "Myth of the Presidential Mandate," which suggests that subservience ought to be a president's lot.

Andrew Jackson was the first president to argue that presidents, the officials elected by national votes, necessarily acquire mandates that put them at least on a par with Congress, which is a conglomeration of representatives of lesser constituencies. Prior to Jackson and for most of the 19th century, the prevailing doctrine was that Congress is the principal representative of the people. Jefferson's first message to Congress was couched in language of a nonpartisan executive: "Nothing shall be wanting on my part to inform, as far as in my power, the legislative judgment, nor to carry that judgment into faithful execution." According to Edward S. Corwin, the constitutional historian, "The tone of [Jefferson's] messages is uniformly deferential to Congress."

So totally did Monroe subscribe to the doctrine of congressional supremacy, he was utterly silent on the burning issue of the day, the admission of Missouri to statehood and the status of slavery in Louisiana Territory. Teddy Roosevelt and, even more, Woodrow Wilson asserted presidential supremacy by invoking the mystique of the mandate. The nation, wrote Wilson, "is conscious that it has no other political spokesman. His is the only national voice."

Dahl doubts that presidential campaigns generate mandates for specific policies. He says a necessary (but not sufficient) condition for claiming a mandate is winning a majority of the votes. Reagan in 1980 (50.7 percent) and Carter in 1976 (50.1) barely qualified and Kennedy in 1960 (49.7) and Nixon in 1968 (43.4) did not. And, says Dahl, even when a president wins a majority there can be competing claims for mandates: Democratic candidates for the House won 50.4 percent of the vote in 1980 and 52 percent in 1984.

But wait. Perhaps it can be demonstrated (as modern opinion research purports to do) that presidential elections usually involve meaningful majority consent to particular policies only at high levels of generality ("Get America moving again," 1960; "Peace with honor," 1968; "Cut taxes," 1980; "No new taxes," 1988). But such a demonstration does not dispose of the concept of a mandate.

Whatever else elections do, they confer offices. Since TR, Wilson and, decisively, FDR invented the modern presidency, presidential elections have conferred a mandate in this limited but not negligible sense: Elections create a public mood of initial deference to acts of presidential discretion.

In 1988 Bush got a mandate for . . . what? For not furloughing Willie Horton? For pledging allegiance? For cutting capital gains taxes? (How many Bush voters were swayed by, or even aware of, that idea?) But even campaigns less negative and vapid than Bush's confer, primarily, an office and initial deference. That is, an election provides less a mandate than an opportunity to fashion a specific mandate while, and by, governing.

"The president," wrote President (of Princeton) Woodrow Wilson in 1908,

> is at liberty, both in law and conscience, to be as big a man as he can. His capacity will set the limit; and if Congress be overborne by him, it will be no fault of the makers of the Constitution—it will be from no lack of constitutional powers on its part, but only because the president has the nation behind him, and Congress has not. He has no means of compelling Congress except through public opinion.

For a few presidents, those with the requisite will and skill, some modern extraconstitutional developments (broadcasting; opinion measurements techniques) compensate for Congress's superior constitutional powers. The kind of presidency ("tribune of the people," "rhetorical," "plebiscitary") necessary for wresting supremacy from Congress is an innovation. "From Washington through Jackson," writes Dahl, "no president gave more than five speeches a year to the general public, a total that was not exceeded by half the presidents from Washington through William McKinley." Presidents spoke primarily to Congress (usually in formal language and deferential tones), and occasionally to the public in the sort of generalities heard in inaugural addresses.

But today's political culture—a maelstrom of interest groups generated by omniprovident government—makes coherent congressional government impossible; hence presidential ascendancy is necessary. However, it may be beyond Bush's capacities.

Bush inherited the presidency from a "conviction politician" who, because he was that, often aroused public opinion to compel Congress. But Bush seems to regard as lèse-majesté the idea that he must constantly earn his claim on the public's continuing deference. Such deference depends on clarity about ideas and principles—"the vision thing." That is why Bush's inarticulateness, although often comic, is not funny. It is not an esthetic but a philosophic failing. He does not say why he wants to be there, so the public does not know why it should care if he gets his way. Until the public does, he won't. Congress will.

October 22, 1990

The Veep and the Blatherskite

The more thoughtful half of the Bush-Quayle team has recently been brimming over with thoughts, two of which merit more amplification than he gave them. Quayle says Perot "has contempt for the Constitution." And Quayle says the election of Perot would deepen the problem of "the deadlock between the elected branches" of the government. "So let us return to the tried and true. Let us elect a president—Republican or Democrat—and give him a Congress that responds to presidential leadership."

Perot, whose preferred rhetorical mode is the murky expostulation, is what used to be called a blatherskite. There is an inverse relationship between the confidence he has in his opinions and the care he has taken in forming them. Consider this doozy of a Perotism: "Germany and Japan are winning. Why are they winning? They got new constitutions in 1945. This was a time when the Industrial Revolution had occurred. Our Constitution was written 200 years ago, before it occurred." Leaving aside the fuzzy, panicky notion that Germany and Japan are "winning," what is Perot's point? That our Constitution is incompatible with industrialism? Tell that to Carnegie and all the other industrialists who had nothing to learn from Perot about making things and money. What does he think the modern world requires that our Constitution prevents?

Ignorance of constitutional values, rather than contempt for them, probably explains Perot's plan to pass "a law" that "says Congress cannot raise taxes," and his desire for referendums (on raising taxes, on use of military force) that would be, to say no more, extraconstitutional. His thinking—or, lacking evidence of such, his talking—does suggest deep-seated impatience with the Constitution's purposeful patterns of indirectness. The principles of representation and separation of powers are supposed to conduce to deliberation—deliberate rather than precipitate behavior. The government's divided structure is designed to produce a measured pace compatible with thoughtful and prudent behavior by the few who are elected to act for the many. Perot's urge to give government a plebiscitary cast conflicts with the Founders' aspirations. But so does Quayle's supposedly "tried and true" theory of presidential "leadership" to which Congress "responds."

The Founders tried to constitute deliberative democracy which would filter the public's unformed sentiments and give them shape and the weight of reasonableness. Such democracy requires that the deliberative body—Congress, as the Founders hoped it would be—enjoy at least equal status with the presidency. It requires presidents to deliberate with Congress rather than expect Congress to "respond" to leadership as a horse responds to a bit and bridle.

What Quayle considers traditional, and people seem to desire, is neither traditional nor desirable. It is what Jeffrey Tulis calls, in his brilliant book with this title, "the rhetorical presidency." It is the presidency serving as the sun around which American government, indeed America's consciousness, supposedly should orbit. But today's clamor for "leadership" would have dismayed the Founders, for many of whom "popular leader" was synonymous with "demagogue." The term "leader" appears 12 times in *The Federalist* papers, and is used disparagingly 11 times. (The other reference is to leaders of the Revolution.) The Founders believed presidential appeals to, and manipulation of, public opinion would be an anticonstitutional preemption of deliberative processes. Thus there was, until this century, " 'a common law' of rhetoric." Presidents spoke infrequently and about little. Washington averaged just three popular speeches a year; Adams, one; Jefferson, five. Madison, president during a war that burned his house, gave none. The 24 presidents prior to Theodore Roosevelt gave about 1,000 speeches, but more than half of these were by three presidents (Hayes, Harrison, McKinley).

Until the 20th century, presidents communicated primarily with the legislative branch, not "the people," and communicated in written messages suitable for deliberative reasoning. Then modern technologies of transportation and communication gave presidents new capacities, and Woodrow Wilson supplied a theory for using them. Presidents, he said, should engage in "interpretation," meaning the discovery of what is in the hearts of the masses—or would be there if the masses were sensible. Soon presidents were everywhere, moving about, by railroad and then airplane. They were in the air by radio, then television. America was on its way to today's notion of the president as tribune of the people, constant auditor of the nation's psyche, molder of the public mind.

Perot's impatience with inhibiting institutions and shaping structures echoes the complaints of many Progressives and New Dealers, who considered the Constitution an outmoded impediment to decisive, vigorous government. Quayle's call for a Congress responsive to presidential "leadership" echoes Woodrow Wilson, who was the bridge between the Progressives and the modern presidency that was consolidated during the New Deal.

The Founders' philosophy has not recently been tried but is still true.

Employing the principle of representation and the separation of powers, the Framers constructed constitutional distance between the government and the governed. Their hope was that deliberative processes could, in Madison's words, "refine and enlarge the public views" and produce "the cool and deliberate sense of the community." This is why they made Congress the First Branch of government, Article One in the Constitution.

But today's slatternly Congress, its members sunk in careerism, exemplifies the degradation of democracy into a mere maelstrom of appetites. As Congress has lost esteem, including self-esteem, the presidency has become the nation's obsession. Trouble is, most presidents are mediocre. And when the weight of Wilsonian expectations is put upon a figure as flimsy as George Bush, the presidency buckles and the nation becomes susceptible to Perot's watery Caesarism. This is the bitter fruit of our disrespect for our 18th-century Founders. And it may be a glimpse of what the 21st century has up its nasty sleeve.

June 29, 1992

Vacuum vs. Resentment

These lead-gray late-winter days are especially dreary for many conservatives. Conservatism is currently being defined either by Pat Buchanan's bad ideas (nativism, protectionism, isolationism) or Bush's lack of ideas. Buchanan says Bush's privileged background precludes his having sympathy with ordinary people, and that Bush has betrayed conservative principles. But Bush's disdain for domestic problems and politics should not be blamed on his background. And the plaintive claim that Bush has betrayed conservatives comes from people gullible enough to have believed that he has beliefs. By the way, who is Buchanan to be checking conservatives' credentials?

Guess who says this about Bush:

The President conveys something seigneurial and contemptuous as a campaigner; it is as if the whole contest were *beneath him*. . . . He kept saying that he "cared" about the economic hardship individual citizens were experiencing, as if his "caring"—his notice—were all the affected people were after. He did not offer substance, as if he didn't really have to, the implication being that these folks could be swayed with less. He was, as he generally is, snobby-dismissive of his critics. . . .

So says *The Washington Post*, which agrees with Buchanan about only one thing: Bush's grating persona.

But conservatives should not blame Bush's condescending disconnection from the country on Bush's Andover-Yale upbringing. A bad attitude is not a necessary result of good schools. The president who engineered the end of the WASP ascendancy grew up cosseted by privilege on a Hudson Valley estate. In winter his parents took him out in a horse-drawn sleigh lined with red velvet and bearing the family crest, a sleigh originally a gift from Tsar Alexander II to Napoleon III. And when Franklin Roosevelt went from Groton to Harvard, all but two of his classmates went with him. Bush could be better, he just isn't.

Conservatives should not be social determinists in explaining character, or its lack. But reverse snobbery has recently been all the rage in Republicans' intramural dust-ups. In 1980 Reagan came out of his tar paper shack in Pacific Palisades to beat up Bush who, Reaganites said, was "a clean fingernails Republican." (Reagan presumably dirtied his nails cutting the brush on his Santa Barbara ranch.) In 1988 Bob Dole ran a more-downtrodden-than-thou campaign against Bush, bragging about his rise from the lower orders in Kansas. This drove Bush to boast that he was a bowling alley kind of guy. Bush in 1988 was the first Republican nominee born to wealth since Taft in 1908. But the emptiness of Bush's politics is not a necessary result of anything. President (and Chief Justice) William Howard Taft had a fine mind and a fine family. And his grandson, the senator, did not let a Yale education incapacitate him for a life of thoughtful conservatism.

Thirty-two years ago Buchanan was moved by Barry Goldwater's *The Conscience of a Conservative*. Fighting faiths make much of the claims of conscience. Buchanan calls his current insurrection an imperative of conscience, an act of fealty to principle. Well now. Buchanan's principles did not prevent him from serving six pugnaciously loyal years in Nixon's White House. Never mind the crime wave there. But Nixon's administration was the second most liberal administration since the New Deal, second only, and not by much, to Lyndon Johnson's.

Nixon's wage-and-price controls constituted the largest peacetime intrusion of government into the economy in American history, surpassing even the dreams of the New Dealers. Nixon saying, "We are all Keynesians now," had an industrial policy (subsidizing the SST) and he got government into running a railroad (Amtrak). He initiated revenue sharing, which weakened spending restraints at state and local levels. He created the Burger Court which did not overturn any major Warren Court precedent. Its 1973 abortion decision was an act of raw judicial power as sweeping and unconnected with constitutional reasoning as any opinion in the Court's history. In 1971 in a Charlotte, North Carolina, case a unanimous Court, with Burger writing the ruling, allowed judges vast latitude to order forced busing to achieve racial balance in schools. Today's racial spoils system gained momentum from Nixon's "Philadelphia plan" for minority contractor set-asides in the construction industry.

The Environmental Protection Agency and the Occupational Safety and Health Administration were born under Nixon. The seeds of today's deficit explosion were sown in Nixon's competition with Wilbur Mills, the chairman of the Ways and Means Committee, to see who could be most lavish with Social Security. But Buchanan, who considers Bush an apostate from the conservative church, still speaks of Nixon as one of the faithful.

The Wall Street Journal's David Brooks writes that when Bush tries to resemble a Reaganite, he clearly feels he is ideologically slumming and "comes out looking like a French kid trying to do rap music—lots of effort, no effect." But Bush is where he is because of the Reagan connection, and that means conservatives have a problem.

The conservative *National Review* says that because Bush is Reagan's heir "in fact, if not in spirit," conservatives must take "decisive distinguishing action" lest recent conservatism be retroactively discredited by association with Bush. But some distinctions Buchanan draws are injurious. Against Bush's lazy, muzzy drift, Buchanan proposes a purposeful march down a descending, crumbling path that the European right took to oblivion decades ago. He blends nationalism with statism, including protectionism against the challenge of change, which he sometimes denounces as "vulture capitalism." And he, like today's campus leftists, encourages a crabbed, defensive, ill-humored definition of America not in terms of shared affirmations of ideas but of a sharpened sense of ethnic identities, some of them preferable to others. (Zulus and Yalies, he suggests, pose severe assimilation problems.)

Caught between the vacuum that is Bush and the resentment that is Buchanan, conservatism faces its worst identity crisis since Goldwater and Reagan, two tough but also generous and amiable Westerners, stepped, almost simultaneously, onstage, smiling.

March 9, 1992

Politics and a Sense of Proportion

Bill Gray's departure from politics for admirable reasons, and the preposterous reasons John Sununu gives for lusting after the perquisites of power, intimate the end of an era.

Congressman Gray of Philadelphia, third-ranking Democratic leader in the House and the highest-ranking black in House history, might have become Speaker, in time. But there are, he thinks, better uses of his time. He is resigning to become head of the United Negro College Fund.

Washington—or, more precisely, the city's predominately white political and media sliver—is uncomprehending and aghast. Many liberals are particularly dismayed by this instance of self-determination by a black man.

Gray's decision, which gestated for two years, involves a mix of motives. True, he can make more money as a private citizen (and he has a handicapped child for whose future to provide). However, Gray also knows that not just political empowerment but social development—particularly enlargement of the black middle class—is the crucial challenge for the black community. In this, Congress can be at most marginally important.

Given the surge of their enrollments—up 17 percent in four years, twice the college average nationally—the 41 colleges served by the UNCF may educate close to one million students in the next decade. The students range from needy inner-city and rural blacks, who for cultural reasons do not test well but who are college material, to upper-middle-class blacks (the Huxtable children) seeking an intensely black experience.

Gray, a preacher who values pastoral duties more than political duties, is a former teacher whose father was president of two black colleges. His career change, as an affirmation of fresh starts and of education, is quintessentially American.

Sununu's comportment expresses a dark side of recent American experience, the grotesque inflation of pretentiousness by presidential appendages. This has become a plague since 1945, as one presidential role, that of commander-in-chief, has come to predominate over all others.

Absurd notions of urgent haste, cockeyed obsessions with secrecy, delusions of indispensability—these have been pathologies of presidential aides during the era of the national security state in a hair-trigger world. They are ingredients in Sununu's insistence on grand travel arrangements even to political fund-raisers, stamp auctions, dentists and ski slopes.

So extreme is his horror of merely commercial aviation, his government chauffeur had to cart him on a five-hour journey to a Manhattan stamp auction. So desperate was Sununu to avoid the hourly flights between Chicago and Washington, he violated rules and misled White House lawyers in his frantic solicitation of private jets from the wealthy.

As his behavior has become that of a buffoon, his explanations have become Napoleonic. They are symptoms of elephantiasis of the ego to which small people orbiting around presidents are prone. Perhaps such people are especially prone when serving a president who believes that seriousness starts at the water's edge—foreign policy is everything.

Sununu, says Sununu, must be constantly able to be in instant voice communication with the President, if at all possible on a secure telephone. (In a dentist's chair? On skis? Gosh.) Does he try to schedule his Boston dental appointments in the likely intervals between nuclear attacks? (Does the dentist dare put those little cotton tubes in Sununu's mouth? What if the President called?) How fortunate the Republic was to survive 20 decades before the policy of instant communication was dreamed up to flatter its adherents.

But perhaps we may hope that the Sununu mentality will go the way of the Berlin Wall. Maybe the government will get off its tiptoes.

Campaigning in St. Louis for the League of Nations in September 1919, Woodrow Wilson warned of habits of mind that might be produced by perpetual high tensions among nations. We would, said Wilson, think of the President not merely as important temporary counselor but as commander-in-chief. Information and plans would be secreted. (In 1989, the year the Wall fell, the U.S. government, according to itself, created 6,796,501 new secrets.) In the world Wilson warned against, "We must be physically ready for anything to come."

Sununu, tootling along the New Jersey Turnpike, or zipping about in mooched jets, with his papers soggy with secrets and safe from the prying eyes of passengers, sure has been ready for anything.

We cannot restore the world in which President Jefferson said he had not heard from his ambassador in Spain for three years and if he did not hear for another year, he would write to him. We are a far piece from even the world of 60 years ago, when presidents elected in November were not inaugurated until March and Congress did not convene until the following December—13 months after being elected.

But the 1990s are ripe for restoration of a republican—small *r*—sense of proportion regarding government. Conservatives, especially, should note that Gray, who is leaving, has it, and Sununu, who is staying, does not.

June 30, 1991

Ross Perot: America's Rorschach Test

Herman Rorschach, a Swiss psychiatrist, gauged patients' mental states by what they saw in inkblots. Ross Perot is America's Rorschach test. His rise reveals America's dangerous cult of presidential leadership.

Perot's popularity is fresh (and redundant) evidence that the public suffers from what psychiatrists call cognitive dissonance, an incongruity between attitudes and behavior. That often is brought on by the mental incoherence of professing, simultaneously and fervidly, incompatible beliefs. The public wants Perot to put an end to what the public's wants have produced—the fiscal crisis caused by the public's demand for increased government and decreased taxes. And while the public claims to want more modesty from politicians, the public flirts with Perot, a politician (especially political in his denial that he is a politician) of stupendous vanity.

Freud was the vainest person who ever lived because he believed that no one prior to him had ever understood anything, his insights being indispensable and sufficient for understanding everything. But Perot's political vanity is impressive. He seems to think America has problems because it has not had the benefit of his willfulness; that compared to him, everyone in public life lacks courage or common sense; that he can assuage conflict and reconcile competing values by establishing, in his person, an electronic communion with "the people" through televised "town meetings." (Never mind that town meetings are supposed to serve a polity the size of a small New England town, not a continental nation, and that such meetings are for discussions and decisions, not gatherings to give a leader information.)

Perot's childlike fascination with gadgetry envisions government as a great telephone answering machine. The evident idea behind his electronic town meetings is that government is not properly responsive because the public's wishes are not well measured. Actually, government today involves minute measurement of public appetites by servile politicians worshipful of those measurements. Such government reflects the decay of deliberative democracy into plebiscitary, answering-machine democracy.

The core principle of our republicanism is representation: The people do not decide things, they decide who will decide. Representatives are supposed to deliberate about the national interest, not just broker demands registered from various factions. But Perot's idea of the plebiscitary presidency reflects Woodrow Wilson's revolution against the Founders' idea of deliberative democracy.

The Perot phenomenon is a consequence of Wilson's mystification of the presidency. Wilson's theory of presidential government makes the president the indispensable catalyst of mass opinion. He defined the primary business of government as the massing of opinion by a strong leader. More than a decade before he became president, Wilson the political scientist wrote:

> A nation is led by a man . . . in whose ears the voices of the nation . . . sound . . . like the united voices of a chorus, whose many meanings, spoken by melodious tongues, unite in his understanding in a single meaning and reveal to him a single vision, so that he can speak what no man else knows, the common meaning of the common voice.

So a Wilsonian president knows "what no man else knows" and his mystical "understanding" and "single vision" supplant all constitutional arrangements and become the sole motor of government. A cult of leadership was in the air here and abroad in Wilson's day. Soon in Italy, and then Germany, the head of government was called simply Leader (Duce, Führer).

In Wilson's 1913 Inaugural he was at it again, having visions: "At last a vision has been vouchsafed us of our life as a whole. . . . We know our task to be no mere task of politics. . . ." "Mere" politics is not enough for a mystical Leader, whose business is the ecstatic transformation of the nation into a melodious chorus.

The Founders' idea of government centered on the deliberation of many representatives has been replaced by the idea of presidential "interpretation" (Wilson's word). The leader interprets what is on the mind of the masses, or would be on that mind if the masses were made to think clearly. What that means today is that the electronic town meeting will come to order.

When Senator Tim Wirth (D-Colo.) recently announced his decision not to seek a second term, he listed many defects of American life, including George Bush, who, Wirth said, "refuses to lead, who does not seem to have a sense of where he wants the country to go, and whose lack of direction in turn pervades the whole government."

Wirth, too, reflects Wilson's obsession with the presidential persona: If a president is inadequate, stasis pervades the government, and the country is threatened by entropy. Bush is a mediocre president, but most presidents have been mediocre. What is new is the notion that the nation's health is held hostage to the genius, or lack of genius, of the chief executive.

The public's pathetic determination to perceive genius in Ross Perot, that political inkblot, is a result of what Wilson wrought.

May 28, 1992

Ross Perot's Pose: The Reluctant Sheriff

Who, besides Bill Clinton and George Bush, is responsible for Ross Perot's remarkable political rise? Owen Wister is. Ninety years ago this week he published a novel, *The Virginian*. It pioneered a literary genre, the Western; it invented the cowboy of popular imagination, and it defined a region, the West, as a repository of American yearnings and regrets.

Perot is a blank book that Americans are judging by its cover. The values they are reading into him were first vivified in *The Virginian*, which in 1902 was avidly read by Americans who had anxieties that seem familiar. Their bumptious America, fresh from the exhilaration of the "splendid little war" with Spain, was feeling its oats and was full of respect for all varieties of virility. But Americans looked back uneasily on the grasping materialism of the Gilded Age and looked ahead queasily to the growth of large entities—teeming cities, arrogant corporations—that could suffocate individualism and personal independence. Into this unsettled society rode Wister's cowboy, "the last romantic figure upon our soil . . . a hero without wings."

In 1902 there was a cowboy—from Fifth Avenue, via Dakota Territory—in the White House. Teddy Roosevelt was Wister's friend and hero. Like Wister, and many other well-bred Easterners, TR was a prep school and Harvard graduate who went west for physical and mental revival and came to regard the West as a sanatorium for the nation's soul. (Another gently born Easterner, a Connecticut Yalie, came to the White House by a roundabout route through the West: George Bush, the oil wildcatter from Midland, Texas.)

America is a product of two immigrations. One brought people to these shores. The other rolled westward, away from the urban wilderness of East Coast congestion, to what Wister called, "these free plains, this wilderness of do-as-you-please." In part, Wister's Virginian was Huck Finn on a raft the size of Wyoming, on a river as broad as the West. Like Huck, the Virginian was short on book learning but long on broadening experience. He possessed a strong code of right and wrong and needed space to keep his character from becoming cramped. But he was not fleeing civilization, he was making one.

Leathery, lean-hipped and long-legged, his strong jaw set against loose talk about any lady ("Stand on your laigs, you polecat, and say you're a liar!"), he was laconic when not reticent, and occasionally epigrammatic. He uttered what would have been a sensational sound bite: "When you call me that, *smile!*" As a Wister fan said, that could be on the Great Seal of the United States.

Wister's narrator resembled Wister. He was a tenderfoot "green from the East" who fell under Wyoming's spell, and the Virginian's. So did the winsome schoolmarm from Vermont. In the novel the Virginian tells some tall tales, punctures the pomposity of a preacher and lynches a few rustlers (including his ex–best friend). The schoolmarm puts her dainty foot down, saying she won't marry the Virginian if he goes out into the dusty street for a gunfight with that varmint Trampas. But in an oft-repeated scene (for example, Gary Cooper and Grace Kelly in *High Noon*) our hero goes anyway, and she sticks with him anyway. This makes feminists cross but is boffo at the box office.

Popular fiction from *Uncle Tom's Cabin* to *The Bonfire of the Vanities* has shaped American sentiments. But no American novel has had the amazing fecundity of Wister's. It was a best-seller for six years and much read for many decades. A long-running play and several movies were made from it. So was an industry, the mass production of cowboy myths, of which the Perot presidential movement is a spinoff.

Okay, so Perot does not toil out in the Western air that Wister said was "pure as water and strong as wine." Perot does not work "swallowed in a vast solitude" but in downtown Dallas. And Perot made his money not punching cows but selling computers to the government. Never mind. A barefoot billionaire, with dew from the grass roots still on his toes, is an idea as American as the Declaration of Independence. The Declaration, wrote Wister, "acknowledged the *eternal inequality* of man.

> For by it we abolished a cut-and-dried aristocracy. We had seen little men artificially held up in high places, and great men artificially held down in low places, and our own justice-loving hearts abhorred this violence to human nature. Therefore, we decreed that every man should henceforth have equal liberty to find his own level. . . . Let the best man win! That is America's word. That is true democracy. And true democracy and true aristocracy are one and the same thing.

Not really, and certainly not in Perot's case, but an immoderate respect for moneymaking makes some people think so. That has made Perot a presidential pretender—money worship, and the mystique of the West. The West, with its promise of rebirth and regeneration, is crucial to America's recurring yearnings for second chances. Americans periodically worry that the nation needs to be picked up by the scruff of its neck and shaken and given a stern talking-to. There is an American hankering, found in many Western novels, for someone who will lay down the law and then throw down the tin star and move on. *High Noon*, again. Maybe that is Perot's role—the Reluctant Sheriff who would rather ride into the sunset but first has to make the town safe for womenfolk and young 'uns.

Today the electorate's mood regarding politicians can be put in words familiar to readers of pulp Westerns: "String 'em up!" So suppose Sheriff Perot says: "I am strapping on this here shooting iron for a limited purpose and a limited time. If I can't clean up Dodge in one term, I'll hightail it out of town anyway." Suppose voters say: "Given the alternatives—Clinton and Bush—how big a mistake can we make by taking Perot for just four years?" If Perot makes that single-term pledge of the Reluctant Sheriff, it will prove that he is a pretty good politician. But when you call him that, *smile*.

June 1, 1992

The Perils of the Politics of Condescension

To be fanciful, suppose Democrats, having lost seven of 10 presidential elections since 1952, want to win in 1992. What should they do? They should begin by picking up (with two hands; it is heavy) Michael Barone's book *Our Country: The Shaping of America from Roosevelt to Reagan*.

Long ago a style of history became fashionable, and like many intellectual fashions it has been impervious to evidence. (Intellectuals are often the last to know things.) The style was materialist and determinist. It taught that the driving force of American politics is economic conflict. But Barone believes politics usually divides Americans along cultural rather than economic lines. The salient question is not who gets what, but rather what kind of (and whose) country is this?

The two nominations of Adlai Stevenson were a turning point for the party. The tone-setting party intellectuals turned away from the party's celebration of the ordinary Americans. Stevenson, the very model, or so many admirers thought, of the intellectual liberal, actually read little and his liberalism was lukewarm. He was less interested in civil rights than Truman was and, says Barone, he was not more intelligent than Eisenhower, only more ironic. But in the Stevenson years condescension became the stance of many who set the course of the party.

When a supporter gushed to Stevenson that all thinking people supported him, he replied, "Yes, but I need to win a majority." Barone says it is inconceivable that FDR would have said, or even thought, such a thing. "Stevenson was the first leading Democrat politician to become a critic rather than a celebrator of middle-class American culture—the prototype of the liberal Democratic who would judge ordinary Americans by an abstract standard and find them wanting." Stevenson's attractiveness to those who fancied themselves (the word was just coming into fashion) "alienated" from American culture deepened after he lost, thereby proving himself too good for the uncomprehending unwashed. What Stevensonians sought from their man, says Barone, was "validation of their own cultural stance." They rejected "American exceptionalism," the belief that America is especially decent because many Old World vices never made the transatlantic passage.

Until Stevenson, cultural elitism found a congenial niche only in the Republican Party, which not coincidentally was the minority party. And until Stevenson the Democratic Party had the more nationalistic foreign policy. (The party represented the most military-minded region, the South.) Stevenson, arguing for less assertive foreign and defense policies, was a harbinger of candidates, and defeats, to come. Twenty years after the first Stevenson nomination the transformation of his party was patent at the McGovern convention in Miami. There the elected delegates from Illinois, including Mayor Daley, were ousted because they lacked the right racial and sexual blend, and were replaced by others, including a young preacher named Jesse Jackson. The convention roll call was conducted in a preselected random order to avoid the sin of alphabetism (discrimination on the basis of alphabetical sequence). The party had lost its mind.

McGovern carried Beverly Hills and Manhattan's wealthy Upper East Side, as Mondale was to do. This was, needless to say, for cultural, not economic, reasons. The conservative era arrived when the composition of the swing vote that was up for grabs changed. In 1930 it consisted of upper Midwest La Follette progressives, and Jews. By 1980 it consisted of Southern whites and Northern blue-collar ethnics. The cultural liberalism of the post-Stevenson Democratic Party made the first two groups solidly Democratic by 1980 and repelled the other two.

Many Democrats have assumed that cultural liberalism would be politically less important than economic liberalism. But Barone demonstrates that the politics of economic redistribution did not really dominate even the New Deal era, other than from 1935 to 1940, and lost most of its saliency in the blast of the postwar boom. The Democratic Party's problem is that its activism worked. It fostered college education, home ownership (subsidized mortgages), suburbanization (highways, water systems)—in short, an upwardly mobile middle class. As economic concerns mattered less, cultural questions mattered more.

But Democrats have continually tried to restore the primacy of economic issues. Remember the 1982–83 flirtation with "industrial policy"? Reagan's riposte was on the cliffs of Normandy, and at the Olympics— cultural affirmations. In 1988 Democrats began in Iowa their long trek to failure. About half the participants in Iowa's caucuses favored unilateral disarmament. That was a cultural stance: America the menace. Bush's riposte was the Pledge of Allegiance and Willie Horton—America is good enough to deserve allegiance and punish those who break its laws. Dukakis toiled to change the subject, to child care, college tuition aid and other economic matters. He won 10 states.

In presidential politics both parties begin with about 40 percent of the voters. Democrats averaged 40.7 percent with three Northern-tier tickets in 16 years (Humphrey-Muskie, McGovern-Shriver, Mondale-Ferraro). Those tickets represented a region that, to many Americans, represents uncongenial cultural values. Economic issues, says Barone, have "become routinized and drained of emotional content." Postwar economic growth has left nothing remotely resembling a majority with a dominating economic grievance. War, hot or cold, with its mobilization mentality, encourages cultural unity. Peace and affluence produce cultural diversity which, in a nation as dynamic as this one, produces anxieties. The party that addresses them best is apt to do best in elections.

Democrats won when the country was morally comfortable but economically troubled. Republicans rose when those conditions reversed. Democrats lose when calling for economic redistribution. Republicans win talking about shared values. So says Barone. Adlai Stevenson's political children, who fancy themselves bookish, should read Barone.

June 4, 1990

Bill Clinton as Henry of Navarre

Is Bill Clinton our Henry of Navarre? Henry, the King of France, who died in 1610, was raised a Protestant but twice embraced Catholicism for political reasons, once with words that could be the credo of many a politician: "Paris is well worth a mass."

Is Clinton a chastened, converted liberal? Or does he just believe the White House is worth a moderate speech? Republicans will say his acceptance speech, sounding themes of entrepreneurship and responsibility, was mere trimming for tactical purposes. That is not a frivolous suspicion about a man who entered politics in the service of George McGovern and who was nominated by a convention composed of delegates more liberal than even most Democrats.

Dukakis learned what happens to a Democratic nominee who runs from the liberal label. When he told the 1988 convention that the election would be about "competence," not "ideology," Republicans pounced. Clearly Dukakis himself thought that his liberalism was a handicap. There is a striking difference between the two parties today. Ask a Republican running for office if he or she is a conservative and chances are he or she will say, "Darn tootin'." Ask a Democrat running if he or she is a liberal and he or she is apt to exclaim nervously, "Labels do not matter!"

Oh yes they do. The words "liberal" and "conservative" denote beliefs that are motives for actions. It is pathetic that Democrats cannot redefine liberalism by reassociating it with popular actions. What is the most broadly and deeply popular thing American government has done in this century? Social Security. Liberals did it. Of all that government has done since the Second World War, of what are Americans most proud? The civil rights laws that liberals wrote before they degraded the phrase "civil rights" into a cover for a racial spoils system. Clinton cannot win unless he rounds on Republicans and defends his liberalism by distinguishing it from other liberalisms. Liberalism is a faith with several sects, and Clinton's recent utterances suggest he is a communicant in what can be called the church of middle liberalism.

Clinton could have usefully taken the country on an imaginary Manhattan walk from Madison Square Garden to where, in 1911, a fire in the Triangle Shirtwaist factory resulted in the deaths by suffocation or jumping—the building had only one fire escape, no fire extinguisher and many doors were locked—of 146 women workers. Michael Barone, in *Our Country*, his history of American politics from 1930 to 1990, says the flames lit the fire of modern liberalism. Watching in horror from the street was a young social worker, Frances Perkins, who 22 years later would become the first woman in a president's Cabinet (FDR's Secretary of Labor). She served on the commission that studied the fire and advocated many health and safety laws that defined a kind of liberalism—the use of government to regulate enterprise and shape society's allocation of wealth, opportunity and security.

American politics can be considered a tale of three liberalisms, the first of which, classical liberalism, teaches that the creative arena of human affairs is society, as distinct—very distinct—from government. Government's proper function is to protect the conditions—life and liberty, primarily—for the individual's private pursuit of happiness. This is now called conservatism, but until the New Deal it was the Jeffersonian spirit of most of the Democratic Party.

FDR knew that New Deal liberalism was significantly more ambitious. He said that until the emergence of the modern industrial economy, "government had merely been called upon to produce the conditions within which people could live happily, labor peacefully and rest secure." Now it would be called upon to play a grander role. It would not just provide conditions in which happiness, understood as material well-being, could be pursued. Rather, it would become a deliverer of happiness itself. Government, FDR said, has "final responsibility" for it. This "middle liberalism" of the New Deal supplemented political with economic rights.

The New Deal—the modern state it created and the class of people for whom that state provided employment—led to the third liberalism, that of the 1960s and '70s. This "managerial liberalism" celebrates the role of intellectuals and other policy elites in rationalizing society from above, using the federal government, especially the judiciary, and the "science" of public administration, meaning bureaucracy. This liberalism promised that government mastery of economic management would end business cycles, thereby guaranteeing a steady flow of revenues for building a good—no, merely good would not be good enough—a Great Society. According to this liberalism the creative agency is not society but government, which molds society like modeling clay.

The result of this liberalism was an overreaching, overbearing nanny government. It caused a proliferation of cranky, dependent factions claiming victimization and demanding entitlements. It also caused a conservative reaction that swept liberals into the political wilderness.

The 1930s taught a majority of Americans to think that the free market is a fragile and sometimes perverse thing, and that government is generally more efficient than private sector institutions. The Second

World War, during which government organized prodigies of productivity, reinforced the public's faith in the public sector. The high tide of that faith came in the 1960s, the politically formative years for Clinton and his running mate. Indeed, Al Gore, something of an environmental hysteric, seems to have boundless confidence in government's ability to organize the future by accurately foretelling and wisely regulating economic and scientific advances.

But now Clinton, leading a liberal party weary of the wilderness, says that an entrepreneurial economy is that on which all other policies depend. He says that the "forgotten middle class" (actually, politicians think of little else) and not various "victims" of American life is the focus of attention. And he says welfare recipients have a responsibility to go to work. So he now says. The question is, has he learned the lessons of America's recent history, or just the tactics of Henry of Navarre?

July 27, 1992

The Republicans Convene: "Dry Sterile Thunder Without Rain"

HOUSTON—The Republican convention succeeded in the sense that the Party clearly spoke its mind. It was, perhaps, a costly success because it proved that there can indeed be indecent exposure of the mind as well as the body. Let us begin with the President's speech, which had the merit of being merely inadequate rather than, as many others were, strange.

His speech was not up to the demands that his political condition placed upon it. Judged, as the speech must be, against the background of behavior that his condition has caused, his speech was (in T. S. Eliot's phrase) "dry sterile thunder without rain."

It is not news that when Nature was dishing up rhetorical gifts, Bush did not hold out his plate. But by the verve of his delivery here he proved, again, that practice makes adequate. Unfortunately, this adequacy was a reminder that his problem has not been his lack of style but rather his abundance of insincerity.

The speech would have been far better for a candidate for a first term. As the umpteenth reiteration of mostly familiar items, from tax cuts to school choice to term limits, for which he has been only intermittently and impotently ardent, it repeatedly raised a ruinous question. For example, when the man under whom domestic spending and regulations have exploded says, "Government is too big and costs too much," people wonder why years five through eight will be better than years one through four have been.

The reasonable suspicion will be that the passion Bush showed at the podium Thursday night was ginned up for, and will not survive, this phase he calls his "campaign mode."

But at least his speech was superior to many given here because it was about things that constitute a recognizable agenda of governance. Viewed against the American political tradition, Wednesday night, that bath in "family values," was extraordinary and, properly understood, unpleasant.

Once upon a time political parties talked about things that were clearly public matters, things government could promote or prevent, things like land for homesteaders, antitrust policies, rural electrification, Social Security, medical care, defense and so on. Not so Wednesday night.

Then Republicans made "family values" their focus. In the process they showed that their view of government is out of focus, and they pounded the phrase "family values" into shapeless mush with a bad odor. Just slightly below the surface of Wednesday's touchy-feely sensitivity session was a serrated edge intended to open in both Clintons wounds that cannot be sutured in 75 days.

Marilyn Quayle's speech was evidence for those who say women should be kept out of combat not because they are too physically frail or morally fine but because they are too fierce to respect the rules of war. In a speech that launched an evening of sustained innuendo, she said—well, tiptoed to the edge of saying—that Bill Clinton "took drugs" and "joined in the sexual revolution" and "dodged the draft" ("ran from his responsibilities" was Lynn Martin's version an hour later). And he probably believes "that commitment, marriage and fidelity" are "just arbitrary arrangements."

As for Mrs. Clinton, well, Mrs. Quayle implied that Mrs. Clinton is one of those women who "wish to be liberated from their essential natures as women" and who in the 1960s believed—may still; can't be sure—that "the family was so oppressive that women could only thrive apart from it."

Next, Barbara Bush said: "However you define family, that's what we mean by family values." Fogginess is, apparently, a Bush family value. Her contribution to the evening's thoughts about government (this was a *political* convention, wasn't it?) was that families are good. But coming hard on the heels of Mrs. Quayle's philippic, and at the end of a day spiced with Pat Robertson's revelation that the Clintons are hatching "a radical plan to destroy the traditional family," Mrs. Bush was just a kinder, gentler coda to one long innuendo: Democrats may hug their children, but probably don't really mean it.

The effect of four days' immersion in this thick soup of values-blather was cloying to the point of gagging. It was akin to being congealed in a traffic jam behind a bus belching diesel fumes, and on the bus's bumper, smack in your line of sight, is one of those nagging stickers asking, "Have you hugged your kids today?"

Yes, I have—not that it is any business of these politicians serving as moral cheerleaders. Is there no public business—roads, schools, national defense, stuff like that—they could attend to?

The Republicans' graceless rhetoric here compelled two conclusions. For all their talk about America's "strength" and "greatness," their tone is of frightened timidity. These are "America the Endangered Species" Republicans, terrified that neither "family values" (see Mrs. Bush's definition, above) nor the nation can survive Mrs. Clinton.

And Republicans have caught a particularly virulent version of the Democrats' quite-virulent-enough tendency (remember the Bork confirmation fight) to turn political disagreement into moral assault.

August 23, 1992

Election, Not Canonization

Voters, encouraged by candidates and by journalists caught up in all the folderol, begin to believe that a presidential election is like a walk along the lip of a volcano: a matter of life and death. Actually, we are just selecting someone for a four-year-stint as head of one of the three branches of one of our governments. That's all. That's enough.

We are not selecting a moral tutor, or a role model for our children. Nothing in the normal lives of politicians specially equips them for those functions, and nothing in our constitutional order or political tradition assigns those functions to politicians. We are not selecting someone to (in the gaseous language of today's politics) "control the economy" or "get the country moving." Presidents can't control the economy. (Who wants to live in a country where they can?) And since 1776 there has been ample motion in America, thank you.

As the first post–Cold War election, this is the first election in the experience of most Americans in which they need not worry that if they make the wrong choice the world will be at risk. If we make a mistake next Tuesday, we can tidy it up four Novembers from now. Presidents aren't apt to do all that much damage in four years, and they can't do much that is irreparable.

A fascinating fact about this election is that the stakes are lower but the electorate's interest is higher. People have paid attention to the 90-minute debates. A century ago Gladstone could hold the attention of working-class audiences for that long in the open air, his voice unamplified, discussing the disestablishment of the Irish church. Back then, political oratory was popular entertainment and there was intense earnestness about public controversies. This year the third debate had the highest rating, which indicates a crescendo of interest almost Victorian.

A correlate of this gravity is widespread impatience with nonsense. Someone once said excessive righteousness is symptomatic of "spiritual diabetes." Voters detected that disease in the Republicans' hugely unsuccessful convention. One night in the Astrodome, when the rhetorical fire and brimstone were flowing like lava, a journalist asked a delegate what she thought about the country's trajectory. "It's satanic," said the delegate. And who, asked the journalist, is to blame? The delegate, looking at the journalist the way an elementary school teacher looks at a backward pupil, said: "Satan, of course." But Republicans have no monopoly on ludicrous righteousness. Al Gore seems convinced that he, almost alone, has pierced the veil of reality and has espied the environmental apocalypse toward which the rest of us are sleepwalking. (How we sleep through his warning shouts is hard to say.)

Bush, too, has been shouting a lot, trying to summon back the salad days of 1988. Then Michael Dukakis, seeing no need to counter Bush's attacks on his veto of the Massachusetts flag salute law, said: "The American people aren't interested in a debate over which one of us loves his country the most." He was mistaken. So were all those commentators who said that the flag salute veto (and Willie Horton) were not "real issues."

Jean Bethke Elshtain, a Vanderbilt University political scientist, rightly says voters and candidates are "coconstructors of issues." Candidates gauge voters' concerns and win when enough voters share their constructions. "To claim, then, that candidates are trafficking in nonissues because they immerse themselves in weighty symbolism is to presume that which does not exist: a clear-cut division between the symbolic and the real, between issues and emotional appeals." This is so because elections concern "not just interests but identities, not just what we are to do but *who we are and what we have become.*"

This year Bush failed to enlist voters as coconstructors of issues about Clinton's activities during his college days. This suggests that Americans have become focused on the mundane: Which candidate is most apt to do a modicum of good? Fine. Elections are not canonizations. Bush also seemed to be mechanically going through old motions when he warned that a Clinton administration would be "Carter II." He was trying to do to Democrats what they did for decades to Republicans regarding Hoover. In 1944, 12 years after Hoover was defeated, FDR was still running against him, recalling "the mess that was dumped in our laps in 1933." And the theme was alive 20 years after that. In 1964, when I tried to convince a crusty steelworker in Donora, Pennsylvania, to vote for Goldwater, he snapped, "I don't like Hoover." Not "I didn't" but "I don't."

It has taken the Democrats just 12 years to get free from the taint of the Carter years. The unpleasantness in 1992 was quite contemporary. Cynical politicians, and those journalists whose idea of sophistication is the languid acceptance of cynicism as normal, say politics has always been like this. That libels the past in order to legitimize the present. Of course, there always have been episodes of unpleasant campaigning. But our politics is unquestionably coarser than it was not long ago. As recently as 1988 Bob Dole seemed stunningly harsh when he said Bush should "stop lying about my record." Four years later it seems almost decorous to call an opponent a liar. Consider these salvos of ads fired by Republican Newt Gingrich and his challenger, Tony Center: "Meet Tony Center, a trial lawyer. . . . Center actually sued to strip a four-year-old and a one-year-old of their child support to pay his own legal fee." "It was Newt who delivered divorce papers to his wife the day after her cancer operation."

The good news about all the bad behavior by politicians is that the country is well immunized against heady expectations and hence against deep disappointments. Virginia Woolf wrote that "in or about December, 1910, human character changed." What had seemed so portentous to her was some exhibit or other of avant-garde art. If, next Tuesday, for only the fourth time in this century, an elected incumbent is chucked out of the White House, there is sure to be a surfeit of overheated overinterpretation. Don't believe it. Human nature won't have changed. The head of one branch of one of our governments will be about to change. That's all. That's enough.

November 2, 1992

The "Rhetorical Presidency"

President Clinton is probably being pelted with advice as he prepares to go to Capitol Hill to deliver his State of the Union address. My advice is: Don't go.

The Constitution requires only that the president "shall from time to time give to the Congress information on the State of the Union" and recommend measures for improving it. Although Washington and Adams had delivered their messages orally, Jefferson in 1801 sent a written message, a practice continued until Wilson went up to Congress in 1913, his first year as president. Jefferson's and Wilson's decisions expressed sharply contrasting understandings of the presidency.

In 1801, in his first giving of "information," Jefferson told Congress that recent "wars and troubles" were largely surmounted, so taxes could be cut and government pruned. As used to be customary, Jefferson put his remarks in a context of constitutional interpretation, stressing that "the states themselves have principal care of our persons, our property, and our reputation, constituting the great field of human concerns." Enterprise flourishes most when most free, and the federal government should feel strictly inhibited by the "limits of our constitutional powers." The idea of such limits now seems quaint, but not more so than Jefferson's concluding pledge: "Nothing shall be wanting on my part to inform, as far as in my power, the legislative judgment, nor to carry that judgment into faithful execution." Jefferson envisioned a modest role for presidents. They are primarily to execute the judgments of the First Branch, and secondarily to help "inform" that branch's deliberations.

It would have been in character if Jefferson, having economized time by not traipsing up to Capitol Hill, had spent the time reading a book. Clinton could profit by doing that, and a particularly pertinent book is *The Rhetorical Presidency* by Jeffrey K. Tulis of the University of Texas at Austin.

Tulis identifies Wilson as the principal progenitor of the modern presidency, the office that has broken many of its occupants, including Wilson. Wilson, who regarded the separation of powers not as the Constitution's genius but as its defect, articulated in theory and vivified in practice what has become the unexamined premise of contemporary politics. It is that the president's primary function is to exercise rhetorical leadership to mobilize the public's "opinion" in order to shatter the gridlock to which a large and pluralistic society, with a government of checks and balances, is prone.

It was grimly apposite that Wilson's health collapsed beneath the weight of this duty, during his Western tour to arouse opinion against congressional opposition to the League of Nations. Wilson cast presidents in a crushing role, one demanding skills that few presidents have in a sufficiency for the post-Wilson office. Tulis warns of, and Clinton should worry about, "an increasing lack of 'fit' between institution and occupant" in the era of the rhetorical presidency. Increasingly "presidential abilities and institutional requirements diverge," now that those requirements involve constant exhortation of an—inevitably—jaded public.

Clinton, who has been campaigning unceasingly since 1974 (20 campaigns since then), vows not to stop, promising more bus trips and the like. The presidency has become a seamless extension of campaigning, at a cost to the deliberative processes of government. Management of the dynamics of public opinion takes precedence over the rhythms of deliberation in representative institutions.

The toll that rhetorical style can take on substantive policy is illustrated by Tulis's analysis of President Johnson's 1964 State of the Union declaration: "This administration today, here and now, declares unconditional war on poverty." War. Unconditional. That bugle call launched the nation on a hurried march to disillusionment.

Johnson promised to "pursue poverty" with "pinpointed" attacks. It would not be an easy "struggle"; no single "weapon" or "strategy" would suffice "in the field." Rather than make a reasoned, deliberative presentation, persuasive about why eliminating poverty should be considered possible and an "unconditional" imperative, Johnson used a metaphor—"war"—as a substitute for argument. Indeed, it truncated debate. The premise—we were at war—drove policy: frantic urgency, quick mobilization. Johnson's subsequent message to Congress bristled with martial metaphors. Poverty is the "enemy" to be "driven from the land," not by "a single attack on a single front" but by all our "weapons" in "many battles," just as in "war against foreign enemies."

The metaphor "worked." Hearings in the poverty program were hasty; dissent seemed like a shirking of wartime duty. But the public's understanding of what it had embarked upon was superficial. And when the "war" bogged down, the public's commitment to it proved to be slight.

The "rhetorical presidency," continuously trying to mold the public mind, suits the temperament of the hyperkinetic persons who prosper by means of peripatetic campaigning. But one result is the loss of indirectness in government—representation, separation of powers. As Congress comes to accept the terms of competition with the "rhetorical presidency," it, too, tries to become a molder of "opinion," but in the unequal struggle Congress becomes a marionette of opinion, a role devoid of dignity. (Witness senators telling Zoë Baird their counts of telegrams and telephone calls.)

There is a tension between rhetoric written to a deliberative assembly and rhetoric spoken to an audience of scores of millions. The former seeks to "inform"—Jefferson's word—the reasoning of a small number of people in a legislative chamber. The latter seeks to inspirit the populace. Prior to this century, Tulis says, presidents preferred written communication with Congress rather than oral addresses to the public. This preference derived from an idea—the Founders'—of the proper functioning of the government. After Jefferson vowed "to inform . . . the legislative judgment," he continued:

> The prudence and temperance of your discussions will promote, within your own walls, that conciliation which so much befriends national conclusion; and by its example will encourage among our constituents that progress of opinion which is tending to unite them in object and in will.

That is representative government, elegantly understood not as a handmaiden of public opinion but as an "example" elevating that opinion. It is still worth trying.

February 8, 1993

So, the Culprits Are Now the Cure?

Our current President, never a slave to the rule "Save your breath to cool your porridge," is particularly loquacious when his subject is, as it usually is, "change." He got awfully wrought up at a recent governors' meeting, calling for "fundamental and profound and relentless and continuing change."

The blizzard of adjectives does not disguise the emptiness of his relentless praise of "change." Anyway, as Heraclitus said and American history confirms, change is one of life's constants, whether or not presidents desire it. Furthermore, today there are only two practical proposals that promise profound social change—term limits for legislators and school choice—and this President opposes both. But the governors, who are this President's kind of people, heard his call and vowed to change.

When the political class, which is more united by interests than divided by ideas, comes to a bipartisan conclusion that it should unite in stopping something, the rest of us should start worrying. The governors promised to stop what they call the "bidding war" in which states compete to lure businesses by offering them tax and regulatory concessions and other enticements. Too bad. Federalism, combined with the increased mobility of capital and labor, has worked to inhibit the growth of burdensome government. Companies have become careful shoppers for the best business climate. Now the governors want less competition among themselves. They prefer more government "investments," meaning spending (on workers' skills, infrastructure and the like). So instead of entrepreneurial federalism by state governments we shall get more of the normal growth of those governments.

Which brings us to the skit staged last week on the White House lawn. There the President and Vice President were surrounded by props, like first-graders ready for show-and-tell. Displaying forklift trucks loaded with forms and regulations, our leaders promised to "reinvent" government. For example, they will, if Congress is willing, prune 7,500 Agriculture Department employees. From a payroll of 110,000. When Lincoln created the department, it had one employee for every 227,000 farms. In 1900 it had one for every 1,694 farms. Today it has one for every 16 farms. Calling a derisory cut of a ludicrously bloated bureaucracy a "reinvention" illustrates this rule: The extravagance of government rhetoric is inversely proportional to the seriousness of the act involved.

The government that cannot bring itself to kill the helium reserve (created in 1925 for the Army's blimp fleet) is going to perform the Herculean task of "reinvention," with the Vice President playing Hercules? Please. Even if, for the first time in the annals of government, everything works out exactly as is optimistically projected, the "reinvention" will cut five years' spending only about 1 percent. Although the administration with its forklift trucks implies that "reinventing" government means shrinking it, this exercise actually is a tactic to facilitate some huge expansions, beginning with health care. The point of the "reinvention" charade is to pump up confidence in government so people will tolerate the growth of it.

Administration officials have had fun histrionically announcing the obvious with a sense of original discovery: Government is often imbecilic. But they seem insensible of the real significance of, say, the government's nine pages of specifications for ashtrays. The authors of such documents are wide-awake, outwardly normal people who commute to work each day to do things like that. When they were children did they dream of writing ashtray regulations? Doubtful. But now it is their vocation. It is what they do, even what they *are*. They make neither shoes, nor butter, nor poetry. They make rules. Because they believe they know best. That conviction defines their class. Besides, most of these people have never been in the private sector, on the receiving end of regulations, and they have no intention of ever suffering that indignity.

Most members of Congress are careerists who have had little if any experience in the private sector and have had all that they intend to have. They like building and bossing around the bureaucracy that bosses around the rest of us. That is why they are in Congress. It is the joy of the job. They are, they really believe, being noble. They wrap us in rules and spend our money for us because they are compassionate. Their compassion is 98 percent condescension: They know best how to pursue our happiness.

Now we are told that this government, which is stuffed top to bottom with such people, is suddenly going to behave quite differently. In the normal dynamic of its organic life it metastasizes, and churns out reams of regulations. Yet it is going to "reinvent" itself under the stern guidance of a Democratic administration, and in collaboration with the Democratic-controlled Congress. Not likely. Democrats believe in the enlargement of government, and hence of bureaucracy. That is why they are Democrats. And their party depends on the support of government employees, who are not convinced that they are too numerous.

The administration's basic "reinvention" goal is to get government to do what it does better, or less offensively, so that the public will let it do even more. But government does so much so badly because it is trying to do much too much. The federal government is doing many things that no government can or should do, or that some other level of government would do better. But for all the presidential enthusiasm for "change" (fundamental, profound, relentless, etc.), the stunning and depressing aspect of his "reinvention" plan is its banality, its refusal to rethink government's basic functions. For example? The Commerce Department's activities almost certainly are a net subtraction from the nation's standard of living. Suppose the Commerce Department were filled with helium and floated away.

What is really newsworthy about the "reinvention" agenda is not that the administration plans to close 10 percent of the Agriculture Department's 1,200 field offices, but that the administration actually thinks that 90 percent of the offices are essential, and considers a 10 percent cut "reinvention."

September 20, 1993

The Miniaturized Presidency:
A Casualty of Peace

In 1878, when football was new on campus, Tommy Wilson, a Princeton undergraduate and informal football coach, wrote, "*Everything* depends upon the character of the captain and president [of the team]." Years later Wilson, then known by his middle name, Woodrow, would think of government the way he had thought of football.

He said that when a president has the confidence of the country, "no other single force can withstand him." He can be "irresistible" in an office that can be "anything he has the sagacity and force to make it." A forthright critic of the separation of powers, Wilson revolutionized the presidential office, treating it not only as the engine of an activist central government, but as the nation's tutor—"the moral, spiritual leader of the country," as a later Wilsonian, Walter Mondale, was to say.

But today Bill Clinton is reduced to around-the-clock dickering with a House of Representatives his party controls, and the House is less than half of his Congressional problem. He is unhappily experiencing the marginalization of the presidency that began under his predecessor. Clinton is powerless to prevent the end of the Wilsonian tradition he aimed to revitalize.

William Leuchtenburg, an admiring biographer of Franklin Roosevelt, says that FDR, who saw himself as picking up Wilson's fallen torch after 12 fallow Republican years, presented himself "as the father to all the people." So did Lyndon Johnson, whose model was FDR. And when President-elect Clinton met with Bill Moyers, who worked for Johnson, Clinton said, "He and I talked . . . about the need to revitalize the office as an institution . . . around which the American people can rally."

Clinton assumes that Americans are, or should be and can be made to be, in a rallying 'round mood. But rallying 'round is what people do in emergencies, particularly wars. That is why contemporary liberals, with their collectivist agendas, seem perpetually nostalgic for wartime—for Wilson's "war socialism" and FDR's domestic mobilization during the Second World War. That nostalgia surfaces in metaphors, as in LBJ's "war on poverty."

The end of the Cold War is one reason America now has its second consecutive president who is notably mismatched to his moment in office. George Bush prepared all his life to conduct the Cold War, only to have it end, leaving him (almost literally) speechless. Clinton, too, is a casualty of peace. He urgently needs the aura that surrounded presidents when the nation was in a permanent state of siege in a hair-trigger world.

Clinton, who has a breathtaking agenda for expanding federal supervision of American life, has reached the White House just as a prerequisite for such an ambitious presidential program is fast draining away. That prerequisite is a national fixation on the presidency, and a predisposition to think there should be a national "agenda" and that the president should write it.

Clinton may seem to be a miniaturized president, but that is because 60 years of emergencies—from the stock market crash of October 1929 to the fall of the Berlin Wall in November 1989—made most presidents seem larger than life-sized figures. However, the office that Wilson thought potentially irresistible has always been much less powerful than it is prominent.

Much of LBJ's domestic agenda failed because he was mistaken in believing that he personally could generate popular support for the sort of government activism that a huge event—the Depression—generated for FDR's activism. Clinton is floundering because his ideology tells him three false things.

It tells him that 12 years of Republican "neglect" must constitute a crisis comparable to depression or war. It tells him that nothing is difficult for the truly moral—that, for example, the reason there are millions of people without health insurance is that until now no one has really cared. And it tells him that the Wilson, FDR and LBJ presidencies are models to be emulated today.

However, a lesson of the first one-twelfth of Clinton's term is that "gridlock" (that overheated description of a normal, healthy outcome of our Constitution—presidents not getting all they want) results not just from "divided government," the legislative and executive branches controlled by different parties. It also results from both branches being controlled by a divided party, which the Democratic Party is. Not only do many members of Clinton's party reject his agenda, they feel no particular need, moral or prudential, to defer to him.

Peace is going to be hell for presidents, at least for those not reconciled to the restoration of what is, when viewed against the sweep of American history, normal: Congressional supremacy. The players on the other side of the constitutional line from the president—in the legislative branch, which is not supposed to be part of the president's team—

dispute Tommy Wilson's notion that everything depends on the president.

May 30, 1993

"The Fatal Conceit"

Clinton's Washington is awash with "the fatal conceit." The phrase is from the late Friedrich von Hayek, Nobel Prize–winning economist. The conceit is the belief that governing elites can make the future conform to their plans, and should do so because the alternative—allowing markets to allocate resources and opportunities—makes the preferences of the untutored many superior to the planning of the expert few.

Today the fatal conceit is expressed in "industrial policy," a specialty of "new Democrats." In the name of industrial policy, the tax code will acquire many curlicues of "targeted" incentives for behavior that disinterested government knows, just *knows,* meets an "unmet need." Government, fancying itself wiser than mere markets, will allocate capital to what it is sure will be "strategic" industries years hence. Solomonic government knows the right number of airlines and the sorts of planes they will need next century. (It is subsidizing research on a supersonic passenger plane.) Government knows the correct market share for this or that import. (It soon may say it knows how many Japanese cars Americans should be allowed to buy under "managed" trade.) Government knows the "fair" share of foreign markets for U.S. exports. It knows what "countervailing subsidies" are required to combat other nations' "unfair" industrial policies.

Government can direct the training of workers because government knows the skills that will be in demand down the road. Government knows the "fair" share of foreign markets for U.S. exports. It knows the precise percentage of GDP that should be spent on health care, the "reasonable" cost for particular medical procedures. Government knows the proper price for pharmaceuticals and insurance. (Bill and Hillary Clinton, although peripatetic campaigners for 20 years, have nevertheless found time to master the intricacies of those last two industries and have pronounced their pricing policies unjust.)

Clinton says his industrial policy will keep America "on the cutting edge" of progress. Never mind the antic implausibility of the government, that author of agricultural subsidies, the welfare system and many other misadventures, serving as a reliable guide to the fast-unfolding future. This government, which hardly excels at such basics as delivering mail and budgeting, is going to divine the rapid evolution of our science-driven economy? Please.

Government has occasionally been a catalyst for technological advance. In *Second Thoughts: Myths and Morals of U.S. Economic History*, published by Oxford University Press for the Manhattan Institute, economist Paul Uselding notes that the technology of mass production—machinery producing standardized products with interchangeable components of high quality and low unit cost—was advanced by the 19th-century firearms industry organized around government armories. And firearms mechanics took their skills to other industries, making clocks, sewing machines, agricultural machinery. War, government's largest undertaking, has always stimulated technologies, from revolvers to computers.

But today the pace of technological, and hence economic, change is swift and accelerating, and the creaking unwieldiness of government is worsening. So is government's entanglement with economic interests resistant to change. Anytime and everywhere, government is unsuited to supervise economic life, and modern government is spectacularly unqualified for guiding a modern economy. Socialism, which fancied itself especially modern, shattered under the strain of modernity because socialism was systemically ignorant. It blundered around blindfolded because it did not have the billions of bits of information, essential for efficient allocation of social energies, that markets signal every day.

Today's "new Democrat" turns out to look a lot like a Gilded Age Republican. Back then, Republicans controlled a government swollen with the confidence and prestige conferred by victory in the Civil War. Industrial capitalism, revved up by the war, was poised for continentwide expansion and Republicans were hot to help it with an industrial policy. That policy included tariffs, land grants and bond issues for railroads, the Homestead Act and Land Grant College Act to spread scientific agriculture and other remunerative knowledge. Even war was industrial policy when used to encourage Indians to see the virtues of the westward migration.

Back then, Democrats, true to their Jeffersonian pedigree, were disgusted by industrial policy. They understood, as had Jefferson, a careful reader of Adam Smith, that tariffs were government devices for transferring wealth from consumers to corporations. Historian Robert Kelley writes that Samuel J. Tilden, that undeservedly unremembered Democrat (New York's governor; scourge of the Tweed Ring; presidential nominee in 1876), understood the primary cause of the carnival of corruption in government in the Gilded Age: "It simply flowed," he said, "from the cozy relations between Republicans and the business community, and the centralist, big-spending doctrines Republicans preached as they sought to aid business in every possible way."

Today it is a Democratic administration that desires relations between business and government more "cooperative" than during the Republican years. Trouble is, the dynamics of democracy are apt to cause "cooperation" to result in "lemon socialism"—government assistance that does not midwife promising new industries but rather props up faltering old ones. *The Wall Street Journal* knows why: Unborn industries do not have lobbyists; old ones do.

The fundamental flaw in industrial policy—in picking industrial "winners" rather than allowing the market to pick them—is this: If the payoff from an investment is clear to government, why won't the private sector pursue it? One instrument of Clinton's industrial policy is called Advanced Research Projects Agency. But how advanced is a project if bureaucrats in Washington can fathom it?

The fatal conceit partakes of the childlike faith that the world is plastic to our touch and the future is transparent to our gaze. This conceit gives rise to government that treats society like Play-Doh, to be toyed with and put into whatever shape we wish. It is a beguiling attribute of children that they do not understand what life does to plans. But that is not a beguiling attribute of a governing class.

March 8, 1993

Purring Along the Potomac

In the intensifying contest to write the gushiest journalism about the two new princes of the executive branch, the competition between *Time* and *Newsweek* has been nip and tuck. *Time*'s Elizabeth Taylor broke from the pack with her apotheosis of Al Gore as "an introspective spokesman for the inner child, an icon for the new manhood." But *Newsweek*'s Jonathan Alter, rising to the challenge, has written of Bill Clinton: "He keeps all of his old friends (even when they are of no political use to him) and makes about 10 new ones a day." Golly, 36,500 new friends every decade. Alter also espies the dim outlines of a New Jerusalem, a city of virtue, arising along the Potomac, and none too soon: "During the Reagan-Bush years, Washington lost its sense of shame." That sense was so acute until noon of January 20, 1981.

Clinton may be coming as Cromwell to purge the capital of impurities, but this has not alarmed the lawyers, some of whom have been

known to lobby. Let's see. Vernon Jordan, lawyer and influence entrepreneur, heads Clinton's transition. The person in charge of budget issues for the transition has lobbied for the AFL-CIO, home builders and
a coalition opposed to cuts in Social Security—27 percent of the budget. As Peter Stone writes in the *National Journal,* "On Election Day, an
eerie silence descended on the offices of Washington's top lobbying, law
and public-relations firms. . . . The clout merchants jetted off to Arkansas to celebrate." A headline in the *Legal Times* sent shivers of delight
along K Street and should send a shudder through the Republic: FOR
LAWYERS, CLINTON IS A CHANGE FOR THE BETTER. The story quotes a leading lawyer: "The one thing everyone agrees on is that the government
will now be more interested in regulating business. We are all expecting
about a 33 percent increase in fees." That will be a handsome return on
the legal profession's huge investment in Clinton's campaign.

Government is by far the nation's largest employer, landlord and
landowner, but that does not begin to measure its metastasizing presence in the nation's life. The government itself (OMB) estimates that
the private sector spends 5 billion hours a year filling out federal paperwork. The cost, even at just $20 an hour, is $100 billion. (State and local
governments involve another $20 billion in paperwork costs.) Lawyers
know government will become even more labyrinthine and burdensome under Clinton than it became under Bush. The Bush administration's number of pages in the *Federal Register,* the publication of
government regulations, surged beyond even the levels of the Carter
administration. Democrats seethe with 12 years of pent-up demand for
government activism, but there is little money left over from entitlements and interest payments. Therefore, the government, which has
shown itself capable of writing a 15,629-word directive on pricing cab-
bages, will get much of its exercise and amusement by writing lots of
litigation-breeding rules.

Clinton came to Washington last week trailing clouds of glory. But the
electorate, seeing him schmoozing with his party's leaders in Congress,
may have had second, or perhaps first, thoughts about unified government. Clinton sealed his friendship with the party's grandees by the
first of what may be many propitiations.

As a candidate he hurt Congress's feelings by saying the president
should have line-item veto authority. Today the president is presented
with 13 gargantuan appropriations bills and has the nasty choice of signing them, or plunging the government into chaos. With a line-item veto,
he would be able to strike out particular items. Congress could not restore them without two-thirds votes in both chambers. The Democratic
Congressional leaders were in Little Rock just a few hours before
Clinton beat a retreat from his line-item veto demand. Suddenly he

called "intriguing" a much weaker alternative, that of "enhanced reci-sion." Under it, the president could veto particular items but simple majorities in each house (where majorities would already have ap-proved the items) could overturn his veto. Even that limp idea will face the probably fatal opposition of His Porkship, Robert Byrd of West Vir-ginia, Chairman of the Senate Appropriations Committee.

Candidate Clinton said he would pressure Congress to cut its staff 25 percent in one year. President-elect Clinton, having been given an ear-ful by Democratic Congressional leaders, says, gosh, Congress has al-ready cut its staff. But a recent government survey concluded that Congress has 38,509 employees, a number virtually unchanged since a year ago and 500 more than five years ago. No one can stop Clinton from keeping his promise to cut the White House staff 25 percent in one year. Arthur Schlesinger, Jr., notes that FDR fought the Depression with a staff smaller than the president's wife has today, and fought World War II with a staff smaller than the vice president's today.

By quickly coming to terms with his party's Congressional wing, on its terms, Clinton may have begun a familiar process, the Gulliverization of himself. Like Gulliver among the Lilliputians, a president can be bound down by countless little cords, none of them particularly strong, but cu-mulatively immobilizing. Clinton and Congress can be counted on to see pretty much eye-to-eye about taxes. Clinton thinks it is very impor-tant to raise taxes on the obscenely opulent, meaning families earning more than $200,000 (about 850,000 or .7 percent of the 115 million tax-payers). There also will be various business taxes, but none of them will molest the sacred middle class unless members of that class buy goods or services produced by businesses. Tax increases, we are told, are nec-essary because of the "reckless" tax-cutting "orgy" of the 1980s in shameless Washington. But Congressional Budget Office economists say the average family's federal tax burden—income, Social Security, cor-porate, excise—amounted in 1980 to a rate (total federal taxes divided by pretax income) of 23.3 percent. Since then the rate has gone as low as 21.7 percent but today is 23.2 percent.

Worried by the welter of change? Don't be. The lawyers are on their toes and on the job, looking out for the welfare of everyone who hires them, Congress is purring with contentment about the pliable president-elect, and Washington has regained its famously inhibiting sense of shame.

November 30, 1992

Here Come the Eager Beavers

James Carville, Bill Clinton's Clausewitz, talks like an Uzi, in bursts. He should do the president-elect a final favor by firing off for him the story of the traffic lights on Florida Street in Baton Rouge.

A decade ago, Carville helped elect as mayor of that city a man who promised to synchronize the traffic lights on the main drag, Florida Street. By God, said the candidate, using a rhetorical trope then fashionable, if we can put a man on the moon, we can smooth out the herky-jerky stop-and-start nonflow of traffic. So the new mayor straightaway turned to Carville and said: Get it done. Carville called the city's traffic engineer and said: Make it happen. The engineer said: OK. But it will cost bushels of money. The computers will have to be jiggered. And there will be these problems with left-turn lanes. And, besides . . .

The traffic on Florida Street still does not flow.

But even if Carville tells this cautionary tale to Clinton and to the swarms of eager beavers now bearing down on Washington, hot to right wrongs, it probably will not do a lick of good. Washington had better brace itself for the arrival of a lot of liberals who really believe that government is a sharp scalpel, and who can hardly wait to operate on the body politic. Or, to change the metaphor, they are eager to go marching as to war.

The Cold War is over, but the governmental hubris that the war engendered lingers on. Liberals, who often have faulted U.S. foreign policy for its alleged bellicosity, are enamored of "wars" on the home front. Burton Yale Pines, a leading conservative, believes the Cold War gave rise to a misplaced confidence in Washington's capacity to do things not related to the Cold War, but which were called "wars" anyway. The powers Washington acquired to run containment of communism seemed to give Washington derivative legitimacy as architect of ambitious domestic undertakings. Washington declared "wars" on poverty, crime, drugs and AIDS, spoke of a "Marshall Plan" for the cities and a "Manhattan Project" for education. The language of war lent spurious plausibility to the idea that the government's skills in foreign policy could be as successfully applied to solving the social problems of an open, individualistic, pluralistic society.

Actually, the importation of martial language into domestic governance began before the Cold War. Franklin Roosevelt, in his first Inaugural Address, said he might ask Congress for "broad executive power to wage a war against the emergency, as great as the power that would be given to me if we were in fact invaded by a foreign foe." Eight months before that, FDR had told the Democratic convention that the nation should resume the "interrupted march along the path of real progress." The 12-year interruption had been the interval of Republican rule between Woodrow Wilson—a war leader—and FDR, domestic "commander-in-chief" treating a domestic difficulty as the moral equivalent of war. Wilson, who disliked the Founding Fathers' purposes in designing the separation of powers, was impatient with institutional inhibitions on government's freedom to alter the balance between "the power of the government and the privileges of the individual."

Before Clinton surrenders to the siren call of the Wilsonian presidency, he should curl up with a good book, Terry Eastland's *Energy in the Executive: The Case for the Strong Presidency.* Eastland traces some problems of the modern presidency to Wilsonian grandiosity in the conception of the president's duties. Wilson, writes Eastland, was the first holder of the office to believe "that Presidents are to lead the people ever onwards and upwards—to an unknown destination only history can reveal, but which, as the decades have passed, inevitably seems to have required larger and more costly government whose reach extends more deeply into the states and the private sector." Wilson declared that "the size of modern democracy necessitates the exercise of persuasive power by dominant minds in the shaping of popular judgments." Thus began the inflation of the presidential function: The president as the public's tutor, moral auditor and cheerleader.

Clinton, who will be the sixth Democratic president since Woodrow Wilson, leads a party still awash with Wilsonian liberalism's desire to conscript the individual into collective undertakings. Wilson presided over the "war socialism" of modern mobilization. Walter Lippmann and other "progressives" thought war could be a healthy antidote to America's excessive "individualism" and "the evils of localism." The public, properly led by a "dominant mind" at the pinnacle of the executive branch of the central government, could be nationalized and homogenized and made into good raw material for great undertakings. The greatest of these was to be what Peter Drucker calls "salvation by society"—society, controlled by government, would perfect individuals. Hence, Lyndon Johnson. One of his aides, Harry McPherson, described how LBJ envisioned the nation as a patient whose pathologies were to receive presidential ministrations:

People were [seen to be] suffering from a sense of alienation from one another, of anomie, of powerlessness. This affected the well-to-do as much as it did the poor. Middle-class women, bored and friendless in the suburban afternoons; fathers, working at "meaningless" jobs, or slumped before the television set; sons and daughters desperate for "relevance"— all were in need of community, beauty, and purpose, all were guilty because so many others were deprived while they, rich beyond their ancestors' dreams, were depressed. What would change all this was a creative public effort. . . .

It is a wonder we did not wind up with a Department of Meaningful Labor, a "war on anomie" and an Agency for Friendly Suburban Afternoons. LBJ promised a Great Society "where the city of man serves not only the needs of the body and the demands of commerce but the desire for beauty and the hunger for community." Today Americans would settle for cities where the most basic needs of the body (such as protection from punctures by bullets) and the rudimentary requirements of commerce (order; adequate education and transportation) are provided.

Clinton's eager beavers should ponder that, perhaps during a herky-jerky drive down Florida Street.

November 16, 1992

The Secret Service and the Truman Stroll

Not long ago, Tom Foley, pride of Spokane and Speaker of the House, squared his shoulders and strode forth to the front steps of the Capitol to do a congressman's basic duty of posing for photographs with students from back home. But what to his wondering eyes did appear? The vast Capitol plaza had been sealed off by that least-secret presence, the Secret Service. Seems the president was out of the country (of course), so Dan Quayle, who was in his Capitol office, was being cocooned with extra protection.

The Speaker was not amused. The plaza was promptly liberated. Photographs were taken. But it is high time to touch, ever so gingerly, a subject many Washingtonians fret about but are loath to address—the bloat and behavior of the Secret Service.

Recently Senator Pat Moynihan and some colleagues had a disagreeable experience at the hands of the elements (it was cold and rainy) and the Secret Service at a presidential bill-signing ceremony in Texas. After the signing, when the president departed, the Congressional delegation could not. Secret Service agents "froze" the site and took their time about unfreezing it. Were the swarms of agents with weapons and walkie-talkies coping with some special threat? No, it was the by-now routine interlocking-overlapping of walls of security between the Republic's chief executive and the public that made him that. A protracted stand in December mud does concentrate the mind, and for Moynihan and some others, herded here and detained there, it was one time too many at the mercy of "strutting agents with high-power rifles." It was one more proof that the Secret Service is becoming too big for its britches.

The Secret Service, which at first was preoccupied with catching counterfeiters, did not begin protecting presidents until after the third assassination, that of McKinley in 1901. It did not protect presidential candidates until the 1968 assassination of Robert Kennedy. Since the 1960s the Secret Service, like government generally, only more so, has burgeoned. This, because its protection mission is not controversial, and no one wants to say "enough, already."

Times have changed. For the worse, naturally. President Monroe was faulted for excessive formality because he complained that diplomats constantly dropped in on him uninvited and expected tea. John Quincy Adams regularly swam stark naked in the Potomac, accompanied only by a servant in a canoe. All day long citizens wandered into his White House to pester him for loans, jobs or other favors. A British visitor shrank from the "brutal familiarity" with which President-elect Jackson was treated when traveling from Tennessee to Washington. It was not as brutal as the treatment White House furniture got from the crush at his Inaugural blast, which was an open house. Tyler founded Washington's metropolitan police essentially to guard the White House but Pierce in 1853 became the first president to have a personal guard (just an old Army buddy).

Enemy cannon were across the river and spies infested the city but almost anyone at any time could wander into Lincoln's White House. Through the late 19th century presidents regularly received the public each day in the East Room. Until FDR there was a New Year's Day receiving line for anyone who joined the queue out on the street. Security became serious during World War I but then until December 7, 1941, the White House lawn was again a public park. Portions of the mansion's first floor were open to everyone. You could even park on the narrow street between the White House and what is now the Executive Office Building.

The world has become more dangerous for leaders because of the lethality of portable weapons and the ideological fevers that inflame individuals. Still, dangers do not justify excesses. There must be limits, even to prophylactic measures against menaces. All government agencies strive, from primal urges of their organisms, to maximize their missions.

The Secret Service's mission is the safety of a few people, particularly the president. Like any agency, it always says more is better. Indeed, it always says more is necessary because any failure of its mission is dreadful.

But such failure is not the only bad thing that can befall a republic. Another is an unrepublican disproportion in the president's traveling retinue, an unseemly grandiosity surrounding leaders, an inflation of the aura of officiousness and majesty. Prime Minister Thatcher was nearly killed by an IRA bomb. Prime Minister Major was the target of an IRA mortar attack, yet British security, although efficient, is scarcely noticeable. Presidents travel around America embarrassingly enveloped in firepower, as though this were a banana republic bristling with plotters. Moynihan believes that a "ubiquitous, overlarge and too frequently inconsiderate Secret Service" is becoming "a praetorian guard." It threatens the quality of American democracy by treating the president "as a person under constant threat, and all others as possible suspects." There are Congressional spouses who stay away from State of the Union addresses because the Secret Service has made these occasions physically and emotionally unpleasant. Thus Moynihan: "This armed intrusion into the simple ceremonies of the Republic is a disgrace and a danger."

But Moynihan ends his philippic limply, with the sort of evasion that begets the problem: "No care can be too great to protect the president and the vice president. But there is such a thing as excess and it ought to be avoided in a republic." The phrase "no care can be too great" is an instance of, and an invitation to, excess. Like the phrase "life is priceless," it sounds good but is inapplicable as policy. If we really regarded life as priceless, we would ban (among a zillion other things) left turns by cars—and then cars. We don't believe that "no care can be too great" to protect life because the price—in money, comity and liberty—would be excessive. The same is true concerning the care we take of leaders.

We have lost the admirable attitude—call it republican relaxation— that once characterized Americans' intimacy with their government. But is it really impossible to recapture the era—this is not ancient history—when President Truman jauntily strolled across the street to his bank? Most Secret Service agents are public-spirited and civil, but there is a lack of moderation in the definition and management of their mission. Enough—no, much too much—already.

February 24, 1992

Scrubbing Political People, and the Green, from the Greenbacks

From Britain comes the germ of a good idea. The Duke of Welling-ton's picture is being replaced on the five-pound note by that of George Stephenson, the engineer who developed steam power. Michael Fara-day, the physicist (electrical induction), is replacing Shakespeare on the 20-pound note.

There is proper indignation about the demotion of Shakespeare, the greatest shaper of that nation's discourse and imagination. But science and technology deserve honors. A British intellectual says sniffily that although Stephenson is "a man of eminence" he "hardly serves to fill you with patriotic fervor." Well, even if making us fervid is govern-ment's proper business, why celebrate so many political figures, such as the Duke? Wellington deserves his ample honors for squishing Napo-leon. But what good is done by reminding people, redundantly, of the glories of their most famous political and military pinups? Better they should be nudged to note that science, commerce and the arts are na-tional glories, and necessities, too. Actually, the British know this. Flor-ence Nightingale and Sir Christopher Wren, the architect, adorn some paper notes.

Many European nations steer clear of political persons on their paper currency, partly because those nations are so old and grumpy no one can praise any political figure from their past without picking a fight. German currency features poets, musicians, scientists and the like, or portraits of unknown people by famous painters (Dürer, Cranach). That is understandable. If our political history were like Germany's, we, too, would dodge the subject. In France, where governance is emphatically not the nation's *gloire,* the currency features cultural heroes such as Pascal, Montesquieu, Delacroix, Debussy. Italians, who regard their government as a disagreeable rumor or a temporary inconvenience, decorate their currency with portraits of some of those who have helped decorate and ennoble their peninsula: Maria Montessori, educator and physician; composer Bellini; Bernini, sculptor and architect. The painter Caravaggio is on the 100,000-lira note, worth about $79.

Until 1969, when bills larger than $100 were withdrawn, 11 political men had their portraits on U.S. paper currency: Washington ($1), Jefferson ($2), Lincoln ($5), Hamilton ($10), Jackson ($20), Grant ($50), Franklin ($100), McKinley ($500), Cleveland ($1,000), Madison ($5,000), Chase ($10,000). Now, it does not matter that most Americans haven't a clue who Chase was (Lincoln's first Treasury Secretary). It matters more, but not much, that the sainted Madison, our subtlest political thinker, was relegated to rare appearances on a large denomination. However, what is seriously wrong with the list is its monomania: Politicians are not the sole sources of a nation's success and grandeur.

There is much more to national enrichment, material and moral, than the people who make its laws and run its institutions of governance. Those important things depend on other things—habits, mores, customs, values, virtues—that are shaped, vivified, nurtured and husbanded by people often working far from the public arena.

So, to tutor the nation in the various sources of its greatness, let's scrub all the political people from the greenbacks. And while we're at it, let's get rid of the green, which is intensely boring. Let's reissue the big bills and liven up the currency with many colors and the following faces:

$1: Mark Twain. The smaller the denomination, the more common the usage. Who deserves this place more than the man who, through Huck Finn, put the American language of common usage into literature?

$2 (Let's print more of these, please—they are convenient, and not just at the racetrack): For our jazzier money, let's have someone representing our distinctive music, jazz and the musical stage—Scott Joplin, W. C. Handy, Louis Armstrong, Duke Ellington, George Gershwin.

$5: Choose a painter for the prettified currency, perhaps Mary Cassatt, or Sargent, Remington, Whistler, Homer.

$10: Someone who exemplifies the American turn of mind—Emerson, or William James.

$20: Alexander Joy Cartwright, who codified the great game, or Willie Mays, who perfected it.

$50: America's inventors democratized science, turning technology to common uses, so pick one: Fulton, Whitney, Edison or the Wright brothers.

$100: One source of America's success is public education. Therefore: Horace Mann.

$500: By the written word, especially novels, America emancipated itself culturally from the Old World. So make room for Hawthorne, Melville, Wharton, Fitzgerald, Hemingway or Faulkner.

$1,000: If money is, as Emerson said, the prose of life, let's put a poet on it, Emily Dickinson or Walt Whitman.

$5,000: Henry Ford (or Charles Kettering or Alfred Sloan). A giant of

American industry, a pioneer of mass manufacturing, should grace a large denomination.

$10,000: Wealth without wisdom is not merely barren, it is a menace. Therefore here, at the pinnacle of the currency that is supposed to serve as a store of value, is the place for philosophy in the form of a man who is not much read anymore, which is our loss: John Dewey.

It is frustrating having so many eligible people and so few denominations of paper currency. Of course, there is no reason why we could not rotate the people portrayed on the paper money. The government constantly changes the value of the currency (always in one direction: down), so the paper could be redecorated periodically. The paper currency could be a slowly expanding honors system—sort of a House of Lords for the eminent departed. Someday—not soon, let us hope—we shall want to make room for, say, some American writers still writing. What fun it would be one day to whip out a wallet and pay for dinner with two Eudora Weltys, three Peter Taylors and a Saul Bellow.

Furthermore, we may not always have just 11 denominations. By the time our government gets done debauching our currency (actually, government's inflationary work is never done), we may be buying loaves of bread with $10,000 bills. We will need bigger denominations, so save the names of those (Frank Lloyd Wright, Aaron Copland, James Fenimore Cooper, Robert Frost, Michael Jordan . . .) who do not make our new varsity 11.

June 3, 1991

A Short History of Greed

The definitive history of greed is yet to be written but the broad outlines are well known. Greed was inserted into the human story a while back by a serpent. Since then it has waxed and waned.

For example, there was little of it during the Dark Ages, when there was little to covet. True, the Visigoths were grasping people, but a distinction should be drawn between their innocent Third World ebullience and the greed Ronald Reagan let loose in America. There were gobs of greed during America's Gilded Age after the Civil War, when robber barons made disgusting amounts of money. They also made railroads, steel mills and a unified nation capable of employing and assimilating millions of immigrants, but that, of course, was no excuse.

Anyway, journalists and Democratic presidential candidates and other historians are agreed that greed seems to vary inversely with the fortunes of the Democratic Party. The sharpest spikes on the graph of greed coincide uncannily with Republican presidencies. At noon on January 20, 1981, greed began soaring to a particularly amazing peak.

Arkansas Governor Bill Clinton says the 1980s were a decade of "greed and self-serving." Iowa Senator Tom Harkin says the 1980s featured "greed and selfishness." Nebraska Senator Bob Kerrey says "greed and cynicism" were everywhere. Former California Governor Jerry Brown says politics then became "a Stop & Shop for every greedy special interest." Former Massachusetts Senator Paul Tsongas says— and to think he has been called boring—"this generation is ready to turn its back on the 1980s and the greed."

But while waiting to see which of these moralists is nominated to drive greed back to wherever it came from, read "Was It a Decade of Greed?" by Richard B. McKenzie of the University of California, Irvine. Published in *The Public Interest*, the essay notes that in the greed-soggy 1980s charitable giving by individuals and corporations increased dramatically.

While Americans were, as everyone knows, wallowing in self-absorption and going on consumption binges, they also were giving to charities at a rate substantially above even the level that would have been predicted from the upward trend established in the previous 25 years. Between 1955 and 1980 giving (expressed in constant 1990 dollars) increased at a compound annual rate of 3.3 percent, from $34.5 billion to $77.5 billion. But between 1980 and 1989 giving increased to $121 billion, an annual rate of increase of 5.1 percent, a growth rate 55 percent higher than in the preceding 25 years.

Giving by individuals, which is more than 80 percent of all giving, grew 68 percent faster in the 1980s than between 1955 and 1980. Giving by individuals grew even faster than did spending on the consumption of automobiles (60 percent), jewelry and watches (41 percent), personal services such as hairstyling and health clubs (38 percent) and restaurant meals (22 percent). In fact, giving by individuals increased faster than total consumer spending (48 percent), which was, everyone knows, at a level indicative of Babylonian decadence.

Does population growth explain away this odd charitableness by the odiously greedy? Nope. Real per capita giving by individuals increased twice as fast as in earlier decades, from $284 in 1980 to $409 in 1989. And private giving as a share of national income increased 29 percent from the late 1970s to the late 1980s.

Giving increased not only in the teeth of the 1980s gale of greed, but increased in spite of lower tax rates, which increased the cost of giving. For a pre-1980s taxpayer in a 50 percent bracket, a $100 gift cost $50 (the gift minus the $50 reduction of his tax bill). But for a taxpayer in

Reagan's top bracket of 28 percent, the $100 gift costs $72 (the gift minus a $28 tax bill reduction).

How can all this be explained? It is, of course, impossible that charitable giving accelerated because people had significantly more disposable income. Everyone knows (because everyone who says there was a gusher of greed says so) that in the 1980s most people were made miserable. Hence it is unlikely that people gave more because they were happy, optimistic and in a giving mood.

The only acceptable explanation—meaning the only explanation compatible with what everyone (journalists, Democratic presidential candidates and other historians) knows—is this: Charitable giving increased because of the *horrors* of the Reagan era. Specifically, the virtual extinction of the middle class and the annihilation of the environment were so gross that not even the anesthetizing effect of greedy consumption could prevent a broad outpouring of charitable giving from horrified Americans.

Call it "the charity of revulsion against conservatism." The explanation of it will be complete when someone explains how the orgy of consumption coincided with general economic misery.

January 23, 1992

The Price of Moral Preening

One Whitewater puzzle is this: Why have the Clintons been so ruinously resistant to revealing everything about what probably are, at worst, dealings too minor and complicated to arrest the nation's attention, and concerning which a political statute of limitations has expired because an election has intervened?

The answer may be: Revelation would disarm an administration dependent on sowing moral disdain for opponents. That is, Whitewater may be trivial, other than as a deflator of moral pretensions.

The Clintons regard disparagement of the 1980s as a means of dominating the 1990s. Their problem was to justify "reversing Reaganism" in spite of Reaganism's results—93 consecutive months of growth, 19 million more jobs, surging exports, declining inflation and interest rates.

Statistical criticism would not suffice. It was said the new jobs were low-skill jobs, but the Bureau of Labor Statistics disagreed. It was said the Reagan years widened income inequalities, but the widening began in the 1970s, slowed after growth resumed in 1982 and was mostly an effect of education differentials in an increasingly knowledge-based economy. So statistical criticism of Reagan's years yielded to moral disdain for "the decade of greed."

The sensibility of the 1960s, the Clintons' formative years, featured intellectual conceit and moral vanity. Both are on display in the Clintons' health care plan, a huge act of condescension that presupposes that personal freedom must be severely restricted to produce rationality and punish avarice.

Vanity is what children of the 1960s learned in college, when professors and other adults who liked the younger generation's politics said it was a singularly moral generation. Taught that their sincerity legitimized their intentions, the children of the 1960s grew up convinced they could not do wrong.

Hence the Clinton administration's genuine bewilderment when accused of ethical lapses. It is a theoretical impossibility for people in "the party of compassion" to behave badly because good behavior is whatever they do. Bad behavior is whatever Ed Meese did.

Whitewater may involve unseemly grasping and corner-cutting and indifference to proprieties while pursuing money. Hence the intense resistance to revelation: It threatens the politics of moral preening, a political style increasingly problematic for the Clintons.

Webster Hubbell, formerly Mrs. Clinton's law partner and currently the third-ranking official in the Justice Department, is under investigation concerning possible overbilling of clients, such as the federal government. Moralists trained by Mrs. Clinton to sniff the faintest whiff of greed may worry about Hubbell's bill for 180 hours of work for one agency in August 1990, including work on 20 consecutive days, including weekends.

Suspicious people, their suspicions attuned to Mrs. Clinton's example as a greed-detector, may recall the acceleration of her payout from her law firm, from January 1993—which would have been the firm's normal payout—back into December 1992. Was she evading the tax increase her husband had not yet publicly discovered was necessary?

People watching Mrs. Clinton worry about the greed of pharmaceutical companies may—their moral senses quickened by her example—worry about her participation in ValuePartners. That investment group suddenly and sharply increased its "selling short"—betting on the decline of—stocks in pharmaceutical companies when President and Mrs. Clinton were castigating, and threatening to punish, such companies.

People inspired by Mrs. Clinton's denunciation of other people's motives may wonder why the Clintons did not put their assets in a blind trust until July 1993. Other recent presidents did so before taking office. Ascribing base financial motives to other people has become, thanks partly to the Clintons, evidence of moral vigor, so some will suspect that the person handling the Clintons' affairs had trouble getting the numbers about their holdings to square with tax filings and other disclosures made during the Arkansas years. That person was Vince Foster.

Now, all these suspicions may be unfair but they are condign punishment for the Clintons. Such suspicions flourish in the accusatory climate the Clintons have cultivated by ascribing disreputable motives to their opponents. Mrs. Clinton is still hard at it, telling *Elle* magazine that her critics' motives are political or personal or "financial." Of course. There can be no honorable disagreement with a child of the 1960s.

Her husband told the slowly resigning—next month—Bernard Nussbaum that this is a time when "serving is hard." Democrats control the executive branch and Congress, which on January 20 last year experienced a sudden reduction of interest in oversight of the executive branch. What, then, is so hard?

Perhaps it is hard serving in a climate of moral posturing of the sort that fueled the Clintons' rise to power. If the outcome of Whitewater is a diminution of their moral vanity, the episode will have been a blessing.

March 10, 1994

Mr. English Stays in Washington

The rural counties of western Oklahoma's 6th Congressional District have lost lots of population since the dust bowl days of the 1930s and soon will lose another person. Their congressman, Glenn English, is retiring, not at the end of his term, but in a hurry, in January, to become head of the National Rural Electric Cooperative Association. It is headquartered here, near where it tills and reaps so successfully, on Capitol Hill.

Elected in 1974, after Watergate, English was part of the bumper crop of freshman Democrats who vowed to usher in a reign of virtue. *The Almanac of American Politics* says Oklahoma's 6th District should be Republican, but English votes conservative on most issues—although he also votes for "generous aid for farm areas," including "the farm credit system, the FmHA (Farmers Home Administration) and REA."

The Rural Electrification Administration, which today subsidizes with cheap loans the cooperatives that are the members of the NRECA, was established during the New Deal to facilitate electrification of the countryside. Then only 10 percent of America's farms had electricity. By the 1950s, 90 percent had it. The problem has long since been solved, but the "solution" rolls right on. Today some of the subsidized power goes to places like suburban Atlanta, Aspen, Colorado, and Hilton Head, South Carolina.

This year President Clinton proposed substantially limiting REA's subsidies. However, English is chairman of the subcommittee that protects the REA. He, with the help of the member co-ops of the NRECA, which contributed $714,930 to Congressional candidates in the 1992 elections, largely beat back the challenge. English says he began negotiating with the NRECA less than three weeks after the House finished reauthorizing the REA. Given the timing, English and the NRECA were courting while collaborating.

So English is passing through the revolving door that connects the public sector with private sector institutions that are parasitic on the public sector. But this will not distress Clinton. He says, "I don't think we should discourage people from moving in and out of government." He made that laconic comment when defending two of his senior aides who are leaping from the White House into greener pastures.

Howard Paster, head of White House Congressional liaison, will make about $1 million in Washington with Hill & Knowlton, the public relations and lobbying firm. Roy Neel, Clinton's deputy chief of staff, will be paid about $500,000 by the United States Telephone Association in Washington.

Candidate Clinton said: "During the 1980s . . . high-level executive branch employees traded in their government jobs for the chance to make millions lobbying their former bosses. . . . This betrayal of democracy must stop. . . . We must stop the revolving door." With Paster and Neel leaving after less than a year, the door has rarely revolved so rapidly. Under Clinton's rules, solemnly announced earlier this year, Paster and Neel cannot immediately lobby, but they can supervise lobbying.

When Republicans spun in the revolving door in the 1980s, Democrats waxed sociological about the era and moral about motives—the "decade of greed" and all that. But cupidity left town last January 20 when the party of compassion took control, so now Dee Dee Myers, Clinton's spokeswoman, is deploying the fallacy of the false alternative on behalf of Paster and Neel: "You can't expect that people in government will never have another job."

"I," says Clinton, "don't think we should have a permanent government class and a permanent private sector . . . across the divide from each other." Fear not, Mr. President, the divide hardly exists.

Of course the President, who has hardly been out of government as an adult, opposes the real solvent of permanent government—term limits. About 40 percent of the 121 senators and congressmen who left office last year have joined the Washington influence industry. Term limits would swiftly devalue such people by steadily rotating their contacts— their old colleagues in Congress—out of Congress.

No one should be shocked by Paster and Neel, any more than by Clinton at a Hollywood fund-raiser scooping up $100,000 contributions for "soft money" accounts of the sort he says should be banned. One reason for occasionally having Democratic administrations is the fun of watching the hypocrisy rise hip deep, and hearing the moral principles get tempered by compassion for those who once professed them but who now would be inconvenienced by them.

One of Clinton's closest confidants insists that Clinton's principles concerning the revolving door are "infinitely better than what we had before." So says George Stephanopoulos, White House savant and former student of theology, who has an interesting notion of infinity.

December 19, 1993

PART 6

International

A 1930s Figure

The anesthetizing tranquility of the post–Cold War world has suddenly been driven away by Iraq's emphatic reminder of the nature of
the pre–Cold War world. This echo of the preceding 30 or so centuries
suggests how much like the past the future may be.

It is tempting, but misleading, to compare the strutting Saddam Hussein to Mussolini, and thereby diminish Hussein, making him seem, as
Mussolini now does through the obscuring mists of history, more absurd
than menacing. Mussolini was the very junior partner in the Axis, and was
last seen hanging from his heels at a Milan gas station. Hussein, too, is
unlikely to die old, venerated, in dignified retirement, or in his sleep. But
he is unlike Mussolini in two significant particulars.

Hussein radiates a more virulent and personal viciousness than
Mussolini did. Mussolini's internal security apparatus was evil but not
as brutal as Hussein's and it is unimaginable that Mussolini would have
used poison gas against Italians as Hussein has against Iraq's Kurds.
And Hussein disposes of far more military might, relative to neighbors,
than Mussolini did.

However, Hussein is a very 1930s figure. He issues ultimata. He
masses troops on international borders ostensibly to give weight to the
diplomacy of ultimata but actually to demonstrate, with contemptuous
clarity, that ultimata are perfunctory preludes to the crossing of borders.

The U.S. response to this, particularly regarding reassurances to
Saudi Arabia, will probably be influenced, and for the better, by the fact
that today's president is the last of a well-schooled line. Unless Lloyd
Bentsen, the former bomber pilot, runs and wins in 1992, George Bush,
the former fighter pilot, will be America's last president from the World
World II generation. For that generation, war was the enveloping, formative experience and the word "Munich" is freighted with warning
when it denotes analogies.

The lesson of Munich was: When it is necessary to confront an expan-
sionist dictator, sooner is better than later. As Douglas MacArthur said,
in war all tragedy can be summarized in two words—"too late." Too late
perceiving, too late preparing for danger.

Democracy is not, as Ronald Reagan and others seem to assume, the
certain solvent of danger. Democracy does not necessarily render a society pacific, just as a dictatorship (for example, Franco's Spain) does not

necessarily manifest aggressive dynamism. But democracy does generally help domesticate nations. Therefore it is well to note the following:

Democracy has recently been sprouting here, there and, it almost seems, everywhere between the cracks in the crumbling concrete of despotisms. It has been sprouting not only in the Soviet Union and Eastern Europe, but in Latin America, too. However, the world still waits and watches, without grounds for near-term hope, for the first democracy in the so-called Arab world.

In the 42 years since Israel was established on one-sixth of 1 percent of the land in "the Arab world," the reaction in the region to the existence of Israel has been unanimously hostile, and this unanimity has obscured the fact that the phrase "the Arab world" is only a geographical, not a political expression. The most envenomed and bloody relationships, and most volatile confrontations, do not involve Israel.

The "blame Israel first (and last, and in between)" brigade is large and growing, here and abroad. But it should be given pause by Hussein. Iraq's act is redundant evidence of this truth: The existence of Israel, and of "the Palestinian question," usually has precious little—and often, as in this case, nothing—to do with the largest and most dangerous doings in the Middle East. Today it is especially apparent that Israel is the all-purpose but implausible alibi for the various pathologies that convulse many Arab nations, and relations between them.

History will record more clearly than did contemporary journalism the fact that in the 1980s Iraq and Iran fought one of the major wars of this century of big wars. The war raged most of the time outside the range of television cameras and therefore largely outside the consciousness of the West.

This week, however, the West should remember with gratitude recent history's single most effective and beneficial act of arms control, Israel's 1981 bombing of Iraq's embryonic nuclear-weapon program. And this week it is wise to acknowledge that the world became more dangerous because nothing much happened after Iraq used poison gas against Iran. The regime of international restraint, sometimes called international law, was significantly weakened by the weakness—the virtual invisibility—of the world's response.

Israel noted that nonresponse and concluded, not for the first time, this: The unthinkable isn't.

Stephen Crane once wrote:

A man said to the universe:
"Sir, I exist!"
"However," replied the universe,

"The fact has not created in me
A sense of obligation."

Hussein has demonstrated the sincerity of his bellicose rhetoric. This demonstrates why Crane's poem expresses the essence, and correctness, of the statecraft of the only democracy in that unhappy region.

August 3, 1990

The Perils of "Legality"

Misery may love company, but for nations there are occasions when company can be misery. We have the comfort of company in the current crisis partly because we have wrapped our policy in the infinitely elastic cloth of "international law." But there will be prices paid, by this President and successors, for this promiscuous recourse to the problematic rhetoric of legality.

President Bush will regret this recourse if he decides his policy requires removal of Saddam Hussein. It is more difficult to give a patina of legality to that goal than to reversing aggression. Subsequent presidents will rue today's reliance on "international law" when they need to use force and find the "international community," the supposed source of such law, fickle. Today's unity has been produced by Arab fear (of Iraq) and allied needs (for oil). It will be hard to replicate such unity in future crises, yet the unity is being adduced as proof of the "legality" of policy.

This lawyerly Republic has long been wont to orient foreign policy to international law, at least rhetorically. In a sprightly new book, *On the Law of Nations*, Senator Pat Moynihan regrets a recent falling away from that tradition, to which Bush, to Moynihan's satisfaction, now recurs. Sprightly means vivacious, cheerful, brisk. But a sprite is a disembodied spirit, a ghost. Like international law.

Moynihan says that adherence to legal norms for nations' acts is intensely practical because it is conducive to domestic support and international leverage for policies. And it often is not optional because international law codified in treaties is "the supreme Law of the Land." But skeptics see problems, particularly when international law might seem to matter most—where force is the issue.

International law—so reverently invoked, so rarely defined—is like God. The threshold question is: Does it exist? Some spheres of international behavior (e.g., maritime matters, the rights of diplomats) are governed by lawlike regimes: There are enduring and widely adhered-to conventions, and institutions for arbitrating disputes. But what has international law to do with what is being done about Saddam Hussein? Who gave whom what legal "right" to do what it seems right to do—deter further aggression?

Some disparagement of international law derives from a visceral reflex for independence, for freedom from fetters. That reflex is not foolish, but neither is it an argument. Intellectually serious skepticism about international law derives from concern about damage that idea does to the concept of law and to the practice of prudent statecraft.

Before congeries of customs, habits, norms and arrangements can properly be called law, questions need answers. If international law is really law, who enacts, construes, adjudicates and enforces it? The phrase "international law" often is virtually an oxymoron. Law without a sword is mere words: Lacking an enforcement mechanism, *soi-disant* "law" is merely admonition or aspiration.

Law must be backed by coercion legitimized by a political process. The "international community" has no such process. Indeed, the phrase "international community" is metaphoric and misleading. A true community exists only when there is consensus about certain matters—the meaning of freedom, the nature of rights and duties, sources of legitimacy. Thus the phrase "international community" denotes no reality. Rhapsodizing about the U.N. as the "international community" incarnate obscures this fact: The U.N. is composed of representatives of regimes most of which rule in ways repellent to the U.N.'s democratic minority.

If "international law" is defined as what the "international community" actually does, the problem deepens. Regarding force, history is clear: Nations do what they think necessary and feasible. And even today, while "experts" on international law spin theories making everything everybody's business, nations whose interests are not implicated in a particular eruption of force do next to nothing.

When Iraq broke the durable and precise convention against chemical warfare, the "international community" was torpid. When Iraq menaced oil supplies, that "community" was galvanized, as it was not when Egypt intervened in Yemen (1962) and in countless other cases. If international law is consensus in action, that law exists concerning especially inconvenient aggression, but not most aggression, and not poison gas. (Oh, yes. The "international community" and its "law" were outraged by Israel's 1981 raid against Iraq's nuclear plant.)

Recently the United States has used force to punish Libya for sponsoring terrorism, has hijacked a plane to capture hijackers, has supported insurgency to change the government of Nicaragua and has changed the governments of Grenada and Panama. The world is a safer, better—in a sense, more lawful—place because of these actions. But each was at best of uncertain "legality."

About one thing Moynihan is right, and rightly disturbed. The interventions in Grenada and Panama violated the supreme law of the land in the form of the Charter of the Organization of American States: "No State . . . has the right to intervene, directly or indirectly, for any reason whatever, in the internal or external affairs of any other State." Moynihan asks: If we do not believe these things, what do we believe? Fair question.

He says we should eschew actions incompatible with our language of law. But it would be better to eschew language that cannot be squared with prudent statecraft. Regarding force, "international law" is often capriciously, meaning politically, defined in ways that serve the ruthless by inhibiting only the scrupulous. It often is invoked by the decent—as by the U.S. government today—to give redundant respectability to policies that are perfectly defensible without the veneer of ersatz legality.

Eager seizure of the label "legal" encourages the fallacy that international law is explicit and exhaustive—that anything not clearly "legal" is illegal. And it puts policy at the mercy of a vague and volatile consensus of an "international community" most members of which are unsuited to serve as ethicists or judges. There will be times when the United States, in defense of its interests, will need to act irrespective of any international consensus. Then the chimera of international law may hold America hostage.

September 10, 1990

Georgia on Our Minds

When in repose, which he rarely is, President Bush reaches for horseshoes and fishing rods rather than reading matter. But before he ricochets somewhere else, someone should immobilize him long enough for him to read the essay by Caroline Ziemke on Senator Richard Russell in the spring 1988 *Georgia Historical Quarterly*. It will help Bush understand another Georgia senator, Sam Nunn, who 30 years ago set out to become what Russell was and Nunn now is, chairman of the Armed Services Committee.

That committee's hearings have demonstrated that Bush cannot produce domestic consensus to match his multinational coalition concerning the Gulf crisis. Some people have been startled by Nunn's skepticism about the scale of the Gulf deployment and the evident slide toward war. Nunn is a Southerner with that region's regard for military values. Is he not a hawk?

Perhaps the only good this crisis will do is discredit the inane dichotomy between hawks and doves. Nunn is a case study of the complexity of American opinion. The pedigree of Nunn's statecraft runs back to Russell, and hence back, in a sense, 126 years. For most Americans today, the Civil War is a television series. For many Southerners, and particularly Georgians, the "lost cause" is a lesson of perennial relevance: Things often do not work out well.

Modern war made its debut in Georgia in 1864, with Sherman burning barns and bending rails and blurring the distinction between combatants and noncombatants. Thirty-three years later, Russell was born in Winder, a short march from Atlanta. In 1933, at 36, he began a Senate career that ended with his death in January 1971.

Only 14 of today's senators served with him. Few Washingtonians remember how he bestrode the Senate, particularly on military matters. It is remembered that Russell, whose protégé Lyndon Johnson was, supported the Vietnam War once many Americans were under fire. But a decade before that he said, "I am weary of seeing American soldiers being sent as gladiators, to be thrown into every arena around the world."

In 1953, when Eisenhower sent $1 billion to the French in Indochina, Russell said, "You are pouring [money] down a rat hole . . . that is going to be one of the worst things this country ever got into." In 1954, when Eisenhower sought (note well, President Bush) Congressional authorization for use of air and naval forces in Indochina, Russell deflected the request (perhaps to Eisenhower's relief). When Eisenhower, himself wary of Asian involvement, sent a few hundred military advisers, Russell warned, "You are opening up a trail today that will be costly in blood and treasure. . . . There will be thousands there tomorrow."

In April 1961, when Kennedy was concerned about Laos, Russell said, "We should get our people out and write the country off." In August 1964 Congress passed (after Senate hearings of less than two hours) the Gulf of Tonkin Resolution authorizing the President to resist Vietnamese Communists "by any means necessary, including the use of arms." Only two senators, Oregon's Morse and Alaska's Gruening, opposed it. But Russell added an amendment: Any Congressional repeal of this grant of power to the president would be immune from veto. In February 1966 Russell joined Morse and Gruening in an unsuccessful attempt to repeal the grant. In 1967 he opposed procurement of 30 Fast Deployment Logistics (FDL) ships, saying, "If it is easy for us to go anywhere and do anything, we will always be going somewhere and doing something."

The South, which did its damnedest to destroy the Constitution, has produced some senators, such as Hugo Black and Sam Ervin, passionate about constitutional propriety. Perhaps Southern senators once were particularly jealous of legislative prerogatives because they could not realistically aspire to the presidency. That is no longer true. Yet regarding the proper working of checks and balances concerning war powers, Nunn resembles Russell.

Russell, writes Ziemke, was a bridge between the nation's two military pursuits that became "lost causes." One was waged on behalf of Southern nationalism; the other, against Vietnamese communism.

> Russell showed an understanding of the nature of civil war, revolution, and the painful process of reconstruction that must have stemmed, in part, from his Southern heritage. Even more importantly, Russell, as a Southerner, had a cultural understanding of frustration, defeat, and national humiliation that was alien to the experience of other Americans.

Is it still reasonable to speak of such regional differences? Does Nunn have in his political chromosomes some Southern wariness about resorting to war? Has he some constitutional punctiliousness that disposes him to keep the most uncontrolled facet of the federal government—the president acting as commander-in-chief—in check? Nunn may someday seek the presidency, but he is a man of the Congress. His great-uncle, Georgia's Carl Vinson, was chairman of the House Armed Services Committee and served a record 50 years and two months in the House. Nunn is a product of Congress's institutional culture as well as a regional culture.

Part of the institutional culture is a prickly rivalry with the executive branch, a vigilance that history warrants and prudence requires when the executive is making decisions that are matters of life and death. Furthermore, if Congress's abiding sin is parochialism, that vice has its virtue: Congress is flavored by regionalisms and particularities that have their own wisdoms. They should assert their right to be heard when, as now, policy is being made by an extremely small coterie in the executive branch.

The obverse of that right is a presidential duty to listen. The duty is not just moral or constitutional, but also prudential. Our hyperkinetic President, who last week hopscotched around the Southern Hemisphere, should have the South, especially Georgia, on his mind. Last week a Georgian who served eight years (1961–68) as Secretary of State affirmed a statement he made 25 years ago: Any large foreign policy undertaking without Congressional support "is in the subjunctive mood."

So says Dean Rusk, who was born 81 years ago, about 30 miles from Winder, on the edge of Sherman's charred path to the sea.

December 17, 1990

Once Again, Ike Was Right

Some people who fancy themselves flinty realists believe that today's concern for Congress's war powers is symptomatic of America's foolish legalism, and of a contemptible preoccupation with process rather than policy. However, it is peculiar "realism" that would launch the most uncertain of enterprises, war ("Every war is going to astonish you," said Eisenhower), with an anticonstitutional act that squanders this democracy's vital military asset, public support.

Many uses of force occur in a constitutional twilight area where the respective rights of the president and Congress are debatable. Most twilight cases should be resolved in favor of the president. But the military offensive that the United States may soon initiate against Iraq is not a twilight case. Constitutionally, Congress must authorize any launching, from a standing start, of one of the largest military operations in American history. Authorization does not mean after-the-fact ratification. Authorization must be formal and explicit, not merely inferred from legislative silence or statements by individual legislators or collateral legislative activity. Congress must do this even though many members are eager to flee from responsibility. It is a duty, not a perquisite.

President Bush will either comply with the constitutional requirement for Congressional authorization for war, or by unilaterally initiating war he will unilaterally amend the Constitution. Surely the Framers' definition of war covers a collision between massed armies involving more than a million people. So as Walter Dellinger of Duke University law school says, "If the declaration of war clause does not apply here, it will have been stripped out of the Constitution."

Many conservatives have defended vast presidential autonomy in conducting an interventionist foreign policy. But concerning domestic policy these conservatives advocate "strict construction" of the Constitution, meaning fidelity to the Framers' "original intent." Such conservatives are now caught in a contradiction.

Although a delegate to the Constitutional Convention proposed giving the president power to initiate war, the Convention embraced Roger Sherman's view, as expressed in Madison's notes: "The Executive shd. be able to repel and not commence war." The Convention substituted "declare" for "make" in defining Congress's power relating to war because "make" might be misconstrued to mean "conduct." The president can "make" (conduct) those wars that Congress, in determining policy, initiates. As explained by Hamilton in the *Federalist Papers* (number 69), Congress's power reflects the Framers' determination not to repeat Europe's history of executive-initiated wars. And the Convention's decision was not controversial.

The modern controversy about these powers began when Truman took the nation into Korea without Congress's assent. He at least had the excuse of urgency—a surprise attack, and South Korea crumbling— and within days after the invasion Congress was enacting supportive measures. Still, Eisenhower understood the damage done to his predecessor by fighting an undeclared war. Eisenhower twice sought and got the kind of Congressional support Bush has not sought. In 1955 Congress declared the President "authorized to employ" forces "as he deems necessary" for protecting Formosa and the Pescadores. In 1957 Congress declared: "If the president determines the necessity thereof, the United States is prepared to use armed forces" to aid Middle Eastern nations threatened by communist aggression.

On January 19, 1956, Eisenhower told a press conference, "When it comes to the matter of war, there is only one place that I would go, and that is to the Congress of the United States, and tell them what I believe." On April 4, 1956, asked yet again about war powers, he exclaimed:

> I get discouraged sometimes here. I have announced time and time again that I will never be guilty of any kind of action that can be interpreted as war until the Congress, which has the constitutional authority, says so. . . . Now, there are times when troops, to defend themselves, may have to, you might say, undertake local warlike acts, but that is not the declaration of war, and that is not going to war, and I am not going to order any troops into anything that can be interpreted as war, until Congress directs it.

Eisenhower, who had studied war all his life and had practiced politics in and for the Army, made a reasonable distinction. Not all uses of force, not all warlike acts, constitute war. But anything reasonably interpreted as war must be "directed," meaning ordered, by Congress.

Today's president is content merely to reiterate the statement that history is "replete" with instances (about 200, he said last week) when presidents have used force without Congressional authorization. Bush apparently believes that incantation of this number suffices as a constitutional argument. But almost all those uses of force, from the sorties Washington ordered against Indians, to the naval action Jefferson ordered against the Barbary pirates, and beyond, were brief and were directed not against sovereign states but against merely episodic threats. Most occurred when communication within America was slow and travel was arduous and Congress was dispersed most of the time. And as Arthur Schlesinger says, when Lincoln in the spring of 1861 and Roosevelt in the autumn of 1941 breached the Constitution with military measures, their excuse was acute national emergency. Neither made the impertinent claim that a right to initiate war is an inherent and routine presidential power.

Could Bush get away with the anti-constitutional act of initiating war on his own hook? Sure. Once the shooting starts, Congress has only two weapons and neither blunderbuss is practical: impeachment or defunding the war. So Bush is inhibited only by his oath of office (about preserving the Constitution) and prudential consideration.

When a war, like the impending one, approaches slowly and not at all stealthily, and when America is not repelling a surprise attack but launching a huge offensive as a matter of policy, the only reason for not seeking Congressional support is that it cannot be got. But going to war without it is not something that real realists do.

January 14, 1991

From Bayonets to Tomahawks

General Schwarzkopf, his voice as flat as Kansas, his language spare, said, "The Iraqis had no concept of what they were getting involved in." Indeed, how could they have known what had begun when the first Tomahawk missile detonated in Baghdad? By making the cradle of ancient civilization a theater of war involving the most modern nation, Saddam was slapped in the face by this fact: Today's weaponry evolves rapidly, sophistication increases exponentially. When a scientific nation like America goes 15 years between wars, it brings to the next battle new weapons never tested in the crucible that counts. America's new array is passing its test and proving this point to Saddam: Modern science makes militarism increasingly untenable for societies that are not comprehensively modern.

The weapons Wellington's men used at Waterloo in 1815 were like those Marlborough's men used at Blenheim in 1704. But America's inventory of weapons today is significantly different from that of the Vietnam War. Saddam, too, has some advanced systems. A bane of the modern world has been the acquisition of sophisticated technology by political primitives. Saddam is a primitive at large in, but not at home in, the modern world. The marriage of a modern military apparatus to a politically and culturally underdeveloped society is bound to fail because of irreconcilable incompatibilities. Saddam struck it rich in the oil business, went on a shopping binge and imported some military modernity. But today he is learning, late, a lethal lesson about the relationship between militaries and societies. Saddam is making disastrous history for Iraq because he knows so little history, particularly of war.

Early in this century Europe bled nearly to death because of ignorance of the new realities of war. In 1914 many Europeans welcomed war. They were gripped by an old, romantic idea that soon would be machine-gunned to death at the Somme. The idea was that in war morale matters more than matériel—three times more, Napoleon said.

In 1914, graduates of the French military academy marched into battle wearing white gloves and pompons. German university graduates marched singing, with arms linked, toward British trenches. Several British contingents kicked soccer balls as they advanced through no-man's-land. For four years generals fought machine guns with young men's chests. The old men did not understand that war, the greatest engine of social change, had unleashed forces that profoundly changed war itself.

We have come a long way from the infantryman's pike, to the bayonet, to the Tomahawk. In the early age of handguns, 16 feet was thought to be a good length for a pike because most pistols were inaccurate at that distance. The bayonet (invented for the protection of hunters who found themselves with empty guns, facing wounded beasts) made armies reluctant to close with one another. That made firepower over distances more important. Today, a sailor in the Gulf programs a computer and minutes later a Tomahawk deals destruction deep in Iraq's interior.

Historian Michael Howard notes that Viking longboats and Magyar ponies made warriors mobile across long distances. Eighth-century Franks developed the stirrup, making horses useful for fighting as well as mobility. The 12th century's technological marvel, the crossbow, shrank battlefield distances and devalued armor. Combustible materials had been hurled by catapults in sieges of cities and naval engagements. Then the process was reversed. Combustion was used to propel things. The age of cannon arrived when Turkish artillery battered down the walls of Constantinople.

Until industrialism produced a social surplus, the scale of war was severely restricted by its expense. The cost of a single mounted and armored soldier could require several years' income of an entire 12th-century village. Henry V had only 6,000 soldiers at Agincourt. Napoleon was to take 600,000 to Russia. With Napoleon's notion of "the nation in arms," war entered the era of mass effects. But it entered slowly, hauled by horses, dependent on fodder.

War did not really get rolling until the coming of the steam engine, and then the internal combustion engine. These spared soldiers long marches, saving their energies for ferocity in combat. In America's Civil War railroads transported mass-produced conscripts who were carrying canned rations and rifles mass-produced from interchangeable parts. Breech-loading replaced muzzle-loading weapons so infantrymen could fire lying down, killing at a range of several hundred yards while not making themselves targets. Rifling of gun barrels improved range and accuracy by a factor of five. Calibrated rifle sights made raw conscripts better marksmen than Frederick the Great's finest grenadiers. And by 1914 a regiment of field guns could deliver on a few hundred square yards more destructive power in an hour than had been fired by all the guns on both sides in all the Napoleonic wars.

Marx said the industrial working class would acknowledge no fatherland and would serve no nation's military efforts. Actually, public education made workers skillful, trade unions made them loyal, sensationalizing newspapers made them fervid. Improved sanitation and medicine made armies more efficient: Before 1870, sickness usually killed five times as many soldiers as enemy action did.

The 19th century's long peace fostered industrial and scientific progress that made possible the horrors of the 20th century, when wars of armies were supplanted by wars of populations. A 19th-century Indiana inventor named Gatling, appalled by Civil War casualties, thought a gun capable of sustained fire would enable one soldier to do the work of 100, thereby making for smaller armies. But the Gatling gun had the opposite effect. In World War I huge armies were driven into trenches, "shovelry replaced chivalry" and war was deglamorized.

Until 1914 the military was the last redoubt of romantics in the industrial age. Then the machine gun enabled "three men and a gun to stop a battalion of heroes." Military romantics—not an endangered species, a vanished one, buried in Flanders Fields—regretted the machine gun and would have regretted the Tomahawk because "you can't pin a medal on a piece of metal." But neither can you bury a piece of metal in Arlington Cemetery.

January 28, 1991

Edging Back from a Moral Abyss

For many centuries, the West derived its martial ethic from a book. Homer's *Iliad* celebrated combat in close quarters, between symmetrically armed adult male warriors, on neutral ground, far from women and children. Individuals' virtues, such as strength and bravery, not differences of weapons, were decisive. Hence the Homeric hero's disdain for the bow: "My way is not to fight my battles standing far away from my enemies."

But long-range killing—by gun, bomb, missile—became approved almost as quickly as it became possible. And it was conducive to a kind of social callousness. The consequences of military action were unclear to the actors. Then came the graphic revolution in journalism.

That revolution—pictures supplementing, and sometimes supplanting, print—produces this paradox: Journalism supplies information to nourish reason, but some pictures, such as those of Wednesday's carnage in Baghdad, stir passions that paralyze reason.

A second paradox is that the pictures of the bombing of what was, in part, an air-raid shelter, had an impact in America that underscores this fact: America is waging this war in a way superior to the tendency of modern war, the tendency of wars against populations to replace wars between armies.

On Wednesday, U.S. fighter-bombers hit the target they sought, using munitions that minimize collateral damage. But the target was more than—not other than—what U.S. targeters thought. And Americans' anguish in the aftermath speaks well of them.

However, moral responsibility also involves facing this fact: When Americans voted for war, as they did through Congress, and when they did so while defining the enemy regime as Hitlerian, they embarked on a course of action that had to include civilian casualties.

Substantial civilian casualties, in spite of discriminating weaponry and targeting, are implicit in U.S. strategy. That strategy was implicit in the tactics used in the war's first hours. Formally, the war is being waged to drive Iraqi forces north from Kuwait. Actually, the war is being waged from north to south because this war is not territorial. Its aim is not to displace an occupier, but rather to damage, perhaps to the point of destruction, a regime.

Until Wednesday's pictures from Baghdad, this war had been for most Americans a bit too bland, too entertaining, the stuff of brisk souvenir sales. There is something unattractive about airport concession stands selling various Desert Storm T-shirts, among those with NFL and NBA logos. America may need to be dealing death, but almost no Iraqi, civilian or conscript, "deserves" to die.

This war, like all wars, and more than many, is full of tragedy. America, enlisting technology in the service of a civilized sensibility, has sought to minimize the tragedy by maximizing precision in the application of force. But although America is resisting the desensitizing effects of this century's wars—long-distance wars of air power—we have not been immune from those effects.

Today's vocabulary speaks volumes about the callousness war has wrought on the world. A frequently asked question is whether Iraq will use weapons of "mass destruction," meaning gas. But the two laser-guided bombs that struck the Baghdad bomb shelter accomplished what once was called "mass destruction."

Observers of the battle of Ravenna in 1512, the first battle decided by an artillery barrage, considered it mass destruction when one ball claimed 33 casualties. A year later, at Novara, also in Italy, cannon killed 700 in three minutes. When in 1784 General Henry Shrapnel developed the first exploding artillery shell containing subprojectiles, that routinized "mass destruction." At least it was massive compared to the killing of Homeric warfare, killing with edged weapons and muscle power, before war was dominated by chemical energy (explosives).

On April 5, 1585, a Dutch ship named *Hope* packed to the gunwales with explosives was set adrift to collide with a pontoon bridge packed with Spanish troops. The Spaniards thought it was just a fire ship. It was a time bomb. It may have caused 2,000 casualties—and the loudest man-made noise up to that point. It certainly produced, as Robert O'Connell writes in *Of Arms and Men*, the largest number of casualties inflicted by a single weapon up to that time.

Indiscriminate force causing vast collateral damage existed before the Second World War, when air power delivered huge tonnages of free-falling bombs from great heights, often at night. What happened Wednesday in Baghdad was a particular tragedy in a context of general tragedy, but it also was part of America's attempt to edge back from the 20th century's moral abyss. That abyss beckons when long-range killing gives rise to abstractness about its consequences.

February 17, 1991

A Land Fit for Heroes?

In 43 remarkable days America's military displayed a proficiency that was produced not merely by months of planning, but by 93 years of hard apprenticeship. America has had a lot of practice at war-making and practice makes, if not perfect, close enough.

America has now fought its sixth significant war since the battleship *Maine* blew up (by accident, it now seems) in Havana harbor in 1898. The war with Spain and two world wars and Korea and Vietnam and the Gulf War are only America's largest combat experiences since the explosion in the *Maine*. That explosion showered sparks on the dry tinder of American nationalism and detonated the "splendid little war" that made a president of the Rough Rider of San Juan Hill.

Victory over Spain led to 14 years of counterinsurgency combat in the Philippines. There was intervention in China during the Boxer Rebellion, and Black Jack Pershing's Mexican Expedition. In just the last 10 years American force has been used in Lebanon, Libya, Grenada, Panama. Some Americans have been involved in combat in about half of the 93 years since the *Maine's* keel settled into Cuba's mud.

It is not invidious to describe Desert Storm as an optional war. So was Korea. America was not attacked by Iraq and was not committed by treaty to the defense of Kuwait, which has never been defined as a vital American interest. Korea was a war of post-Munich deterrence, an attempt to discourage future aggression by being prompt and early with collective security. Desert Storm was similar, but was more. It was America's first post-1989 act, its first act as the world's only superpower. (One month into the crisis President Bush flew to Finland for a five-hour luncheon summit to stroke Gorbachev. In the last weeks of the crisis America's dismissive response to Gorbachev's mischievous diplomacy proved that the Soviet Union often can be as irrelevant as America wants it to be.) Desert Storm was a didactic war, waged to instruct potential aggressors in new rules for the game of nations.

If the teaching takes, the new world may be so orderly that America can allow its well-oiled combat arms to become rusty. If not, Americans, who have not been so happy since V-J Day (August 15, 1945), probably will be willing, even eager, to lead other coalitions into combat. If so, one reason will be that a generation of younger Americans has been taught a quite false lesson by Desert Storm: wars usually work out this way, short and one-sided and telegenic.

Another reason Americans are so happy, and so ready to do more great works abroad, is that things, especially things done by government, have not been working so well at home. Americans have found domestic problems intractable and foreign commercial competition daunting. The production of many things—cars, engineers, high SAT scores, low budget deficits, livable cities—has faltered. (During the 43 days of Desert Storm, violence in America killed many times more Americans than war did.) Americans are delighted to find a few things that work—weapons, the military generally. In recent years it has become a sardonic jest to say of something not done right, "Well, it's close enough for government work." But the armed forces are government work.

In one dreadful decade, 1965–74, government's stature was radically reduced. Great Society initiatives coincided with extreme disorders among the intended beneficiaries of the initiatives. This stimulated skepticism about government's competence. Then Vietnam and Watergate spread cynicism about government's motives. Since then the American left has been caught in a contradiction, and conservatives have been producing a paradox.

The left wants strong government to engineer social change. But the left's critical stance defeats its political program: By defining America as greedy, corrupt, racist, etc., the left undermines the consensus that is required for strong collective action. Furthermore, because of its hostility toward the military, the left has forfeited the fundamental game of American politics—capture the flag. The party that identifies with American nationalism wins.

For conservatives, today's military success compounds a paradox. Ronald Reagan climbed to the pinnacle of government by teaching distrust of government. But by putting a smiling face on government, and by curbing inflation (government's damage to the currency as a store of value), and by making the military conspicuous, competent and usable, he did much to rehabilitate government's reputation. Reagan's successor, by his deft diplomacy and his selection of superb colleagues, has consolidated the conservative party's position as the party of executive government.

For 40 years most conservatives have had a bifurcated vision of government: It should be bold abroad but tentative at home. Conservatives believe government is a blunt instrument, not a precision tool—a hammer, not a scalpel. It is good at big, broad strokes—digging a canal across an isthmus, waging war—but clumsy at intervening in the organic processes of a complex society such as ours.

This principle, distilled from many historical judgments, is broadly right but not sufficient. Government is not irrelevant to or impotent against the biggest threats to American preeminence, which are here at home. They are inadequate schools, scandalous numbers of children in poverty (one in five), public choices that produce spending wildly in excess of revenues, and private choices that produce a destructive ratio of consumption to savings and investment. If America's government is not smart enough to contribute to the correction of such strength-sapping defects, then America has a long-term problem of progressive anemia from which no weapons, however smart, can protect it.

Today George Bush stands at the sort of pinnacle few presidents have experienced. He has earned the nation's trust and, almost as important, he has the nation's attention. This is a perishable moment, and a propitious moment to say: As we welcome home the heroes from their sacrifices, let us make some symmetrical sacrifices to make this a land fit for heroes. The business of America is not business. Neither is it war. The business of America is justice, and securing the blessings of liberty.

March 11, 1991

The War's Fourth Stage

The peace is not nearly as much fun as the war was. American enjoyment of the war was supposedly a partial vindication of the war, which was supposed to be therapeutic, making us "feel good about ourselves." But the aftermath is depressing.

We are in the war's fourth stage. The four have been: diplomatic blunders that brought on the war; preparing to fight; fighting; enjoying Charlton Heston and Whitney Houston television specials celebrating the war that had been the nation's favorite television program. The fifth stage—scrubbing the pitch off our hands—will last longer than the other four combined.

Some people want to shove America up to its elbows in Iraq's civil war in order to stop Saddam's slaughter of insurgents whose insurgency coincided with American calls for just that. But it is a crashing non sequitur to say that if party A urges party B to overthrow a tyrant, then party A is obligated to participate in the overthrowing.

An Army lieutenant in occupied Iraq says, "There is not a man who would not go north and finish this job." But "the job" is done, at least as the job was defined by the agency to which we delegated the defining of it. The United Nations said the job was to liberate Kuwait. Kuwaitis have been restored to the misrule of their feckless royal family.

The United States stressed that the legitimacy of the war derived substantially from U.N. resolutions. Hence the United States is, as critics warned that it would be, now inhibited from unilateralism, including unilateral intervention in Iraq's civil war. Besides, what are we supposed to do, unilaterally or otherwise, with the ripped flesh of Iraqi society?

Nations are not machines, they are organisms, living things. When their flesh is torn, they bleed, get virulent infections, run raging fevers. We knew this, or had no excuse for not knowing it, when we went to war.

Is it America's interest or duty to become protector of Kurds, Shiites and other minorities now suffering the sort of terrors they might inflict, if they had minorities at their mercy? Kurds and Shiites seem united under Saddam's pounding, but there are factions within factions within these factions, and complexities we cannot comprehend, let alone control.

Kurds bet their lives on, and now feel betrayed by, the "international community." Blather kills. We went to war pretending the United Nations, or our coalition (featuring the Saddam-like Assad), was that "community" incarnate. Such propagandistic chatter leads people like the Kurds to entrust their lives to a fiction.

When Iraq capitulated, many Americans crowed that we had knocked "the Vietnam syndrome" into a cocked hat. But there actually were two Vietnam syndromes, one of which is, alas, very much alive.

Syndrome II, which came at the end of the Vietnam War, was the false and dangerous "lesson" that military power could accomplish little. But a decade before that there was Vietnam Syndrome I, which is proving to be a durable weed in the national garden. It was—is—the supreme political hubris of believing in "nation building." This belief, contradictory to every syllable of Burkean conservatism, is that nations are like Tinkertoys, to be rearranged by Americans who have a right to be rearrangers because they are such clever social engineers.

America is a nation in which, once every four years, armies of clever journalists and opinion-measurers flood placid, open, democratic Iowa. They study it carefully—and then are surprised by the results of decorous political caucuses.

But now America is supposed to sort out Iraq's murderous tribes on the zany premise that there must—why must?—be a bunch of democrats in there somewhere. This ambitious undertaking is being advocated by some conservatives who are not famous for their confidence in the ability of the U.S. government to do much of anything right on the North American continent.

A *Wall Street Journal* columnist, advocating deeper American involvement in Iraq's fate, argues that "42 days of bombing create some obligation to play a role in what happens next." Oh? And then in the next next after the first next?

Such an "obligation" tends to be perpetually renewing, deepened by each intervention taken to fulfill it. Remember, U.S. complicity in the 1963 coup that killed President Diem embedded America's hands deep in the pitch of the Vietnam tar baby.

Iraq, currently convulsed, is an improvisation ginned up after the First World War, which began in Serbia, which is currently part of convulsed Yugoslavia, another improvisation by the diplomats who thought the First World War launched a new world order. When will we learn that wars sow disorders that last twenty times longer than the wars do?

That does not mean wars should not be fought, only that their therapeutic value—making people "feel good"—is evanescent.

April 7, 1991

A Gaullist Foreign Policy

Fifty summers ago, an austere French soldier in his 50th year sat before a microphone in BBC studio 2B and told France that she had lost only a battle, not the war. It was June 18, 1940, the day of Churchill's "finest hour" speech. And the 125th anniversary of the battle of Waterloo.

History has recently been histrionic. The 200th anniversary of the French Revolution coincided last year with the collapse of the husks of Europe's supposedly "revolutionary" tyrannies. This year, while Europe experiences the rebirth of nations, and while Britain's prime minister is punished politically for resisting the dilution of national sovereignty in the name of the abstraction "Europe," France commemorates the 100th anniversary of a prophetic nationalist, Charles de Gaulle.

Other than in their implacability, Margaret Thatcher and De Gaulle are radically dissimilar. She rose through Parliament, he through "treason." His noble broadcast was a call to disobedience against France's government, which condemned him to death in absentia. Thatcher revels in party skirmishes. De Gaulle disdained "the ballet of parties," practicing a Caesarism of plebiscitary democracy, claiming "the individual authority of the state," personally. (Being Caesar is hazardous: He was the target of at least 30 assassination plots.)

Thatcher has the brusque, hectoring manner of a national nanny.

De Gaulle had what a biographer calls a baroque style of leadership suited, De Gaulle thought, to a nation "made by 40 kings over 1,000 years." De Gaulle, who kept spiritual company with those kings (and Joan of Arc), was forever in flight from banality. Thatcher's goal is to bang elementary arithmetic into British heads—the costs of life, the calculations of capitalism.

De Gaulle was both Washington and Lincoln—founder and preserver—of the Fifth Republic, which simmered with the threat of civil war. Thatcher's more mundane aim has been to make Britain efficient.

Thatcher wants the British to be better shopkeepers. De Gaulle used the myth of French grandeur therapeutically, to purge disgrace—the collapse in 1940 that was followed by collaboration.

He would "make use of dreams to lead the French," to seduce them away from the passions of private interests, to national glory. Intoxication by myth was his answer to a perennial dilemma of democracy: How do you exercise the art of leadership amidst the brokering of interests that is the basic business of government by consent?

De Gaulle, wrote Henry Kissinger in his memoirs, was "the son of a continent covered with ruins testifying to the fallibility of human foresight." But because he understood the political primacy of nations (he spoke of "the so-called United Nations"), he had foresight. He saw, over the horizon, Germany reunified and the Soviet Union again being Russia.

Because De Gaulle's mind had a retrospective cast and his rhetoric had a mystical tinge, detractors dismissed him as an anachronism oblivious to the wave of the future. Spotters of such waves were sure the next one would wash away much of the sovereignty and distinctiveness of nations, producing a fuzzy federalism of homogenized peoples.

Thatcher is similarly condescended to by advanced thinkers who stigmatize her as a "reluctant European." But her reluctance partakes of De Gaulle's farsightedness about the increasing, rather than decreasing, saliency and utility of nationalism.

And in one particular, she is De Gaulle's superior. She knows that the nub of the matter is parliamentary sovereignty, meaning that great good by which mankind's political progress is measured: representative government.

De Gaulle understood that among all of Marx's failed prophecies, the most failed was the most fundamental. It was the notion that industrialism made man a merely economic creature and that all noneconomic forces—religion, race, culture, ethnicity and especially nationalism—had lost their history-making saliency. Today's rebirth of Europe's captive nations, including those imparting centrifugal force to the overdue disintegration of the Soviet Union, is refutation of Marx and confirmation of De Gaulle.

Today, socialism's old aspiration, the warm broth of proletarian internationalism, has been supplanted by liberalism's still more watery soup of "Europeanness." Thatcher recoils from the drip-by-drip dilution of national sovereignty through the incremental transfer of power from national parliaments to the supranational bureaucracy in Brussels. There is a steady attenuation of control of lawmakers by elections, a weakening of the crucial criterion of legitimacy: consent of the governed.

As De Gaulle's nationalism was, so Thatcher's is the face of the better future. And what has this to do with Americans' lives today? Today, the threads connecting public consent with the gravest governmental decisions touching life and death—war and peace—are being tangled, frayed, perhaps even severed.

U.S. officials are seeking Ethiopia's, the Ivory Coast's, Zaire's forbearance—permission?—for Americans to sacrifice blood and treasure in an enterprise supposedly swathed in special legitimacy because of 10 resolutions from the United Nations ("the so-called United Nations"), all to advance an abstraction: "the new international order."

America needs a more Gaullist foreign policy, a more stabilizing contact with concreteness: U.S. national sovereignty, U.S. national interests, U.S. national decisions.

November 22, 1990

"Ethnic Self-determination" and Other High Explosives

The Balkans, again. There this century's fuse first sputtered, leading, in 1914, to the explosion that blew to smithereens the Hapsburg, Romanov and Ottoman empires. In 1992, from Sarajevo to Iraq to central Asia, the world is still struggling with the still-smoldering debris of those empires, which died in the aftermath of pistol shots in Sarajevo 78 summers ago. Is it still true that, as was then said, the Balkans produce more history than they can consume locally? That depends on whether other nations decide to regard Bosnia's bleeding as of merely local importance.

Americans watching Serbia's aggression also are watching the presidential candidates' responses to it. Margaret Thatcher, who favors air strikes and weapons for Bosnia, says to Americans, "This is mainly a great moral question. And if there is one country in the world which came to life on a moral basis, it was America." Our foreign policy has indeed been intermittently influenced by the fact that our nation's founding document affirms the universal validity of certain truths that are "self-evident," meaning clear to minds unclouded by superstition and ignorance. So Americans constantly feel tugged in two directions. One is to keep clear of quarrels that arise from superstitions and primitiveness rooted in ancient social soil. But we relish our role as bearers of a bright torch lit by our Founders.

Bosnia's sorrows are occasioning another installment in the argument between America's foreign policy "moralists" and "realists." The moralists ask, "Do we or do we not believe in self-determination?" Realists respond, "Be careful how you use those words. Serbians say they are fighting for self-determination and could invoke the ghost of a moralist, Woodrow Wilson."

Pat Moynihan, in his forthcoming book *Pandaemonium: Ethnicity in International Politics*, says ethnicity makes the world go 'round. And bleed. This is a nasty surprise, not least to all the advanced thinkers who knew, just *knew* that modernity would mean the eclipse of ethnicity. The "liberal expectancy" was that ethnic attachments would weaken, even disappear. Such attachments are (or so the theory was) anachronistic, primitive, transitional—echoes of mankind's infancy. Also mistaken was the Marxist prediction that all preindustrial components of identity—cultural, religious, racial—would be superseded by social class.

Didn't happen. The breaking of nations by ethnic fragmentation dominates world politics today. Many an ethnic group thinks it is a "self" entitled to "self-determination." The 19th century was a century of consolidations. The United States bound a continent together by steel rails and a strong central government. Germany unified. Italy did, too. But given the centrifugal forces loose in the late 20th century, Moynihan wonders: Would Germany or Italy unify today? Might Bavaria and Tuscany and other . . . what? "peoples"? . . . seek "self-determination"?

Americans injected into the discourse of diplomacy the idea that "self-determination" is a universal "right." Before the First World War ended Woodrow Wilson told a cheering session of Congress that "self-determination" is "an imperative principle of action." But self-determination by what sort of entities? Wilson said, "National aspirations must be respected; peoples may now be dominated and governed only by their own consent." He was sowing dragon's teeth. He seemed to assume that the phrases "nation-state" and "a people" are synonyms, or that these entities are coterminous. But in many cases they were not; are not. Ask the Serbian "people" living in, and carving up, the state of Bosnia.

Six of Wilson's 14 Points concerned self-determination. There was to be, for example, "autonomous development of the peoples of Austria-Hungary" and also of "other nationalities under Turkish rule." Peoples, nationalities. And ethnicity. Wilson, says Moynihan, revised the rules of international society "to accommodate, indeed to legitimize and even hallow the principle of ethnicity." But ethnicity is not the same thing as nationality, so the principle of ethnicity disrupts the game of nations. The world would be calmer if history had caused ethnic groups to coincide neatly with national boundaries. But the distribution of peoples does not always fit political borders, particularly when those borders have been drawn by diplomats confident of their ability to tidy up the world and make it rational. Rationalism in politics is risky; when combined, as in Wilson's statecraft, with moralism, it is downright dangerous.

One man worried about it. Wilson's Secretary of State, Robert Lansing, warned that "certain phrases" of Wilson's "have not been thought out." Wilson, said Lansing, "is a phrase-maker par excellence," but when he speaks of self-determination, "what unit has he in mind? Does he mean a race, a territorial area or a community?" While Wilson was enunciating this "imperative" principle, a German corporal, recovering from a gas attack, was planning a political career. And on September 26, 1938, the former corporal said, "[A]t last, nearly twenty years after the declarations of President Wilson, the right of self-determination for these three and a half million [Germans] must be enforced." So spoke Hitler as Czechoslovakia was dismembered. A nation was sacrificed for the "self-determination" of a "people"—Sudeten Germans.

Lansing had seen such trouble coming. The "undigested" phrase "self-determination" is, he had said, "simply loaded with dynamite. . . . It will, I fear, cost thousands of lives. . . . What a calamity that the phrase was ever uttered!" Undeterred, FDR and Churchill affirmed, in their Atlantic Charter of August 1941, the rights of "peoples." And the U.N. Charter endorses self-determination of "peoples." The Serbs and Kurds and others have been listening.

In 1915 Walter Lippmann wrote, "When you consider what a mystery the East Side of New York is to the West Side, the business of arranging the world to the satisfaction of the people in it may be seen in something like its true proportions." But just two years later Lippmann, just 28 years old, was an earnest arranger. He was working for the Inquiry, a small, secret group serving Wilson. From the New York offices of the American Geographical Society it planned a rearrangement of the world that would make the 20th century rational. Ronald Steel, in his biography *Walter Lippmann and the American Century*, writes:

The Inquiry, working from maps and piles of statistics, attacked the question of frontiers by drawing up charts showing the concentration of national groups within Europe. Lippmann then coordinated these charts and lists with national political movements to determine how these ethnic entities could be granted self-determination without triggering new European rivalries. Then he correlated this blueprint with the secret treaties—deciding which territorial changes were acceptable and which defied justice and logic. Once the Inquiry team . . . had matched the aspirations of the ethnic groups with the geography and economics of each region, Lippmann organized the conclusions into . . .

Enough. Has there ever been quite such a spectacle of naiveté and hubris? Soon Wilson was off to the Versailles peace conference. A member of his delegation sent home a letter containing one of the most telling vignettes of this century:

We went into the next room where the floor was clear and Wilson spread out a big map (made in our office) on the floor and got down on his hands and knees to show us what had been done; most of us were also on our hands and knees. I was in the front row and felt someone pushing me, and looked around angrily to find that it was [Italian premier] Orlando, on *his* hands and knees crawling like a bear toward the map.

What were they working on? Perhaps that soon-to-be-born state, Yugoslavia. Perhaps on the basis of the Inquiry's work. Harold Nicolson, a British diplomat at the conference, wrote to his wife, "But, darling, it is appalling, those three ignorant and irresponsible men [Wilson, Lloyd George, Clemenceau] cutting Asia Minor to bits as if they were dividing a cake." Thus was rationality arranged for the Middle East.

The aged Oliver Wendell Holmes once said to the young Lippmann, "I don't want any of this onward-and-upward stuff. You young men seem to think that if you sit on the world long enough you will hatch something out. But you're wrong." Actually, much has been hatched from the well-meaning overreaching of people unwilling to leave bad enough alone. With steady hands they would redraw maps on the basis of ethnic data. But the principle of ethnicity that Wilson (in Moynihan's word) "hallowed" got out of hand. Again, Moynihan: "Fascism, Italian, then German, was much about 'blood.' The Second World War was as much a pogrom as anything else, and far the greatest incidence of violence since has been ethnic in nature and origin." (Not counting—why not?— blacks attempting an "ethnic cleansing" of Koreans from South-Central Los Angeles.)

Bosnia, showing the disintegrative force of ethnic strife, may be an archetype of our foreign policy preoccupations for years to come. So: Does George Bush or Bill Clinton have a Wilsonian itch to fix the world? Clinton's moderately aggressive pronouncements regarding force on Bosnia's behalf may be partly an attempt to solve a Democratic Party problem. Since the Tet offensive of 1968, Democrats have seemed unwilling to countenance force in the service of foreign policy. Be that as it may, Clinton also is the nominee of Wilson's party. Bush is unclear about Bosnia, as about most things, but he has Wilson's sort of WASP moralism and Wilson's penchant for glistening abstractions ("New World Order").

Americans wonder: Does our possession of the military capacity to strike at evil (such as Serbia's) confer a duty to do so? Does our failure to act make us complicit in evil? Those are serious questions, but so are these: Bombing Serbian mortars might make Americans feel good, but is catharsis a suitable reason for military action? Would limited military intervention reform Serbian behavior? The Balkans are not a promising laboratory for a therapeutic foreign policy. Must we intervene to "teach" other would-be aggressors that aggression does not pay? Desert Storm was, in part, such a tutelary policy. Serbia evidently was not paying attention.

The Cold War is history and history itself has been declared at an end, but the world is still too much with us. So as we sift the cinders and ashes of so many of this century's good intentions, let us fix in mind the cautionary examples of Lippmann with his charts and statistics and Wilson on his hands and knees. Realism is not an alternative to moral action. Rather, realism is a moral duty—the duty to know what we do not understand and cannot do. If we do not know those things, we will find ourselves in Pandaemonium. Which, Moynihan reminds us, is the name Milton gave, in *Paradise Lost*, to the capital of Hell.

August 24, 1992

Yugoslavia Dying

The Bush administration's response to the predictable, irreversible and not deplorable disintegration of Yugoslavia underscores three problems with its notion of a New World Order: It involves a misplaced faith in newness. There is an indiscriminateness in its focus on the whole wide world. And it stresses order at the expense of better values.

Ronald Reagan adored one of the most unconservative and incorrect thoughts ever to issue from a pen, in this case Thomas Paine's: "We have it in our power to begin the world over again." Wrong.

Paine, brimming with Enlightenment rationalism, and most Americans, settled along the edge of a continent they considered a blank slate on which to write, thought they had escaped the curse of history's inertia. Today, the ancient peoples overthrowing the legal fiction "Yugoslavia" are caught in an especially concentrated form of that inertia.

Although Yugoslavia is older than most states (most are less than 40 years old), it is dying young at age 73. Cobbled together by strangers as the First World War ended, it forced intimacy upon peoples who were worse than strangers, they were ancient rivals.

To expect Yugoslavia to continue to exist but in a radically loosened confederation is to expect it to accomplish, with none of America's advantages, a more delicate and dangerous task than America undertook between 1776 and 1865. Americans, with a shared social culture and political vocabulary, moved from the Declaration of Independence, through the Articles of Confederation and Constitutional Convention, through Alexander Hamilton's nationalizing policies and John Marshall's nationalization of the law, to the climacteric of the Civil War. This was a storm-tossed voyage from a loose association of states to a unitary nation under a strong central government.

Those were 89 vexing and finally bloody years. But that political journey was facilitated by a common American consciousness formed in the crucible of revolutionary struggle. America's transformation was immeasurably easier than the one in the opposite direction that strangers are urging, from a safe distance, on Yugoslavs. The U.S. government urges for them a modulated movement from close to attenuated association. But developments there are driven by hatreds intensified by being long suppressed by a central government that is a source of unity only as an object of nearly universal disdain.

In March 1861 Lincoln, struggling to preserve the nation, appealed to Americans' "bonds of affection." He invoked "the mystic chords of memory" heard by Northerners and Southerners alike—by Lee as well as himself. He was invoking real things. Those things were not sufficient to avert war but they were a basis of postwar reconciliation. Yugoslavs have no such bonds and hear no such chords.

Any real nation is an ethical association, organized around shared sentiments about important values. Yugoslavia, a manufactured rather than organic entity, is a "prison of nations" (Lenin's description of the Tsar's empire). A nation has been called a daily plebiscite, renewing itself from the everyday acts and sentiments of its people. For seven decades Yugoslavia has been powerless to suppress or win those daily plebiscites.

Deputy Secretary of State Lawrence Eagleburger says, "What we want is a new confederation." Has anyone notified history of the Bush administration's disapproval of the centrifugal tendencies of the late 20th century?

While in Belgrade last month, Secretary of State Baker said, rather grandly, "We will not reward unilateral actions." The ghost of Lord North nodded approvingly. But who assigned the United States the office of Great Rewarder? When did the United States, which resulted from a famous unilateral action 215 July Fourths ago, adopt this sniffy disapproval of unilateral actions?

Order is only generally, not invariably, desirable. (Remember the disorderly farmers who by the rude bridge that arched the flood fired the shot heard 'round the world.) Anyway, in the post–Cold War world, the insistence that Yugoslavia's unity is an important U.S. interest reveals an inability to draw important distinctions.

Wisdom is knowing what you do not know. The Bush administration, which may not know sufficient American, let alone Balkan, history, is investing U.S. prestige in a cause that is and deserves to be doomed—an attempt to preserve the chimera of Yugoslav nationhood.

The administration's post–Desert Storm hubris regarding the external world, and its congenital lack of imagination regarding problems at home, are now reinforcing each other. The administration has a swollen sense of its potency on the world stage and an inability to imagine things to do domestically. The result is gratuitous—and bad—advice for turbulent peoples who are completely uninterested in our distant interest in them.

July 7, 1991

America's Inoculation by Somalia

A policeman's lot is not a happy one. —*The Pirates of Penzance*

What the lyricist W. S. Gilbert wrote, Somalia underscores. The United States, in danger of haphazardly acquiring random assignments as policeman of various tumultuous precincts in today's disorderly world, is having an increasingly disagreeable time in the Horn of Africa, whither it went, nine months ago, to facilitate the distribution of food for a few, perhaps two, months.

The intervention in Somalia has had elements of opéra bouffe. Remember the Marines splashing ashore in December in the dead of night but not in darkness, bathed by the bright lights of waiting camera crews? And there is a grimly comic aspect to the sophisticated aircraft of the world's mightiest military power making Third World rubble bounce during the (so far unavailing) pursuit of someone currently described as a "fugitive warlord." Not long ago he was described as a statesman. But this is not a Gilbert and Sullivan operetta spoofing imperial misadventures. This is real life, and death.

Last week about 400 Army commandos, described as specialists in urban warfare and "stealthy and unconventional warfare," including "snatch missions," were dispatched to chase the warlord. A State Department official said, "This will be a wake-up call that we're playing for keeps." Presumably he meant that turbulent Somalis should wake up to America's seriousness, and simmer down. But perhaps Americans ought to wake up and wonder what "playing for keeps" means in a place that not one in 10 Americans could point to on an unmarked map.

Regarding the warlord, a Pentagon official said, "We think he's in southern Mogadishu. But looking for one guy in a robe among 200 people at a time all dressed the same way is tough." It is hard not to hear in such words the recurring lament of even well-intentioned imperialists: The natives all look alike! Deucedly inconvenient, that. Roman centurions on the Rhine and along Hadrian's Wall probably said the same.

Some people will say that in Somalia, America is only doing its duty. After all, a great nation's capacities generate duties. But America's capacities are not that great. It is a principle of moral reasoning that there can be no duty to do what is impossible, or beyond one's capacities, to do. Therefore there can be no U.S. duty to undertake what various U.S. officials say we have undertaken.

Robert Oakley, former special envoy to Somalia, says we are supporting a U.N.-led program of "total pacification and nation building." David Shinn, another U.S. diplomat, defines the U.S. mission as "recreating a country," and he seems exhilarated by the challenge: "This has never been done before in the history of the world, at least the modern world." Well, there's a first time for everything, right? Actually, no there isn't.

The December 1992 U.N. resolution under which President Bush sent thousands of troops to Somalia ordered them to establish a "secure environment." That is something that the U.S. government has signally failed to establish in many jurisdictions, from the South Bronx to South-Central Los Angeles. And that U.N. resolution's stipulation that the Somali environment is insecure is germane to a U.S. law—the War Powers Resolution of 1973.

That resolution mandates certain Congressional involvement, on a stipulated timetable, when U.S. forces are introduced "where imminent involvement in hostilities is clearly indicated by the circumstances" or "while equipped for combat, except for deployments which relate solely to supply, replacement, repair or training." Enacted by a Democratic-controlled Congress over President Nixon's veto, the resolution attempted to codify matters that ideally should be left to regulation by constitutional language, prudently construed, and the political process, responsibly conducted.

The Constitution vests in Congress the power to "raise and supply" armed forces and to "declare" war. The president is commander-in-chief. Institutional rivalries, occasionally leavened by a soupçon of disinterested reasoning, could produce a satisfactory *modus vivendi* in which Congress formally authorizes, and helps to define, all uses of military force other than those to repel sudden attacks. But in the climate of suspicion produced by Vietnam, Congress passed the resolution, the history of which has hurt the rule of law.

Every president since the passage of the resolution—Ford, Carter, Reagan, Bush and now Clinton—has not only not complied with it, each has made his noncompliance patent. Clinton has hardly needed to notice the resolution, so invertebrate is today's Congress regarding foreign policy responsibilities. It was predictable that a Democratic president would have an anesthetizing effect on the foreign policy assertiveness of a Democratic Congress. Still, the resolution, which by now is stone dead, deserves decent interment in the form of repeal. That might be one of several benefits from the Somali misadventure.

There are in the lives of nations harmful successes and helpful failures. In 1979, when the Carter administration was cobbling together the Chrysler bailout, Alan Greenspan, then a private citizen, warned that the bailout was a bad idea because it would succeed, thereby encouraging government to try to forestall many of the rationalizing failures that are aspects of dynamic capitalism's creative destruction. U.S. intervention in Somalia may prove to be, on balance, beneficial because it will be so discouraging. Perhaps, given the intermittent learning processes of our forgetful society, we now need a prophylactic failure to prevent a spate of similar episodes.

A medical analogy is apposite. Public health owes much to immunology, the science which sometimes uses small doses of disease to stimulate resistance to diseases. The Somalia experience may inoculate America's body politic against the temptations of humanitarian interventionism. If so, Operation Restore Hope, as it was called at the outset, may one day be remembered as a constructive failure. The dialectic of political life is like that.

September 6, 1993

PART 7

People

Man of the Millennium

With 991 years down and just nine to go, let's limber up our mental muscles and think millennially.

Time magazine soon will announce its "person of the year," surely either Bart Simpson or Saddam Hussein: The tone of life this year was set by underachieving at home and overreaching abroad. And *Time* reports receiving nominees for person of the century, and of the millennium. Let's choose for *Time*.

Surely, this century belongs to Einstein or Churchill. Einstein altered how we think about the most basic things—space, time, matter, energy— and hence how we think about, and even how we see, everything. Nothing—not politics, not art, not literature—has been unaltered. Churchill understood the two great, and related, social inventions of this century, total war and totalitarianism. Because of his understanding, and courage, free nations survived both.

Now, who is the most important person of the millennium? It is salutary and oddly bracing to realize how thoroughly time enforces a leveling perspective. How few are the persons whose deeds will be spoken of, or whose words will be read, even a century or two hence. There are remarkably few really tall silhouettes against the time horizon of ten centuries.

The two great, and related, developments of this millennium are the nation-state and political freedom, which involves limiting the state. Therefore, the five finalists for Person of the Millennium are: Machiavelli, Luther, Washington, Jefferson and Lincoln.

Machiavelli disturbed the Western mind as an early, vivid example of modern masterless man, obedient to no god and only to the rules he wrote. But, as has been said, Machiavelli is no more "the father of power politics" than William Harvey was "the father of the circulation of the blood."

With astonishing matter-of-factness, Machiavelli said vice is needed in politics if virtue is to stand a chance. And the purpose of politics is not to make men virtuous, but to make the state (he more than anyone else gave that word currency) safe. In him was the embryo of modern politics, the individualism of self-interested strivers: Every man a prince.

In 1513 Machiavelli stamped a new notion of political reasoning on the European mind. In 1517 Luther nailed his 95 theses to the church door. The Reformation was both cause and effect of nascent nationalism. And the Reformation's central idea was the grain of sand around which formed, in time, a political pearl. The central idea was the primacy of private judgment—conscience.

"Here I stand," said Luther. "I cannot do otherwise." Luther had little interest in political freedom, but the fuse he lit led to political dynamite: the importance of consent. There is, therefore, a direct road from the church in Wittenberg to Independence Hall in Philadelphia and Jefferson's formulation: Governments derive their just powers from the consent of the governed.

Machiavelli and Luther were merely parts of the prologue of modernity. Each was a hammer that helped shatter suffocating systems of thought and governance. But those systems were doomed; there would have been other sufficient hammers.

However, America is the most important thing that ever happened, both because of the vision of good it has presented and the evils it has prevented. America need not have happened, or lasted.

The arguments for Washington or Lincoln as Person of the Millennium are that each was indispensable. Subtract Jefferson from America and American independence would nevertheless have been achieved, if less ringingly. But subtract Washington the soldier, and the Revolution might have been extinguished. Subtract Washington the politician, and the transition to the Constitution might not have happened: Disintegration might have occurred.

Washington not only wielded power well, he provided the imperishable example of available power not wielded, a refusal to achieve unwholesome eminence.

Lincoln, by winning, as only he could have done, the Civil War, prevented the proliferation of petty, unlovely little nations in what is now the United States. He prevented the victory of, among other bad things, the idea of secession. That idea would have caused the disintegration of even the Confederacy, and perhaps what remained of the Union, too.

Lincoln was the last Founder, completing the founding by forcing the issue: America could be defined by its dedication to a proposition. Whose? Jefferson's. Speaking in Independence Hall en route to Washington in 1861, Lincoln said, "I have never had a feeling politically that did not spring from the sentiments embodied in the Declaration of Independence."

The argument for Jefferson is that history is the history of the human mind, of ideas. Jefferson was, preeminently, the mind of the Revolution that succeeded. It resulted in the birth of the first modern nation, the nation that in the 20th century saved the world from tyranny.

Jefferson expressed the American idea: political and social pluralism; government of limited, delegated and enumerated powers; the fecundity of freedom. He expressed it not only in stirring cadences, but also in the way he lived, as statesman, scientist, architect, educator.

Jeffersonianism is what free persons believe. Jefferson is what a free person looks like—confident, serene, rational, disciplined, temperate, tolerant, curious. *In fine*, Jefferson is the Person of the Millennium.

December 16, 1990

Hawkeye: Still with Us

If you crave relief from the tedium of 1992, spend a few hours in 1757. The new movie made of James Fenimore Cooper's *The Last of the Mohicans* is not restful, but it is a bracing immersion in some great American themes, and in the company of a mythic figure who flits soundlessly across the forest floor of our national dreams.

The movie made from Cooper's remarkably cinematic novel (it is all pursuit and rescue, with the rustle of gingham skirts in the wilderness) illuminates today's politics. It illustrates a tension—think of it as the call of the forest against the claims of community—that still conditions our politics.

The movie opens with a panorama of (supposedly) the New York wilderness beyond Albany 235 years ago. Actually, the setting is the Great Smoky Mountains of North Carolina, in one of the few remaining old-growth forests. But this Arcadia is not Eden. It is infested with British and French forces enlisting rival Indian tribes in their contest for control of the continent.

One brief scene in *The Last of the Mohicans* concisely explains the first of the Americans. A dandified British officer is haranguing some buckskin-clad colonials, hectoring them to join the fight against the French. One man in particular is skeptical. The officer becomes furious:

"You call yourself a patriot and loyal subject to the crown?"

Hawkeye, laconic: "Don't call myself subject to much at all."

Hawkeye was a political problem. Still is.

A distinctively American consciousness was quickened during the struggle of the British with the French in North America. One young Virginian, name of Washington, acquired in that struggle military experience that soon would be put in the service of that consciousness. Ever since then, America's political problem has been that most Americans do not feel, or want to feel, subject to much at all. It is hard to govern a nation of Hawkeyes.

The Last of the Mohicans was published in the magical year of 1826, the 50th anniversary of the Declaration of Independence, the year when, on the Fourth of July, the second and third presidents died hours apart. The passing of the Founders' generation plunged the young Republic into anxiety about the malleability of its character and the perishable nature of its virtue. Everything precious seemed as liable to vanish as the wilderness was vanishing under the assault of ax and plow.

Cooper was born to wealth and raised in America's Bethlehem: Cooperstown, New York, mythic birthplace of baseball. He went to Yale and then to Europe, the expatriate's path taken by many other Americans worried that American society was too thin, too lacking in material for literature. But it was on the frontier, where society was thinnest, that he gave America its first and most enduring romance. It is the romance of life lived on the edge, on the frontier where law and social convention barely constrain, and where the individual can step entirely away from both, into the fringe of the forest.

The movie is rated "R" because of the violence which, although graphic, is not gratuitous. It is part of the movie's meticulous realism, a convincing re-creation of premodern war comparable to the battle scenes of *Henry V* and *Glory*. This was a heroic age because beyond the mostly coastal settlements America could be a terrifying place. But transcending the hair-raising (literally: the scenes of scalpings are not for the squeamish) adventure story is the figure of Hawkeye, casting a shadow forward over our political history.

Hawkeye, America's first great popular hero of fiction, is the man between—between forest and settlement, between tepee and drawing room, leading a life that is one long declaration of independence.

Based in part on Daniel Boone, Hawkeye foreshadowed some similar spirits, such as Huck Finn thinking it might be time to "light out for the Territory." Huck going down the Mississippi and Thoreau going up the Merrimack recall restless Hawkeye, heading out, tending west, toward "Can-tuck-ee." When Shane's solitary profile, tall in the saddle, follows the setting sun, Hawkeye is seen again.

The frontier lives in our national memory, as does an ambivalent stance toward civic life. Hawkeye and his many cultural echoes express a perennial American tension. It is between nature and culture, between the idea of a self-created individual acknowledging no social bonds or debts to society, and the individual as a citizen, obligated to the society that shapes him.

This is why politics is such a difficult business in America. Politicians must tread lightly lest they arouse the Hawkeye—"'Don't call myself subject to much at all"—who sleeps lightly, when he sleeps at all, in all of us.

October 8, 1992

Andrew Jackson Is Not Amused

Seeing the use to which his name is being put, the ghost of Andrew Jackson cannot be amused. But, then, Old Hickory—brawler, dueler, warrior, Indian remover, slayer of the Second Bank of the United States—rarely was of a mind to be amused. Because this Inaugural features an open house at the White House, comparisons are drawn with the riotous reception on Jackson's first day. Orange punch soaked the rugs, muddy boots ruined damask upholstery, drapes were torn and china was smashed until the mob was lured out onto the lawn by pails of liquor. It would be nice if, after his slightly Jacksonian open house, William Jefferson Clinton would emulate Jackson's Jeffersonian principles.

Jackson believed that active, interventionist government will, regardless of what it says or intends, be a servant of the strong. Today's Democrats need a dose of Jackson's disapproval of the scramble to make public power serve private interests. Today's Democratic Party stands for anti-Jacksonian governance. The party that celebrates itself at annual Jefferson-Jackson Day fêtes should be embarrassed about this, and perhaps it is.

Consider *Democrats and the American Idea*, a nifty new book of essays. Historian Harry Watson argues that today's party is not as at odds with Jacksonianism as "appearances might indicate." In spite of "the seemingly conflicting rhetoric of the Jacksonians and the New Dealers," Jackson and FDR "had similar purposes in mind," principally maintaining the "material social conditions" requisite for republicanism—independence and equality.

Please. Both Jackson and FDR did indeed see themselves as battling a business elite. But the New Deal's premise was that economic expansion and opportunity require government ascendancy over commerce. Jackson's premise was that the expansion of opportunity was threatened by regulations, subventions and privileges bestowed by ascendant government. The culture of democracy would be deepened by divorcing government from capitalism.

Jackson subscribed to the luminous creed Jefferson enunciated in his first Inaugural. All that "is necessary to close the circle of our felicities" is "a wise and frugal government, which shall restrain men from injuring one another, shall leave them otherwise free to regulate their own pursuits of industry and improvement." It was a Jacksonian editor who in 1837 declared that "the best government is that which governs least." The motto of the *Washington Globe,* the foremost Jacksonian newspaper, was "The World Is Governed Too Much." For Jackson, politics was less about creation than prevention. Indeed. He used the veto more than his six predecessors combined.

Jacksonians wanted to make the promise of capitalism—material progress and upward mobility—compatible with Jeffersonian virtues, personal and civic, that Jefferson had said depended on preservation of a simple agrarian republic. Jacksonian reform aimed to extirpate policies that conferred advantages on special interests. Jackson, who rose from destitution to wealth, objected not to wealth but to certain ways of becoming wealthy. He feared the effect of favor-dispensing government on the citizenry's habits, morals and character. He thought that if government became a trough, politics would become a feeding frenzy. If you doubt Jackson's prescience, look around.

Clinton now says he can't keep his promise to halve the deficit in four years. Jackson said, "I stand committed before the country to pay off the national debt." The whole debt. And he did. Why is Clinton's modest goal impossible? Because professional politicians, sunk in careerism, will do nothing that might jeopardize reelection. This is an argument for term limits. Clinton opposes limits.

Jackson favored them. He believed in "rotation in office" because "I cannot but believe that more is lost by the long continuance of men in office than is generally to be gained by their experience." Experience, he thought, is overrated because public duties are, or should be made, "plain and simple." Today's career politicians, and the parasite class of lawyer-lobbyists who batten on them, want government made arcane and complex so that they can claim to be necessary. But in his ringing veto message regarding the recharter of the bank, Jackson thundered:

> It is to be regretted that the rich and powerful too often bend the acts of government to their selfish purposes . . . Equality of talents, of education, or of wealth cannot be produced by human institutions . . . but when the laws undertake to add to these natural and just advantages . . . to make the rich richer and the potent more powerful, the humble members of society . . . who have neither the time nor the means of securing like favors to themselves, have a right to complain of the injustice of their government.

Modern government arises from a maelstrom of grasping by interests that are inflamed by government's myriad regulating and subsidizing activities. Modern government is made possible by two sentimentalist fallacies. One is that because there is majority rule, government acts only for the interests of majorities. The second is that government is disinterested and so does not have the human tendency to maximize one's own interests. Jackson knew better.

Today, as 160 years ago, government's favors are grasped primarily by organized factions that can afford to be articulately represented in the capital on the fringe of this continental nation, far from where most Americans live, minding their own business. That is why interventionist government inevitably tends to aggravate civic and social inequalities, making "the potent more powerful." That also is why the people most pleased about the restoration to power of today's extremely un-Jacksonian Democratic Party are members of Washington's parasite class. They know that activist government, busily allocating wealth and opportunity, generates opportunities for them to become wealthy by brokering favors. The more interventionist the government is, the more Congress and the bureaucracy become arenas in which career politicians and lawyer-lobbyists barter influence for affluence.

There are broad smiles today along Washington's K Street corridor, which is thick with "influence entrepreneurs," but there is a scowl on the gaunt face of the ghost of Andrew Jackson.

January 25, 1993

Henry Clay and the Limits of Politics

A *New York Times* book review.

In 1832 a gangly 23-year-old grocery clerk was occasionally seen in a skiff on the Sangamon River in central Illinois, charting depths and wondering how improvements might bring steamboats and prosperity to New Salem. Politically attuned people would not have needed to ask about his politics: Young Abraham Lincoln obviously was a Henry Clay man. When in the winter of 1837 the Illinois legislature passed an enormous ($10 million) appropriation to subsidize construction of railroads, canals and turnpikes, there were bonfires and dancing in the streets of the state capital, Vandalia.

To understand why such things engaged such passions and why they should have, read Robert V. Remini's fine biography *Henry Clay: Statesman for the Union.* One of the master builders of modern America, Clay was a man of the middle, and not just politically, in his role as "The Great Compromiser" of sectional disputes. His career flowered smack in the middle of America's protracted founding. How protracted was it? Precisely fourscore and nine years. The process of coming together, institutionally and emotionally, from a loose aggregation of colonists to a single body politic—citizens of a nation with a competent central government—began in Philadelphia in early July 1776, and was punctuated with an exclamation mark in April 1865, at Appomattox.

Clay was 29 years old and constitutionally underage when he was first sent to the United States Senate by the legislature of Kentucky. But he preferred the turbulence of the House, to which he won election at the age of 34. He became Speaker on his first day as a member. He, together with the other two-thirds of "the great triumvirate," Daniel Webster and John C. Calhoun, was a star of "the next generation," the one that would build a commercial society on the political foundations the Founders had put in place.

Clay came as a young man to a Washington where rain often made Pennsylvania Avenue impassable. It was a Washington where President Thomas Jefferson agreed to sign the bill authorizing federal construction of roads, but admonished Congress that the Constitution should be amended to authorize such activities, lest the doctrine of "implied powers" become a large loophole and the Constitution itself mostly a loophole. Clay quickly became what the country became and still is. Rhetorically he was a Jeffersonian; actually he was a Hamiltonian, asserting implied powers sufficient for his "American System." That system involved enactment of tariffs, "internal improvements" (roads, canals, railroads) and other elements of the infrastructure of a unified commercial nation with an energetic central government "adequate to the exigencies of the Union" (Hamilton's words).

Mr. Remini, a historian at the University of Illinois at Chicago, has spent most of his professional life in the company, as it were, of Clay's most formidable enemy, Andrew Jackson. He has written many books about the general, his era and the ideology to which Jackson gave a name: his own. Jackson's name became an adjective; Clay's never did. Clay was a legislator; Jackson was a leader.

Clay's name is usually near the top of lists drawn up to support the assertion by British political theorist Lord Bryce that America's greatest statesmen generally do not get to the White House. But reading Mr. Remini's book leaves one far from certain that Clay, although unquestionably a great man, was suited to the presidency. Clay, who had an acute sense of the dynamics of America's rapidly evolving society, was remarkably blind to the public's changing political values and expectations.

Clay is primarily remembered for relentlessly pursuing an ambition that went unfulfilled, and for meticulously crafting and doggedly enacting compromises that ultimately failed. He burned with presidential ambition, burned so fiercely that he irrevocably blighted his chances early on, in the presidential election of 1824—or, more precisely, the election of February 1825.

Today, as this nation sleepwalks into a remarkably dull presidential season, it is instructive, diverting and amusing to read Mr. Remini's account of the events of 1824, when John Quincy Adams, Andrew Jackson, William Crawford and Clay competed for the presidency. Clay wildly misjudged his strength in the various state procedures that selected presidential electors. When these procedures failed to produce a majority for any candidate, the choice went to the House, which had to pick from among the top three. Speaker Clay had finished fourth. There was bargaining galore, some of it involving trivialities that were ludicrous in light of the great office at issue (the man who alone would cast Missouri's vote presented Adams with a list of printers he wanted appointed to print the laws in Missouri). And Clay supposedly made the "corrupt bargain" that was to haunt him the rest of his life.

Was there an explicit agreement between Clay and Adams? It is hard to say for sure. But against the instructions of the Kentucky legislature, which favored Jackson, Clay supported Adams, who had not officially received a single popular vote in Kentucky. When Adams became President he named Clay his Secretary of State, an office Clay craved because he was sure it was a stepping-stone to the White House.

Reading Mr. Remini's book it is hard to avoid the conclusion that Clay, when operating outside of legislative chambers, was a lousy politician. He was comfortable in Congress; indeed, he was an artist in Washington's ways. But he was barely conversant with what was just then beginning to matter: public opinion. A century before there was a Washington Beltway, Clay had what is now known as the "beltway mentality."

He had a melodious voice, a flair for self-dramatization and a sense of style that he acquired in his youth (he had heard Patrick Henry speak) and modified with appropriate anecdotes and profanity for Kentucky tastes. Mr. Remini's descriptions of Clay, the consummate actor, evoke an era when rhetoric, sent forth by the unamplified human voice, was a vital instrument of governance.

He was full to brimming over with the juices of life, frequently injuring his own political interests by acts of inadequate calculation. But his incaution makes him particularly alluring to any student of today's politicians. Clay, you see, was utterly unmanaged and unpackaged. He had what the 41st President was to call "the vision thing." He created it from his own observations and passions, without the help of polls or "focus groups" massaged by committees of consultants. Furthermore, he was on speaking terms with the English language, which he wielded energetically, sometimes as a club, often as a stiletto, occasionally one too sharp for his own good.

Clay not infrequently drank too much and gambled recklessly. Westerners, as Kentuckians then were, were thought susceptible, and even entitled, to such behavior. His strenuous conviviality, which political enemies insisted was much more unsavory than that, included a conspicuous enjoyment of the company of various women when, as was frequently the case, Mrs. Clay was away. It is as impossible to know the truth of the innuendos that swirled around him as it is to know their consequences, but they cannot have helped his career.

Part of the poignancy of Clay's life is that we can now see that his clever attempts to legislate compromises concerning slavery amounted to attempts to lasso a locomotive with cobwebs. Consider, for example, Clay's last great work, the Compromise of 1850, which addressed conflicts concerning the treatment of slavery in the several jurisdictions within the vast territories acquired in the war with Mexico (1846–48). Mr. Remini believes, reasonably, that the Compromise postponed the Civil War for a decade, and may thereby have saved the nation. Thanks to Clay, the nation had 10 more years to enlarge its manpower, develop its industrial might, find that good Clay man, Lincoln, and thereby prevail.

It is a measure of Mr. Remini's thorough yet understated scholarship that he notes, but does not dwell on, the fact that after winning passage of the Compromise of 1850, Clay "left Washington on Saturday, September 28, and arrived back in Lexington on October 2, a journey of incredible speed, thanks to the railroad." Seven hundred pages earlier Mr. Remini had written of Clay's trip from Kentucky to Washington in December 1806, "traveling by boat up the Ohio River and then by stagecoach over almost impassable roads."

By the 1850s the roar of steam powering steel wheels over steel rails was the sound of American society—meaning, primarily, the economy—preparing to settle what politics and legislatures could not. The supposedly prosaic (as we are apt mistakenly to think) matter of "internal improvements" was crucial to the improvement of the nation's inner, meaning moral, life—and to the showdown over slavery. Railroads carrying conscripts, who were carrying weapons mass-produced from interchangeable parts, would be the North's decisive riposte to the South's constitutional arguments. Railroads, and the steel mills and coal mines and immigrant labor behind them, closed the question that could not be compromised.

Clay's "American System" helped to save the American experiment.

Thus the life of the Great Compromiser illustrates the practical importance of political programs. But it also illustrates the limits of politics as a leash on large, rushing events.

October 27, 1991

Mayor Curley, a Well-balanced Irishman

BOSTON—It is, as the young say, a no-brainer, this question of whether to name this city's new tunnel for Ted Williams, who hit .406 in 1941, or for James Michael Curley, who was mayor four times, twice as often as he went to jail. The Hall of Famer or the felon? Please.

But consider Curley's career. It cast a shadow forward.

A wit once said an urban boss dreaded three things—the penitentiary, honest industry and, most of all, biography. Curley's biographer, Jack Beatty, an editor of *The Atlantic Monthly*, began writing *The Rascal King* more in admiration than aversion but ended in judicious disgust.

Curley was the catalyst of a class conflict unusually raw because it pitted a particularly passionate ethnic group against the most dominant upper class in American history. Curley killed Boston's "deference democracy," the alliance between Harvard and the slums, the former governing, the latter supposedly grateful. He pulverized that with the hammer of what is now called "identity politics." By inciting Boston's Irish to vote their angry ethnicity, he made politics fit Henry Adams's definition—the systematic organization of hatreds.

Born in 1874, when "Brahmins" ruled Boston, Curley died in 1958, as a Boston Irishman sought the presidency. He left school after the ninth grade but read voraciously—especially in jail: "I read 14 hours a day"—and admired the flamboyant Disraeli, the Jew who captured the aristocrats' party. Curley became a mesmerizing orator, whose campaigning would swell his neck size from 16½ inches to 18.

He did not merely make a fortune on kickbacks from contractors and other graft, he flaunted it, building a mansion staffed with servants, taking lavish European tours during the depth of the Depression, golfing in Florida using Massachusetts state troopers as caddies. All was forgiven by the poor, who felt he was on their side. But Beatty believes Curley was ultimately an affliction to his supporters.

Curley, says Beatty, who is himself the son of an Irish-American janitor, sculpted a constituency from the clay of collective resentments.

The Irish, driven to America by a potato famine and British policies they considered genocidal, were regarded by Boston's upper crust as "the human equivalent of locusts." And, says Beatty, "eating regularly filled the horizon of desire."

These immigrants, made pessimistic by their history and fatalistic by their religion, were converted by Curley to the politics of the unreconciled. His career of 32 campaigns—for alderman, State Assembly, Congress (five times), mayor (10 times), governor (three times) and U.S. Senate—began in an age of political volcanoes such as Theodore Roosevelt and William Jennings Bryan, and in a place rich in collective rancors. But what did the poor get from Curley other than catharsis?

Curley detested welfare. During the Depression he tried to prevent a minister from distributing food to the unemployed. A theme of the novel based on Curley's life, *The Last Hurrah*, was that welfare-state entitlements stopped Curley's kind of politics: When people are entitled, they do not need, or do, favors, which are the grease of political machines. Beatty believes that today's "impersonal, dependency-inducing" welfare system, purged of politics, has "broken a contract beneficial to the whole society."

"Our dependent poor," says Beatty, "are not citizens. They get their benefits by formula, not according to their behavior. They have the rights to these 'entitlements,' but no responsibilities."

But Beatty also argues that Curley's kind of contract—public jobs exchanged for political support—caused Boston to fall as Curley rose. Curleyism was funded by high commercial tax rates, so public jobs were paid for by private-sector jobs not created. It would have been a bad bargain even if graft had not diverted so much revenue away from public services.

"Many Bostonians," says Beatty, "were worse off in 1950 than they or their families had been in 1914, and Curley was a major reason why." And at the end Curley was so remote from reality he asked his chauffeur about signs he saw everywhere: "Who is this fellow 'Pizza'?"

Beatty recalls how a supporter of another ineffective paladin of the poor, Juan Perón, explained his support: "Before Perón, I was poor and I was nobody; now I am only poor." Today the politics of "I am somebody!" is practiced by Jesse Jackson and various grievance groups stressing their victimization and seeking a racial and ethnic spoils system. Curley can be seen as more a harbinger than an anachronism.

He was the "well-balanced Irishman—a fellow with chips on both shoulders," and his career was Homeric in scale. But as to the name for that tunnel, three words say it all: Four Oh Six.

March 3, 1994

Harry Truman:
The Office Did Not Make Him

Publishing poetry has been likened to tossing rose petals into the Grand Canyon and waiting for echoes. You might think that would also describe publishing (when the public thinks politicians are valuable only as a source of protein) a biography of an unglamorous president who was deeply unpopular most of his time in office, who left office not merely disliked but disdained—and before most of today's readers were politically awake. What, then, explains the astonishing, even though merited, success of David McCullough's *Truman*?

Americans just now are going through a particularly intense version of an almost quadrennial fascination with what can be called the Truman Paradigm. Americans cling to the memory of Truman because they think it vindicates a comforting hope, a hope they entertain whenever confronted with actual presidential candidates. The hope is: Oh well, "the office can make the man." That hope is as urgent regarding Clinton as it is difficult to maintain in the light of Bush's years in office. But McCullough's affectionate biography demonstrates that the office did not "make" Truman. Life did, and character, that mysterious compound of nature and nurture, of experience and something innate.

It has been said that a biographer should be a conscientious enemy of his subject. That axiom smacks of the spirit of this sophomoric age, an age that equates cynicism with sophistication. That spirit has produced a style of biography called (by novelist Joyce Carol Oates) "pathography"—a dyspeptic chronicle of waste, dysfunction, neuroses and disaster. The premise of pathography is that familiarity breeds contempt, so absence of contempt proves a biographer's unfamiliarity with his subject's private or (surely sordid) inner life. McCullough is no pathographer. His narrative is agreeably free of licentious speculation, and thus it dismays critics who are partial to "psychobiography." In "psychobiography" the large deeds of great individuals are "explained" with reference to some hitherto unsuspected sexual inclination or incapacity, which in turn is "explained" by some slight the individual suffered at a tender age—say, seven, when his mother took away a lollipop.

McCullough's premises—individuals' decisions matter; things could have turned out quite differently—offend those historians who think the idea of great individuals is undemocratic and therefore must be wrong. Such historians say history is made by vast impersonal forces (e.g., the class struggle) or trivia, such as fluctuations in the price of pepper. This is "history with the politics left out"—left out lest egalitarian sensibilities on the left be shocked by evidence that not everyone is equally good or consequential.

Truman's greatness was a product of his goodness, his straight-ahead respect for the public, respect expressed in decisions briskly made and plainly explained. The man from Independence had none of Willa Cather's impulse to flee from, or Sinclair Lewis's contempt for, small-town life in the middle of the nation. Truman generally felt "as good as an angel full of pie." This son of the middle border illustrated the often disorientating—although not to him—acceleration of American history. He was born into a household of Confederate sympathies in 1884, when memories of "bleeding Kansas" were still fresh. He would cause the thunderclap that announced the nuclear age. He died three years after Americans left footprints on the moon.

In 1901, when Truman was in high school, the local paper editorialized: "The community at large need not be especially surprised if there is a Negro lynching in Independence. The conditions are favorable at this time. There are a lot of young Negro men in town who do nothing." Truman became the first president to address the NAACP. He desegregated the armed services, backed a civil rights plank in the Democratic platform strong enough to provoke the Dixiecrat revolt, and became the first major party candidate to campaign in Harlem. Of course, many liberals didn't much like him. Liberals are like Matthew Arnold, of whom, when he died, a friend said, "Matt's gone to Heaven—but he won't like God."

Like most Americans who were young when the automobile was, Truman loved roads. He built lots of them when he went into politics at the behest of Kansas City's Pendergast machine. Its breathtaking corruption made his honesty legend. He could have skimmed a million dollars from contractors, but he left office poorer than he entered it.

He left to win election to the Senate in 1934, to serve the New Deal and his state, where 90 percent of the farms had no electricity. Roads, rural electrification—these were the stuff of governance in the bad old days. Truman was silent about "family values." Must have hated families.

The men who in 1944 engineered the replacement of Henry Wallace by Truman as FDR's running mate knew FDR was dying. So did Truman after August 18, 1944, when he took lunch with FDR at the White House, beneath a magnolia tree said to have been planted by Truman's hero, Andrew Jackson. That day Truman, from the Missouri of

Mark Twain and Jesse James, watched FDR, from the New York of Edith Wharton and J. P. Morgan, unable to pour cream into his coffee, so badly did his hands tremble.

Truman was the last president we shall have who spent adult years handling a horse-drawn plow. He may have been the last president not educated beyond high school. However, he certainly was more learned—better read—than any subsequent president has been. He read Plato and Cato and other classics and devoured histories. The high-octane rhetoric of his 1948 campaign welled up from his passionate identification with Andrew Jackson and William Jennings Bryan. That is, it came not from polltakers and campaign consultants but from convictions (many of which this columnist considers mistaken) rooted in long-lived American themes. Thomas Dewey's speeches were pablum beyond caricaturing. "Our streams abound with fish." "The miners in our country are vital to our welfare."

Which brings us to another reason why so many people today are seeking the company of McCullough's *Truman.* George Bush's linguine syntax precisely expresses his thinking. Bill Clinton's truth-shading and hairsplitting rhetoric of crafty precision is calculated to produce purrs from the maximum number of factions. McCullough's readers have retreated into *Truman* to seek relief from two Deweys.

September 7, 1992

Lyndon Johnson and the Heroic Presidency

The President was lecturing a group convened because he was distressed by conditions in nursing homes. "And when you design toilets . . ."

Let Joe Califano continue the story. Lyndon Johnson

leaned on his left rump, put his elbow on the arm of his chair, took his right arm and hand, and strained to twist them as far behind himself as he could, and while grunting and poking his hand out behind his back, he continued, ". . . make sure that you don't put the toilet-paper rack way behind them so they have to wrench their backs out of place or dislocate a shoulder or get a stiff neck in order to get their hands on the toilet paper."

The Triumph and Tragedy of Lyndon Johnson is Califano's memoir of four years' toil as principal domestic policy aide to the President who worried about placement of toilet-paper dispensers. To read it as today's Democrats campaign tepidly for the office Johnson filled to overflowing is to see how far we have come from the heroic conception of the presidency that Johnson did so much to discredit.

Paradoxically, it is greatly to Johnson's credit as a man that he pushed a political style into disrepute. He seems, in retrospect, an anachronism, at once grotesque and quaint, but also more admirable than many people can comfortably acknowledge.

The adjective "heroic" is here descriptive rather than normative, conveying no approval of style or substance, only a scale—a hugeness of energy and presumption. Johnson was the last president of the Age of Political Confidence, when America's economy and society seemed transparent to the gaze of, and manageable at the hands of, the central government. The presidential style—part Caesar, part national nag—pioneered by Teddy Roosevelt died at Johnson's hands.

The volcanic energy that drove Johnson to dwell on such details as toilet paper derived from two beliefs, both of which now seem childlike: Government can be as precise as a scalpel, and a president can wield it as a surgeon would.

Return, in Califano's uncritical company (the prosecution has had more than its share of whacks at Johnson), to those days of yore when a guns-and-butter President tried to wage war abroad while building a Great Society at home, and tried to hold inflation at bay by holding down the price of steel. How? By locking up and hectoring labor and management negotiators until exhaustion did the work of persuasion.

Then aluminum prices: Sell government stockpiles. Copper? Dispatch Averell Harriman to Chile to roll back the world price. Shoes costing more? Slap export controls on hides. Lamb? Order the Pentagon to buy New Zealand lamb. Eggs? Johnson ordered the Pentagon to purchase medium rather than large eggs and directed the Surgeon General to talk up the cholesterol problem. Lumber? Order the government to stop buying wooden desks.

Johnson, who understood—who felt—the facts of poverty and racial injustice more than any other president, had the generous heart that comes from sensing life's contingencies, and the large role of luck. Seeing a drunk in Johnson City, he held his thumb and forefinger a hair apart and told Califano, "Don't ever forget that the difference between him and me and him and you is that much."

Hence his unsleeping overreaching, which Califano chronicles. ". . . Johnson turned to designing a program to rebuild America's slums. . . . Johnson told me he wanted to turn America's cities into gems. . . ." No Democrat talks like that now.

Many of today's arguments and problems, from racial quotas to entitlement-driven budget deficits, from subsidies for offensive "art" to subsidies for failing schools, trace their pedigrees to LBJ's presidency, the most consequential since that of his hero, FDR. The civil rights acts, the idea of racial preferences, Medicare, Medicaid, federal aid for education at all levels, environmental and consumer-protection laws, the National Endowments for the Arts and Humanities and on and on and on—the list is too long for one column.

The anti-Goldwater landslide of 1964 produced the 89th Congress, 1965–66, the first since 1938 with a liberal majority sufficient to trounce the alliance of Republicans and southern Democrats. But Califano's long list of the results of the 89th ignores one: the Reagan presidency.

Califano regularly went on idea-harvesting trips to universities, foundations, the office of *Scientific American.* "We produced a three-inch-thick book of ideas." But by the time these liberal ideas had become law, the country had acquired some conservative ideas: that government is a blunt instrument; that it often is the problem to which it pretends to be the solution; that it is partial to the unworthy.

The word "liberal" was on the way to becoming an epithet.

October 27, 1991

Lyndon Johnson and Life's Untidiness

Robert A. Caro, the indefatigable and unforgiving biographer of Lyndon Johnson, has now published the second of his projected four volumes. It is, as Caro intended, fascinating and dismaying. It also is something he did not intend, a case study of flight from the inescapable ambiguities of political judgment.

Caro, 53, is a liberal devoting the prime of his professional life—14 years so far—to pulverizing the reputation of the most consequential liberal politician of the postwar era. Caro probably voted for Johnson rather than Goldwater in 1964. It is probably good that Johnson was President when the racial crisis reached a roily boil because, as Caro writes:

Abraham Lincoln struck off the chains of black Americans, but it was Lyndon Johnson who led them into voting booths, closed democracy's sacred curtain behind them, placed their hands upon the lever that gave them a hold on their own destiny, made them, at last and forever, a true part of American political life.

That true tribute appears in the introduction to *Means of Ascent,* this volume dealing only with Johnson's life from 1941 through 1948. Nothing in the more than 400 pages that follow gives the reader an inkling of how Johnson was capable of any goodness.

This volume tells three dismal stories: how Johnson lied about his brief military service, how he used political power to begin making a fortune in the federally regulated broadcasting industry and (this consumes half the book) how he acquired a Senate seat by winning the 1948 Democratic primary. Caro demonstrates, with sledgehammer force, how Johnson stole the election, defeating Coke Stevenson, whom Caro reveres and romanticizes.

But had Caro been a Texas voter in 1948, he probably would have done what most Texas liberals did: voted for Johnson.

Coke Stevenson was a rancher and lawyer whose character may have been, as Caro insists, a splendid distillation of frontier individualism and rectitude. But in his political life, he was a familiar Southwestern type of his day, well to the right of the ground Barry Goldwater was later to occupy, and racist in a way common then but that Johnson never was.

Caro makes a plausible case that Johnson saved his career by stealing 35,000 votes. But the verb "steal" must be used gingerly in this context.

These were not 35,000 votes that otherwise would have been cast after the free deliberation of informed and uncoerced individuals behind democracy's sacred curtain. Many—almost certainly most—of those votes were going to be delivered as a block, at some boss's discretion, to someone. (In other elections they had been delivered to the sainted Stevenson.) The precincts that had better than 90 percent turnouts and larger than 90 percent landslides for Johnson had been "voting" that way for a long time, for other candidates.

Johnson got 494,191 votes, Stevenson 494,104. Subtract 35,000 votes from Johnson's total (never mind that Caro acknowledges that votes were stolen from Stevenson) and it would still have been a close race, largely because of Johnson's support among poor, labor and liberal voters. It is not extenuating but it is interesting that, as President, Johnson did as much as anyone to make impossible the kind of electoral corruption that flourished in Texas, and not only there (see Chicago, 1960). He did it by fostering a dramatic expansion of federal power over the electoral process.

Caro believes that many more than 35,000 Johnson votes were tainted by his "modern" campaign techniques (campaigning by helicopter, and with a broadcasting blitz). Caro's rhapsodical account of Stevenson meandering from one small town, and tiny audience, to another has a misty romanticism to it, until you ask: Why, precisely is it good to campaign in a way that communicates to such a tiny sliver of the electorate?

It is fun to execrate the frequent superficiality—and worse—of media politics. But broadcasting helped put bosses out of business by enabling candidates to talk directly to voters. Caro may pine for the days when a candidate had "no electronic devices to mediate between himself and them" (the voters). But then, the mediating was apt to be done by the bosses so repellent to Caro.

Caro's narrative prompts this thought: Perhaps something in liberalism, or the liberal temperament, disposes liberals to make esthetic judgments about politics, subordinating substantive judgments to the romance of style.

Johnson was a bullying vulgarian, often crudely unethical, sometimes corrupt. He also was the most potent promoter of the liberal agenda since Franklin Roosevelt. Reality is often messy that way, and perhaps something in the liberal mentality has trouble coming to terms with such untidiness.

March 22, 1990

Barry Goldwater: Conservatism's Catalyst

PHOENIX—Looking down on his valley and back on his career, Barry Goldwater, who 30 years ago was en route to a creative defeat in the presidential election, has no regrets. Nor should he. He lost 44 states but won the future.

Today his walk is slower, his emotions are mellower and his features, after 85 years of squinting into Southwest sunsets, are more than ever a craggy map of Arizona. But he is content. He should be. He catalyzed conservatism's breakthrough.

The protests of the 1960s did not begin at Berkeley. The most consequential protest came from the right, beginning at the podium of the 1960 Republican Convention in Chicago when Arizona's junior senator said, "Let's grow up, conservatives! If we want to take this party back, and I think we can someday, let's get to work."

In 1912 civil war erupted among Republicans when a former Republican president, Teddy Roosevelt, challenged an incumbent Republican president, the conservative William Howard Taft. Having failed to win the nomination, Roosevelt ran a third-party campaign, finishing second to Woodrow Wilson, ahead of Taft. The two factions, conservatives and "moderates," fought until 1964, when Goldwater's nomination sealed the conservatives' ascendancy. No one strongly opposed by them has been nominated since then.

As is usually the case, cultural ferment preceded political transformation. In 1953 Russell Kirk published *The Conservative Mind*, which introduced a generation raised on Rooseveltian liberalism to the disturbing thought that Kirk's title did not constitute an oxymoron. William Buckley's *National Review* was launched in 1955. His *Up from Liberalism* was published in 1961. Three years later conservatism made the transition from a cultural critique to a political force on a national rather than merely local scale.

Just as William Jennings Bryan lost three presidential elections but brought invigorating new elements into the Democratic Party, Goldwater precipitated the Republican reorientation that would produce victories in five of the next six elections. Furthermore, in one of history's odd caroms, Goldwater inadvertently hastened the crisis of liberalism by giving it an opportunity for overreaching.

LBJ's landslide broke the rough balance in Congress between liberals and a coalition of conservative Republicans and Southern Democrats, a balance that had existed since 1938. For two years liberalism was unconstrained. It is still trying to rehabilitate its reputation.

Goldwater remembers receiving, while campaigning, a draft of a speech to be delivered on a nationally televised campaign broadcast. He said to aides: It's good but doesn't sound like me. Get Ronald Reagan to deliver it.

And the torch was passed. Goldwater cared more about carrying the torch of conviction than about capturing power. Asked today if he ever really burned to be president, he said, "Not exactly." Besides, after November 22, 1963, he felt that the Republicans' 1964 campaign was bound to be futile. But he felt impelled to make the race because of the support of young people. He could not then know that they included Hillary Rodham and Sam Donaldson, both of them then at the apogee of their political wisdom.

Theodore White wrote that Goldwater offered "a contagious concern. . . . He introduced the condition and quality of American morality and life as a subject of political debate." Actually that subject recurs regularly in American history. Goldwater's contribution was to freshen the argument with strong doses of Sun Belt individualism and an optimism deriving from the exhilarating experience of whirlwind change.

When Goldwater was born in Arizona territory, as it then was, 10,000 people were scattered across the valley where today Phoenix is the hub of a metropolitan area of more than 2 million. At age four he was ring bearer in a wedding that waited for the fast-pedaling Western Union bicyclist to bring word that statehood had been achieved and the couple would be the first married in the 48th state. At age 10 Goldwater rode his horse up into the hills and slept on the spot where he later built the house in which he now lives.

Today Goldwater is comfortable in his role as the Republicans' ranking curmudgeon, expressing views (pro-choice on abortion, for gays in the military) that exasperate some conservatives but should not surprise any who have heard Goldwater's consistent libertarian message about government: When in doubt, get it out of people's lives.

Thirty years ago he was the cheerful malcontent. Still is. When he got to the famously defiant passage in his convention acceptance speech—"Extremism in the defense of liberty is no vice!"—someone in the press gallery exclaimed, "Good God, he's going to run as Goldwater!" Always did. In 1949, when he decided to dabble in politics—he was dragooned into running for the city council—he wrote to his brother: "It ain't for life and it may be fun." Sure was.

March 27, 1994

Margaret Thatcher's Handbag

LONDON—People who confuse changing fashion with advancing wisdom are pleased that Margaret Thatcher is behind in the polls. But she has been there before, and has then won three elections. She probably will win a fourth, but not because of any factor as flimsy as affection. Most voters feel about her as a critic did about Hugh Walpole: "You are glad he lived, but very grateful that you didn't know him." Not since the younger Pitt in the 1790s—not, that is, in the democratic era—has a prime minister held office through an entire decade, as she did in the 1980s. She is in her 12th year as prime minister, the longest run since the 1832 reform bill began, gingerly, the democratic era. The secret of her success is, paradoxically, her annoyingness.

She set out to be a disruptive influence, to enlarge and energize the engine of social change in modern society, the middle class, that vessel of commercial values. As *The Economist* says, she is the only postwar prime minister who has tried to use her office for "Zeitgeist politics." She has toiled to change the temper of the times by reeducating the public, to teach the virtues of striving and the vices of government intervention. Capitalism's revolution came first to Britain but was never finished. It did not sweep away aristocratic lassitude or habits of deference, replacing them with a money-driven meritocracy. Thatcher is capitalism's follow-through.

Columnist Peregrine Worsthorne says Britain in 1979 was a more compassionate society, just as a hospital, concerned with the sick, is more compassionate than a soccer team organized to win. For decades before Thatcher, people went into politics for the same reason people went into the Salvation Army, to help the helpless. But, writes Worsthorne, "while it is perfectly proper for a society to think about the unfortunate, it must never be encouraged to think like them."

A decade, although a long electoral run in a democracy, is a blink in a nation's life. Still, Thatcher has changed her party from one of hierarchy and paternalism to one of egalitarianism and meritocracy. And the experience of being shellacked by her three times has changed the Labour Party from socialism to sentimentalism, a misty middlingness. Intellectually the party accepts the rationality of markets, but regrets it, and thinks counting costs is "uncaring."

The *Salisbury Review*, a conservative journal ambivalent about Thatcher, takes its name from the 19th-century prime minister whose greatness, says the *Review*, "consisted in doing as little as possible for as long as he could." That does not describe Thatcher, whose energy arouses in the *Review* both "admiration for her will, and alarm at her determination to assert it." As a Conservative M.P. has said, "She cannot see an institution without hitting it with her handbag."

She has a restless mind, voracious for information and constantly curious about how things work. But as regards ideas, she considers her pantry quite sufficiently stocked already, thank you. Her sergeant-major political style is an extension of her personal manner, and both arise from her stern doctrines. They have made her the most consequential peacetime prime minister since Disraeli and the only P.M. whose name denotes an "ism." David Marquand calls Thatcherism a British Gaullism born out of a despair comparable to that which engulfed France's Fourth Republic. Like De Gaulle, she is a charismatic conservative nationalist. Max Weber put into currency the word "charisma." He said modern societies generate iron cages of bureaucracies that suffocate change until charismatic leaders emerge.

In the 1960s and '70s governments' hubris grew and competence shrank. While complacent Keynesianism made governments confident they could manage economies, new forces (in Britain, growing union power) were preventing that. Thatcher came to power just as the Carter presidency was giving rise to theories of government overload: Democracies were becoming ungovernable because competing demands were producing gridlock.

Welfare states were embryonic in the 1880s. By the 1980s governments had to face the fact that entitlements expand more constantly and rapidly than do the economies on which they depend. In the 1980s the politics of wealth creation at last took precedence over distribution. This sunburst of common sense has coincided with Thatcher's tenure, which began in May 1979. In May 1981, François Mitterrand became President across the Channel and began keeping his socialist campaign promises—nationalizations, enriched entitlements, reflation to pay for it all. This was Europe's first serious socialist program in a long time, and probably the last for at least as long. Reality forced Mitterrand to make a U-turn that eroded consent.

The lady is not for turning. She is called "confrontational" but Britain is less riven by conflict than it was when governed by socialists, who constantly speak of communitarian values. Socialism and Tory corporatism—two elements of the postwar consensus—produced what can be called the individualism of aggregates. Unions, bureaucracies and industries scrambled to capture the state, to bend public power to private purposes. Thatcherism, by expanding the sway of market forces, has reduced divisiveness by reducing the political dimension of the allocation of wealth and opportunity.

It has been said that for Americans time is linear, connoting advance and progress, whereas in Britain time is circular, a constant returning. A Cambridge don says, "America is total possibility. Britain is total remembrance." Thatcher says: Forget it. The antecedent of the pronoun "it" is the postwar consensus. Intellectuals call her an outsider, but outside of what? From the center of power she has treated the intelligentsia as peripheral. She prefers the practical, energizing middle class that thinks concretely, as does she, the former chemistry student at Oxford. The cult of the amateur, with its disdain for science and commerce, has been rejected by the politician who has come closest to making a profession of being P.M.

She will not be there forever. She is mortal. She has much heart, but all hearts stop. However, she does resemble that gruff Englishman who, when he suffered palpitations, would thump his chest and bellow "Go *on*, go *on!*" until his heart obeyed. She intends to go on and on.

July 2, 1990

The Windsors: Gussied-Up Snopeses

In 1932, when George V gave the first Royal Christmas Broadcast, he coughed, and Britain sighed contentedly. "A king who coughs is a fellow human being," reported *The Spectator* for any readers in doubt about that.

Today a mesmerized world sees enough of the Windsors' divorces, extravagances, assignations, embarrassing photographs, suicide attempts, press leaks, paternity suits, etc. to know that royalty are just like the rest of us. Swell.

This batch of lumpenroyalty—Faulkner's Snopeses gussied up for a pageant—are cruel to each other and contemptuous of the public that is footing the bill for their coarse lives. They are demystifying monarchy more rapidly than any republican could dream of doing.

Republicans have traditionally relied on turgid arguments about monarchy being a retrograde reliance on parental figures for political cohesion. But today the case against Britain's disheveled Royal Family can be stated briskly:

For people in the magnificence business, kitsch is bad business, not just bad taste. If you are (adopting Walter Bagehot's dichotomy) part of the "dignified" rather than the "efficient" aspect of the state, you don't dare to be tacky. If your job is to leaven ordinary lives with elevating spectacle, be elevating or be gone.

Time was when monarchists defended monarchy by claiming that the vice that defines it is actually a virtue: "Of course it is irrational—it's supposed to be." That is, monarchy would not have its supposed power to provide social glue, its magic to fuse the nation into a family, if it relied on mere reason. But today the fissionable Windsors, that no-longer-nuclear family, are giving bourgeois morality even more of a bad name than the bourgeoisie is giving it.

Britain's royalty, with their mistresses and illegitimate children (William IV, who died in 1837, had 10 by one actress—a sort of monogamy, I suppose), has a record that would cause blushes in a brothel, but until recent decades the press averted its gaze. When in the 1930s the Prince of Wales was besotted with Baltimore's Wallis Simpson, Britain's press kept quiet, thereby encouraging his ruinous sense of invulnerability. However, those who live by publicity, as the Windsors have lately chosen to do, and as a modern monarchy probably must, can be fricasseed by it, particularly when the monarchy is invested with religious gravity.

A few decades ago an Archbishop of Canterbury, asked about the Windsors' theological tastes, said, "They're all Low Church. It's because they come from abroad." The Sovereign is "defender of the faith," whatever that means this month in the politically trendy Church of England. It means precious little in England, where mosques are apt to be more crowded than Church of England services are. A lot of the Sovereign's subjects are from abroad. The Windsors know what that is like. The name Wettin, the family name of Albert of Saxe-Coburg-Gotha, Victoria's consort, was changed to Windsor in 1917, when things German were in bad odor.

The world could use a few stodgy, boring, transplanted monarchs just now, if they could be unifying forces in the shards of what once were Yugoslavia and the Soviet Union. Monarchy is a residue of mankind's primitive past, but in parts of Europe's backyard, mere primitivism would be a distinct improvement on barbarism.

For the unenthralled, meaning for grown-ups, the only justification of monarchy is mere utility. But Britain does not need its monarchy for any practical purpose. It is said the British masses like it and so should have it. That sort of non sequitur did not wash when the subject was gin, and it begs the important question: Does monarchy help or hinder Britain's attempt to like what it ought to like? The British must decide if the monarchy, a "link to a glorious past," encourages a retrospective cast of mind and is a subliminal endorsement of snobbishness and class hierarchies. If so, it makes a glorious future more difficult to achieve.

The monarchy costs sacks of money (it is hard to say exactly how many scores of millions of pounds). It is a sound investment only if the Crown really does pull in tourists by the planeloads. Perhaps the British don't mind a governmental system justified by the sort of business thinking suited to the management of a theme park.

Getting rid of the monarchy might be more fuss and distraction than it would be worth. That, essentially, is the remarkably tepid defense *The Economist* today offers: The institution is too trivial to waste time talking about. But as Walter Bagehot, *The Economist*'s great 19th-century editor, said, "Above all things our royalty is to be reverenced, and if you begin to poke about it you cannot reverence it. . . . We must not let in daylight upon magic."

The magic is gone. When the current occupant of the throne is done, they should turn off the lights at Buckingham Palace.

June 25, 1992

Pat Buchanan: Irish Confetti

Pat Buchanan is "Irish confetti" for George Bush.

Parts of Manhattan were paved with extremely hard Belgian stones (Romans used such stones on the Appian Way), which first served as ballast in lightly loaded ships coming to America. Irish immigrants, including some as turbulent as their descendant Buchanan, expressed disagreements with cops by chucking Belgian stones at them. The cops called these bone-breaking showers "Irish confetti."

Buchanan, the pugnacious political aide (to President Nixon and Reagan) and commentator, is challenging Bush for the Republican nomination, beginning in New Hampshire, where a *Boston Globe* poll gives Bush an approval-disapproval rating of 42–47. Republican discontent is finding many forms of expression. For example, Democratic candidate Bill Clinton received a respectful hearing last week from influential Republicans in Southern California's Orange County. Buchanan may be particularly troubling to Bush because he is two things Bush is not: articulate and ideological.

Consider Buchanan's budget-cutting strategy. It is to propose deep cuts and when Congress rejects them, to veto Congress's appropriations bills or continuing resolutions. The result will be havoc, recrimination, polarization: President Buchanan will be in his element. Then the government shuts down. Bliss! Social Security recipients raise hell. Buchanan tells Congress: I'll sign only what it takes to keep Social Security flowing.

Buchanan favors "the politics of confrontation. Consensus, compromise haven't done it for 25 years. Why not try something new." Grab a stone.

Buchanan's style may appeal to working-class and lower-middle-class former Democrats who recently have voted Republican and now, polls show, are the most disaffected Americans. David Duke is after them, too.

Buchanan rightly insists that David Duke's use of such issues as welfare dependency and racial quotas does not make those issues off-limits for decent politicians. Hitler built autobahns; Eisenhower was not Hitlerian because he built the Interstate Highway System. Anti-Communism was right even though Joe McCarthy was an anti-Communist.

Furthermore, one function of insurgent candidacies, within and outside the two parties, from Robert La Follette, Eugene Debs and Norman Thomas through George Wallace and Eugene McCarthy, is to put topics on the table that more conventional politicians are too timid to touch. One such topic today is immigration. It brings out Buchanan's strength—his eagerness to talk about whatever is troubling people—and his weakness: Do not expect from him nuances of thought or delicacy of expression.

He correctly warns that there can come a point when indiscriminate diversity in a population produces national incoherence by blurring identity and diluting community feelings. He is right that "culture, language, background are not illegitimate criteria for us to discuss when we discuss legal immigration."

But it won't do to say, as he does, that a million English immigrants would be easier for Virginia to assimilate than a million Zulus. The English are not knocking at the door. The real policy questions concern people of many other cultures.

"Who," he asks, "speaks for the Euro-Americans who founded the U.S.A.? . . . Is it not time to take America back?" In what sense "take back"? Back from whom?

"No one," he says, "questions the right of the Arabs to have an Arab nation, of China to be a Chinese nation. . . . Must we absorb all the people of the world into our society, and submerge our historic character as a predominantly Caucasian Western society?" Gracious. "All the people of the world"? "Submerge"? Such hyperventilating is not helpful.

Besides, Buchanan evidently does not understand what distinguishes American nationality—and should rescue our nationalism from nativism. Ours is, as the first Republican president said, a nation dedicated to a proposition. Becoming an American is an act of political assent, not a matter of membership in any inherently privileged or especially appropriate group, Caucasian or otherwise. The "Euro-Americans" who founded this nation did not want anything like China or Arabia—or any European nation, for that matter.

Buchanan formally launched his "America First" campaign two days after the Soviet Union formally expired. His most lurid liability is his wrong, sometimes mean and occasionally crackpot ideas regarding Israel, the Holocaust and the politics of American Jews. These ideas will not matter immediately for three reasons: The Jewish vote is not crucial in Republican presidential primaries; no foreign policy questions will be central just now; and Bush is semi-Buchananesque regarding Israel.

Bush has made the executive branch into a megaphone to turn American attitudes against Israel. Besides, voters will, at least initially, look at Buchanan not as a potential president but as a megaphone for hollering in Bush's ear.

Bush may come to envy New York's 19th-century cops. They got the city to put asphalt over the Belgian stones. Bush's solution to his "Irish confetti" problem may not be so simple.

December 11, 1991

George F. Kennan's Conservatism

A *New York Times* book review.

A person's political philosophy is apt to be an effect as well as a shaper of that person's temperament and sensibility. As *Around the Cragged Hill: A Personal and Political Philosophy* makes clear, George F. Kennan's conservatism is a product of his almost visceral recoil from many aspects of modern American life.

This book is, Mr. Kennan acknowledges, not systematic philosophy but "essentially a collection of critical observations." However, from their pattern flows something recognizable as conservatism. To call Mr. Kennan's conservatism anachronistic is not to disparage it: There is something bracing about a man so unreconciled to so much. And to note that his thinking is, strictly speaking, un-American is not to question his attachment to his country, which attachment he movingly affirms.

His conservatism is a curious and not quite coherent blend of two traditions long since relegated to the losing side of American history. One is the anti-Federalist suspicion of great size in a polity, and fear of the concentration of political power in the central government. The other tradition is a high Federalist, even Tory, belief that the central government should be staffed by a disinterested elite and must be strong enough to supervise the base habits of the turbulent masses.

The "cragged hill" of Mr. Kennan's title is from Donne: "On a huge hill,/Cragged, and steep, Truth stands." The truth, as Mr. Kennan apprehends it, is that man is a "cracked vessel" whose distresses can be palliated only slightly by government, which "is simply not the channel through which men's noblest impulses are to be realized." He believes the American portion of mankind is especially flawed and rapidly becoming more so.

For 27 years Mr. Kennan was an intellectual engaged in diplomacy. For four subsequent decades, mostly at the Institute for Advanced Study at Princeton, New Jersey, he has written distinguished books on history and diplomacy. But in *Around the Cragged Hill*, the two chapters on foreign policy reflect primarily his preoccupation with what he considers America's domestic sickness. He pleads for a "self-effacing" stance toward the world, not just because the world is largely beyond our comprehension (never mind our control), but also because all of the country's energies are required at home if regeneration is to be even remotely possible.

The United States, he says, is in "critical shape" because Americans have become "a people of bad social habits." Furthermore, the government's incompetence is such that "one has no choice but to question the adequacy of Western democracy itself" for responding to today's challenges.

Mr. Kennan grounds his thinking in an unblinking acknowledgment of humanity's "animalistic" dimension. His assessment of sexuality is particularly chilly. Given the fissure between man's physical and spiritual natures, "he staggers through life as best he can," bedeviled by an insoluble conflict between what he is and what the interests of civilization require him to be. Mr. Kennan affirms, with characteristic tentativeness, a tepid religious faith in a Spirit, though one acquitted of any responsibility for the mess mankind is in.

Mr. Kennan believes that large nations—he calls them "monster countries" (the United States, the former Soviet Union, China, India and Brazil)—are "problems to themselves." To achieve a greater "intimacy" in civil life, he advocates, with a sort of earnest whimsy, a radical devolution of the federal government's authority to 12 constituent republics, to be organized on regional lines. He does not explain why the 50 states are not suitable receptacles for authority shed by Washington.

His other proposal is notably unpersuasive: a nine-member "Council of State" to be chosen by the President to render advice on "long-term questions of public policy"—but not about "matters of current contention." This notion is offered perfunctorily, as though as a mere reflex by a man of government who really knows the foolishness of suggesting institutional tinkering as a solution to problems of the nation's soul.

The columnist Joseph Alsop called Mr. Kennan "an almost too-sensitive man." Certainly contemporary America lacerates his sensibilities. He deplores, among many other things, "plebiscitary tendencies" in governance, forced desegregation ("people should be allowed to do what comes naturally," and policies should be "responsive to local feelings, local customs and local needs") and egalitarianism generally (because "every attempt at social leveling ends with leveling to the bottom, never to the top"). It is nowadays rare, and for that reason rather entertaining, to read something like Mr. Kennan's lament about the servant shortage:

A society wholly devoid of the very institution of domestic service is surely in some ways a deprived society, if only because this situation represents a very poor division of labor. There are people for whom service in or around the home pretty well exhausts their capabilities for contributing to the successful functioning of a society. There are others who have different and rarer capabilities; and it is simply not a rational use of their abilities that they should spend an inordinate amount of time and energy doing things that certain others could no doubt do better, and particularly where these are just about the only things the latter are capable of doing. . . . I find it hard to picture a great deal of Western culture without the institutions of domestic service that supported it. . . . I cannot, somehow, picture Tocqueville combining his serene meditations with the washing of the pots and pans and the removal of trash from the kitchen premises.

Neither can one so picture Mr. Kennan.

Well stricken in years and well seasoned by life, the 88-year-old Mr. Kennan has standing to complain, and he gives good value as a curmudgeon. There is an echo of the 1920s in his condemnation of "great monopolies," and there is the flavor of the 1940s in his worries about "automation." He considers the computer useful primarily "to speed the manifold processes of a life that is plainly already proceeding at a pace far too great for the health and comfort of those that live it." And his loathing for the automobile is almost majestic. The automobile is a "mass addition" that he associates with many evils, from the increase of crime to the decline of cities and the spread of loneliness. He contrasts automobile travel "with the color and sociability of the English highway of Chaucer's time, as reflected in *The Canterbury Tales*, or with the congenial atmosphere of the railway compartment of the Victorian novel."

Mr. Kennan is apprehensive but firm in wanting the federal government to reform the citizenry's offensive "habits of daily life," including the uses made of automobiles and television. But what, then, of his dour disbelief in government as an instrument of noble impulses?

This is a book to be enjoyed not for its analytic rigor but for the sparks struck from a strong personality. Mr. Kennan quotes, not disapprovingly, his first ambassadorial chief, William Bullitt, saying that mankind is "a skin disease of the earth." But, paradoxically, a species that can speak so harshly of itself is not so bad. Similarly, as long as the United States produces critics as astringent yet affectionate as George F. Kennan, it will not be so fallen as Mr. Kennan thinks it is.

January 3, 1993

George Stigler:
Laissez-faire and Laughter

Journalism, according to a mordant practitioner, involves reporting the death of Lord Jones to people who never have heard of him. Although George Stigler won the Nobel Prize for economics, few Americans knew of him last week when he died, full of years—80 of them—and honors. What should have pleased him most was this fact: The Cold War is over and the University of Chicago won it.

Stigler exemplified the "Chicago school" of economics, named for the university where he taught with Milton Friedman (another Nobel laureate), Friedrich von Hayek (another), Frank Knight (who should have been one) and Ronald Coase (this year's winner), among others. Economics shares a long, open border with politics, and hence with philosophy. Stigler always knew, as the world now does, the serious stakes of the intellectual defense of markets.

However, he may have been the wittiest serious man since Gibbon. Hence the irresistible appeal of his writings to young intellectuals chafing, in the 1960s, under the statist orthodoxies in universities.

In 1962 Oxford, "home of lost causes," was home for a few partisans of what then seemed to be another such cause, the moral defense of capitalism. We were American graduate students enthusiastic about Friedman's *Capitalism and Freedom* and Stigler's essays in praise of laissez-faire policies.

Like most young intellectuals, we were given to going too far, debating whether government, which obviously should privatize schools, courts and roads, must operate lighthouses. Moderates said: Yes, regrettably it must because you cannot price lighthouses' services. Purists rejoined: Rubbish! When light sweeps the water's surface, the lighthouse operator is (in Locke's words) mixing his labor with the water, improving it and making it his property, so he can charge ships whatever the market will bear for the right to pass through it.

Ah, but did the property right lapse when fog blocked the improving light? And so on, and on.

Such intellectual playfulness was part of the genesis of the conservative ideas which, when much matured, produced Reagan and Thatcher, and market economies amidst the rubble of Marxism. The core ideas were given mature expression by Stigler in essays accessible to lay readers.

In 1963 Stigler published *The Intellectual and the Market Place and Other Essays* (foreword by the dean of the Chicago Business School— George Shultz). The subject of the title essay was the revulsion intellectuals express toward economies organized around the self-interested search for profits in the marketplace. That place, say many intellectuals, is for vulgar people with base motives.

Acknowledging that he, too, was an intellectual (buying "more books than golf clubs"), Stigler noted that "we professors are much more beholden to Henry Ford than to the foundation which bears his name and spreads his assets." Ford contributed mightily to mass production. Intellectuals are expensive to maintain. Professors need universities at which to profess. Universities need endowments and tax support. So a large social surplus, the product of private-enterprise economies, is a prerequisite for a large, comfortable (although constantly complaining) intelligentsia.

Intellectuals' disparagement of the system that supports them is ostensibly moral but actually as much esthetic. It is that the "profit motive" ratifies "materialism." And because economic illiteracy is especially high among intellectuals, many of them consider commerce comparable to poker, a zero-sum transaction where one person's gain must be another's loss. In response Stigler said, "Sears, Roebuck and Company and Montgomery Ward made a good deal of money in the process of improving our rural marketing structure, but I am convinced that they did more for the poor farmers of America than the sum total of the federal agricultural support programs of the last 28 years."

It was, Stigler wrote, the industriousness of self-interested profit-seekers in the marketplace that was doubling America's per capita wealth every 25 years. The fact that wealth creation has slowed since Stigler wrote that testifies to two phenomena which Stigler understood. One is the intellectuals' disdain for wealth-creators, disdain that produces ignorant or punitive public policies. Another is the economic illiteracy that causes intellectuals and their public-sector echoes to consider wealth creation easy, even spontaneous.

Stigler later said that his essay, written to encourage intellectuals to reexamine their hostility toward capitalism, had been "more successful in reaffirming businessmen in their faith. This is not an undesirable effect, but a lecturer denouncing cannibalism naturally must view the applause of vegetarians as equivocal evidence of his eloquence."

Regarding the intellectuals' contempt for the vulgarity of market choices, Stigler, his whimsy sheathing a stiletto, said, "When a good comedian and a production of *Hamlet* are on rival channels, I wish I could be confident that less than half the professors were laughing." Stigler's death subtracts from society's supply of two scarce commodities, wisdom and laughter.

December 8, 1991

Lewis Thomas's Amazement

"Statistically," wrote Lewis Thomas, "the probability of any one of us being here is so small that you'd think the mere fact of existing would keep us all in a contented dazzlement of surprise." Thomas seems to have been constantly in such a pleasant condition until, recently, in his 81st year, death came to draw the material of him back into randomness.

A quiet but insistent voice has been stilled at a moment when public life is much preoccupied with subjects Thomas wrote about elegantly—health and medicine. He had been dean of the schools of medicine at Yale and New York University and head of the Memorial Sloan-Kettering Cancer Center. And he won two National Book Awards for the collections of essays he called "notes of a biology watcher." He watched in amazement undiminished over the years.

Human beings, he reminded readers, have been around for only a few thousand years. These rookies, like all of life, are descendants of something that got going three thousand million or so years ago when, Thomas supposed, some single cell was fertilized by a bolt of lightning as the earth cooled. Everything, from bacteria to redwoods to shortstops, started then.

Any one of us results from the chance encounter of an egg and one sperm from among lots of competitors. From that encounter comes first a single human cell. "People," said Thomas, "ought to be walking around all day, all through their waking hours, calling to each other in endless wonderment, talking of nothing except that cell."

And all the really essential information needed for testifying to Congress or turning a double play or leaning against a tree is, Thomas said, in that first cell. It divides, and then the two become four, and ere long from that single cell has come a trillion-cell apparatus that thinks, inquires and worries.

"Worrying," Thomas wrote, "is the most natural and spontaneous of all human functions." Nowadays we worry, he thought, inordinately about health.

Most of us are healthy, most of the time, yet we do not respect the durability and sheer staying power of the human organism. "It is a distortion, with something profoundly disloyal about it, to picture the human being as a teetering, fallible contraption, always needing watching and patching, always on the verge of flapping to pieces." As most internists know, "most things get better by themselves. Most things, in fact, are better by morning."

Which is not to say that Thomas was complacent, or a fatalist. He was a scientist, and a passionate practitioner of medical research. But he had a sense of history and hence of limits.

Time was, and not so long ago, when doctors were valued primarily for their "bedside manner." Their job was primarily to make patients as comfortable as possible until nature either cured or killed them. That sort of medicine was an improvement over the nearly blind injuriousness of medicine during several millennia.

The prerequisite of progress began in the 1830s when a few disturbers of the medical profession's peace discerned that the greater part of medicine was, Thomas said, nonsense. All the bleeding and purging, all the infusions of every known plant and solutions of every known metal, the use of every conceivable diet—all of it was, Thomas believed, an unrelievedly deplorable story of mostly blind guesswork, each wrong guess stubbornly adhered to for decades, even centuries.

It was not until around 1900 that probabilities shifted so that active medicine was apt to do more good than harm. The sort of medicine we take for granted, and increasingly demand as an entitlement, began in the 1930s when sulfonamides and penicillin were added to the pharmacological arsenal. Then doctors became markedly more confident of curing. But only up to a point.

There are more than 5 billion people alive now, and all will die more or less on a known schedule. Thomas thought that one day human beings may be largely free of diseases. Then we shall, each of us, be like the "Wonderful One-Hoss Shay" of Oliver Wendell Holmes, Sr.'s, poem:

> . . . it went to pieces all at once—
> All at once, and nothing first—
> Just as bubbles do when they burst.

Sooner or later, Thomas said serenely, all our particles will return to randomness. Our particles, yes. But Thomas whimsically thought that when his life ended, "I may find myself still hanging around in some sort of mid-air, one of those small thoughts, drawn back into the memory of the earth: In that particular sense I will be alive." He is.

December 12, 1993

Rabbit Angstrom: At Rest, at Last

Rabbit has come to rest as he should have, from heart failure at an early age, a death brought on by his undisciplined surrender to the temptation of petty indulgences. The question is: Is Rabbit us?

Rabbit at Rest, John Updike's fourth and very final novel about Harry "Rabbit" Angstrom, begins at a Florida airline terminal. Rabbit, 55 years old and 40 pounds overweight, is simultaneously suffering intimations of his terminal illness—chest pains—and an irresistible craving for a candy bar. The book ends, many such surrenders later, with Rabbit hospitalized, sagging toward a death that might have been forestalled by sensible habits or serious surgery, which he rejected.

The preceding installments in this unique literary genre—this epic of the mundane—were *Rabbit, Run* (1960), *Rabbit Redux* (1971) and *Rabbit Is Rich* (1981). Updike is not a novelist of ideas but of mingled domestic atmospheres and social intimations. But the mingling makes it reasonable for the readers who have made these books best-sellers to ransack them for social diagnoses. Furthermore, Updike's timing causes them to be seen as summations of decades.

When we first met Rabbit, he was 26. It was 1959 and Updike remembers that "Kerouac's *On the Road* was in the air, and a decade of 'dropping out' about to arrive, and the price society pays for unrestrained motion was on my mind." Updike kept returning to Rabbit to explore America's "unease."

The Rabbit we now rejoin (it is December 1988) is preoccupied with disasters, such as the terrorist destruction of the airliner over Lockerbie and, later, Hurricane Hugo. "He, too, is falling, helplessly falling, toward death." Death by potato chips.

The unbearable heaviness of being Rabbit is both physical and spiritual. He is fat, emotionally logy and oppressed by his vulgar gluttony. He has taken to the desultory reading of history, "that sinister mulch of facts our little lives grow out of before joining the mulch themselves, the fragile brown rotting layers of previous deaths."

Updike has now written 1,700 pages about this emotionally stunted, intellectually barren, morally repulsive egotist whose self-absorption lacks even the fascination of large scale. His life's work is an inherited Toyota dealership ("Who could ask for anything more?") that is taken from him by the no-nonsense Japanese after his son embezzles from it to feed his cocaine habit. That addiction is convincingly depicted in all its hair-raising squalor, but it is, in a sense, less unnerving than Rabbit's collapse of will as he nibbles himself to death.

Rabbit, like all of us, is moved by a mixture of physical and moral promptings. But in Rabbit, the latter are so weak and the former so base, it is a tribute to Updike's craftsmanship that we want to watch as Rabbit becomes a comprehensive failure, as husband, father, business-man, man.

Updike is a realist in the American tradition of Theodore Dreiser, Sinclair Lewis and, recently, Tom Wolfe. Updike does not believe, as many less-read writers seem to, that American life is so absurd that it defeats the conventions of realism.

Realism can be angry, but only up to a point. There must be a residue of caring, even affection, to move a writer to engage reality. Sinclair Lewis may have loathed George F. Babbitt and his home town of Ze-nith, or the smallness of Gopher Prairie's Main Street, but Lewis was angry because they fell short of hopes he had and standards they should have had.

However, realism is not literary photography: It need not be literal, or even in a sense, realistic.

The *New York Times* reviewer calls *Rabbit at Rest* Updike's "power-ful critique of America" and also a "supremely eloquent Valentine to his country." The *Washington Post* reviewer calls it "a happy book; an exult-ant hymn to the inexhaustible vitality of America." Well.

Updike calls it "a depressed book about a depressed man, written by a depressed man." Updike knows that a novel is like a child: It has life of its own. The author cannot control how it and the world affect one an-other. Toward the end, Updike has Rabbit leading the Fourth of July pa-rade dressed as Uncle Sam, and Rabbit occasionally lets loose political sentiments, about falling bridges and rising debts. But Updike may not have much on his mind other than the literary challenge of casting a cool eye on the life, and now the death, of a middle-class man.

But not a representative man—not a metaphor for America. Perhaps *Rabbit at Rest* can be read as a cautionary tale for America the sclerotic, its arteries clogged by dumb consumption. But Updike, who is one year older than Rabbit and grew up where Rabbit lived, in southeastern Pennsylvania, may just be interested in, and perhaps depressed by, mortality.

Is America mortal? Maybe, even probably, but not imminently. As Updike once said, "People run down, and they confuse their condition with the world's."

October 28, 1990

F. Scott Fitzgerald's Literary Jazz

ROCKVILLE, MARYLAND—About a dozen miles north of Washington's sparkling monuments, which celebrate American successes, one of America's saddest stories is commemorated by this inscription: "So we beat on, boats against the current, borne back ceaselessly into the past."

The last words of *The Great Gatsby* mark the grave of F. Scott Fitzgerald, who died 50 years ago, December 21, 1940. He was emblematic of an era and his life is a cautionary tale for this one.

Success (*This Side of Paradise*) came to him suddenly, at 23. At 28, he published *Gatsby*. At 43, he was dead. (In 1919, Gatsby was poor. In the spring of 1922, he was rich. In late summer, he was dead.) Fitzgerald spent most of his adult life dissipating his talent and health in drug abuse. He was an alcoholic.

Not long before his fatal heart attack, he wrote, in a heartrending past tense: "In a small way, I was an original." In a big way, he was. He not only named, he incarnated, the Jazz Age.

His way of living ruined his talent but rose, like his talent, from romanticism. It was the romanticism of style, flair, extravagant gesture. And in the 1920s, as in the 1960s, the cultivation of intensely felt experience was bound up with drugs, a category properly understood to include alcohol. (Gatsby refers to his bootlegging as "the drug business.")

The decade in which Fitzgerald was born marked the closing of the frontier. The virgin West no longer beckoned. The year he was born, 1896, saw the victory of McKinley over Bryan, city over country. The East beckoned. He went from Minnesota to Princeton to become a chronicler of urban America's new manners (the urban America of Jay Gatsby, who was Jimmy Gatz before he left North Dakota).

Fitzgerald was born when ragtime, movies and airplanes were born, amidst an expansive sense of possibility. World War I, said one veteran of it, had taught disdain for civilian virtues (thrift, caution, sobriety) and taught instead extravagance, fatalism and fear of boredom. The war punched history's fast-forward button, revving up the 1920s.

Production soared; speculation soared even more. Producing goods lost stature next to marketing, advertising, salesmanship. Hence the new virtues were poise, self-assurance, personality. "If personality is an unbroken series of successful gestures, then there was something gorgeous about [Gatsby]. . . ." Gorgeous, if you overlook the fact he was a gangster.

Suddenly youth—Flaming Youth, it was called—came knocking at the door. And when the older generation answered the door, it saw out at the curb a roadster. In 1920, the year the presidency was won by a man promising a return to "normalcy," Fitzgerald published *This Side of Paradise,* announcing a new sense of the normal.

"None of the Victorian mothers—and most of the mothers were Victorian—had any idea how casually their daughters were accustomed to be kissed." It was an age of saxophones, women wearing makeup, bobbed hair and "eating three-o'clock after-dance suppers in impossible cafés, talking of every side of life."

Now, that seems impossibly quaint in 1990, the year the *Boy Scout Handbook* was revised to include this counsel: "You owe it to the women in your life to keep their best interests in mind. . . . Don't burden yourself and someone you care for with a child neither of you is ready to bear." However, the giddiness of the 1920s arose from the exhilaration of not knowing where, or if, the carnival would stop.

Part of it came to a screeching halt on Wall Street in October 1929. For Fitzgerald, the carousel closed December 21, 1940. But there is a sense in which the carnival of modernity never closes here, and the nation is more wary, less exhilarated by that fact.

Fitzgerald's life and writings conveyed the idea that the Old World, congealed in its heavy, viscous history, inhibited "freedom" by too much inheritance. But here on the fresh green breast of the New World, people could live "honestly," unconditioned and true to impulses. Fitzgerald's crack-up tells a new-old story: Being unconstrained carries its own burdens, the heaviest of which is self-creation. He was not a skillful author of himself.

"The expression of bewilderment had come back into Gatsby's face, as though a faint doubt had occurred to him as to the quality of his present happiness."

Fitzgerald's writings are like jazz: improvisations on a short theme. The theme is dreams dissipated by indiscipline. His grave is in a churchyard now crowded by commercial clutter and enveloped in roaring currents of traffic. But his life, like his best writing, reverberates out where the dark fields of the republic roll on under the night.

December 20, 1990

Michael Jordan's Athletic Jazz

Basketball may be "the city game," but its greatest performer soared out of Wilmington, North Carolina. That is how it should have been. As *Hoosiers*, one of the best sports movies, made vivid, basketball often means most in small towns where the community gathers in a cramped gym on winter nights, imagining their boys teaching humility to some team from an arrogant metropolis. By the time Michael Jordan stepped away from the game, he had given Chicago the inestimable pleasure of several times slam-dunking in the playoffs the team from the most arrogant of metropolises. The Knicks represent the city that produced the smarty-pants journalist (A. J. Liebling) who hung on Chicago the label the "Second City." The stacker of wheat and hog butcher showed the Big Apple how to play hoops.

Jordan caused Chicago to square its broad shoulders, and he helped make professional basketball boom. The NBA came of age because of three players. One was called Magic. Another, "the hick from French Lick"—a Hoosier town—seemed to have 360-degree vision, peripheral vision with no periphery. The third was Michael. Baseball once had the stars known merely by first names or nicknames—Babe, Willie, Mickey, the Duke.

One reason for the NBA's success is that the pleasures of professional basketball are so immediate, so accessible to spectators. It fits an age in which people seem to want their music illustrated by videos and expect life to have a soundtrack by Metallica. The NBA is MTV as sport—entertainment as sensory blitzkrieg. Many of the pleasures of baseball require a trained eye and a sense of strategic choices in particular situations that arise in a game of constant pauses. The kaleidoscopic spectacle of professional basketball—muscular swirl in a small space—requires no mediating thought.

Explaining why basketball is a simple game, Red Auerbach, philosopher-king of the Boston Celtics, said, "The ball is round and the floor is smooth." Yes, but. Basketball may be the athletic equivalent of another American invention, jazz, but just because jazz often is improvisational does not mean jazz is simple. Because basketball is a game of flow rather than, like baseball or football, of episodes, and because today's basketball players combine balletic grace with furious speed and stunning strength, it is easy to believe that the game is all adrenaline and instinct, with no mind involved. That is not true. But basketball at the NBA level does require a consistency of high energy that cannot long exist without joy. For Jordan, the joy is gone, for now.

The ethics of excellence can be construed in several ways. Jordan's way is: I've done my best and been the best, so I have nothing left to prove. However, another way is: There is a special virtue to continuing to perform at a high level after you have nothing to prove, just for the sake of the craft, and out of respect for anyone who, seeking refuge from a world full of the slipshod and second-rate, will come out on a cold winter night to an arena to see excellence.

But in *Henry IV*, Shakespeare's Prince Hal says, "If all the year were playing holidays,/To sport would be as tedious as to work." The grinding everydayness of sports like baseball and basketball takes a toll on the players' zest, and zest is an indispensable ingredient of consistent excellence. So when, two weeks ago, George Brett, perhaps the greatest hitter of his generation and still a star, announced his retirement after 20 years with the Kansas City Royals, he said simply, "The game had become a job for me, and I thought baseball deserved better than that." If only the sort of respect that America's best athletic craftsmen have for their crafts were infectious. If it were, our entire society could catch a wholesome contagion from the men and women who rise to the top of the stern meritocracy of sport.

Some of Jordan's performances—"the shot" at the buzzer that crushed the Cleveland Cavaliers in the 1989 playoffs; the 54 points that brought the Bulls back against the Knicks last May—are etched in America's sporting history as deeply as Red Grange's 265 yards and four touchdowns for Illinois in the first 12 minutes of the Michigan game in 1924, or "the catch" by Willie Mays against the Indians in the 1954 World Series. But Jordan's manner of leaving the game was also memorable.

His decision was in part an act of filial piety, a way of preserving the bittersweet satisfaction of knowing that his father, who was murdered last summer, saw his last game. Jordan's farewell press conference was satisfyingly rich with talk of father and family, subjects much in need of celebration in the unhappy sections of our cities where Jordan's glittering career in "the city game" has exerted hypnotic fascination.

Jordan's greatness is attested by the "Oh, you must mean who other than" test. A few years ago, while writing a book on baseball, I would ask managers and coaches who they considered the best player and the best pitcher they had ever seen. Often I got first a quizzical look, as though the question could not be serious, and then I got this response: "Oh, you must mean who other than Mays and Koufax." Today, when basketball people are asked to name the best player they ever saw, that quizzical look flickers on their faces, and then they say, "Oh, you must mean who other than Michael."

An ailing arm forced Koufax to retire when he was Jordan's age, 30, and at the peak of his powers, so no one ever saw him, as they saw Mays, in seasons when his skills were sadly diminished. Poignancy is inherent in sport because so much of life's trajectory—the birth, flowering and withering of capacities—is compressed into a short span. By retiring now, Jordan controls our retrospection, leaving only memories from the apogee of his career.

What he cannot control are the consequences of the emulation a career such as his inspires. Somewhere, perhaps on a playground along the mean streets of some city's concrete canyons, where the rusted rims have no nets and where the in-your-face-style of play is captured in the rule "no autopsy, no foul," or perhaps in a small town beneath a basket hung over a driveway that is illuminated only by light spilling from a nearby kitchen window, there is the 11 P.M. slap-slap-slap-swish, slap-slap-slap-swish of a boy practicing a jump shot that someday will have people saying that he is like Michael—maybe even a bit better.

October 18, 1993

PART 8

Sunshine and Showers

Pearl Harbor Plus Forty

Flying over Nebraska in the summer of 1943, an Englishman was struck by the "normality—hundreds of miles of it and not a sight or sound to remind one that this was a country at war." Then his lunch tray arrived, and inscribed on the pat of butter was an injunction: REMEMBER PEARL HARBOR. When Americans pause (if they do pause) to remember what happened 40 years ago, they should ponder the fact that less than two years after Pearl Harbor, advertising arts were employed to remind Americans of the war happening elsewhere.

An American who wants to see a place where a foreign nation inflicted violence on American soil in this century of "total war" must travel 5,000 miles and five time zones from his nation's capital, 2,000 miles from the western edge of the continent, to a state that was not a state when attacked. But what happened there initiated events as transforming to the nation as the events initiated 80 years earlier by an attack on another island military installation (Fort Sumter).

Forty years ago this nation was dragged into world history. It is arguable that the dragging happened earlier, on, say, October 23, 1917, near Nancy, France, when an artillery piece of the First American Division fired the first American shot at Germans. But immediately after the armistice Americans spun a cocoon of complacency.

Unlike World War I, which had a clear beginning in the summer of 1914, the conflagration called World War II began in separate blazes. Arguably, it began in April 1932, when Mao Tse-tung, in the name of the Kiangsi Soviet, declared war on Japan. As early as 1932 the United States supported Chinese resistance to Japan. But as late as 1937 isolationism was so strong that Congress barely rejected an Indiana congressman's proposed constitutional amendment that would have made any declaration of war subject to a national referendum.

Five years after Pearl Harbor, Senator Arthur Vandenberg, the Michigan Republican who helped wean his party from isolationism, said the attack "drove most of us to the irresistible conclusion that world peace is indivisible. We learned that the oceans are no longer moats around our ramparts. We learned that mass destruction is a progressive science which defies both time and space." The era of (in Walter Lippmann's phrase) "effortless security" was over. That "progressive science" meant the end of security, as traditionally understood, forever. And we now must hope that in an age of constant regional conflicts, peace can be divisible.

Four days after Pearl Harbor, Hitler declared war on the United States and, immediately, photographs of FDR replaced those of Mussolini in many store windows on Mulberry Street in New York. The attack punctuated a dreary dozen years. An 18-year-old in 1941 had been six when the stock market collapsed. Suddenly 18-year-olds had jobs, some of them dangerous jobs.

By the Depression, Americans were (in Daniel Boorstin's words) "cheated of our uniqueness." Pearl Harbor completed the process of ending the belief in "American exceptionalism." Americans were not after all guaranteed by their physical setting either easy prosperity or easy security. Suddenly, they had to take soldiering seriously.

D. W. Brogan, the historian, wrote that until Pearl Harbor the regular soldiers, the "30-year-men" of James Jones's novel *From Here to Eternity*, were more isolated from the national life than were the British soldiers Kipling knew in Lahore. As Brogan also wrote about America, "No nation more cheerfully turns its swords into plowshares . . . (and) no nation plowshares into swords with such speed or has so many plows to turn. The Army that was using wooden model weapons in maneuvers in 1940 and 1941 was a great military power by the end of 1942."

Japan's hope that Pearl Harbor would shatter American morale was one of history's huge miscalculations. But events also refuted the Allies' assumption that saturation bombing of civilians would shatter enemy morale. Indeed, compared with the indiscriminate forms of violence eventually used by both sides in both theaters of war, that first Japanese attack seems almost gallant and archaic: military power used against military targets.

Japan made its attack the way it subsequently turned to making consumer goods: brilliantly. Then they ran off a string of victories more brilliant than Hitler's generals gave him.

Forty years on, the great warrior nation is a Jewish state that did not exist in 1941, and the great commercial nation is Japan. History, although frequently horrible, is endlessly surprising.

December 3, 1981

Pearl Harbor Plus Fifty

Surprise is a substantial military asset and one way to achieve it is by doing something irrational. Japan did 50 years ago.

The attack on Pearl Harbor was an exquisitely executed calamity for Japan. It battered American battleships, thereby necessitating the rapid rebuilding of the Navy, this time with more relevant weapons—aircraft carriers—at its heart. The rapidity was the result of another American benefit from Pearl Harbor: rage.

Every war must end, so before launching war you should consider whether you can conceive, let alone achieve, a successful end. Bright people often ignore banalities such as this. Almost all the clever Japanese who planned the attack did ignore it. One did not.

Directed to make it happen, Admiral Yamamoto said: I will do it. Then I will run wild in the Pacific for six months. But then what?

He knew that, having mildly crippled and mightily energized an industrial giant, there would be no plausible outcome involving U.S. submission to Japan's designs. Furthermore, there was no reason to expect a less than ferocious American response.

If Japan's leaders knew much American history (they should have; some, including Harvard's Yamamoto, attended Ivy League colleges), they knew that total war was an American invention, pioneered by soldiers marching through Georgia and South Carolina.

In 1864 total war meant only (the ashes of Columbia, South Carolina, attest to its sufficiency) industrialism, conscription and tactics that blurred the distinction between combatants and noncombatants by attacking the farms, factories and transportation on which modern armies depend. By the 1940s the fury of total war was growing exponentially because of three additional ingredients—the modern state's organizational bureaucracy, propaganda and forced-draft science (as at Los Alamos, New Mexico).

Americans who are now older than 60 remember the instant they heard the news of three events—Kennedy's assassination, FDR's death and Pearl Harbor. We who have lived all our lives in the long shadows cast by ballistic missiles cannot fathom the trauma felt by Americans when a few Sunday morning minutes revealed that broad oceans and pacific neighbors no longer guaranteed the nation's physical safety.

The study of history, or even of one great event, is chastening because it teaches the unpredictable relatedness of things, and the inability to subdue life's contingencies. That is why history is the best undergraduate major and should be a prerequisite for political life. Consider the fact that the attack on Pearl Harbor was just one large event in the most momentous week of this century.

On December 7, 1941, a Soviet counterattack on the outskirts of Moscow pushed back German forces a few miles and shocked Hitler: Blitzkrieg had failed where failure would be fatal. Quickly killing the Red Army had been the key, he still thought, to a negotiated peace with Britain that would keep America out of the war.

The Wehrmacht's failure to achieve that quick kill freed Hitler from the need to moderate his criminality out of concern for British and American sensibilities. Therefore, he made a choice he had put off making. Germany could not win, so it would—and should—perish. Four days after Pearl Harbor he declared war on the United States.

"In December 1941, within a few days," wrote historian Sebastian Haffner, "Hitler made his final choice between two incompatible aims he had pursued from the outset—German domination of the world and extermination of the Jews. He abandoned the former as unattainable and entirely concentrated on the latter."

Hence his strange lethargy in the second half of the war. Politics was now nothing, the murder machinery was everything. The Wannsee Conference, where Nazi officials formalized plans for the "final solution," occurred January 20, 1942.

The Soviet troops that stopped the Wehrmacht in front of Moscow were Siberians transferred from the Russo-Japanese military frontier in Manchuria. The transfer occurred after the neutrality treaty Japan signed with Russia when preparing for war with the United States.

Pearl Harbor was folly, but magnificently executed folly. When Japan began planning the attack it had not yet developed the essential weapon, shallow-running torpedoes. More than 100 officers knew of the plan even before preparations, including simulated attacks, made it possible for many more people to surmise the target. Yet secrecy was maintained all the way across the broadest ocean. Surprise was achieved.

But on Saturday morning, December 6, a new U.S. government committee, code-named S-1, had met in Washington. Its subject: the feasibility of constructing atomic weapons. More surprises were coming.

Still, 'twas a famous victory from which elements of Japan's fleet returned to harbor, at Hiroshima.

December 5, 1991

D-Day and the Braided Cord

NORMANDY—"Old men forget," said Shakespeare's Henry V before the Battle of Agincourt, during an invasion of Normandy. But not the old men who as young men stormed the beaches here half a century ago.

By June 6, 1944—two days after U.S. forces reached Rome, the first Axis capital to fall—the cream of the Wehrmacht, 2 million men, had been killed in Russia. And still the Normandy invasion was a hard-won success. If Hitler had not been a habitual late sleeper, if that morning he had unleashed the panzer divisions north of Paris, which Rommel might have got him to do if Rommel had not been in Germany for his wife's birthday, the war could have been even longer. But even before D-Day the defeat of Germany was certain.

Any war is a braided cord of related battles. In the autumn of 1940, in the Battle of Britain, the Royal Air Force ended whatever chance Hitler had of invading the island. Hence he had to guard the Atlantic Wall with forces that could have been decisive if moved to the Eastern Front. The disastrous raid on Dieppe on August 19, 1942, from which only 2,500 of the 6,000 mostly Canadian raiders returned to England, lulled Hitler. But by November 3, 1943, in Fuehrer Directive 51, he told the Wehrmacht that the likelihood of "an Anglo-Saxon landing" precluded further weakening of German defenses in the west. However, the war was won in the east, by Russians.

Most Americans say the war began December 7, 1941. Actually, that is the day the war that began September 1, 1939, began to end, because of two events 7,000 miles apart.

One was the attack on Pearl Harbor, which brought U.S. industry into the war. Churchill, whose greatness included a gift for seeing the sweep of things, said he slept "the sleep of the saved" that night, knowing the war's outcome: "So we had won after all!"

Also on December 7, a Soviet counterattack drove back German forces that had advanced to the outskirts of Moscow. That night Hitler drafted Directive 39: "The severe winter weather which has come surprisingly early in the East, and the consequent difficulties in bringing up supplies, compel us to abandon immediately all major offensive operations and to go over to the defensive." There would be other German offensives, but the grinding down of Germany had begun.

The easy drive to Paris in 1940 convinced Hitler that his offensive revolution in arms—tanks, motorized infantry with radio coordination, dive-bombers functioning as flying artillery—could negate the manufacturing weight of the democracies. He was wrong. In 1939 the U.S. Army of 170,000 was smaller than those of 15 other nations, including Romania. On D-Day that many Allied soldiers crossed the Channel. In 1939 America manufactured 800 aircraft, civilian and military. In 1940 it manufactured 40,000.

Hitler's racialist theories told him that America, enervated by prosperity and degraded by a polyglot population, could not produce worthy warriors. Wrong again.

Stephen Ambrose, Eisenhower's biographer and president of the D-Day Museum being developed in New Orleans, calls D-Day "a love song to democracy." German soldiers were magnificently obedient to orders, as befitted young men socialized by 11 years of totalitarianism. But Americans, with the talent for spontaneous self-organization that Tocqueville considered a national characteristic, adapted to the chaos of combat in a confined coastal strip.

Bold in conception and heroic in execution, the invasion was an astounding exercise not only of logistics but also of secrecy. Germany, misled by Allied intelligence services, did not know on which part of the coast the blow would fall, even though in May 1944 a gust of wind blew 12 copies of invasion plans out of a window of the British War Office in London. Eleven copies were quickly recovered by scrambling aides. Two agonizing hours later, a civilian, never identified, returned the twelfth to a military sentry, and walked away.

D-Day came 30 years into the 75-year crisis that began in June 1914, with pistol shots in Sarajevo, and ended in Berlin, November 9, 1989, when the Wall crumbled. Arguably, the invasion was the third of the three most consequential battles in American history—Saratoga, which saved the Revolution; Gettysburg, where the Confederacy crested; and Normandy, where the United States stepped forward as the leader of the West.

The invasion hastened the end of the war, and hence of the Holocaust. So let there also be remembrance of something else that happened June 6, 1944. That day Germans on Crete packed 400 Greek hostages, 300 Italian POWs, and 260 Jews on a boat, sent it to sea and scuttled it, killing all.

Such murderousness, writ large across a continent, was why they went ashore that day, those young men now grown old and those who did not get to grow old.

June 5, 1994

Making the Mall a Monument to Mars

Have you ever been to Gettysburg battlefield? It is a solemn carnival of marble, granite and bronze, a jumble of monuments to particular states, military units and heroes. These material residues of 19th-century passions are a kind of noble clutter. Well, war is untidy and perhaps battlefields should be, too. But do we want the center of the nation's capital, and especially the Mall, to look like that?

My trembling hand holds before my disbelieving eyes documentary evidence of our national knack for wretched excess. The documents concern legislation to create a Desert Storm memorial, perhaps for the Mall. Given the fact that we may be only at the intermission in that war (Saddam is still behaving badly and President Bush is cross), this seems premature as well as inherently silly. It also is part of a process that has become absurd and reflects the distemper of the times.

This proposal for yet another memorial comes from the American Battle Monuments Commission, which is just doing what government agencies do—maximizing its product. (A National Pickle Commission would try to put a tiny tub of pickles on every American table.) The ABMC proposes a Desert Storm memorial that "could give recognition to the other United Nations Forces of the coalition." Oh? Perhaps a statue of some sheik using the hood of his Mercedes as a desk, on which he writes a check to rent the U.S. military?

It is, of course, impossible to conjure up an idea too nutty to attract Congressional sponsors, so there never is a shortage of proposals for more monuments. In addition to a slew of proposals for memorials to particular military units, the infectious fever of "monumentitis" has recently produced proposals for memorials to Native American veterans, Hispanic veterans (surely Asian-American veterans will be heard from soon), Peace Corps volunteers, victims of Pan Am Flight 103 (a bit sticky, given that Syria is our new best friend), the American housewife, Thomas Paine, John Adams, George Mason, Francis Scott Key, John Muir, Martin Luther King, Gandhi and General Draza Mihajlovic, a Yugoslav whose monument would last a lot longer than Yugoslavia will.

While there is a statue and fountain honoring Christopher Columbus in front of Washington's Union Station, building such a thing today would be next to impossible, now that the politically correct doctrine is that Columbus was merely a bringer of genocide and air pollution. But there still are ideas for, well, enriching the Vietnam Veterans Memorial. Women have won a representation-through-statuary battle. Now there is a move afoot to put a bronze dog there. (Do K-9 vets vote?)

Monumentitis makes us see the good side of recessions, which slow fund-raising, and of bureaucratic procedures that make precipitous action impossible. Consider the case of the Korean War Veterans Memorial, destined for the Mall near the Lincoln Memorial.

It is notoriously difficult to get consensus, let alone unanimity, among opinionated people concerning esthetic matters, so it is noteworthy that the Commission on Fine Arts was unanimous in rejecting the proposed design for the Korean memorial. The design might be a satire on today's tendency to define justice as the proliferation of group entitlements. It includes 38 seven-foot-tall statues of ground troops (all male, but ethnically varied) leading to a pool, an inscribed stone and a flag plaza, backed by a granite wall covered with military photographs etched in Benday dots.

You wonder why there is to be a Korean memorial when the Mall has no World War II memorial? The ABMC told Congress that, notwithstanding the existence of a score of cemetery and other World War II memorials in America and around the world, Washington needs another. Actually, the continued existence of our democracy is the best possible memorial to those who fought that war. But if a material memorial is built, it will have to be shoehorned into the Mall or elsewhere in Washington's "monumental core" that extends west from the Capitol to the Lincoln and Jefferson memorials, Arlington Cemetery and the Pentagon. The following projects are already at least past the site-selection stage: the FDR Memorial Park, the National Peace Garden, the Memorial to the Black Patriots of the Revolutionary War, the Women in Military Service Memorial and the Law Enforcement Officers Memorial. Fortunately, the memorial to the victims of crime has been derailed.

More proposals will bubble up as the grievance industry—a growth industry for the 1990s—produces more complaints about under-representation in the statue sweepstakes. Joseph E. Brown, a landscape architect and scourge of monumentitis, rightly says that "new proposals seem to focus almost exclusively on victims, casualties and those who consider themselves unjustly ignored." There is a generational difference here: Ever heard a World War II veteran complain about an insufficiency of memorials? Given all the ethnic ingredients in the American stew, there are limitless possibilities for politicizing the commemoration process. That is a melancholy thought for this bicentennial of Pierre L'Enfant's great master plan for the Federal City.

We shape our physical environment, then it shapes us. Washington's monumental core serves the nation's civic liturgy, using material things to articulate precious sentiments—gratitude, admiration, love. It should be lovely. It has not always been.

When Lincoln "came out of the wilderness" in February 1861, Washington was worse than any wilderness. Biographer Stephen Oates says sewage marshes festered at the foot of the White House grounds. At the northern edge of the garbage-strewn Mall there flowed an open drainage ditch with dead cats floating in the putrescence, the odor of which was even worse than that of the pigs rooting in the streets off Pennsylvania Avenue. In this century, the "temporary" World War I and II buildings were not scrubbed off the Mall until the 1976 Bicentennial.

It has taken time and care to make the Mall what it is, one of the world's most splendid public places. Its satisfying geometry is an analogue of our society. Its orderly vistas open receptive minds to the symmetry, balance, proportion and temperateness of our political institutions and the civil society that sustains our common purposes. This shrine, to which Americans come as pilgrims, should not become a monument to Mars or to grumpy factions.

August 26, 1991

Michael Crichton's "Conservative Realism"

The sexes, already at daggers drawn about so many things, now have something new to scrap about. It is Michael Crichton's novel *Disclosure*, number one this coming weekend on *The New York Times* best-seller list, with about one million copies already in print and the movie rights sold for $3.5 million.

Its subject is sexual harassment of an employee by his boss. A woman boss. Batten down the hatches.

Crichton has sold more than 100 million books worldwide—30 million in the United States in the last 18 months alone—because his raw material (the adjective is just right) touches anxieties of the age. These include menacing science (*Jurassic Park*), menacing Japanese (*Rising Sun*) and now women who are menacing because they are as libidinous as many men are and powerful enough to behave as badly as many men do.

What do you call a steamy novel that is like those novels known as "bodice-rippers," but with the sex roles reversed, a novel in which what gets ripped is a man's shirt? Whatever, Crichton has written one, with a political pamphlet embedded in it.

A young executive anticipating ever greater glory at a high-tech Seattle corporation, DigiCom, is disappointed when a woman with a high ratio of political skills to technical knowledge gets promoted over him by the corporation's CEO, who is "progressive" about promoting women. She is not only a former lover of the disappointed executive, but treats subordinate men as sex objects. Her first day in power she summons her former lover to an evening meeting, makes extremely aggressive advances— "He felt dominated, controlled, and at risk"—and when he spurns her they both file sex harassment complaints.

Here we go again: He says . . . she says. Who will believe him? His lawyer, that's who. The lawyer is a woman named Fernandez, which scrambles the calculus of political correctness. She says:

> Harassment is a power issue. And power is neither male nor female. Whoever is behind the desk has the opportunity to abuse power. . . . About 5 percent of sexual harassment claims are brought by men against women. It's a relatively small figure. But then, only 5 percent of corporate supervisors are women. So the figures suggest that women executives harass men in the same proportion as men harass women.

Crichton's premise—that there is no difference between the sexes regarding abuse of power—may or may not be true. But it certainly is a provocation to "victim feminists," whose premise is that the world would be pretty much perfect if it were scrubbed clean of all vestiges of patriarchy.

With so many perfectionist dreams, from Rousseau's to Marx's, thoroughly discredited, it is late in the day for serious people to believe that something straight can be made from the crooked timber of humanity. But there always is a supply of credulous people, and one of Crichton's useful purposes in *Disclosure* is to annoy them.

A young female associate of Fernandez says, "I just can't believe a woman would act that way. So aggressively." Fernandez replies: Suppose this were a case of conflicting claims about, say, money—about a contract. "Would you assume that the man was lying because a woman wouldn't act that way?" The associate says of course not, and Fernandez asks, "So you think women are unpredictable in their contractual arrangements, but stereotypical in their sexual arrangements?"

Crichton's novels are not deathless literature but they are terrific thermometers measuring social fevers. *Disclosure* is symptomatic of the fact that many men evidently feel set-upon and eligible for a slice of the status of victim. Hence the broadside delivered by a Crichton character against affirmative action:

Look: when I started in DigiCom, there was only one question. Are you good? . . . Now, ability is only one of the priorities. There's also the question of whether you're the right sex and skin color to fill out the company's HR [human resources] profiles. And if you turn out to be incompetent, we can't fire you. Pretty soon, we start to get junk. . . .

In the 1930s a didactic, even preachy kind of novel called "socialist realism" was all the rage among novelists on the left. But the world turns and today Crichton has produced a work of what can be called "conservative realism," presenting the world the way many conservatives want readers to see it. *Disclosure* is a better broadside than a novel, but between you, me and the lamppost, the pamphlet in the novel is a good thing for a few million readers to run into.

January 20, 1994

Sexual Harassment in Kindergarten

Some liberal senators seeking wrongs to right have found a bountiful supply of them around playground teeter-totters, on school buses and wherever else kindergartners and grammar school children congregate and misbehave with Babylonian abandon. The senators—the usual suspects: Harkin, Simon, Moseley-Braun, Mikulski—have authored "gender equity" education bills which attack, among other "crises," that of sexual harassment among the young. The very young. Senator Kennedy, a co-sponsor of the bills, says:

> You have first-, second- and third-grade harassers. You have kindergarten harassers. We're reaching out and identifying them at the earliest grades, disciplining these individuals. As with every aspect of health care, early intervention can have a big impact.

Kennedy is indispensable for illuminating the premises of contemporary liberalism. Leave aside the question of whether he is accurately depicting sexual goings-on in grammar schools. But note his use of the phrase "health care." Even if sexual harassment is as rampant as Kennedy says from kindergarten on, why call this a "health care" problem?

One answer is that health care is the hot topic in Washington, a city that has at most a one-track mind. So today people push their pet projects by claiming they are health care projects. This tactic has often been tried using the phrases "civil rights" or "children's issues," as in: "A strong infrastructure is important for minorities (or children), so this highway bill is really civil rights (or children's) legislation."

But the significance of Kennedy's use of the phrase "health care" is more ideological than tactical. It expresses the mentality behind liberalism's faith in therapeutic government.

Sexual harassment, in kindergarten, or anywhere, must be a health problem because all problems are health problems. Sexual harassment must be a species of pathology, a psychological rather than a characterological defect. Otherwise liberals will have two horrid dilemmas. They will have to speak the language of personal faults and responsibilities. And they will have to join cultural conservatives in denouncing the contributions of popular culture, including the regnant sensibility of the permissive 1960s, to the corruption of character among the young.

(In Florida, where a 13-year-old arrested in connection with the killing of a tourist has a record of 56 arrests, juvenile criminals come under the jurisdiction of the Department of Health and Rehabilitative Services. Note the title. There is no mention of crime or punishment, which may be one reason why there is such a high ratio of the former to the latter.)

The idea that conflict between grammar school boys and girls might result from jealousy, conflicting interests or plain bad behavior would allow the idea that not everything that passes between the sexes is sexual. That idea is repellent to people making careers in the burgeoning "gender equity" bureaucracies which the senators' package of bills would further enlarge. These bills would spend money on "leadership training" for girls, on an Office of Gender Equity in the Department of Education and on much else. The caliber of the reasoning behind the bills can be gauged by this from Kennedy: "Despite the provisions of Title IX prohibiting sex discrimination in schools receiving federal funds, we continue to see differences in the educational achievement of boys and girls."

The legislation echoes two reports from the recently radicalized American Association of University Women, reports long on alarm and low on plausible data. "How Schools Shortchange Girls" said that teachers have always "unconsciously" treated girls and boys differently and are eager to do better but need federal money. "Hostile Hallways" reported a "pervasive climate of sexual harassment," with 81 percent of all students, boys and girls, reporting themselves victims. The report found a need for federal money.

Here is what has been happening without Kennedy patrolling the hallways:

By 1979 there were as many women as men in colleges. Today women get most of the B.A. and master's degrees, and probably soon will be majorities in medical and law schools. (In the last 20 years the percentage of medical degrees awarded to women has risen from 8 percent to 33 percent, the percentage of law degrees from 5 percent to 41 percent.) By the eighth grade more boys than girls have flunked a grade and among secondary school students more boys are assigned to special education classes than girls. Although girls do not test as well as boys in math and science, they test better in reading and writing.

But Asian-American eighth-grade girls score significantly better then white males in science. How inconvenient. Families, not schools, make this difference, and many other differences that derive from the families' values, not the families' wealth or the nature of the schools. So, what is the Office of Gender Equity going to do about that?

September 23, 1993

Journalism When Congress Ruled the Roost

A *New York Times* book review.

Nations are naturally forgetful, and democracy makes them more so. Democracy's insistent message is that all arrangements rest on the shiftable sand of opinion, customs and mores, so democracies focus on the fluid future. Washington, a city of frequent comings and goings and many short leases, is so busy trying to divine the future it has little energy left over for learning about its past. A pity, that. It is well to be reminded that things could be worse. They were, not long ago.

Fortunately, Congress has hired a few people like Donald A. Ritchie to take care of its institutional memory. He is an associate historian in the Senate Historical Office and the author of a dandy book. *Press Gallery: Congress and the Washington Correspondents* is sometimes startling, sometimes dismaying and constantly illuminating. Mr. Ritchie's intelligent idea, deftly executed, is that a history of Washington journalism, organized around sketches of emblematic correspondents from particular epochs, can reveal the slow transformation of journalism from a craft into a profession. It also can help explain the evolution of America's democratic values and practices, and the struggle for supremacy between the legislative and executive branches. Mr. Ritchie's narrative, rich in astonishing details, demonstrates that through most of Washington's history the relationship between the press and the politicians has been more intimate than adversarial. "Intimate"? The word barely does justice to the many, often unseemly, entanglements.

For a century and a half Capitol Hill, not 1600 Pennsylvania Avenue, was the epicenter of Washington journalism. The federal government was constructed by a constitutional convention that met in secret. Even the windows of Independence Hall were kept closed during the steamy Philadelphia summer of 1787. And beginning in 1789, and for a long time thereafter, the government wanted privacy. This preference accorded with Federalist Party philosophy favoring government by an elite insulated from the turbulent masses. Journalists might have been expected to find, from the first, a congruence between their vocational interests and liberal (meaning Jeffersonian) ideology. However, Mr. Ritchie shows that the sociology of American journalism was not nearly so simple.

Washington journalism began as stenography, the recording, or summarizing, of Congressional debates. Until the Senate voted in 1848 to hire impartial reporters of its proceedings, Henry Clay and John Calhoun and others would stroll down to newspaper offices at the foot of Capitol Hill to edit newspaper reports of their remarks. Edit and polish. Mr. Ritchie says that while Daniel Webster was speaking he would sort through synonyms aloud: "Why is it, Mr. Chairman, that there has gathered, congregated, this great number of inhabitants, dwellers, here; that these roads, avenues, routes of travel, highways, converge, meet, come together, here? Is it not because we have a sufficient, ample, safe, secure, convenient, commodious port, harbor, haven?" The Senator later pruned the excess verbiage for newspaper "reports." Mr. Ritchie says Webster's famous philippic in reply to Senator Robert Hayne— "Liberty and Union, now and forever, one and inseparable"—was not nearly so impressive in actual delivery.

As soon as there were parties, there were party papers. None were neutral, and no editor wanted objectivity from his man in Washington. The passions of the Jacksonian era stimulated the proliferation of papers, Jacksonian and Whig. The number of papers doubled between 1830 and 1860. The connection between them and parties made journalism a path to Congress. Schuyler Colfax, James G. Blaine, Horace Greeley, William Randolph Hearst and Joseph Pulitzer were only the most prominent people who used papers as springboards to office. Congress's freshman class from the 1864 election included 10 journalists.

The sound of journalism's future was the staccato clicking of an invention tested in Congress. "What hath God wrought?" was the message Samuel F. B. Morse sent on May 24, 1844, from the Capitol Building to Baltimore. Baltimore's reply: "What is the news in Washington?" That increasingly insistent question from out in the country would change everything.

The compression of time and the annihilation of distance by electronic journalism had begun. Technology often is a solvent of mores, and the telegraph helped subvert the cozy relationships between politicians and the party press. The new speed of communication sharpened the appetite it fed. Editors pressured Washington correspondents for more news to fill papers that were expanding to accommodate a new American industry—advertising. The imperative need was now for information, not partisan promotion.

In Washington information was rationed by governmental secrecy, and, as usual, governmental rationing produced black markets. Throughout the 19th century, and until 1929, the Senate debated treaties and nominations in secret session. This put a premium on personal relations between reporters and Congressional sources. Then, as now, the ship of state leaked from the top. The secrecy of government and the penury of journalists—most were paid poorly, and not at all when Congress was not in session—combined to produce arrangements that corrupted both journalists and politicians: Legislators found jobs for friendly journalists, usually in Congress, occasionally in executive departments. Often the jobs were fictitious. Mr. Ritchie says one reporter was listed as assistant horseshoer for the horses of Congressional messengers. Another was paid for work he never did, folding documents in the Senate Folding Room. Placement of journalists in Congressional jobs led to the selling of inside information by journalists to other journalists.

The transformation of the party press into more adversarial journalism was accelerated by scandals of the Gilded Age. The possibility of scandal grows as government grows. After the Civil War, which turned Washington into a bazaar for contractors, government grew because it was fostering growth—giving land to railroads, enacting protective tariffs. As it became more active allocating wealth and opportunity, timely information acquired more cash value. Many journalists cashed in. Mr. Ritchie says it was not until World War I that members of the press gallery were barred from providing news tips to stockbrokers, a practice that enriched some Civil War correspondents.

Mr. Ritchie argues that after the Civil War the cooperative relationship between press and politicians was disrupted first by a scandal too lurid to ignore, and then by a new form of competition that prodded newspapers to adopt a more skeptical stance toward Washington power. The Credit Mobilier scandal oozed from the company created for construction of the Union Pacific Railroad. Reports about the way its stock had been spread among legislators chilled cordial relations between Congress and reporters. And, says Mr. Ritchie, just when those wounds were healing, relations were disrupted by a new force—newsmagazines.

Magazines, competing with newspapers for readers and advertisers, flaunted their exuberant disdain for the deference the Congressional press corps displayed toward the tight little political community on

Capitol Hill. Magazines were homes for muckrakers. Teddy Roosevelt put that term into America's political lexicon with his "Man with the Muck-Rake" speech denouncing a magazine series attacking Senate corruption. Magazine writers made national reputations writing on many subjects from many places. They were not dependent on long-term relations with sources in government. The magazines' successes reporting scandals provoked newspaper editors to press their Washington correspondents for similar vinegar.

Some of the coziness of correspondents with their subjects survived well into this century, and shifted as institutional supremacy did. As late as 1930 the head of *The New York Times*'s Washington bureau, and a few other favored journalists, had the privilege of tossing around a medicine ball with Herbert Hoover each morning on the White House lawn.

No newspaper had posted a reporter at the White House in the 19th century. President Grover Cleveland underwent cancer surgery on board a yacht in New York Harbor without the press knowing anything about it. But presidential ascendancy was well advanced by the time one of William McKinley's secretaries began briefing the press at 10 o'clock each evening. McKinley's successor, the first President filmed by a movie camera, was the first charismatic President. Twenty-five years later Teddy Roosevelt's cousin would master a medium—radio—that reached over the heads of Congress and journalists, directly to the electorate.

As in so much else, war has been the great catalyst of change. The Civil War completed the slow creation of a Washington press corps by quickening the country's thirst for news. World War I, and the peace conference, produced, Mr. Ritchie says, a dramatization of Woodrow Wilson exceeding that of any previous president. Since 1917 Congress has been able to reclaim coequal status only briefly, and only when reacting to policies or proposals or misconduct from the executive branch. Its moments in the sun have come when it was debating the Versailles Treaty or the Robert Bork nomination to the Supreme Court, or when it was investigating the Teapot Dome or Watergate or Iran-contra scandals.

Mr. Ritchie ends on a slightly elegiac note. He seems to regret, somewhat, the fact that the nation's focus, and that of the press corps, has shifted irrevocably, 16 blocks west on Pennsylvania Avenue. However, he is a scrupulous historian whose fine book brings back the powerful aroma of a past too raw to be romanticized. Thus does memory help reconcile us to current discontents. It is an old axiom: Ignorance of the past causes us to libel the present.

June 30, 1991

The Game of Basketball and the Drama of Black Inclusion

SPRINGFIELD, MASSACHUSETTS—Displayed here like the sacred relic it is—like those supposed fragments of the True Cross that filled an implausible number of medieval reliquaries—is a small piece of varnished wood. It is from the floor of the old gym where 100 years ago this week basketball was born.

Winter in western Massachusetts was vexing to Dr. James Naismith, 30, whose responsibility was physical education for young men at the International YMCA Training School. So he hung two peach baskets from the lower rail of the gym's balcony. The rail was exactly 10 feet high, which is why you and I can't get our wrists over the rim.

The old gym is long gone, replaced by (this story gets more American as it goes along) a parking lot. But basketball is everywhere. Just as the Civil War spread baseball across the country like butter over bread, young YMCA administrators carried the gospel of basketball.

It is hard to believe now, with the NBA awash in cash and playing in palaces, but in the 1930s and '40s some professional players developed flat-trajectory jump shots because they played in dance halls with low ceilings. Today's balletic and ballistic players would hit those ceilings with their foreheads.

Basketball is a team game in which the aim of the teamwork often is to produce, for a fleeting instant, a favorable one-on-one mismatch—to reduce the game to what happens on the playground or beneath the hoop above the barn door. Basketball is the team game that can be practiced alone. Its sound is not just the screech of sneakers on hardwood but, before that, a distinctly outdoor urban sound, the rattle of a ball as it caroms around a loose rim and drops through a metal chain net onto an asphalt playground illuminated only, and badly, by a street lamp.

Basketball has two archetypes—the small-town Midwestern white kid with a crew cut and a jump shot, and the black kid in the city, playing the game of inexpensive equipment and confined spaces. Basketball in its early urban incarnations was considered a Jewish game. Then some other of society's outsiders got inside, and the game was transformed.

Many of the milestones along the march of blacks toward inclusion in

American society involved athletics. One milestone was reached March 19, 1966, in College Park, Maryland. There, in the NCAA basketball championship game, Texas Western College (now the University of Texas at El Paso) played the mighty University of Kentucky coached by Adolph Rupp, a great coach and a bad man.

In 1966 there was not a single black playing varsity basketball in the Atlantic Coast Conference, the Southwest Conference or the Southeast Conference in which Kentucky plays. When pressured by Kentucky's president to recruit minority players, Rupp exploded to an assistant, "That sonofabitch is ordering me to get some niggers in here. What am I going to do?"

He was going to get beaten 72–65 by Texas Western College. TWC started five blacks—the first time that had happened in an NCAA championship game—and played just two substitutes, both black. Afterward Rupp reportedly said, "TWC. . . . TWC? What's that stand for—Two White Coaches?"

Sports Illustrated's Curry Kirkpatrick reports that a few months before Rupp learned more than he wanted to know about TWC, Rupp said to his players, "When you go home tonight, I want you to look long and hard at these [national] rankings. One. Two. Three. Kentucky, Duke, Vanderbilt. All from the South. And all white. You'll never see it happen again." Rupp got at least that right.

Unlike baseball and football, basketball is a game of flow, with much room for improvisation, so comparisons to another American invention, jazz, are irresistible. It is the most purely American game in the sense that it has no evolutionary connections, as baseball and football do, with other nations' games. It is, therefore, suitable that basketball has become such a showcase for black talent. And it is a distinctive form of expression—a kind of language—for many young black men. This is as it should be because blacks are, in a sense, the most purely American Americans. As W.E.B. Du Bois wrote:

> Once for all, let us realize that we are Americans, that we were brought here with the earliest settlers and that the very sort of civilization from which we came made the complete absorption of Western modes and customs imperative if we were to survive all; in brief, there is nothing so indigenous, so completely "made in America" as we.

Actually, there are a few—a very few—other things, such as basketball.

December 19, 1991

Turning Back the Football Clock

Big-time football, for which the brittle human body is unsuited, flourishes on campuses, where it is inappropriate. This season began, as all seasons seem to, with several schools' football "programs"—the preferred noun; a synonym for "fiefdoms"—penalized for infractions of rules regulating the recruitment and compensation of players. Coaches frequently blame "boosters" for bad behavior, not always plausibly, as a recent *New York Times* editorial implied: "At the University of Washington, Don James resigned as head coach after failing to notice that his quarterback owned three cars."

Now the college football industry claims that the end of civilization as we have known it is nigh. Why? Because shrinking budgets, which often expand reasonableness, and laws requiring equity for women's athletics, have produced a rule restricting the number of football scholarships to 88, and next year to 85.

Until 20 years ago scholarships were unlimited and some schools gave more than 130. Eighty-five might seem sufficient for teams that field only eleven students at a time, but Ray Goff, head coach at Georgia, says fewer scholarships mean less talent, more fumbles, more broken plays, more penalties, fewer fans and—coming to the point—fewer dollars. "We are fighting against the pros for the limited entertainment dollar. We want to keep putting 80,000 people in our stadium on Saturdays."

Joe Dean, athletic director at Louisiana State University, frets about competition from the NFL's New Orleans Saints, "only one hour away, interstate all the way." The Saints "are putting on a show down there and we have to compete with that." "Have to"? Says who?

When college football first flourished it was unlike today's contests between vast throngs of players, some with narrow specialties (third-down-and-short-yardage blockers, etc.). The evolution of football into its current elephantine squads (some teams have 150 players, counting nonscholarship "walk-ons"), with minute divisions of labor, is explained in a new book, *Reading Football: How the Popular Press Created an American Spectacle*, by Michael Oriard, formerly of the Kansas City Chiefs, currently of Oregon State University's English Department.

As American football developed from rugby, blending elegance and violence into contact ballet, the seminal change was abandonment of rugby's "offside" rule that prevented any teammate from preceding the ball carrier down field. This change guaranteed a satisfying quantity of mayhem—blocking and tackling—and the need for pauses after each play while the teams regrouped. Because of the constant pauses, coaches can exercise close control.

At first, coaching during a game—even walking up and down the sidelines—was forbidden as unsportsmanlike. When in 1921 Coach Bob Zuppke of Illinois invented the offensive huddle, referees joined huddles when substitutes entered the game, to prevent sneaky coaching. But football developed "coach-centrism," the celebration of coaches as master manipulators meshing players like cogs in a clock.

Walter Camp, the Yale player and coach and a businessman (head of the New Haven Clock Company), dominated football's formative years. He wanted brains to matter more than mere muscle—the brains of coaches. Coaches would mold the raw material of players into teams modeled on that supposed paradigm of efficiency, the modern corporation. Football would train America's corporate elite.

Here are the *New York Herald*'s headlines about the 1892 defeat of coach Arthur Cumnock's Harvard team by Camp's Yalies:

MOST SCIENTIFIC FOOTBALL BATTLE ON RECORD

IT WAS A CONTEST BETWEEN COACHES

WALTER CAMP AND HIS COLLEAGUES WORSTED ARTHUR CUMNOCK IN THE
STYLE OF PLAY THEY HAD HAMMERED INTO THEIR APT AND WILLING PUPILS

Today's coaches, wired to talk to lieutenants high in the stands, stalk the sidelines like Napoleon at Austerlitz, and with about as many troops and as much modesty, being "scientific" and the center of attention. As usual, attempted improvements have made matters worse. Football improvers legislated a two-stage (in 1964 and 1975) transition to unlimited substitutions. This has meant unlimited opportunities for coaches to fuss and fiddle with each play.

We conservatives are constantly lectured about the impossibility of "turning back the clock." Such lectures come from people whose interests are threatened by the idea of a superior and recoverable past. Such people run today's big-time football "programs."

Suppose colleges returned to severe limits on substitution, with many players playing both offense and defense. Colleges could cut scholarship costs, coaches might stop their General Patton imitations and recede into the background, and if some LSU fans were unreconciled to this, there would still be the NFL alternative, "only one hour away, interstate all the way."

October 3, 1993

All Change Begins *Where?*

In the soothing ointment of President Clinton's words, one element was especially welcome to people who worry about the political giddiness encouraged, inevitably, by the civic liturgy of an Inauguration. The element was the emphasis placed by Clinton, who as candidate stressed "change" propelled by government, on the autonomy of change: "Profound and powerful forces are shaking and remaking our world. . . ."

The forces to which he was referring—forces of communication, commerce, science, intellectual and religious conviction—are always doing that. But because an Inauguration is a festival of government, it is apt to make the political class, and perhaps even normal people, susceptible to a fallacious notion about the importance of politics.

The political class, in its egotism and self-absorption, is particularly apt to find this notion plausible. It is a notion especially pleasing to Democrats, who are disposed to think of government as the sun around which life revolves.

It is a notion stated last summer by Ted Kennedy: "The ballot box is the place where all change begins in America." There is hardly a page of American history that does not refute that insistence, so characteristic of the political class, on the primacy of politics in the making of history.

Change begins in America when a Yale graduate, Eli Whitney, serving as a tutor on a cotton plantation, gets interested in inventing a machine to separate cotton fibers from cotton seeds. Eli Whitney's cotton gin helped produce the economic foundations of slavery. Another change began in America when, in the 1940s, the descendants of slaves, displaced by new cotton-picking machinery, began their migration to Northern cities.

Change begins in America when John Fitch makes the first American vessel powered by steam, and when a Connecticut inventor, Samuel Colt, patents a revolving-breech pistol. Change begins in America when a young blacksmith in Grand Detour, Illinois, makes a "self-scouring" steel plow suitable for turning the thick black topsoil of the Middle West. Today you can read the blacksmith's name in yellow print on green machines: John Deere.

Change begins in America when young John Rockefeller, who went to work at a produce-shipping firm in Cleveland at age 16, at age 20 starts trading products, including the black fluid being pumped from under western Pennsylvania.

Change begins in America when a voice crackling down a wire from a nearby room says, "Mr. Watson, come here, I want you." Change begins in America when in a garage in Detroit, the young Henry Ford conceives not only a vehicle for the masses but a mode of mass production that will make Americans mobile and prosperous. Change begins in America when two brothers in a Dayton bicycle shop tinker with a contraption that eventually will change how Americans experience America's vast distances.

Change begins in America when Thomas Alva Edison in Menlo Park, New Jersey, says he has not failed because 80 materials have proved unsatisfactory for making filament for an electric light bulb—he has succeeded in learning 80 things that don't work.

Change begins in America when a 36-year-old Illinois inventor produces a substance that will make possible new ways of experiencing the world. John Wesley Hyatt produced celluloid—which, in due time, produced Hollywood.

Change begins in America when in 1954 a traveling salesman of six-spindled milk-shake machines called Multimixers visits the McDonald brothers' restaurant in San Bernadino, California, where eight Multimixers were kept busy. The idea Ray Kroc got that day produced not only a great corporation but an entire industry.

But wait. Material change is not more consequential than intellectual, moral and spiritual changes, which also do not begin at the ballot box.

Change begins in America in 1734 when Jonathan Edwards, a clergyman in Northampton, Massachusetts, ignites the Connecticut Valley, and other preachers throughout the colonies spread the religious revival called the Great Awakening, which stimulated Americans' sense of their distinct identity.

Change begins in America when Harriet Beecher Stowe writes a novel. Meeting her in the White House, Lincoln supposedly said, "So you're the little woman who wrote the book that made this great war." Change continues in America when, in 1960, another woman publishes another novel on the subject of race: Harper Lee, *To Kill a Mockingbird*. Change begins in America when Lincoln Steffens writes *The Shame of the Cities*, Ida Tarbell writes *The History of the Standard Oil Company* and Upton Sinclair writes *The Jungle*.

Change begins in America when Mark Twain, Stephen Foster, Scott Joplin, Edward Kennedy Ellington and others invent American sounds in language and music.

Change begins in America when . . .

But enough. In a good society some change, some of it very important, begins at the ballot box. But in a good society politics is peripheral to much of the pulsing life of the society. It is in America, where, without the instruction or supervision of the political class, change is continuous.

January 24, 1993

Freedom Isn't Restful

It is axiomatic that people who worship the sun will resent people who proclaim the scientific laws of heat. And as long as Americans believe their prosperity is linked to the fortunes of familiar old corporations, Americans will resent the laws of economic change. Consider the case of Sears, Roebuck.

Retailing has become rough sledding for Sears, which reportedly is thinking of closing up to 100 of its smaller stores and shrinking its famous "Big Book" catalogue operations. Bad news? Not necessarily. Times have changed, as usual.

Time was, in 1886, Richard Sears was a 22-year-old railroad agent in North Redwood, Minnesota. Having on his hands an undeliverable consignment of watches, he discovered that he could sell such merchandise to agents down the line, who sold it in their towns. Sears paid the manufacturers when the agents paid him, so he needed no capital. He made $5,000 in six months, quit his $6-a-week railroad job and, working with Alvah Roebuck, by 1898 was sending 583-page catalogues into the prairie.

Sears, Roebuck's path had been blazed by another Midwestern merchandising genius, Aaron Montgomery Ward. As a traveling salesman of dry goods, Ward had discovered what railroads and the Homestead Act had wrought—a vast, thinly settled inland empire of lonely farm families. Ward's catalogue drew them into what historian Daniel Boorstin calls a "consumption community."

Ward's catalogue customers did not just send orders, they sent letters. One farmer proposed marriage to the girl modeling the hat "on page 153 of your catalogue." Other letter-writers chatted, as over the backyard fence:

> I suppose you wonder why we haven't ordered anything from you since the fall. Well, the cow kicked my arm and broke it and besides my wife was sick, and there was the doctor bill. But now, thank God, that is paid, and we are all well again, and we have a fine new baby boy, and please send plush bonnet number 29d8077. . . .

Sears, Roebuck prospered with the help of Rural Free Delivery, which made the Big Book as central to many rural lives as the Good Book. Indeed, in an oft-told story a boy who was asked by his Sunday school teacher where the Ten Commandments come from replied, "Sears, Roebuck."

In 1907, Sears mailed 3 million fall catalogues; in 1927, 75 million catalogues and other mailings. There were lots of satisfied customers, and resentful competitors. Some Main Street merchants paid children to turn in their families' Sears catalogues for burning.

In 1991 Sears' long run as the nation's largest retailer was ended by a company born and still headquartered in Bentonville, Arkansas (population 11,000). Wal-Mart built an empire on an insight: The dispersal of Americans from central cities would enable a chain of discount stores to grow by starting in small towns and moving toward suburbs.

Just 12 years ago Wal-Mart had less than 12 percent of Sears' revenue. Today Wal-Mart is as resented as Sears once was by many merchants in the small towns. They have seen their downtowns wither as the small stores lose customers to the Wal-Marts out along the highways.

Small stores lack Wal-Mart's muscle in negotiating advantageous relationships with vendors. Hence small stores, so important for so long to the social fabric of their communities, lose the price competition with Wal-Mart. Over time, and not much time, price competition overwhelms community traditions.

Wal-Mart is just one part of Sears' problems. Competition has become fiercer because many of today's most skillful retailers are specialists—The Limited (fashionable apparel), The Gap (basic apparel), Circuit City (consumer electronics), Pier 1 and Ikea (home furnishings), Trak Auto (auto supplies). Furthermore J. Crew, L. L. Bean, Victoria's Secret and thousands of other firms enable customers to shop by mail or by 800 numbers. Such companies put severe price pressure on Sears. And consumers know what they stand for, which is hard to say about Sears, which sells snow tires and baby clothes and power tools and cosmetics.

Sears has various strategies for coping with its changed environment, and in some form or other Sears will be around for a while. But whatever the future fluctuations of Sears' fortunes, its path from the prairie to the present says something about how to read economic news.

Americans read about the travails of, say, GM and IBM and other giants and become anxious. But behind the difficulties of an IBM may be the exciting story of a Microsoft.

Economic history, like the history of the Earth's species, is a story of adaptations and extinctions. In dynamic capitalism, the pace of change is generally rapid and usually accelerating. But freedom is not supposed to be restful.

January 3, 1993

Wild in the Streets: What Ails BMW Drivers?

You see them coming several blocks back. Your rearview mirror reveals cars driven with a nervous, jerking, lunging, spastic intensity, clinging to the bumpers of the cars ahead, weaving across lanes, rushing toward the next red light. Toward, and often right through.

The spreading lawlessness of drivers in Washington, and not only here, is more than a nuisance, although it is that: Traffic moves more slowly because prudent drivers hesitate to enter an intersection even after the light has turned green, so frequently are red lights disregarded. And manic drivers are more than amusing, although as fools usually do, such drivers have a comic dimension: Even the most aggressive driving can cut but about 10 minutes from a 10-mile commute. Have they thought of leaving home 10 minutes earlier? Or are 10 minutes more abed really worth risking life, limb and driver's license?

Actually, lawless commuters face decreasing risks of arrest because police are increasingly preoccupied with the slow-motion riot that is life in the inner city. Thus do the lawless from suburbia benefit from the lawlessness of the urban criminal class. But let us not be judgmental.

Instead, let us be advanced thinkers who study the increasingly, shall we say, *interesting* driving habits as evidence of America's increasing "diversity," and as a flowering of new "values." Let us begin, anthropologically: Even if this new lawlessness is just fallen humanity misbehaving again, why now, and why this way? What has happened to other ways of venting pent-up aggressiveness, like fighting Redcoats, clearing forests or watching football?

Lunatic driving in the evening may—although I doubt it—express an intense longing for hearth and home. But aggressiveness in the morning is mystifying: To what work are they rushing headlong? In Washington, often to government jobs, which in many cases means they are rushing to the sluggish river of paper that someday will result in some decision to which American society will be magnificently impervious. Perhaps the numbing everydayness of many people's work, in the private sector, too, explains the rip-roaring behavior behind the wheel going to and from.

Recently Joseph Epstein, the essayist and professor (of English, at Northwestern), put to me a startlingly simple question: "Do you know anyone who makes anything?" Epstein had recently met a man who makes pajamas. Epstein was struck by the realization that it is rare for him to encounter anyone whose days are filled with making *things*—things you can heft, hold up to the light, take to the cash register, take home, put to practical use.

Around campus most of the people Epstein sees make seminars and lectures—true, the occasional article and book, too, but it's somehow not the same, not as real, as pajamas. In Washington we make hearings, laws, litigation, lunch appointments and journalism. All of it is, of course, terrifically important, but perhaps the evanescence of it produces demented drivers. Just a thought.

Driving probably will become even wilder now that Christmas (in P. G. Wodehouse's words) has us by the throat. Holidays and homicide go together like eggnog and nutmeg, so 'tis the season to study the wildness in the streets. I have not noticed—are we still allowed to notice?—what nowadays are called "gender differences." Men and women are equally represented among the demented drivers, which probably is heartening evidence of the emancipation of women. BMWs are disproportionately driven by red-light runners, but I make no judgments. (*New York Times* headline, December 2, 1993: IMPATIENT DRIVER SHOOTS MOTORIST FOR MOVING TOO SLOWLY IN BRONX. The shooter was driving a BMW.)

No judgments, so I will not dwell on the possibility that lawless driving by commuters from suburbia is of a piece with that inner-city behavior commonly called "crime in the streets." Let others wonder whether lawless BMW drivers, like young predators in Nike high-tops, represent the barbarian belief that they have a right to do what they like to do, and whether those drivers and those predators are all creating themselves in the way the writer Margaret Halsey meant when she said that "identity is not found, the way Pharaoh's daughter found Moses in the bullrushes. Identity is built. It is built every day and every minute throughout the day."

However, here is a minimally judgmental thought.

Years ago, when Washington's Redskins were owned by Edward Bennett Williams, they had an unreliable kicker who, Williams said, "had put the excitement back into the point after touchdown." In a well-functioning society, some things are supposed to be dull. Driving through an intersection, for example.

December 5, 1993

Scrooge, a Prince of a Guy

The invention of modern Christmas got a boost 150 years ago from a book that begins with three unfestive words: "Marley was dead." In 1843 Charles Dickens, that volcano of Victorian sentimentality, erupted with *A Christmas Carol*. Christmas was making a comeback.

When Oliver Cromwell was Lord Protector he protected England from Christmas which, Puritans said, was "an extraeme forgetfulnesse of Christ, by giving liberty to carnall and sensuall delights." Of course to Puritans a fruitcake was a dangerous delight.

Christmas in Merrie England had become a rollicking good time after the Norman Conquest imported French flair. By 1252 Henry III was slaying 600 oxen to go with the salmon pies and roasted peacocks. By the 1640s Cromwell was not amused.

Besides, the second syllable of "Christmas" suggested a popish plot. So the House of Commons sat on Christmas days and sheriffs were sent forth to require merchants to open for business. Pro- and anti-Christmas factions rioted.

The Puritans were bullies but were not wrong when they said that Christmas observations in December had their origins in pagan festivals of the winter solstice, and no one knew in what season Christ was born. Some say that if shepherds really were tending their flocks in the fields that night, it must not have been winter, when sheep in Palestine were penned at night. Some early Christians in Egypt fixed Christ's birth at May 20, and dates were suggested in every month before December 25 became the consensus choice.

That choice coincided with some rival religions' celebrations of the rebirth of the sun, symbolized by candles and by what would come to be called yule logs. Pagans had traditionally decked their halls with boughs of holly, evergreens and mistletoe to symbolize winter's inability to prevent the renewal of life. In one of life's nice caroms, Christmas trees, a German tradition, may have been introduced to America during the Revolutionary War by Hessian mercenaries of the sort that George Washington routed from Trenton after crossing the Delaware on Christmas night, 1776.

The Puritans brought to New England a Cromwellian detestation of Christmas, the celebration of which was made a crime in Massachusetts in 1659. That edict was repealed in 1681, but in 1686 the governor needed two soldiers to escort him to Christmas services. In 1706 a Boston mob smashed the windows in a church holding Christmas services. New Yorkers, dissolute even then, and Southerners, always sensualists, celebrated Christmas from the 17th century on, but as late as 1874 Henry Ward Beecher, America's most prominent preacher, said, "To me, Christmas is a foreign day."

The birth of Christmas in its modern form, as a festival of sentiment and material comforts, was made possible by the cooling of religious passions. In 1823 the Troy, New York, *Sentinel* published anonymously Clement Clarke Moore's decidedly secular poem beginning, " 'Twas the night before Christmas . . ." Forty years later Thomas Nast, the illustrator and political cartoonist who gave us the Democratic donkey and Republican elephant, popularized the modern image of Santa Claus, a jolly one-man shopping mall.

It was not until 1885 that all federal workers were given Christmas Day off. President Chester Arthur, an otherwise sound fellow, signed that law. Franklin Roosevelt discerned Christmas's potential as a countercyclical program and moved Thanksgiving from the last Thursday to the third Thursday in November in order to get Christmas shopping humming sooner. (It was moved back to the fourth Thursday in 1942.)

Dickens, who did so much to define the modern Christmas, did so with virtually no reference to religion. He was just 31 in 1843, still tormented by memories of a youthful privation—his father in debtors' prison, himself toiling in a blacking factory—and intensely interested in child labor and the conditions of the poor. *A Christmas Carol*, written in haste and rapturously received by the rapidly expanding reading public, epitomized the Dickens whom Orwell was to describe as "generously angry."

Orwell distilled Dickens's doctrine into 10 words: "If men would behave decently, the world would be decent." On the eve of a revolutionary era in Europe—1848 was just five years away—Dickens said that a change of hearts was the key to changing society.

Scrooge did not need to be trundled in a tumbrel to a guillotine or even have his property expropriated. A few ghosts and a winsome child named Tim would suffice for a conversion experience. In the end Scrooge was still a capitalist, but a prince of a guy.

Karl Marx, who in 1849 settled in London not far from Dickens, ardently admired Dickens's depiction of social ills. But if Marx understood the writer's message, he must have gagged. Count that among the good that Christmas has done.

December 23, 1993

Me, Fifty

In the Middle Ages a particular Pope was so deeply revered that once a year he paraded through Rome's streets wearing a ridiculous hat to discourage excessive veneration. In our children's eyes, we are always wearing such hats, but especially on our 50th birthdays, when we have long ceased to be young and are a long way from being venerable.

When the mail arrived the other day, the Prodigy, a.k.a. Victoria Will, age 10, was amused, with malice. There, just as she had delightedly warned that it soon would be, was a copy of *Modern Maturity* magazine. That is the monthly publication of the American Association of Retired Persons, which sends it to you as your 50th birthday impends, whether you want the magazine or not. You don't, trust me.

It is full of pictures of gray-haired but sinewy seniors, brimming with energy and banging the kettle drum of their sincerity about the glories of the golden years. They are supposed to reassure you. They don't.

Looking forward from age 50 is no bowl of blueberries and looking back, and distilling lessons from things, is difficult to do without sounding like Polonius when he was loading down Laertes with bromides. However, from among the bric-a-brac of experience, I have plucked a few strategies for living.

For example, I have a telephone-answering machine. I never turn it on. Part of the fun of venturing out and about is to return home to that cold machine and think of all the calls I was able to miss. The world is too much with us anyway without allowing it to ambush us on tape.

Let us hope the world beyond America's borders will be less intrusive for a while. To have been born seven months before Pearl Harbor and to turn 50 two months after Desert Storm is to know the centrality of war in America's modern experience. The jubilation about our most recent war—the biggest parades will be in June; the celebrations are lasting five times longer than the war—suggests we have become a bit too fond of the narcotic of mass experiences.

I began my professional life as what my father was, a college professor, doing, as he did, philosophy. It has subsequently been my fate, chosen but not planned, to live as a writer in this political city.

Washington often seems dizzied by the rush of little events. If we did not notice them the day they happened, we would never notice we had missed them, so swiftly do they sink beneath the surface of serious history. In Washington I have learned that it is symbolically correct that the Capitol is on the edge of the continent. In a good society, politics is a dignified profession with a vital jurisdiction, but in most lives it is and should be at the margin. Unhappy is the country in which people cannot talk about themselves or their relations with others without recourse to political categories.

When someone called William Butler Yeats's attention to Thomas Mann's ponderous assertion that "In our time, the destiny of man presents its meanings in political terms," Yeats demonstrated the superiority of the Celtic to the Teutonic temperament by writing a short poem, "Politics," which begins:

> How can I, that girl standing there,
> My attention fix
> On Roman or on Russian
> Or on Spanish politics?

One pleasure of becoming stricken in years is that almost all strong passions centered on politics seem disproportionate. This is particularly so since the defeat of totalitarianism, which tyrannized us, too, by making us think about politics constantly.

It is marvelous to imagine what was going on in the mind of the woman who so detested William Gladstone that she sent a wreath to the grave of the heifer that knocked him down. Politics is not crucial to the principal ingredients of happiness—cheerful children, feisty friends, fulfilling work and a strong bullpen.

We who came to social consciousness in the 1950s acquired, with every breath, the sense of America's vigor, the "glittering in the veins" and the "crush of strength" that Wallace Stevens sensed one night on the Connecticut Turnpike in 1954. America has not done badly in the struggle to achieve that elusive balance of freedom and security that characterizes a society in which the strong may freely strive and the weak need not feel fear.

Boil my experience down and the residue that remains in the pan is this: To be paid for the privilege of writing about the American pageant is bliss. As Henry James lay dying, his hands made writing motions across the sheet that covered him. I hope that will be true of me, but not soon.

May 5, 1991

Why Is There No Surgeon General's Warning on Family Vacations?

Having just now, with the help of the healing arts, recovered enough use of my right arm to grip a pen, I wield that pen to write this warning (to be pondered all winter) against the folly of summer vacations.

The phrase "family vacation" is, of course, an oxymoron. Children, with their unresting energy, overwhelm the adult pleasure from vacations—the delicious feeling of truancy from everyday bustle. But for children, summer is supposed to be a soufflé of delights, both diverting and instructive. To that ambitious end I spared no expense of time and treasure.

I took the three Will siblings—boys 18 and 16, and the Prodigy, 9—first on an Alaskan cruise, then to California. There, disaster, having bided its time, struck, to the delight of the children.

The cruise—a Dutch ship magnificently crewed by Indonesians with exotic names like (really) Bambang—suited father who, lost in a deep deck chair and a shallow novel, knew the children would not leave the ship or, while on it, escape the captain's dread sovereignty. (I took the precaution of explaining to them, in hair-raising detail, the maritime punishment of keelhauling, and the eligibility of children for it.) The cruise was grand, but nothing lasts forever, alas, and a few days after docking I and the three were in Southern California, at the top of a water slide in one of those infernal amusement parks featuring water tortures that people inexplicably find fun.

Amusement parks refute the notion that ours is a species suited to self-government. What can be said in extenuation of people who pay to be whirled and flung about in ways that wrench joints and induce headaches and queasiness? Water parks are particularly Dantesque. There, you broil in long lines in the sun for the pleasure of plunging—buffeted and sandpapered—down a plastic chute into cold water.

When seating myself at the top of one such slide—the Wipeout or Cobra or Nairobi Express, I forget which—I tore something, or several somethings, in my upper arm. The next day that arm was useless, but the bicep was a pretty shade of indigo, with bright yellow trim. Soon I was in the fell clutches of modern medicine and fitted with a sling. Then

I was subjected to the merciless merriment of the three ingrates to whom I improvidently helped give the gift of life.

Human beings differ in tastes. Some do and others do not like operas, popsicles, democracy, poetry. But there is one uniformity: All children adore seeing father brought low by injury. Not too low or for too long, but sufficiently to be semi-incapacitated and awkward.

This allows them to poke the injured portion of him, inquiring with feigned innocence, "Daddy, does that hurt?" And they miss no opportunity to explain, loudly, to friends and even strangers, the silliness—"It was on a water slide!"—that got daddy the injury that they clearly think serves him right.

The pleasure children derive from a father's physical incapacity is political. Power is linked to authority, which is inextricably bound up with competence and dignity. An injury, particularly one that father suffers in ridiculous circumstances and that makes him fumble with doorknobs, subtracts from parental majesty and thus advances the emancipation of children.

Which is bad enough. Worse is the encounter with medicine and its intimation of mortality.

"Let me show you," says an orthopedist whose patients include Washington Redskins, heroic gladiators. He leads this victim of a parenting injury to a corner of his office and there patiently explains the shoulder mechanism by manipulating an alarmingly lifelike (deathlike, actually) skeleton. Just what I least want: another reminder of the skull beneath the skin of life.

There is nothing like a little bodily breakdown to make a middle-aged man feel the cold grip of withering age. "The bloom is gone and with the bloom go I." Another doctor, preparing to pump air and dye into the shoulder joint (for a CAT scan), says something Torquemada probably said to victims of the Inquisition on the rack: "You are going to feel a certain tightness in the shoulder." This doctor says he is just a year younger than I, and last year he suffered a herniated disk. "We are just at the age," he says cheerfully, "when we begin to fall apart."

Where do doctors learn to say these things? Are there medical-school classes that teach banter calculated to supplant physical with mental suffering?

The prognosis is that if I am diligent at physical therapy, by the time next summer's vacation rolls around I should be, so to speak, ready to rip. Meanwhile, although the calendar says summer still has several weeks in which to inflict injuries, it is time to close the book on this season of suffering, while I still have one arm healthy enough to close a book.

September 6, 1990

Family Travel, as in "Travail"

THIRTY THOUSAND FEET OVER WYOMING. OR PERHAPS OHIO. HEADING
EAST, PROBABLY—Vertigo, a normal consequence of vacationing, can be
combated by looking out the airplane window and focusing on the far
horizon. But the horizon is a line one never reaches, so the mind fills
with melancholy thoughts about Moses on Mt. Pisgah, seeing the Promised Land that he would never enter. Never mind. Just over the horizon,
cool and beckoning, lies Labor Day, and release from the rigors of
vacationing.

The annual family vacation is not merely obligatory, it is fun. But it
involves too much heavy lifting to be really restful.

It is a law of family life that the amount of baggage—what armies call
a logistical tail—accompanying a traveling child is inversely proportional to the child's age. The older Will children will, unless reminded
and then threatened, leave for a three-week vacation with one change
of socks. But David Will, 13 months old, embarks for California the
way Eisenhower embarked for Normandy in 1944, with lots of equipment.

David makes few requests, other than a steady supply of Ritz Bits,
those tiny cracker sandwiches glued together by peanut butter which
may require United Airlines to redecorate several 757s. But David is a
high-maintenance creature requiring diapers and bottles and a portable
playpen and a collapsible stroller and several collapsible adults. You
might think the portability of children's stuff is a convenience. Think
again.

The experience of traveling with the Will children is not like Bos-
well's experience traveling with Dr. Johnson in the Hebrides. The dia-
logue is different. When, five summers ago, in Rome I announced that
we were going to Florence for a few days, the children exclaimed in
spontaneous chorus: "The hotel had better have cable." Comity hangs
on the thin thread of such contingencies.

It has been said that the choice of vacation spots is a common dis-
rupter of marital bliss, so what America needs is an ocean in the mountains. All the Wills, save one, love beaches, the most detestable places
on the planet.

Beaches are sun, sand and surf. The first causes cancer. The second
sticks to every patch of skin that has been coated with the gunk that

provides protection from the sun. The third, the surf, is a hostile element that mankind, or at least that portion of mankind that has actually evolved enough to hate beaches, has been trying to get away from ever since our biological antecedents emerged from the oceans and began crawling inland, shedding gills and acquiring civilization.

Perhaps, said Chekhov, the universe is suspended on the tooth of some monster. While at a beach, I believe that. But this year, as usual, my reasoned objections to beaches were met by my family's spacious yawns. Truth be told, I am glad, because the sight of a 24-pound boy meeting the Pacific Ocean was worth the trip. David had been more or less walking for more than a week. Thigh-deep, meaning nine inches, into the surf, his confident body language proclaimed to the Pacific: "It is a question of who's boss!" He learned.

For him in the surf, travel was what travel used to be for most people, arduous and tinged with the thrill of danger. Historian Daniel Boorstin notes that the old English noun "travel," meaning journey, comes from "travail," meaning trouble or work or torment. And the word "travail" seems to have been derived, through French, from the Latin word "trepalium," which meant a three-staked instrument of torture. To journey, or travail, or later travel, meant to do something strenuous.

Thirteen years and two children ago I knew this. I wrote that vacations, although a hard-won entitlement for toiling humanity, come under the category of progress that may have gone too far. However, there is this to be said for vacations: They rob winter of its sting. Someone shoveling snow is consoled by the thought that things could be worse. He could be at a beach. Of course vacations enable parents and children to get to know each other better, but time heals such wounds.

Next summer is still far over the horizon, but it is never too soon to begin summoning up the stoicism that vacations require and that Robert Frost distilled into six words: "The best way out is through."

September 5, 1993

Jon Will's Aptitudes

Jon Will, the oldest of my four children, turns 21 this week and on this birthday, as on every other workday, he will commute by subway to his job delivering mail and being useful in other ways at the National Institutes of Health. Jon is a taxpayer, which serves him right: He voted for Bill Clinton (although he was partial to Pat Buchanan in the primaries).

The fact that Jon is striding into a productive adulthood with a spring in his step and Baltimore's Orioles on his mind is a consummation that could not have been confidently predicted when he was born. Then a doctor told his parents that their first decision must be whether or not to take Jon home. Surely 21 years later fewer doctors suggest to parents of handicapped newborns that the parental instinct of instant love should be tentative or attenuated, or that their commitment to nurturing is merely a matter of choice, even a question of convenience.

Jon has Down syndrome, a chromosomal defect involving varying degrees of mental retardation and physical abnormalities. Jon lost, at the instant he was conceived, one of life's lotteries, but he also was lucky: His physical abnormalities do not impede his vitality and his retardation is not so severe that it interferes with life's essential joys—receiving love, returning it, and reading baseball box scores.

One must mind one's language when speaking of people like Jon. He does not "suffer from" Down syndrome. It is an affliction, but he is happy—as happy as the Orioles' stumbling start this season will permit. You may well say that being happy is easy now that ESPN exists. Jon would agree. But happiness is a species of talent, for which some people have superior aptitudes.

Jon's many aptitudes far exceed those few that were dogmatically ascribed to people like him not long ago. He was born when scientific and social understanding relevant to him was expanding dramatically. We know much more about genetically based problems than we did when, in the early 1950s, James Watson and Francis Crick published their discoveries concerning the structure of DNA, the hereditary molecule, thereby beginning the cracking of the genetic code. Jon was born the year before *Roe* v. *Wade* and just as prenatal genetic tests were becoming routine. Because of advancing science and declining morals, there are fewer people like Jon than there should be. And just in Jon's generation much has been learned about unlocking the hitherto unimagined potential of the retarded. This begins with early intervention in the form of infant stimulation. Jon began going off to school when he was three months old.

Because Down syndrome is determined at conception and leaves its imprint in every cell of the person's body, it raises what philosophers call ontological questions. It seems mistaken to say that Jon is less than he would be without Down syndrome. When a child suffers a mentally limiting injury after birth we wonder sadly about what might have been. But a Down person's life never had any other trajectory. Jon was Jon from conception on. He has seen a brother two years younger surpass him in size, get a driver's license and leave for college, and although Jon would be forgiven for shaking his fist at the universe, he has been equable. I believe his serenity is grounded in his sense that he is a complete Jon and that is that.

Some of life's pleasures, such as the delights of literature, are not accessible to Jon, but his most poignant problem is that he is just like everyone else, only a bit more so. A shadow of loneliness, an irreducible apartness from others, is inseparable from the fact of individual existence. This entails a sense of incompleteness—we *are* social creatures—that can be assuaged by marriage and other friendships, in the intimacy of which people speak their hearts and minds. Listen to the wisdom whispered by common locutions: We speak of "unburdening ourselves" when we talk with those to whom we talk most freely.

Now, try to imagine being prevented, by mental retardation and by physical impediments to clear articulation, from putting down, through conversation, many burdens attendant on personhood. The shadow of loneliness must often be somewhat darker, the sense of apartness more acute, the sense of incompleteness more aching for people like Jon. Their ability to articulate is, even more than for everyone else, often not commensurate with their abilities to think and feel, to be curious and amused, and to yearn.

Because of Jon's problems of articulation, I marvel at his casual everyday courage in coping with a world that often is uncomprehending. He is intensely interested in major league baseball umpires, and is a friend of a few of them. I think he is fascinated by their ability to make themselves understood, by vigorous gestures, all the way to the back row of the bleachers. From his season-ticket seat behind the Orioles dugout, Jon relishes rhubarbs, but I have never seen him really angry. The closest he comes is exasperation leavened by resignation. It is an interesting commentary on the human condition that one aspect of Jon's abnormality—a facet of his disability—is the fact that he is gentleness straight through. But must we ascribe a sweet soul to a defective chromosome? Let us just say that Jon is an adornment to a world increasingly stained by anger acted out.

Like many handicapped people, Jon frequently depends on the kindness of strangers. He almost invariably receives it, partly because Americans are, by and large, nice, and because Jon is, too. He was born on his father's birthday, a gift that keeps on giving.

May 3, 1993

Acknowledgments

When publishing books, as when playing baseball, a strong bench is a joy, as is this opportunity to thank mine. Erwin Glikes brought to the making of many books, including this one, an elegant craftsmanship. Olga Barbi, nearing the 60—that's not a typo—year mark at *Newsweek*, has for nearly 20 years helped make my columns fit and flow. At the Washington Post Writers Group Alan Shearer and Anna Karavangelos do the same. In my office Dusa Gyllensvard and Mary Moschler are excellent constants. Mike Andolina, Joe Erlinger and Tim O'Brien serve my office when their college studies permit, and sometimes when their studies don't. And when it is time to produce a book, Gail Thorin is indispensable.

Index